DON'T YOU KNOW THERE'S A WAR ON?

The American Home Front,
1941–1945

DON'T
YOU KNOW
THERE'S
A WAR ON?

*The American Home Front,
1941–1945*

RICHARD R. LINGEMAN

A PERIGEE BOOK

Copyright © 1970 by Richard Lingeman
Perigee Books
are published by
G.P. Putnam's Sons
200 Madison Avenue
New York, New York, 10016

First Perigee Printing, 1980
Library of Congress Catalog Card Number: 79-127721
Printed in the United States of America
SBN: 399-50359-5

To my mother and father

Acknowledgments

Due credit for originating this book should go to Harvey Ginsberg of G. P. Putnam's Sons, whose idea it was; he has been a most helpful and patient editor throughout its execution. The author's gratitude is also due to Mary Schilling, who typed perseveringly through the various versions the manuscript assumed on its way to completion, and to my wife, Anthea, who designed the book, among other things. Thanks also to my agent, Lynn Nesbit of the International Famous Agency. Finally, any book which attempts to relate the story of what ordinary Americans thought, did, endured during the war years owes a good deal to the memories of the people who lived through it; to the dozens of here anonymous home front "veterans" who informally shared these memories with me on various occasions, my thanks for the pleasure of their company.

Grateful acknowledgment is hereby made to the authors and publishers for permission to quote from the following copyrighted works, which are further cited in the Chapter Notes and Bibliography:

Brave Men by Ernie Pyle. © 1943, 1944 by Scripps-Howard Newspaper Alliance and Holt, Rinehart and Winston, Inc.

"Dream" words and music by Johnny Mercer. © 1944, 1945 Michael H. Goldsen, Inc. Used by Permission.

"G.I. Jive" words and music by Johnny Mercer. © 1943 Capitol Songs. Copyright assigned 1960 to Commander Publications, Hollywood, Calif.

"The House I Live in" by Lewis Allan and Earl Robinson. © 1942 by Lewis Allan and Earl Robinson. Used by permission of Chappel & Co., Inc.

"I'm Getting Tired So I Can Sleep" by Irving Berlin. Copyright © 1942 by Irving Berlin. Copyright © renewed 1969 by Irving Berlin. Reprinted by permission of Irving Berlin Music Corporation.

Journey Through Chaos by Agnes E. Meyer. © 1943, 1944 by Agnes E. Meyer. Reprinted by permission of Harcourt, Brace & World, Inc.

"The Lonesome Train" by Millard Lampell. © 1944 Sun Music Company, Inc. Reprinted by permission of MCA Music.

"My Sister and I" by Hy Zaret, Joan Whitney and Alex Kramer. © 1941. Reprinted by permission of Screen Gems–Columbia Music, Inc., and Whitney, Kramer and Zaret Publishing Company.

On a Note of Triumph by Norman Corwin. © 1945 by Norman Corwin. Reprinted by permission of Simon & Schuster, Inc.

"Saturday Night Is the Loneliest Night of the Week" by Sammy Cahn and Jule Styne. © 1944 Barton Music Corp.

The State of the Nation by John Dos Passos. © 1944 by John Dos Passos. Originally published by Houghton Mifflin Company.

Contents

DON'T YOU KNOW THERE'S A WAR ON?

The American Home Front, 1941–1945

I

PRELUDE: SATURDAY

Sunday, December 7, 1941, was a red-letter day, a where-were-you-when day, that historical lightning has etched permanently in memory. Such is the clarity of its recall that a shadow of obscurity is cast over the days immediately preceding. Many have marked in their memories where they were when they heard about Pearl Harbor, but how many could remember where they were the day before the attack, Saturday, the last, unmomentous prewar day?

As 1941 drew to a close, the United States had some 134,000,000 people. Its chief occupations were manufacturing, steel, copper and coal extraction and processing, and farming. There was a civilian labor force of some 56,000,000 plus armed forces of about 1,500,000.

The median income was around $2,000 a year, so the contemporary song was being a bit modest when it said:

> Twenty-five bucks a week tho' it may be hay to Vanderbilt
> It'll pay the way from day to day for you and me.
> Twenty-five bucks a week tho' it wouldn't build a battleship
> It'll keep us filled with pork-chops from the A & P.
> Ten for food, ten for rent, five for the phone and clothes
> Something for the pictures shows and the laundry man
> and the Morris Plan.

Forty bucks a week, of course, was more like it, though there were 18,000,000 families (more than half the 32,000,000 families in the country) living on less than that amount. A family of five making right around the median was living within what the Labor Research Association termed the "minimum health and decency budget." A much more frugal "maintenance level budget" devised by the Works Progress Administration and aimed at blue-collar families of four, called for a little more than $1,500 a year, which provided food, clothes, rent and no savings. By that standard something like 40 percent of American families were living below maintenance level. The average income in this bracket was $900 a year.

During 1940 and 1941 the *Ladies' Home Journal* conducted a survey of American families in various parts of the country which it called "How America Lives." Buried in the excelsior of the magazine's chummy prose and resolutely cheerful outlook was a reasonable portrait of American family life just beginning to emerge from the Depression economically, if not psychologically. Most of the families were in the middle two-thirds of the population who made between $1,000 and $3,000, just beginning to pay off some debts or acquiring better homes and better-paying, steady jobs; most bore scars of recent bad times, and most were living modestly, just on the edge of genteel shabbiness. (The two poor families the magazine selected—one a Mississippi Negro share-cropper, the other a Brooklyn slum family—were living very badly indeed; they were among the 4,000,000 families in the country with an average yearly income of only $312 a year or abject poverty by whatever standards you use.) Most lived on fairly tight budgets, like the mother of four who was lauded for her ability to feed her family on $1 a day (not counting milk). Meals were barely nourishing, averaging 2,500 calories a day for each person. A typical weekly menu, provided by one such middle-class lady, went as follows:

BREAKFAST
Orange juice, oatmeal and milk; bacon and eggs once or twice a week, toast and coffee.

LUNCH
Soup, bread and butter, raw celery or carrot strips, sandwiches occasionally, milk and fruit for the children; a couple of cheese sandwiches, cake and fruit for father's lunch pail.

DINNER
An inexpensive main dish, such as macaroni and cheese or to-matoes and frankfurters, or escalloped potatoes with bacon or

frankfurters; vegetable beef soup; vegetables; and a fruit salad or Jell-o for dessert, or, infrequently, pies or cake; and a Sunday pot roast or chicken, but not every Sunday.

Despite this frugality, most families were still better off than in the Depression years 1935–39. A good bit of the rising level of prosperity was trickling down from the national defense program, which had got under way in earnest after the fall of France in June, 1940. More than 5,600,000 workers in heavy industry (about half the total) were working on defense contracts by the end of 1941, averaging around $40 a week. In twenty-five leading industries the average hourly rate was 85.3 cents in October—the highest on record and 10 percent above October, 1940. Farm income for the year, reflecting spiraling farm prices, reached an all-time high.

A gloomier part of the picture was the 7,500,000 wage earners who were making below the legal minimum wage of 40 cents an hour or a total of $16 a week; for the 6,000,000 of these who were in businesses not covered by the law (agriculture, retail trade, domestic service, fisheries and so on), wages of less than 15 cents an hour were not at all uncommon.

These pockmarks of poverty on the face of America aside, the economy as a whole was semibooming. The gross national product stood at $125.3 billion, more than twice the low-water mark reached in the depths of the Depression; national income was at a record high of $95 billion; total industrial production was up 66 percent from the 1935–39 average, aided by the injection of $8.3 billion in defense spending by the federal government, reaching a crescendo of $75,000,000 a day by December. Already the economy was feeling the pinch of material shortages (while making no particular effort to increase productive capacity of such scarce materials as aluminum and magnesium). Steel scrap, for example, which we had sold to the Japanese as late as 1940 (a total of 200,000,000 tons between 1935 and 1940) and which was essential to open-hearth steel production, was dwindling—according to the *Wall Street Journal* there was only enough on hand to last five or six weeks. Manufacturers were calling for "a national appeal to householders, farmers, everyone to join in a government-led and directed campaign to salvage scrap from every back yard and corner lot." A similar campaign to collect aluminum scrap had been tried, but it turned into a fiasco, with great piles of pots and pans languishing in collection points because no one would cart the scrap away, and anyhow, its value in plane production was nonexistent. Chromium and other forms of special steels were scarce, yet the auto makers, having a banner year and seeking to sell all they could before things worsened, slapped chromium on their 1942 models as if there were no tomorrow.

Those sharing in the new prosperity—such as the defense plant janitors who were being paid more than college professors, the Washington lawyer-lobbyists raking in $10,000 fees—were eating, drinking, being merry as if there were no tomorrow too. Nightclub grosses were up 35 percent. Fifty-thousand-dollar weekly grosses in the plush New York night spots were considered average; one week, with Jimmy Durante as headliner, the Copacabana took in $62,500; strictly dining places like 21, Toots Shor's, Lindy's and Dempsey's averaged $20,000 a week on food; the Stork Club, where the patrons were the floor show, shot from $15,000 to $35,000 weekly gross. Showman Monte Proser tried to cash in on the boom on a mass basis with his Dance Carnival in Madison Square Garden, where dancers lindy hopped, shagged and fox-trotted to the orchestras of Benny Goodman, Larry Clinton and Charlie Barnett in a tripleheader, admissions from 44 cents; but the overhead was too high, and the operation folded after a month—despite a crowd of 31,553 on the first weekend.

Only fifteen shopping days to Christmas, and the department stores were in the throes of the biggest shopping spree in years. Retail sales for the entire year would total $54,000,000—$10,000,000 above 1940 and $6,000,000 above 1929, the previous record year. Goods were plentiful, although a bit higher in price than last year (the cost of living had risen 12 percent). Nylons, for example, were replacing silk hose which had been made scarce by the embargo on Japanese silk thread; Stern's of New York offered them at "one special buy all you want price" of $1.75 a pair. A fifth of scotch could be had in St. Louis for $3; Rittenhouse Rye for $2. Two Christmases hence, these items and many others would be rare gems, and people would kick themselves for not stocking up.

A smattering of patriotism appeared amid the traditional symbols of the season. One store advertised its " 'Blue Star' Girls . . . ten intelligent girls gaily done up in star-spangled dresses" who assisted shoppers. There were red, white and blue "patriotic mules" and "personal blackout sleep shades" to be had, and gifts for the servicemen, such as a Hickok belt buckle embossed with the Great Seal of the Republic: "The young chap in Service will get a bang out of this gift." For the fastidious selectee, Brooks Brothers, the venerable men's store, was offering custom-tailored private's blouses in olive drab serge at $75. Children's war toys took a defensive posture, like the country. A model Defense Fort resembled those Maginot Line pillboxes made obsolete in 1940 by the German blitzkrieg; a remote-control toy plane which dropped bombs on a battleship was dubbed U.S. Air Defender.

Despite the prosperity in the Yuletide air, luxury goods did not seem overly in evidence; most gifts were under $100. Good men's suits could be had for $35–$40, while women's furs were mainly of the cheaper breeds, including one called Jap Munk. Of course there were more substantial purchases such as platinum watches for $500 or radio phonographs for $200–$400 or the new Oldsmobile with hydramatic drive in the $1,100 range. Yet little of the advertising appealed to a greedy affluence. Even Cadillac (after suggesting a "Cadillac for Christmas") emphasized practicality: "To insure your family's motor car needs for the duration of the emergency give them a Cadillac. It's good common sense for their protection."

In the first full year of the defense program, the nation's Christmas stocking was full of civilian goods; as one government official put it: "We have our guns and we have our butter." The shortages caused by defense production were few; for example, RCA, overburdened with defense work, couldn't keep up with the demand for Victrolas, so it took a jolly ad urging people to buy from its rivals—"of course we know you're disappointed, madam, but our competitors make good phonograph-radios." Defense contract dollars were just as good as free enterprise dollars, so RCA wasn't exactly complaining. At the convention of the National Association of Manufacturers held that weekend in New York different sentiments came from business leaders. Some of the speakers groaned about increasing government regulation of the economy, comparing it to "Nazi collectivism," while another business leader was worrying about the sad plight of those engaged in defense contracts if the government was suddenly to cancel them when the present emergency ended. He maintained that the businessman, lured into switching to defense production by government spending which some estimates said would run as high as $50 billion annually, faced ruin and the nation a depression unless the government made plans to tide them over the peacetime transition.

Still, there were 4,000,000 men out of work. The defense program gave jobs with one hand; with the other it took them away. Matériel shortages resulting from accelerated demand for weapons caused civilian goods industries to curtail production. A new phrase entered the language: "priorities unemployment"—unemployment caused by a business inability to obtain a priority from the government's Supply Priorities and Allocation Board, in charge of diverting raw materials to the defense industries under a materials rationing system. Poor planning also hindered the priorities system. There was not enough to go around. A typical matériel-starved business was Talon, Inc., of Meadville, Pennsylvania, maker of zippers. Unable to buy any copper since August, Talon had laid off 800 men. Since it employed 5,000 of Meadville's 9,000 workers, its cutbacks affected the entire economy of the city. Throughout the nation, the Congress of Industrial Organizations estimated, one and a quarter million men were victims of priorities unemployment. Business had gripes about the priorities system, and so labor too had grievances against the inequities of the defense program.

The news was full of muffled but ominous portents. From the Far East came reports of Japanese troop movements in Indochina. The objectives of the Japanese high command were cloaked in ambiguity; the barometer of war fell threateningly. In Washington, Japan's two diplo-mats, cartoon clichés in striped pants and winged collars, went to and fro for talks with Secretary of State Cordell Hull, but as a satirist of the day summed it up, no one knew what real intentions they carried concealed in their briefcases—or their real thoughts behind the grinning façades. That night the President would make a last appeal to the Emperor for direct talks between them, but the rickety diplomatic bridge between the two countries was sagging near to collapse. While the talks continued, the people remained in a limbo between peace and war. The New York *Times'* Washington correspondent wrote Saturday: "an impression prevailed in diplomatic circles that something approaching a status quo may have been reached temporarily that might permit the exploratory conversations between the United States and Japanese emis-saries to continue with less disturbance. Time also would be afforded each side to take any desired steps to strengthen their military forces against a possible future breakdown of negotiations." On Friday the House of Representatives appropriated an additional $8 billion for defense, increasing the Army to 2,000,000 men. Senator Robert Taft of Ohio found it hard to believe that the country needed such a large force. The past week the Chicago *Tribune* had leaked a classified War Department plan calling for an American Expeditionary Force of 5,000,000 men and a total armed force of 10,000,000 by 1943. The War Department said the document was hypothetical, but the isolationist forces in Congress said the document proved that the President intended to intervene in the European war, despite the 1940 Selective Service

Act prohibiting draftees from serving anywhere outside the continental United States.

The news from the Russian front seemed hopeful but confused. The Soviets announced a winter counteroffensive which wrested back hundreds of villages with tongue-spraining names. The phrase "as clear as the news from the Russian front" was a popular simile.

Attention focused on the Japanese shadow play in Southeast Asia. As Japanese military power lazily uncoiled itself toward the Dutch territories—Java and Malaya, for two; the chief sources of our rubber—and the British base at Singapore and Hong Kong and perhaps Australia and even the Philippines, soberer heads were increasingly calculating the conditions for some kind of American involvement in the Pacific alongside the ABCD powers (Australia, Britain, China, the Dutch). *Time* magazine had recently reported that in Washington the odds for war with the Japanese were 9 in 10. Walter Lippmann's Saturday column stated flatly: "For the first time the country is now really on the verge of an actual all-out war" with Japan. Glamorous foreign correspondent Vincent Sheean in a speech in New York predicted war with Japan very soon—if not within ten days. Sheean also predicted "spectacular" Japanese successes against Pacific outposts and the fall of Thailand and Burma.

If Americans did not expect to be at war the next day, or the next week, or the next month, they knew it would come. *When* was a question whose answer lay behind the opaque curtain hiding the intentions of the enemy.

College students poised on the brink of the future looked ahead and saw the iron gate of war lowering across their path. A professor at Bryn Mawr summed up the prevailing mood: "Students seem to be waiting for something to force the issue—for whatever is going to happen, whether it's war or not, to become more *imminent*."

Americans saw the coming of war through a glass darkly, but they overwhelmingly agreed that it would come. By the summer of 1941 a Gallup Poll showed 85 percent of the people believing we would be drawn into the European war; another poll shortly before Pearl Harbor had two-thirds of the respondents predicting war with Japan shortly. The isolationist–Roosevelt-hating coalition in Congress, which bitterly fought FDR's defense measures, was out of touch with the preponderant weight of public opinion, its prominence caused by its noisiness and inordinate Congressional power. The people did not want war, but they had overwhelmingly supported the President every step of the way on what *Time* called his "thousand-step road to war." They, by preponderance of the polls anyhow, had favored aid to China and an embargo of war goods to Japan as far back as 1938; they favored allowing American ships to carry aid to Great Britain, armed convoys to escort these ships, the stationing of American troops on Iceland, the "undeclared war" in the Atlantic and peacetime military conscription (64 percent favored it before France capitulated to Germany and three months before Congress finally passed the Burke-Wadsworth Selective Service Act—the "fishbowl" draft). The country was overwhelmingly in favor of aiding England in late 1941, even though it meant getting into the war. Asked by Gallup which was more important: that the United States stay out of war or that Germany be defeated, 68 percent said it was more important that Germany be defeated. The public was consistent in its support of the various measures taken to aid England, even though they ran counter to our official stance of neutrality.

Yet no one was at a fighting pitch. The government was demanding little in the way of sacrifices; the Civilian Defense program under Fiorello LaGuardia was a joke, and government direction of rearmament was riddled with bungling. People knitted bundles for Britain or attended showings of "Defense Dresses" but otherwise were only sporadically engaged in any sort of preparedness measures. The letters *OHIO* found scrawled everywhere around Army bases meaning "Over the Hill in October" summed up their mood. The men felt their training was a waste of time, and they wanted to go home—even if it meant desertion. But this had altered by winter. A series of maneuvers had been held, and this activity (plus the ominous war news) bolstered morale; further, the men were beginning to have more adequate equipment to train with. In the summer, because of munitions shortages, they had trained with wooden rifles and logs representing mortar and cannon (indeed the Army seriously considered ordering artillery from Britain, so belated were American manufacturers). Still Saturday's St. Louis *Post-Dispatch* could print this filler:

YOLK'S ON YOU

Camp Funston, Kan.—It was a mock parachute attack on cavalry troops, ordered to defend themselves with hand grenades. No ammunition was available, so they used mock hand grenades—eggs.

Although the Army's readiness was steadily improving, thanks to the organizational efforts of General George C. Marshall, it was estimated that only 600,000 men out of 1,400,000 were adequately trained. One general flatly predicted that if the American Army were thrown into battle with the Germans, it would lose a half million men. (On the other hand, in a report to the nation released on Saturday, Navy Secretary Frank Knox was more reassuring, saying: "The American people may feel fully confident in their Navy . . . the U.S. Navy is second to none.")

The armed forces were grossly unready for any full-scale or even partial involvement in war for the next three to six months. The General Staff counseled delay.

Antiwar voices continued to sound in Congress and before German Bund street-corner rallies. The America First Committee, the castle keep of isolationism, was under investigation by the Justice Department and the Dies Committee for acting as a front for German propaganda. General Hugh S. Johnson announced his resignation, opening another crack in the America First Committee's façade of respectability. Johnson's immediate opposition was to the committee's political activities—running candidates for Congress in the next election. He also protested against the "curious hodgepodge of Communists, pacifists and exponents of various other 'isms' [for some reason, perhaps blindness, he omitted the committee's increasing echoing of the German propaganda line and the Communist Party's flip-flop to a "popular front" in favor of U.S. intervention against Hitler]" and to the speeches of some members which had expressed "a tone of religious and racial intolerance"—referring, of course, to the anti-Semitic speeches of Charles Lindbergh, among others. Probably considerably less than one-quarter of the American people supported America First, largely because of the crackpot, pro-German image it was acquiring.

Aside from the diehards, such isolationism as existed among the public at large was in the form of escapist yearning, the understandable wish that the rest of the world, with all its horrors and miseries, would stay away from our door. Americans were saying, in the words of the contemporary song:

I don't want to set the world on fire.
I just want to start
A flame in your heart.

But the world was on fire, and tomorrow Pearl Harbor would be ignited.

The antiwar movement known as America First still had powerful friends, both at home and in the *Reich,* but peace, symbolized in cartoons as a harried dove or bedraggled young lady, had few champions.

On Saturday, a New York organization called Peace House took out a notice in the papers calling on Americans to write immediately to their Congressmen urging them "to keep U.S.A. out of war." At the end of the ad was this announcement:

CLOSED
Until Further Notice
On Account of Illness

Also closing was the Japan Institute, a Japanese propaganda agency. The agency blamed the shutdown on its difficulties in obtaining operating funds after Japanese assets in the United States were frozen. The Japanese bade *sayonara* on a graceful note: "In saying farewell we earnestly hope that it shall be our pleasure again to take up our work among you in the not too distant future when conditions will have returned to normal."

Peace's last public advocates on the eve of war were Norman Thomas, the perennial Socialist candidate, and Dr. George W. Hartmann of Teachers College, Columbia, who spoke out against intervention in a debate Friday night before the Conference of Progressive Educators at the New Yorker Hotel. Asserting that our national interests in the Far East were really economic, Hartmann said: "There is not enough tin and rubber in the world for me to go to war with Japan." The preservation of the American system, even, was not worth going to war, Hartmann added: "There is not a single social order in the world which is worth the certain destruction of five to ten million human beings that will be necessary to defeat the Axis powers." (For a radical pacifist, Dr. Hartmann was a conservative prophet of doom. Military and civilian deaths in World War II would total at least 35,000,000 people.)

So the American people went about their business that Saturday, while the six carriers of the Pearl Harbor Striking Force under Vice Admiral Chuichi Nagumo sliced through the cobalt-blue waves of the Pacific a few hundred miles north of Hawaii. Saturday night in the cities, Christmas shoppers and pleasure seekers streamed to the restaurants, nightclubs, theaters. Reminders of war in the popular amusements of the day were softened through sentiment or laughter. In New York one might hear the popular *chanteuse* Hildegarde at the Savoy Room singing "The Last Time I Saw Paris," which she had popularized, or "My Sister and I," which told of two Dutch children, refugees, who have come to live in America. The war that made them refugees is referred to in the song only as "the fear that came from a troubled sky." Now, in their new lives, they are almost happy, except the "times we awake and cry" as they remember:

> A tulip garden by an old Dutch mill
> And the home that was our own until—
> But we don't talk about that.

Songs of the period didn't "talk about that" but merely sadly recalled tulip gardens or Paris when her heart was young and gay. Or perhaps, like a new song just becoming popular, they dreamed rosy dreams of a vague, distant postwar world of peace:

> There'll be bluebirds over
> The white cliffs of Dover
> Tomorrow just you wait and see.

But the nightclub merrymakers mostly danced to the harmless, cheerful little tunes of the day—"Chattanooga Choo Choo," "The Hut Sut Song," "Maria Elena," "Why Don't We Do This More Often?", "Scatterbrain" and "Elmer's Tune." Movie audiences laughed at the Army through the screen antics of Abbott and Costello in *Buck Privates* or *Keep 'Em Flying* or Bob Hope in *Caught in the Draft*—the only popular movies with a martial theme. Theatergoers met a similar dearth; only Lillian Hellman's *Watch on the Rhine* and the London blitz drama *The Wookey* mentioned the war. Most Broadway offerings were warm comedies, mysteries or light musicals.

So the night went. Those in the crowds debouching along Broadway who picked up the Sunday *Herald Tribune* on their way home would read in the rotogravure section an article about the naval base at Pearl Harbor, "the point of defense of our West Coast." The pictures of silver sands mingled with war planes flying over Diamond Head were a pleasant blend of escapism and preparedness. As the article pointed out, the tourist disporting there would scarcely notice the Army pillboxes, they were so well concealed.

The American people got ready for bed, and if they thought of the future at all, it was with reluctance and, at bottom, with pessimism. Perhaps a reflection of this mood was the results of a poll released only that week asking people what they thought the world would be like after the war. Nearly 70 percent of those asked thought they would have to "work harder after the war." Some 60 percent thought everyone would be paid less after the war than before it started and that there would be "lots of unemployment." Only 37 percent thought that their sons' opportunities to succeed after the war would be better than their own. These were not dreams of a brave new postwar world. Or perhaps all the poll showed was that the American people—whatever may be said of some of their leaders or past wars—do not go to war for economic gain. Most of the polled saw a long and grim war and only uncertainty, perhaps another depression, after it.

Or perhaps Robert Sherwood summed up the national temper best —and certainly most succinctly—when he wrote in *Roosevelt and Hopkins* that World War II was "the first war in American history in which the general disillusionment preceded the firing of the first shot." An amateur poet put it less succinctly, though no less accurately, in a poem printed in Saturday's paper:

> If we should take that crimson road again,
> We will not need the bugle nor the drum
> To lead us blindly unto death's terrain.
> To learn that fame is but a tasteless crumb.
> For we shall know and knowing cannot shun
> It is but one more task that must be done.
> To quench the flame that would engulf our world.

II

IN THE EVENT OF
AN AIR RAID
WALK, DO NOT RUN

Monday morning, December 8, dawned like a hangover from a lost weekend. In San Francisco, the night had been one of restless alarms. Three times in the Bay Area sirens sounded (they were fire engine sirens; the city had no air raid sirens); then the radio abruptly went dead. No one knew whether it was an air raid for sure, or a drill, or, indeed, anything at all. People looked out their windows, saw the streetlights on, and decided that perhaps it was a big fire at the radio station.

The city's rudimentary civilian defense forces went into action, and one woman complained to police: "There's a crazy man prowling around my place shouting, 'Lights out!'" By the time the third alarm shrilled the city authorities ordered the Pacific Gas and Electric Company to pull the master switch. The downtown lights were controlled by individual switches, however, and men had to go around extinguishing them one by one. Some people, awakened from their sleep, lost their tempers and called police headquarters to demand the noise be stopped. One complainant, told that it was an air raid warning, asked angrily: "If there are Jap planes around why aren't they dropping any bombs?"

And that indeed was the crux of the mystery. Lieutenant General John L. DeWitt, commanding officer, Fourth Army and the Western Defense Command, told newsmen after the first alert that strange planes had been over the city, adding: "I don't think there's any doubt the planes came from a carrier." Fifteen huge searchlights along the bay and at the

Presidio wove a crisscrossing latticework of beams across the night sky, but there were no hostile planes. The official explanation was that thirty enemy planes had flown in from the south, passing over Mare Island Naval Base, then split up into two groups over the city, one group flying north, the other south. Army pursuits tracked the northbound group for a time but lost it; the southern group was never located. Actually, there had been no hostile planes.

Without direction from their radios and any adequate air-raid warning system or previous practice, San Franciscans reacted with confusion to their first blackout. Worst was the driving. Police ordered motorists to use only their parking lights, and buses and streetcars followed suit. Enormous traffic jams developed, and the night was marred by the sound of automobile accidents.

The next morning at an emergency meeting of the city defense council, General DeWitt had angry words for those who didn't believe that the enemy had been in the skies: "There are more damned fools in this locality than I have ever seen. Death and destruction are likely to come to this city any moment. These planes were over our community for a definite period. They were enemy planes. I mean Japanese planes. They were tracked out to sea. Why bombs were not dropped, I do not know. It might have been better if some bombs had dropped to awaken this city."

In Seattle, the night and early morning were more harrowing. When the alert—which had spread, patchily, up and down the entire West Coast—reached Seattle, a crowd of nearly 1,000 people gathered in the downtown area and spontaneously, in the manner of mobs, set out to "enforce" the blackout. By 11 P.M. all lights were out except a glaring blue neon sign at the corner of the city's busiest block. The mob surged toward it, led by a nineteen-year-old woman whose husband was a sailor on a destroyer. (Later she explained her zeal: "We've got to show them they can't leave their lights burning. This is war. They don't realize one light in the city might betray us. That's my patriotism.") The mob began hurling anything that came to hand at the sign—bottles, rocks, tin cans and old shoes—as a squad of police stood by. The mob began throwing at other lights, then turned to looting. Before police stopped them, they had left a wake of shattered glass and looted stores over a six-block area.

The Eastern seaboard was quiet that Sunday night. Most people gathered about their radios, as they were to do for the next day in the largest numbers in history, listening for the meager news of Pearl Harbor or perhaps just relieving the tension with old favorites such as *Jack Benny, Edgar Bergen and Charlie McCarthy* and *One Man's Family*. In Washington the President had called a Cabinet meeting for eight thirty, which was joined by the Congressional leadership at nine. As the officials arrived, cheering crowds were lining Pennsylvania Avenue, "another evidence"—wrote a reporter fervently—"of the national determination to defeat Japan and her Axis allies which every official is confident will dominate the country from this moment forth." Showing up at the nine o'clock meeting was Senator W. Lee "Pappy" O'Daniel of Texas, though he had not been invited. Pappy explained that he wanted "to make sure Texas is represented at this conference." In his zeal he had forgotten that the chairman of the Senate Foreign Relations Committee, the senior Senator from Texas, Tom Connally, would be present by invitation to look after the foreign relations of the sovereign state of Texas.

As the President met with his advisers, then retired to work over his address to tomorrow's special session of Congress, his wife's voice stood in for him, over radios in millions of American homes. Broadcasting to the women of the nation, she said: "I have a boy at sea on a destroyer—for all I know he may be on his way to the Pacific; two of my children are in coast cities in the Pacific. Many of you all over the country have boys in the service who will now be called upon to go into action; you have friends and families in what has become a danger zone. You cannot escape anxiety, you cannot escape the clutch of fear at your heart and yet I hope that the certainty of what we have to meet will make you rise above those fears." She concluded: "I feel as though I were standing upon a rock and that rock is my faith in my fellow citizens."

In New York City, another man was in the spotlight—Mayor Fiorello LaGuardia. Of his two large hats, one was the hat of the national chairman of the Office of Civilian Defense. But his first duty was to his city, and all Sunday he had issued orders throwing up security guards around bridges, tunnels and factories and alerting the auxiliary firemen and air raid wardens. At five he held a press conference, broadcast over the city station WNYC, in which he called "Nazi thugs and gangsters" the "masterminds" of the bombing of Pearl Harbor. New Yorkers, he warned, should have no false sense of security because they lived along the Atlantic, for it was an extreme crisis and anything could be expected.

Monday passed without incident. There was little overt anti-Japan-

ese hostility. The previous night about 200 Japanese considered dangerous had been rounded up by the FBI and the police and placed in detention on Ellis Island after questioning at the Federal Building.
Japanese restaurants were closed. Their patrons were allowed to finish
eating; then the staff and owners were convoyed home. All Japanese
trying to leave the city by plane were turned back by police. Consul
General Morishima Morito was apprehended as he left his office at
5:15 P.M. He was carrying some newspapers, and an aide was carrying
a briefcase. A police search of the briefcase revealed that it contained
twenty film strips of scenes in Washington and New York, including the
Washington Monument, bridges, the New York skyline and one that
appeared to be either a dam or a reservoir. The police confiscated the
films as possible evidence. The FBI switchboard was swamped with
calls from people reporting suspicious Japanese lurking about.

Anti-Japanese violence was sporadic. Teddy Hare, forty-two, was
beaten up by three men in front of his house, and stones were thrown
through the plate-glass windows of the Taijo Trading Company. The
owner of a Yonkers curio shop became so infuriated that he took an
ax and a hammer and broke every item in his store bearing a "Made in
Japan" label. He piled the shards in a window along with a sign that
read: THIS IS OUR STOCK OF JAP GOODS. In White Plains, Matsuabo
Matsushita, a janitor, made an abortive hara-kiri attempt employing a
pocket knife and a needle and causing only superficial wounds. "My
country has done wrong in attacking the USA," Matsushita explained.

The roundup of Japanese followed a nationwide master plan, directed by Attorney General Francis Biddle and executed by the FBI,
which had compiled dossiers on a number of Japanese considered potential saboteurs. Early on the morning of the eighth, Biddle had
dismissed the possibility that all Japanese aliens in the country would be
rounded up. "Less than 1,000 Japanese nationals will be affected," he
told newsmen. "Procedures are being established to provide a fair hearing for all."

Most New Yorkers went to their offices Monday, still numb, gos-
siping about what had happened, exchanging scraps and tatters of information—"Wake Island has fallen"; "the radio said the battleship
Oklahoma was set on fire"; "Clark Field was wiped out"—and so on.
Many wondered at how lax the armed forces at Pearl Harbor had been
and demanded punishment of those responsible. Others were more fatalistic—the Japs had come out of nowhere to strike a sneaky, treacherous

blow, and nothing could have prevented it. Most hearts turned silently toward the White House, and when the President addressed Congress at noon, 60,000,000 Americans were at their radios—a record number of listeners—to hear him speak briefly and simply of the "day that will live in infamy."

Thousands were determined to do more than talk. By 7 A.M. there were thirty men in line at the Army recruiting center in New York waiting to enlist; the total for the entire day was three times that of April 6, 1917, when the First World War began. The Navy had 700 enlistments by midafternoon, the Marines 500. Processing was slow, though. Because of a shortage of doctors, the Navy turned away 1,000 men that day.

The Civilian Defense Volunteer office on Fifth Avenue was similarly swamped as people came in to register as air raid wardens or for other war jobs. The overburdened personnel closed the office at five so that more interviewers could be trained, promising to work around the clock from then on.

Despite the shortage of manpower, the director of Civilian Defense's city seemed fairly well organized, at least on paper. No one would know until the real thing came, of course. There were 115,000 wardens, and the city had been divided into zones and sectors and individual warden posts. Police Commissioner Lewis Valentine, whose department was directly over the wardens, said on Monday that he hoped to have them on twenty-four-hour duty at every post as soon as possible. This was to begin at midnight, Monday. Superintendents were also on twenty-four-hour air raid protection duty in their buildings. When the wardens were ordered to report to their sector commanders on Monday, in lower Manhattan there was a 100 percent turnout—10,000 men in all. Like San Francisco, the city of New York had no air raid sirens as yet, and any air raids would have been signaled by police and fire sirens in alternate long and short blasts. The wardens' duty was to assist the fire and police departments to see that lights were put out in a blackout, turn out streetlights, and summon aid where there was bomb damage.

Meanwhile, the Army's First Interceptor Command based at Mitchel Field, Long Island, was in action by dawn, Monday, when planes began taking off and patrolling the air, in company with Naval Air Force reconnaissance. Forty thousand civilian aircraft spotters manned 1,300 posts along the Eastern seaboard and District of Columbia, and the 62d Coast Artillery set up antiaircraft guns around New York City.

Tuesday, December 9, New York had its first air raid alarm. It came during the day and was not nearly so mysterious as San Francisco's. A man who remained unidentified but whose credentials were official enough to impress the military called First Army Headquarters on Governors Island and said he had heard on a radio broadcast originating in Washington that enemy bombers had been sighted off the Eastern seaboard. Would First Army please confirm or deny this report? Thank you. The Governors Island man had missed the broadcast but said he would telephone Mitchel Field to see if they knew anything. From then on events followed the script of an Abbott and Costello comedy routine. Somehow, the man at Mitchel got the idea that Governors Island was telling him that enemy bombers had been sighted. Whatever was said, it was somehow decided that the enemy would arrive at 2 and the alert was sounded, at approximately 1:25 P.M. in New York City and on up through the New England states.

In New York there was no panic. Indeed, people stood out on the streets gawking up at the sky—those who heard the police sirens. Air raid wardens moved out in desultory fashion to take their posts. Just that morning the Board of Education had distributed a booklet called *The Schools in Civilian Defense,* stating its conclusions about students. Assuming that air raids on New York would be brief and sporadic, the board decided that evacuation of children from the city would be unnecessary. (It had surveyed eighteen upstate counties, though, for available accommodations.) In the event of an air raid warning it would be best to send the children home from school. When the sirens sounded on Tuesday afternoon, the schools were notified, and classes dismissed. Within twenty minutes New York's one million schoolchildren had cleared the schools. Many, however, did not reach home but, making the most of their reprieve, began playing in the streets. Parents kept the school switchboards jammed with anxious calls or else rushed to school to claim their offspring.

Throughout New England similar exoduses were taking place. Hundreds of schools were evacuated. Workers in defense industries and civilians at military bases were sent home—wasting valuable production time.

Finally, in midafternoon, the Army, which had been maintaining all along that "Washington" had alerted it to the presence of enemy planes, admitted (through Major General Herbert A. Dargue, commander, First Interceptor Command) that there were "definitely no enemy planes." In Boston, J. W. Farley, director of the Massachusetts Commission of Public Safety, said that "the Army and Navy now informs us that it was a dress rehearsal." To crown the confusions, the stock market, which had held fairly steady Monday, considering the attack on Pearl Harbor the previous day, plummeted.

About eight o'clock the next morning, Nassau County police on Long Island were notified by Mitchel that unidentified planes were approaching. Later there was some conflict over what kind of warning was given. Mitchel said it had merely given a routine alert, and when the planes were identified as U.S. Navy patrol planes, the all clear was sent out.

Whatever the story, the police cars wailed alternate long and short blasts. It was 8:41 A.M., and thousands of New Yorkers were on their way to work—in subways, on buses, arriving on commuter trains. Those who heard the sirens were pouring out of subways or hurrying along the streets. Being New Yorkers, they paused (if they heard the sirens at all), glanced up at the sky, and hustled on to work. In Sunnyside, Long Island, where the students had been sent home from school, the youngsters returned at noon, only to find that their teachers had decided to take advantage of an afternoon off to do their Christmas shopping.

The planes were ours. They had first been detected at 5:33 A.M. by the Mitchel radio detection unit while they were still 150 miles out to sea. Mitchel warned Suffolk County, then Nassau, then Brooklyn and Queens.

By this time Wednesday's papers were displaying pictures of New Yorkers in Battery Park, at the height of Tuesday's alert, gaping up at the sky and pointing. This caused their mayor some embarrassment, since, as national head of Civilian Defense, he would have expected to have had a model city. Indeed, the "Little Flower" was out of the city. He and Mrs. Roosevelt were on a tour of civil defense preparations on the West Coast. Said LaGuardia in Seattle when queried about goings-on in his own bailiwick: "Am I embarrassed. Am I humiliated. Won't somebody catch hell about this when I get home? Here I go around the country telling people they must stay inside, during air raid alarms. And right in my own city—this happens!" When asked what he thought of the state of the nation's civilian defenses, LaGuardia replied: "This is the time to speak frankly. So, frankly nowhere in the country is civilian defense operating to my satisfaction." The mayor of New York was not noted for understatement, but here he seemed to have made a rare one.

All the false alarms, the New York Hotel Association announced, were hurting the hotel business. Guests were checking out, and convention groups were canceling their future reservations. The association petitioned Newbold Morris, who was acting mayor in LaGuardia's absence, to dispel the false rumors that New York City was now unsafe to visit.

Tuesday night it was Los Angeles' turn to deal with the ubiquitous enemy planes. These planes (probably from the same ghostly aircraft carrier that had bothered San Francisco Sunday) were reported due "over" Los Angeles at 8:15 P.M. Angelenos had a scant five minutes' notice, for the alarm sounded at 8:10. Police, fire department, air raid wardens, and even Boy Scouts moved up and down streets, turning off lights. Los Angeles also had no sirens and made do with police and fire engine alerts. But the people were cooperative. They were jittery and had already experienced two radio silences Monday, plus partial blackouts. A thunderstorm on Monday had sent thousands of nervous citizens to their windows, thinking that Japanese bombs were already exploding. Further, war was already taking its toll. During the blackout of the previous two nights, four deaths had resulted from automobile accidents. Tonight, lights blinked out quickly; by nine the city was lying dark and still under the clear night sky.

San Francisco, the Bay Area and Sacramento had a similar alert the same night. This time San Francisco blacked out almost completely. Associated Press reporters were filing their dispatches by kerosene lanterns, with steel helmets at their sides. Downtown, zealous citizens went around breaking store windows where lights were still burning. The Army refused to explain the cause of the alerts but said that at the yellow signal all its planes had scrambled.

Later Lieutenant General John L. DeWitt scotched any thoughts the citizens might have that the Army was playing games in order to get them to practice their blackouts. "This is war," he said, "death and destruction may come from the skies at any moment." Persons who doubted the reality of the Jap planes tooling around California skies were "insane, foolish, idiotic. It is damn nonsense to assume we would practice an alert." (Nonetheless, there were no Japanese planes over California, and it seems probable that General DeWitt was taking advantage of some erroneous reports to emphasize to Californians that This Is War.)

Even though the early alarms had proved false, people in California were nervous. Already they were seeing signs of enemy spies among them. A woman in San Francisco observed regularly flashing lights across the bay. She made a movie of them and sent it to the FBI, which ran it again and again in a vain attempt to break the code or whatever it was. On Tuesday night, other San Franciscans reported that six flares had been dropped over the city during the blackout.

Rumors were rife, and *some* of the people believed some of the time that:

1. The Japanese consulate gave a banquet the night of December 6 for U.S. Army and Navy officers and served them unprecedented quantities of alcohol in order to incapacitate them for the morrow.

2. A small army of Filipinos invaded Los Angeles' Little Tokyo and slaughtered hundreds of Japanese. The police immediately roped off the area and kept it sealed for a week afterward and newspapermen killed the story lest it touch off a wave of Japanese lynching on the West Coast.

3. A Los Angeles housewife, mistakenly deciding her Chinese groceryman was a Japanese, smashed a bottle of club soda over his head, killing him.

4. A man in Del Monte was so furious when the Army moved some artillery onto Cyprus Point the night of December 7 that he ordered the commanding officer to take his "damned guns someplace else" because this was "private property."

5. Twelve thousand Japanese who had once lived in the United States but who had returned to Japan before the war were being trained as a special invasion force.

At the time of Pearl Harbor, the state of the nation's civilian defense was barely adequate. The concrete accomplishments during the prewar period were few. There were the traditional state-federal government and local-state conflicts to hamper the establishment of any centralized, nationwide system of civilian defense. LaGuardia wanted a national system with the Washington office of the Office of Civilian Defense over the regional offices, which in turn would be over the local offices. But the state governors, jealous of their perquisites, were loath to relinquish control over an organization potentially affecting the lives of so many. They resisted federal domination of the OCD, and were reluctant to subordinate state and local government to the role of carrying out any and all federal programs the OCD might originate. Ultimately each state organized a central defense council—not always by that name—of which the governor was usually ex officio chairman, and with specialists in various areas (public health, fire prevention, etc.) heading up the various divisions. At the same time, there were nine regional OCD offices (based on the nine domestic Army commands), and municipal units were set up, at least in part. Chicago, for example, was designated a separate area, and Mayor Raymond J. Kelly ran its civil defense as though it were his own satrapy, calling it the Chicago Committee on National Defense.

In effect, the saying that federal authority in civilian defense was "about the strength of an armband" was true. The office never had the power to enforce any of its policies, nor could it even withhold funds and equipment from an uncooperative locality. A model defense council plan was promulgated by the OCD, and many states followed it in setting up their own civilian defense; but enforcement of blackouts and penalties for violation of a blackout were carried out through state law or municipal ordinance.

So civilian defense sputtered along quaintly in the confused months immediately prior to the war. LaGuardia generated a whirlwind show of activity, thus undeniably drawing attention to civilian defense but also fanning a brush fire of criticism not only for his conduct of office, but also for staying on as mayor of New York. Some of it was due to apathy (as late as December 5, the Chicago *Tribune* would write: "There is no need for these white helmeted air raid wardens"); many people thought practice air raids silly, and LaGuardia sounded like a false Cassandra in his calls for civilian readiness in the face of possible enemy attack.

LaGuardia's philosophy of civilian defense was simplicity itself: It should be confined solely to air raid protection—that is, air raid wardens, auxiliary firemen and so on. "An auxiliary fire department medical department—that is all there is to it. We go out when the alarm is sounded . . . and our task is to train the people to follow rules for their own protection and our air-raid wardens see to it that traffic stops, that the streets are cleared and that people get undercover; and if it is at night, darken the rooms in the general blackout effort."

According to the President's initial executive order, however, that was not all there was to it. Also called for was a Voluntary Participation program, which would enroll civilians in community service work connected with health, welfare, child care, physical fitness, morale and so on. These plans LaGuardia dismissed as "sissy stuff," until the Bureau of the Budget announced that it would withhold all further funds of the OCD unless LaGuardia complied with the entire executive order. The upshot was that Mrs. Roosevelt, who took a strong interest in the Voluntary Participation program and pressured LaGuardia to do something about it, was appointed director in charge of Voluntary Participation. Under her were four units: Women's, Youth and Veterans Activities and Physical Fitness.

By November, 1941, all the states and 5,935 towns and cities had at least set up defense councils. Many air raid wardens had been trained. Plans for taking care of casualties, clearing debris and repairing water mains, gas mains and other vital services were in being. True, local defense councils had no equipment—not even armbands for their wardens, let alone the supplementary fire-fighting equipment that would presumably be needed in the event of air raids. LaGuardia had asked Congress for $99,000,000 worth of such equipment, but by the time of Pearl Harbor, this request was stalled in the House Military Affairs Committee. There still another philosophy of civilian defense prevailed. Several members who were anti-LaGuardia urged that all civilian defense protective functions be placed under the War Department and the Voluntary Participation programs be abolished or transferred to other government agencies.

There was no air raid shelter program, and LaGuardia had said rather vaguely before the war: "It hasn't been definitely decided that air shelters are the answer." On the other hand, he wanted 50,000,000 gas masks after Pearl Harbor, although his previous appropriation request provided only for an "educational order" of 1,000,000 masks.

LaGuardia defended his organization with his usual pugnacity. In a speech, forgetting what he had said in California a week previously ("nowhere in the country is civilian defense operating to my satisfaction"), he maintained that civilian defense was "magnificently organized" and lashed out at his critics, calling them "swivel chair scribes," "two by four editors," "liars" and "some Jap or friend of a Jap." Those critical of the OCD were practically traitors engaged in a "new technique, to seek to create confusion, to continue fear and terror in the minds of the people."

At the same time he delivered a sober warning to New Yorkers, flatly predicting that the city would be attacked. "The war will come right to our cities and residential districts. At the present time, under the present relative position of the enemy, we may not expect long-continued, sustained attacks such as the cities of Great Britain have suffered, but we will be attacked—never underestimate the strength, the cruelty of the enemy—and we must prepare for that." (On New Year's Eve, LaGuardia issued a combined greeting and a warning: "Rejoice, be happy, make merry, but please do not use any sound-making device, any siren or horn that would resemble the alarm in your community.")

When war came, the Washington office of the OCD had only seventy-five full-time people in the Protective Division (the Voluntary Participation was even more skeletal). Undermanned though it was, the OCD swung into immediate action. The seventeen-hour day became the rule. One officer worked forty hours straight; another, thirty-four; and one, beginning December 8, worked against two shifts of stenographers daily until May 8. One of the office's first missions was preparation of a pamphlet called *What to Do in an Air Raid*. Fifty-seven million were rushed into print in December, and in addition, newspapers all over the nation reprinted the pamphlet in their pages. "The safest place in an air raid," instructed the pamphlet, "is at home." In case of attack, people were to retire to their previously prepared "refuge room" in the center of the house and lie down under "a good stout table." If one's house was hit, one was reminded to "Answer tapping from rescue crews," though "You most likely won't be hit or trapped, but if you are, you can depend on rescue squads to go after you." One was reminded also to stay away from windows. In the absence of air raid shelters Americans were comforted by the thought that "you can do all these things without any special equipment, other than what you now have in your home." The pamphlet closed stirringly: "You can lick the Japs with your bare hands, if you will do just these simple things. . . . Do not be a wise guy and get hurt."

By January, 1942, there were 5,601,892 Americans enrolled in civil defense programs—though most of these had to wait for room in a training program to open up. There were also 7,031 defense councils in existence. Then the roof fell in. Restive, frustrated over the gloomy news from the war fronts, and mindful of "unpreparedness" at Pearl Harbor, Congress turned its wrath—or some of it—on the OCD, and more specifically on LaGuardia and Mrs. Roosevelt.

Silly as it may sound, Mrs. Roosevelt came under attack because of an actor and an eurythmic dancer. The dancer was a young lady named Mayris Chayney who had caught Mrs. Roosevelt's eye back in 1938 when she invented—and demonstrated before the First Lady—a dance called the Eleanor Glide. In December, 1941, Miss Chayney was appointed head of the Children's Activities Section of the Physical Fitness Division of the OCD—which, of course, was Mrs. Roosevelt's area of concern—at a salary alleged to be $4,600 a year. (Miss Chayney later said the figure was "all news to her" and that in her two months she had received no pay.) Miss Chayney interpreted her job as one of providing recreation for children during air raids and developing programs of dancing and rhythmic exercises that could be performed by people confined in an air raid shelter. What program she had devised was still not apparent by early February when the storm broke in Congress.

The actor was Melvyn Douglas, an ardent New Dealer who was appointed head of the Arts Council of the OCD's Voluntary Participation branch, at a salary of $8,000 per year. (Later it developed that Douglas was not expected to work full time and would be paid on a per diem basis of $22.22 a day when he actually performed OCD tasks.) On February 5, Thomas Ford, Democrat from Los Angeles, launched his attack on Chayney and Douglas during the House debates on the OCD appropriation bill. Criticizing "frills" in the OCD program, Ford pointed to the hiring of Miss Chayney, who he seemed to think was a "fan dancer" and a "strip teaser." He also criticized the appointment of Douglas, who he said had "communist tendencies," and called for a Congressional inquiry into OCD spending. Representative Carl Hinshaw (R., Calif.) chimed in that "glamour is not needed to inspire our people to the defense of the country." The next day the angry debate continued. Representative Clare E. Hoffman (R., Mich.) suggested a Bundles for Eleanor Roosevelt movement be launched in tribute to Mrs. Roosevelt's ability to get jobs for her friends. Representative Marion T. Bennett (R., Mo.) was equally sarcastic. He thought that if a "fan dancer" like Miss Chayney was worth $4,600 a year, then Miss Sally Rand, the noted fan dancer from his district, should be worth at least $25,000. Asserting that the only qualification Miss Chayney had for her job was that she had created the Eleanor Glide, Representative Bennett continued, with heavy-handed rancor: "If that is the prime requisite for such an important job, I promise you that I will persuade Sally Rand to name six of her ostrich fans, Captain Jimmie, Captain Elliott, Lieutenant John, Ensign Franklin, Sistie and Buzzie, respectively." Other members chimed in, and one summed up the Congressional mood: "Enemy raids on the continental United States are to be expected—what can actors and dancers do about them?" The upshot of the debate was that the appropriations were authorized but a rider was attached prohibiting the use of OCD funds for "instruction in physical fitness by dancers, fan-dancing, street shows, theatrical performances or other public entertainment." Further no person working for the OCD could be paid more than $4,500 a year unless he had been appointed by the President with the advice and consent of the Senate, and only $3,000,000 of the appropriation could be spent on administrative expenses—the rest going for protective equipment. FDR signed the bill on February 21; the previous day

Mrs. Roosevelt had resigned as head of the Voluntary Participation division and Jonathan Daniels had been appointed her successor. Miss Chayney also resigned, as did Melvyn Douglas, who enlisted in the Army as a private a few months later—but not before the Senate Appropriations Committee, holding a hearing on the authorization, queried whether or not Melvyn Douglas wasn't really a German named Melvin Douglas Hasselberg. "He is a Jew," replied the OCD.

Even before the Congressional blowup, the President, it appeared, was already dealing with the LaGuardian aspect of the program (he did not foresee that his own wife would precipitate the major Congressional hostility). In January, when the House and Senate were leaning toward abolishing the OCD entirely and putting air raid protection functions under the War Department (on January 8, the House had voted to strip LaGuardia of his powers and place the OCD under the War Department), the President had appointed James Landis to the position of executive director of the OCD. Landis, an expert in administrative law, was dean of the Harvard Law School and regional director of the OCD for New England. He was an experienced administrator as well, having served under the New Deal as chairman of the Securities Exchange Commission. A *modus vivendi* with LaGuardia was worked out by which Landis was to be in charge of day-to-day administration of the OCD, while LaGuardia ostensibly remained in charge of large policy decisions. This effectively forestalled favorable Senate action on the House measure. After the storm had passed, LaGuardia was able to resign face-savingly on February 10, proclaiming that his work was done; the appropriations he requested had gone through. Then, Landis, who was in *de facto* charge of the office, was made director on April 10. (LaGuardia remained in command of New York City's Civilian Defense program—and was subjected to the same "part-time" criticism.)

Landis took over the OCD facing a hostile Congress and a skeptical press. The latter, especially the Chicago *Tribune* and Cissy Patterson's Washington *Star,* found the OCD—or "Ocey Docey," as it had come to be known—great sport. There was, for example, the time the lights burned late in the OCD headquarters at DuPont Circle in Washington. Did the press take the occasion to praise the long hours the office's personnel were working? No, they cruelly pointed out that on the particular night that the OCD's lights were burning late the rest of Washington was undergoing a blackout—the OCD was one of the few violators. (The OCD explained that the blackout was under the jurisdiction of the local civilian defense authorities and claimed immunity.)

Among Landis' first acts was to abolish the ten inspector generals, appointed by LaGuardia, whose job was to watch over the several regions and report the progress being made at the local level. They had been resented by the local defense councils and had to go. In something of a paper move, Landis also abolished or transferred to other agencies the Voluntary Participation program activities that Mrs. Roosevelt had set up. The notorious Physical Fitness Division was transferred to the Office of Defense Health and Welfare Services—but not before Senator Harry Byrd, the Virginia Democrat, had raised the roof because he learned the OCD had appointed a bowling coordinator.

By the end of January Landis reported that 5,601,892 Americans, including 334,666 auxiliary police, 670,673 air raid wardens and 265,580 medical personnel, had volunteered for civil defense (training them and actually putting them on the job were another matter) and 8,478 defense councils had been organized. Still, flash fires of criticism continued to flare all over the nation. In New York City air raid wardens were calling the early precautions "a perfect farce." A Wisconsin newspaper said in late February that "Civilian Defense in this state is a mess" and blamed the mess on the federal government. Los Angeles in April reported the city needed 50,000 auxiliary firemen and fire watchers but had enrolled less than 5,000. In Buffalo the local civilian defense chief resigned over political interference with the civilian defense program and privately predicted that there would be panic and chaos if the bombers were to come. In the Bronx and Queens in New York there were reports of mutiny among the air raid wardens. Police Commissioner Valentine refused to comment, but it was reported that some of the initial dissenters were being investigated by the police for possible ties with the Christian Front or the German-American Bund. In March, 15 wardens whose territory was the DuPont Circle area in Washington where the national OCD had its headquarters resigned protesting the shortage of equipment, and 105 more threatened resignation. The men received a reprimand from Colonel Lemuel C. Bolles, head of the Washington OCD: "There are a number of men under MacArthur in the Philippines who are not resigning and who are not getting equipment either."

But Washington was not unique. All over the nation the most crippling problem was the shortage of equipment. It was not until March 6 that the OCD received its $100,000,000 for equipment, and not until March 16 that the Bureau of the Budget informed Landis that funds were actually available. Contracts were let as quickly as possible, but priorities posed another snag. In the distribution of priorities the

OCD was relegated to the end of the line, just ahead of consumer goods industries. The equipment specifications formulated under LaGuardia were now obsolete, for they called for critical matériel upon which the Army and Navy had a higher priority. Fire hose couplings, for example, called for precious copper and had to be redesigned so that cast iron, which was less critical, could be employed.

Ironically, one of the first to jump on the OCD's neck for these delays was its old boss, LaGuardia himself. The mayor accused his successor of "bungling" and observed: "I want to tell the OCD that you cannot put out a fire with an armband."

When the OCD failed to deliver on LaGuardia's demand for 22,000 air raid wardens' helmets, Fiorello unleashed volley after volley of criticism. Where were those helmets? The OCD could well reply that they were in the works, have patience. This was true: The McCord Radiator and Manufacturing Company was turning them out as fast as possible. Soon New York's quota was sent to Akron, where the B. F. Goodrich Company was to install rubber and cork linings. After about 300 were completed, an employee tried one on and discovered that the helmets had been designed three-quarters of an inch too small.

New York air raid wardens, tackling their jobs *sans* helmet, armband, flashlight and gas masks, made do with what they had as best they could. During an early blackout many men provided themselves with police whistles, the kind that is sold in any dime store. Never mind that the whistles bore the legend "Made in Japan"; at least they blew, and a man with a police whistle is a man with some authority. Uniforms were being designed for the wardens (which they had to pay for themselves and were optional), but in the meantime a man had to dress as comfortably as he could for those cold early-war nights. The *New Yorker* magazine devoted an "As to Men" section to advising Manhattan exquisites on warden fashions:

> Abercrombie and Fitch recommends its long woolen underwear for the night trick, taking the sensible point of view that a warden trudging the streets wants to feel comfortable rather than natty. . . . For unobtrusiveness, and at the same time real warmth, there's nothing better than a hug-me tight fleece-lined vest at Brooks. . . . Of course no one knows whether a blackout will descend upon us. If and when it does, though, some luminous cloth that I came across at Brooks ought to help prevent human collisions. It is cut into brassards and hatbands which have buttons at one end and buttonholes at the other for adjusting their size.

The shortage of air raid sirens was also a hindrance. Police and fire engine sirens which most large cities resorted to in the early months of the war were unsatisfactory. People either couldn't hear them or else confused them with normal fire or police department activities. In New York, big factories volunteered their whistles, and the city accepted gratefully. Other towns showed ingenuity and the variety of noisemakers used was colorful. Sepulveda, California, used a 100-year-old cast-iron Mississippi riverboat bell, while Reading, Pennsylvania, simply used auto horns (three shorts and a long blast—the "V for Victory" sound) to alert the citizenry. Milwaukee utilized fifty-five factory whistles, nineteen stationary sirens, plus air horns, emergency vehicle sirens and a Foster steam siren.

To end the siren shortage, the OCD let a contract to Bell Telephone Laboratories to design a standard model. The result was christened the Victory Siren and could be operated by an ordinary automobile engine which powered compressed air through whirling metal blades. Touted by its designers as "the loudest sound in the world," its blast was said to be able to break the eardrums of a man standing 100 feet away, and the Army considered using it as a weapon for a time. The Victory Siren blanketed an area 10 miles square with its wail, but many communities refused to purchase it because it was too loud.

The threat of an enemy invasion of our shores, though increasingly remote as time went on, was a real possibility to many local authorities. California's coasts were well manned by the Army and coastal defense guns, but the Atlantic coast was relatively undefended—if Hitler couldn't cross the Channel, how was he going to get across the Atlantic? Still, who knew?

Before the war most states had organized State Guard units after the President had federalized the National Guard. These were composed of men with deferments, men too young for the draft and old-timers up to sixty-five years of age. Their mission was mainly to combat subversive activities and civil unrest and to provide assistance in emergencies, including air raids, when the civil authorities might have their hands full. But in at least one state, Georgia, the State Guard was actively preparing to repulse an invasion. Attorney General Lindley W. Camp had organized a small citizens' army made up of World War I veterans and other able-bodied Georgians, and during the early months of 1942 they spent most of their time patrolling the coast and readying their defenses. Convicts from Tatnall Prison were set to work night and day building bridges and improving roads for the transport of men and supplies. The little army utilized whatever manner of trucks and cars and makeshift weapons it could assemble, and its mission was to hold off any German invaders as long as possible in a delaying action, then to retreat slowly to Baxley in Appling County and hold out until help arrived from the real Army training camps at Fort Benning and elsewhere in the state.

In January and February people living along the East Coast saw German submarines operating offshore, although official sources gave out little information. Flashes of explosions appeared against the night sky, and beaches became littered with a grisly flotsam and jetsam—bodies, charred lifeboats, empty lifebuoys, and fish and waterfowl that had died in oil-fouled waters. Cape Hatteras, long a graveyard for storm-tossed ships, received a new kind of marine carcass: the torpedoed merchantman. As early as December 14, aircraft spotters and residents on the Delmarva Peninsula heard "sounds like rolling thunder . . . accompanied by red flashes far at sea to the northeast shortly after midnight." In June vacationers at Virginia Beach watched as two freighters were blitzed by the methodical U-boats. Perhaps the show bore out the prediction of Mayor Clifford B. Cropper of Baltimore four months earlier. Scoffing at gloomy forecasts that the war would hurt tourist business on Maryland beaches, the mayor said submarine activity off the Atlantic seaboard would be one of its greatest tourist attractions. But the lights from the unblacked-out cities at night cast a faint but deadly emanation over the littoral waters—what Brigadier General Thomas A. Terry, commanding officer of the Second Service Command, termed a "murderous mound of light"—silhouetting targets against the night sky for the lurking subs.

In Georgia rumors were rife that U-boats were putting ashore at Brunswick and Savannah under cover of darkness to land espionage agents and bring back spies; also, small boats operated by traitorous Americans were reportedly plying between the coastline and the lurking subs, conducting a profitable trade in gasoline and other supplies. Presumably Camp's army was hunting down these poltroons, but the possibility of air attacks carried out by small planes catapulted from the decks of subs still remained.

In Charleston, South Carolina, a local citizen expressed the prevailing view of the Nazi menace to a sojourning journalist: "We're close enough to the Caribbean," he said, "and close enough to everything to

feel that we're right at the head of the enemy's list."* Charleston's civil
defense measures had moved forward accordingly. There were sandbags
on the roofs of hotels, and refugee and casualty centers had been published in the local papers. Public bomb shelters, located in schools,
gymnasiums, parish halls, markets and churches had also been designated. Those west of King Street (Main Street) were for whites; those
east of King Street were for Negroes. One local citizen told a visiting
journalist that the town was divided up about half and half between
those who expected some kind of an attack someday and those who
"never give the war a thought." Although "people down here don't get
excited as quickly as they do in some places," he said, the city would
give a good account of itself if trouble came: ". . . if any of them ever
come falling out of the sky over Charleston harbor and try to do any
landing on that beach out there or on Sullivan's Island, they'll never
live to be pampered by our government and hustled off to luxury at
White Sulphur Springs [Japanese diplomatic personnel were interned at
the resort]. No sir! We'll take care of them right here in our own way."

An editorial appearing in *Collier's* in March cautioned:

> It may come to pass, as has been predicted, that enemy air-
> men will fly over here occasionally during the war, drop bombs on
> important industrial spots, then bail out, let their planes crash and
> give themselves up. In case such things do happen, we'd like to put
> in an earnest plea now, to any civilians who may reach these air-
> men ahead of police or soldiers, not to obey the human impulse
> to lynch them, shoot them, or kick them to death.

The Midwest was less fearful of German or Japanese raids though
the possibility was alive. In Illinois a local civilian defense pamphlet declared that "Chicago can be bombed" and contained a map showing
that Chicago was closer (via the polar route) to Nazi-occupied Norway
than was New York City. And then there was the jittery lady in Elgin
who wrote a letter to President Roosevelt protesting the locating of defense
plants in her area without any provision for bomb shelters to protect
civilians from the raids that were sure to follow. She said that departing
servicemen should shed tears for the civilians who were left behind at the

---

* "The enemy's list" was a popular status symbol in those days; cities were always
announcing that because of their vital war production and all around importance, they
were "number one on the enemy's list" of targets to be bombed. Where these "lists"
originated is unclear; certainly, the enemy had a large number of top-priority targets on
that list, if various city fathers were to be believed.

enemy's mercy "for were they not evacuating a city far less prepared to meet the enemy than they will be a few weeks hence?"

In Wisconsin the state commander of the American Legion called for the formation of a guerrilla army made up of the state's 25,000 licensed deer hunters. These sharpshooters "would be a formidable foe for any attackers," the minuteman in chief declared. Arizonans for the most part felt protected by the mountains and desert that lay between them and the Pacific; still—as one citizen put it—"California can handle those Japs, can't they? We've got the [Mexican] border to worry about. Things are liable to pop down there any time." And in Tillamook, a city on the Oregon coast, a group of farmers led by Stewart P. Arnold, a blind veteran of the First World War, had organized a guerrilla band. *Life* gave them a write-up with pictures of men aiming guns at a mythical foe from behind giant tree stumps. The magazine said approvingly: "They are prepared to defend their heritage with bullets and the frontiersman's lore. Sworn to die fighting if need be, they plan to hide their dairy herds deep in the woods, to combat forest fires started by incendiary bombs, and to harry the invader who dares penetrate their trackless timberlands. To a man they are dead shots."

Japanese ships remained as spectral as the *Flying Dutchman,* however. The garbage scow of the Oakland Scavenger Company which claimed to have rammed and sunk a Japanese sub in San Francisco Bay had its kill scoffed at by the Navy, which wondered why the scow's skipper had waited two weeks before reporting the incident. Then, on February 23, as if in partial answer to General DeWitt's prayers, a Japanese submarine surfaced off the California coast and lobbed a few shells in the general direction of an oilfield near Santa Barbara. No major damage was done, but the small shell pocks made good pictures for the newspapers. The shelling incident was repeated in June when another sub fired a half dozen or so shells onto a sandy Oregon beach and repeated the performance the next day. Residents of nearby towns heard the cannonade and the whistle of the shells and could see orange-colored flashes against the sky.

But it was in Atlantic waters, where enemy subs were operating with most deadly effect, that the OCD was able to render its first major service. Immediately after Pearl Harbor all civilian planes were grounded lest they be mistaken for enemy planes or employed by indigenous saboteurs for bombing missions. Soon, however, the OCD realized that the nation's 100,000 private pilots were a potential asset. As a result, the Civil Air Patrol, which had been established as an independent arm of the Office of Civilian Defense on December 1, was activated on December 11. These civilian sport fliers were given 200 hours of special training, and when, by March, 1942, it became clear that the Army and Navy needed help in dealing with the U-boat menace, the CAP's planes were drafted for patrol duty. The first CAP base, known as Coastal Patrol Base Number One, was organized near Atlantic City. All the personnel were civilians. They used their own planes and received no pay for their services (though they received a per diem subsistence allowance and rental for their planes and were reimbursed by the government for crash liability). Planes from Coastal Patrol Base Number One began flying over coastal waters from New York harbor to Cape May, reporting any subs in the vicinity and spotting wreckage and lifeboats as well.

This unit was so successful that CAP organization and training in the other coastal states was accelerated. With a few months there were twenty-six coastal patrol bases up and down the entire Eastern seaboard, and CAP planes were sallying forth as far as 100 miles to blanket the entire area. Their auxiliary coverage of the offshore waters released Army and Navy aircraft for long-range surveillance. By July the CAP planes had been armed with bombs and actively engaging submarines. By war's end the CAP sky pickets had bombed fifty-seven submarines in all, mostly inflicting minor damage but sinking a handful of Nazi raiders. The work was hazardous; piloting their small planes as much as 100 miles out to sea in winter, the CAP men faced almost certain death should they ditch in the chill, steel-gray Atlantic waters, unless quickly rescued. Twenty-six of them were killed in action and five more seriously injured. Others were forced down and rescued.

At its peak, the CAP numbered 80,000 men and women, plus 20,000 air cadets—boys and girls between fifteen and eighteen who received preflight training. There were units in the hinterlands, as well as along the coast. Throughout the country CAP men performed a wide variety of functions, including searching for downed aircraft, acting as industrial couriers, towing targets for antiaircraft gunnery practice, patrolling forests on the lookout for fires, impersonating enemy planes in air raid drills, patrolling the Mexican border, inspecting camouflage from the air, and, in emergencies, flying in food or plasma to backcountry areas.

But the Civilian Air Patrol enlisted only a small elite in its coastal defense activities. Of greater impact on the average American living along the Eastern seaboard was the dimout. There the submarine menace was a vivid reality.

In March, 1942, the Third Civilian Defense Region ordered a coastal dimout along the Virginia and Maryland shore and southward. The dimout regulations prohibited any direct rays of light or fixed lights shown seaward and encompassed an area 12–16 miles inland. Signs were posted along roads within one mile of the coast ordering all autos to put out their headlights when proceeding toward the water. There were strict penalties for violators—up to one year in prison and a fine of $5,000.

By June New York City, slow to comply voluntarily, was dimmed out by military order. The ban on all outdoor advertising signs drained Times Square of its incandescence; theatergoers had to grope their way to performances. Lucius Beebe described in the *Herald Tribune* the havoc wrought upon Manhattan's *haute monde*:

> The opening night of Ray Bolger's new musical "By Jupiter" saw [theatergoers] completely baffled by the lack of familiar West Side landmarks and feeling their way from Sardi's to the Shubert Theater and back by an elaborate system of navigation based on the Braille system and dead reckoning. In some instances, the staff of Sardi's went into action as harbor pilots, guiding customers to their seats in a sort of pallid gloom and this department and Mrs. Fred Wildman, after the entr'acte, found themselves for a time in the right seats but in the Broadhurst Theater where "Uncle Harry" rather than "By Jupiter" was in progress.

At the Stage Door Canteen on Forty-fourth Street, perhaps Romney Brent was taking hats in the checkroom or Katharine Cornell was pouring coffee at the food counter, while in the kitchen, Shirley Booth and Alfred Lunt might be scraping plates into the garbage. On a given night there would be lines in the street outside the canteen, and 500 young men from at least six different nations inside, flirting with the pretty starlet hostesses.

Nightclub trade initially was down: The Latin Quarter estimated its business was off 25 percent. As one restaurant owner summed it up: "People come [to Times Square] to see lights." Broadway, once so profligate with its kilowattage, was now a pinched miser.

Up and down the coast it was the same—and along the West Coast too. In November, stricter dimout rules were issued. The gay resorts lost some of their sparkle. In Ocean City, New Jersey, the beach closed after sundown. Buildings near the ocean were equipped with light traps—double doors, the outer of which was opaque to seal in the light inside. Windows facing the beaches had to be heavily curtained and the curtains drawn at night. In Manhattan the streetlights were shielded on the ocean side; Coney Island was dark. Bridges along the coast were guarded now, and the beaches were patrolled by Coast Guardsmen, sometimes on horseback.

On the West Coast, after the initial panic, the blackout became effective. By January, 1942, San Francisco was answering its tenth alert —and seventh blackout—of the war. Two minutes after the sirens sounded, observers on the roof of the San Francisco *Chronicle* building reported that the city's darkness was practically entire.

Flying Officer Nobuo Fujita of the Imperial Japanese Navy, the only enemy pilot to bomb American soil, dropped incendiary bombs on an Oregon forest in November, 1942. Fujita flew a modified Zero, equipped with pontoons, which was housed in a special watertight compartment on the submarine I-25. His mission was to set fire to the tinder-dry forests, setting off a fire storm that would spread and ultimately sweep down the coast. Fujita made two attacks, the first by day, the second by night. Though he was flying over a relatively uninhabited stretch of America, he noted that the small town of Brookings Harbor was "completely blacked out" (perhaps they were all asleep). Yet he had no trouble navigating, for the Cape Blanco lighthouse cast its resolute beam steadily out to sea. Homing in on the light, Fujita flew inland and dropped his bombs, then managed to return to his sub. The raid, of course, did not accomplish its objective.

So the dimout became a way of life, and the periodic blackout drills became a mild annoyance. At first, though, blackouts had, especially in the large cities, an undercurrent of romance. To see the darkened buildings and the deserted streets was a newly minted experience for the city dweller. Many commented on how odd it was to see the stars.

Certainly, the air raid warden's nagging cry—"Get those lights out!" —became a familiar sound in many towns during the war years. The extra-zealous warden would keep up the din until the residents complied, or if the residents were out, he might even break in and turn out the lights. Of course in the big city, there was a limit to what you could do, and one foreign journalist in New York watched while a lone air raid warden raised his puny cries against an offending square of light twenty-six flights up in a giant apartment house. Finally, he saw the absurdity of his activity, smiled sheepishly, said, "Guess they've gone out for the night and left the lights burning," and walked away. But for the most part, Americans—even those living in small towns whose military importance was practically nil—took their blackouts seriously, at least during the first year of the war.

More philosophic souls found blackouts a time for patriotic introspection. One warden saw the blackout as a symbol of the "blackout of civilization" caused by the war, while the Chicago *Tribune* saw it symbolizing "the awesome night that war has brought to the world." A Chicago warden said that the blackout "does something to you. It is a personal experience. . . . There is no physical fear. But the war is no longer far off in London or Chungking." The *Tribune* proposed that future anniversaries of the "armistice" terminating the current conflict be memorialized by turning down the lights as a reminder of the perpetual darkness against which men in many parts of the world were fighting. So eager were Chicagoans to do their part in their blackout of August, 1942, that even the altar lights that had burned steadily since the Great Fire of 1871 in the Virgin Holy Family Church (in gratitude for its being spared by the fire) were extinguished. A lawyer found the absence of noise salubrious and recommended blackouts as a cure for jangled nerves. One lady air raid warden became a grandmother during the blackout and urged the parents to name the child OCD.

In the small towns of Princeton and Williamsfield, Illinois, however, there was some grousing among the farm folk about the August 12 blackout. They objected to its beginning at 10 P.M. and ending at 10:30. By that late hour most of them were in bed, and how could you have an honest blackout if everybody is already in bed?

On July 30, a blackout of downstate Illinois was held to test the ability of civilian defense people to go out on short notice. In Spring Valley, considerable confusion resulted because the War Production Board had refused to give the town a priority for a siren. In Springfield, signals got crossed, and when the warning came, the streetlights were turned on. Folks in Rockford took the whole thing as a big joke and gathered in the downtown area to make wisecracks at the civilian defense people as the latter bustled about their duties. The situation in Galesburg was the same, and town officials suggested that the next blackout come as a surprise so that people would be caught at home and unable to treat it as a carnival staged for their amusement.

With coastal cities permanently dimmed, the Pacific Gas and Electric Company reported a reduction of 60,000 kilowatts nightly in electricity demand. In New York it was predicted that the dimout would save the city $200,000 annually in electric power; actual savings the first year amounted to $1,000,000. Blackout curtain material was popular everywhere, as were special light-opaque window shades. Apartment owners searched about for window coverings that were decorative as well as lightproof; monk's cloth and various heavy drapes were preferred. *House & Garden* offered its readers tips on how to black out without sacrificing chic. "Bedrooms need not go into mourning," advised the magazine cheerily. "Make a blackout shade by seaming together two pieces of fabric, one black and one to match your curtain. . . . If long sheer bedroom curtains over Venetian blinds are your delight don't give them up. . . . Venetian blinds with slate closed, will afford a certain amount of protection from flying glass splinters." As for the bathroom windows, the solution was to "abandon your pastel window and shower curtains for the duration and put up, instead, a completely opaque black shower curtain. Use another to make window curtains." But the magazine qualified this advice with the caveat *"if your color scheme permits."* As for the black window shades, readers were advised to "stencil them with a colorful design to harmonize with the furnishings of your room or paste a large chintz motif in the center."

The blackout way of life spawned a host of other special blackout products, some useful, some frivolous. In the latter category were the shoes offered by a New York store christened "Dimout Suedes . . . golden background discreetly twinkling through the screen of perforated decor on these newest originals for fall." There were blackout candles, which had a pedestal type of bottom so that they would stand up without needing candlesticks. To provide a quickly installed "light lock" on store or business entrances, Folding Blackout Partitions made of special flameproofed material were offered by one manufacturer. There was also a "blackout glue" for attaching heavy paper, cloth or other blackout materials to windows. And for groping his way through blacked-out streets, the man about town had a Safe T Cane which had a flashlight hidden in its knobbed plastic handle which pointed downward and shone through the transparent plastic red that made up the lower part of the cane.

The blackout raised some unique legal problems. In one factory, the workers demanded to be paid for time spent at the job during a blackout. But Acting Wage-Hour Administrator Baird Snyder ruled: "Time spent by employees on the premises of an employer covered by the Wage-Hour Law during blackouts or air-raid alarms where no work is done need not be compensated for as hours worked." It was left to collective bargaining or employer decision at each plant to decide whether anybody would get paid while standing around in his darkened plant waiting for the all clear. (More commonly, during practice blackouts, factories engaged in war production were excused.) Naturally, people who got arrested for violating blackout regulations had a legal problem, and an ingenious Houston attorney in one such case defended his client by pointing out that those same regulations required that the chief of police must publish a legal notice of the blackout in a daily newspaper before 5 P.M. on the day one was to occur. This he had not done, the attorney contended, and therefore "there was no blackout. There was only an apparition."

Another coastal measure that was largely the responsibility of the civilian population was the Ground Observer Corps, which was under the War Department and the Army Air Forces Aircraft Warning Service. Ground Observer Corps members were civilians who manned aircraft spotter posts along both coasts and in "first priority" regions for 300 miles inland. Their function was to report every single plane in the sky to the Army's Filter Centers located in major coastal cities. The Filter Centers determined if the planes were friend or foe, through various procedures, and would relay warnings, if necessary, to the appropriate local civilian defense control points, which in turn would alert the civilian population.

Ground observers (or spotters, as they were more commonly called) were required to spend many lonely hours in a variety of observation posts, scanning the skies. The War Department had in prewar days envisaged an army of 500,000 of them, with each post manned in shifts by 19 men in good physical condition. But as the war progressed, the posts were increasingly manned by women, youths and sometimes even blind people (it was enough to report the presence of a plane in the area, not the type, and for this purpose hearing was as effective as sight). At its peak, the GOC mobilized 600,000 such citizens. Many of them were farm or rural people.

Several states had completed a skeletal GOC before Pearl Harbor, with much of the groundwork being laid by the American Legion working closely with the Air Force. Delaware was perhaps typical. By July it was 100 percent organized, and on December 8, eighty-nine observer posts manned by 9,000 observers were on twenty-four-hour duty. It was not easy in those early days. Shelter for the observers was rare, and most stood out in the cold and rain to perform their duties. As rapidly as possible, each community built shelters for the observers or located them in already-standing structures. There were no state or federal funds available for this purpose, so the posts were financed by the

communities themselves through socials, dances, donations, profits from
the scale of scrap or allocations from the municipal governments. As a
result, spotting became a rather more civilized activity. The Arden
Spotters Post in Brandywine Hundred, Delaware, was a 30-foot-high
tower—high enough to spot planes as far off as the Delaware River—
with a widow's walk at the top for spotters on duty and a small steam-
heated house where people could thaw out. At Seaford the local American
Legion post donated its headquarters and provided money to rebuild it
as an observation post two stories high with an observation platform
around the second story. The Delaware City post was manned by 175
observers and purchased a three-room building with a lookout tower. A
sun porch was constructed for added comfort. Security was tight at the
spotter posts; all personnel were required to have ID cards. Logbooks
were kept and regular reports filed. To the spotters anyhow, this was
serious business.

The spotters and the Aircraft Warning Service served at least one
useful function besides insurance. By keeping track of all the planes in
the area and systematizing their identification, they put an end to the
false reports of enemy planes; at the same time, the improved chain of
command ensured that it would be highly unlikely that an identified
friendly plane could trigger a full-scale alert, as had happened in New
York on December 9 and 10. (There was only one other such occurrence
on the East Coast, in 1943.)

Still, the backbone of any civilian defense system was the warden in
the street and the other auxiliary emergency workers trained to deal
with the various effects of wartime disasters. A galaxy of specialists
was created—each with its distinctive armband consisting of a circle in
which was a diamond containing the symbol of the particular specialty.
Air raid wardens had a striped diamond inside the circle; messengers, a
lightning bolt; nurse's aides, a red cross; demolition crews, a pick; gas
and decontamination corps, a beaker; and so on. By the end of April,
1942, the U.S. Citizens Defense Corps, embracing these protective spe-
cialties, had been established. To qualify for the corps, one had to take a
training course of a minimum number of hours. Upon completion, one
was eligible to take an oath of allegiance to the U.S. government (although one's appointment was made by state or local authority). The
oath went as follows:

> I solemnly swear [or affirm] that I will support and defend
> the Constitution of the United States against all enemies, foreign

and domestic; that I will bear true faith and allegiance to the same: that I take the obligation freely, without any mental reservation or purpose of evasion; that I will well and faithfully discharge my duties as a member of the U.S. Citizens Defense Corps; and that I do not advocate and have not advocated, the overthrow of our constitutional form of government in the United States by force or violence.

The successful candidate was then awarded a certificate of membership signed by the governor of his state. In 1942 the attempt was often made to hold an important ceremony upon induction. In Chicago, for example, 16,000 block captains were administered the oath of allegiance at the Coliseum in April by OCD Director Landis, who then made a speech assuring them that Chicago could be bombed—like the college commencement speaker who assures the graduates that they may well have to earn a living in the outside world.

Universities provided facilities and instructors for civilian defense training; in Chicago the local radio station gave a crash course for air raid wardens that was well received, and in New York the new medium television was used (since there were only about 15,000 sets in the New York area, wardens assembled at local police stations to watch); the Red Cross participated widely in first aid instruction; and other specialists came forward as they were needed. For example, the chemists in Decatur, Illinois, set up their own gas warfare course without waiting for the state to inaugurate one. Earlier the American Legion had organized a traveling unit which went about the state showing people how to use gas masks—Illinois had two gas masks at the war's beginning, eventually received a total of 22,000 for the entire state.

Though women were enrolled in the civilian protection aspects of OCD, it was largely man's work. In some of the smaller communities, indeed, civilian defense took on some of the characteristics of a stag party, providing the menfolk with a pretense to get out of the house and away from the wife and children. In the large cities, in the anonymity of the blackout, men who otherwise would never have met felt a camaraderie as they made shoptalk about goings-on in their sector or block, griped about the lack of equipment, speculated whether that light would go out or not and how long the blackout would last and philosophized about the larger issues of when the war would end and what the postwar business outlook appeared to be. Discipline and training were informal and face to face; though the higher-ups and the Washington big shots might bungle, down here among the wardens in the street there was a feeling of usefulness and purpose and the shared thought that the job was important for, well, it *could* happen, and, if it did, would their block be ready? For retired men there was an opportunity to get back into harness, if they had some usable skill. Important executives could take pride in applying their business skills to the seemingly life-or-death matters of civilian defense. For others, it became almost a hobby. And for many or all of these, it was an outlet for one's vague sense of shame over not being young enough or fit enough to participate in the war.

At the higher level, for those officials in charge of whole cities, there was something perhaps a bit godlike in watching the lights winking out for a blackout, knowing that one had played an important role. One director of civilian protection for a large city in the East referred to the "personal thrill it gave him to watch the lights go out, one by one, as far as he could see and realize that in that demonstration was represented the fruits of months of work, late nights, long conferences and [the] successful cooperation of thousands of human beings."

For all the growing OCD activity, the fact remained, as one historian later remarked, that "all through 1942 the accent was upon fear and self-preservation [for] in time of disaster people would in a large measure have to help themselves." What information the government disseminated to the ordinary civilian had a tendency to be contradictory—a confusion compounded by the statements of those who were supposed to be authorities. Take the great How to Fight an Incendiary Bomb controversy. In its original broadsheet to the homeowner of December, 1941, the OCD had warned him: "If incendiary bombs fall, play a *spray* from a garden hose (never splash or stream) of water on the bomb. . . . *A jet splash, stream or bucket of water will make it explode* [original italics]." Later, officials discovered that the incendiaries tested had been different from the kind the Germans actually used. The former contained pure magnesium and would apparently explode under a jet (as opposed to a coating spray) of water, while the latter would not. Snuffing out the bomb with sand had also been recommended, but it was learned from British experience that the Germans were arming their incendiaries with a delayed-action hand grenade, calculated to go off several minutes after the bomb hit, thus killing the civilian defense worker trying to extinguish it. So the OCD changed its technique and advocated the jet method, preferably from a considerable distance and while standing behind some shield. The irrepressible LaGuardia, perhaps thinking this change in policy reflected unfavorably on his own stewardship, for his administration had recommended the spray method, publicly challenged the OCD to a "race" to determine which method was faster. The race was duly held in New York, and the jet method won by a few seconds, and nobody was really satisfied. Then, to confuse the issue thoroughly, the Chicago fire department announced that *its* method—dunking in water—was by far the most effective. In a democracy at war, each citizen had a choice of how he put out that incendiary bomb sputtering away in his attic.

The ordinary citizen was later to be faced with real bombs—but these were Japanese, not German, and all instruction, such as it was, had been geared toward the latter. Beginning in November, 1944, the Japanese released a series of large paper balloons, some 30 feet in diameter and bearing Japanese ideographs. Each carried a 30-pound bomb set to go off forty hours after launching. The program, which had been in preparation over two years and conceived as revenge for the Doolittle B-25 raids on Tokyo in 1942, assumed that the balloons, carried by prevailing westerly winds, would drift over America. Upon exploding they would start forest fires and create panic among the civilian population. In all, some 9,000 bombs were launched, of which a tiny percentage reached the United States. Most landed in the western part of the country, but at least one made it as far as Maryland. The bombs were singularly ineffectual in carrying out their intended mission: civilians spotted and captured many of them before they went off, others were duds, and, anyhow, over the period of time they were launched (November through April) the forests were not dangerously dry, as they would have been in August and September, when the forest fire danger is at its peak.

The bombs did, however, cause deaths. A few people, not realizing what they were, came too close to them, just as their timing devices ignited the explosion. But the OCD—and the government—clamped a lid of secrecy on the bombs, after one newspaper story about a bomb discovered in Wyoming in December was published. The purpose of the news blackout, of course, was to keep the Japanese from gauging the success, if any, of their balloons. In this sense it was effective; after the war, Japanese military men admitted that they had abandoned the program because they did not know if any of the balloons were reaching their destination. The only report they had they picked up from Chungking radio—the same AP story about the Wyoming balloon that appeared in this country. Yet here was a case of actual danger in which the government's failure to warn civilians probably resulted in some deaths. The War Department sought to institute a word-of-mouth campaign; luncheon clubs, fraternal organizations and the like were told about the bombs by guest speakers. A Wyoming editor did not miss the irony of this. Refusing to abide by the censorship, he wrote in May, 1945:

> A word-of-mouth campaign is under way throughout this part of the country, warning residents against tampering with Japanese bomb balloons or fragments thereof which may fall in the area. Information is being told verbally which censorship forbids the newspapers to publish.
>
> Presumably the censorship theory is that Jap spies can read but can't hear.

Americans were also dubiously advised about a number of other measures to take in the event of an air raid—measures which were usually only sketchily explained but pounded home with the force of the revealed word of God. Not infrequently, these articles of dogma were soon doused by a splash of acidic common sense. For example, New York City's Board for Civilian Protection advised New Yorkers to fill up their bathtubs, washtubs and any other handy receptacles if an air raid was imminent, the water being for fire-fighting purposes. The Board for Civilian Protection thought over its proclamation for a couple of months, then suddenly realized that if, when the sirens sounded, everybody started filling his bathtub, there would be a considerable strain on the city's water pressure. So it reneged just a little, saying, at the end of January, 1942, that maybe the homeowner should just keep a quart bottle full for drinking purposes in case the water mains were severed by bombs.

Another bit of shady advice was to turn off the pilot light and any other gas source in the home. But down in Baltimore the local civilian defense committee, which was noted for sailing an independent course often at odds with official OCD policy, said that turning off the gas created an even greater danger of explosion. It won, too, finally; the OCD admitted it had been wrong.

Before the war, OCD Chairman LaGuardia had dismissed the necessity for civilian air raid shelters with a sort of vague wave of his hand. After Pearl Harbor, the erection of public shelters in the large cities was never a serious possibility. In point of fact, there was a critical shortage of materials needed to build them, for in 1942 the country plunged into a massive construction program, erecting defense plants, workers' housing and new Army camps at a prodigious rate. Still, people on city streets when the sirens sounded had to have somewhere to go (to get them out of the way), and so they were herded into doorways, under theater marquees and into buildings previously designated as shelters by a luminescent yellow *S*.

For those civilians caught on the street who could not reach a shelter, the commonest advice was "Cover your head and put your handkerchief between your teeth to keep them from being broken by bomb shock." Those in their homes, of course, had that heavy table with the mattress underneath recommended by the OCD, or if they cared to, they might go in for more elaborate shelters. *House & Garden* was ready with hints in its March issue showing how to convert the basement into a passable shelter with sandbag-filled bulkheads. It approved of the efforts of Mr. Frederik Rehberger, a Wall Street lawyer, who had constructed in the middle of his basement a 10-by-15-foot sandbag and board shelter which was considered large enough for both work and play. Its nearness to the cellar stair not only made it more accessible but also made it easier to hear any incendiary bombs that had landed upstairs and to rush up to spray-not-jet—or was it jet-not-spray?—some water on them. Sand-filled wood partitions 24 inches thick served to support the first floor, which was reinforced over the shelter. Sandbags covered basement windows, but care was taken to leave an exit hole, in case that uninvited incendiary bomb upstairs entered unheard and burned its way through to the basement.

House & Garden did not allow its imagination to be fettered by a narrow utilitarianism, however. Its most stunning suggestion was the "reinforced concrete garden or pool shelter." This was a large concrete cube, located poolside, with 2-foot walls and a 3½-foot-thick roof. The shelter also had a large concrete overhang, beneath which was a patio complete with chaise longues and a fireplace. Inside, however, the place was a veritable *Führerbunker,* with various sections of the diagrammed interior identified as the "gas lock," "air filter," "books" (books?), "water tank," and "airtight metal doors." This Taj Mahal of air raid shelters cost only $2,500 to build. So that this money would be doubly well spent, *House & Garden* advised its readers: "In building shelters consider their peacetime role. They may do double duty as bathing pavilions, wine cellars, root cellars, etc."

Preparations for raids varied from city to city. In Seattle, the sky bristled with barrage balloons, and there were sandboxes on every street corner for incendiaries, interceptor planes on the alert and well-marked air raid shelters. Even people's backyards were conscripted. As a Seattle taxi driver complained to a visiting journalist: "Remember what I was telling you about those machine guns? Well, the soldiers came to my house yesterday and put one in my back yard. My kids won't stay away from it and my wife is going nuts. . . . Funny, ain't it? The Navy wouldn't have me, the Army couldn't use me, and now they've gone and brought the goddam war right to my kitchen door."

Even in Wyoming, the least populous state in the Union and not exactly the arsenal of America, a vocal minority was urging that shelters be built, and in some communities they were seriously studying caves and mine shafts as shelter possibilities. A Casper newspaper columnist complained: "Have we got to wait until lives are needlessly sacrificed before we at least begin to plan air raid shelters?"

Other Wyomingians retained their composure—perhaps because they realized that all most of them had to do was head for the nearby sagebrush in the event of an air raid. The editor of the Laramie *Republican-Boomerang* warned against carrying the civilian defense program "beyond the realm of credulity" and thought that shelters were one of the least pressing needs in his state at the moment.

In New York, no great hue and cry for shelters were raised, even though the New York subway system was much too shallow (unlike the London Underground) to provide mass shelter. One lady, in a letter to the *Times,* timidly suggested that she be allowed to go into her closet in the event of an air raid, rather than under the dining-room table. "I would be better protected from flying glass," she wrote, "by going into this closet, leaving the door slightly ajar, than I would be lying face down on the floor in the middle of the room as had been suggested." Still, she sighed resignedly, "In my own case, I know that, if a bomb struck my apartment building there would be little chance for its survival because it is a two-story structure."

Another Manhattan worrier complained in the *Times* that at a recent air raid protection meeting in her building (at which only ten of the twenty families were represented) they spent the entire time discussing what to do about incendiary bombs, and she queried: "Why are we sure it's going to be incendiaries? Why not gas?" No one at the meeting apparently knew anything about gas either, but the superintendent consoled her by saying that, since she lived on the tenth floor, her family would survive. Still, the lady thought, she would like to buy a gas mask and wondered where to get one.

It was not until shortly after the Battle of Midway in 1942, however, that the first and only gas scare of the war occurred. The Navy announced that it had found poisonous gas cylinders aboard a captured

Japanese cruiser. The Japanese propagandists countered by saying they had found poisonous gas among American stores captured on Guam, and Japanese radio said ominously that President Roosevelt had "abrogated the poison-gas clause of international law" and predicted that "Uncle Sam's boys will be given a smell of their own DuPont gas which the Japanese captured at Guam." This threw the West Coast into a gas tizzy. San Francisco staged a practice alert which incorporated gas instructions for its air raid wardens into the program. Civilians were told that if the gas alarm was sounded, they were to close doors and windows and get as high as possible above the street level, even though it meant leaving a comfortable, work and recreationally suitable basement shelter. In Los Angeles the city health officer gave the following advice to residents caught out on the street in a gas attack: "Immediately before entering any house remove your outer clothing. Don't hesitate to do this. It is better to have a red face than a burned body." And in Washington, the Army Chemical Warfare Service took a leaf from Great Britain and developed a Mickey Mouse-face mask for children. The idea got as far as the publicity photo stage (Charlie McCarthy wearing one), when it was decided that it used up too much rubber.

Industrial accidents and sabotage involving companies manufacturing gas were also stressed. This aspect of the program took on a concrete reality when a man in Brooklyn dropped a chlorine gas cylinder in a sewer and fifty people had to be hospitalized. Cities such as Niagara Falls and Rochester, where various types of gases were manufactured, were most concerned. The gas program, spotty as it was, did provide another way of dramatizing the realities of war to the home front and possibly helped sell War Bonds, if nothing else. The pot was kept mildly bubbling by the capture, in 1943, of a new kind of poison gas from the Afrika Corps. Offshore submarines and, later, the robot bombs provided, in theory at least, a way for the enemy to deliver the gas if it so chose.

Despite false starts and contradictory instructions, the people at the grass roots were proceeding doggedly ahead in forming their civilian defense organizations. A counterpart to the Citizens Defense Corps, known as the Civilian Voluntary Services, was established to swear in volunteers for such activities as Victory gardens; salvage campaigns (which, after the first one, came under the War Production Board); Victory Speakers, who delivered canned talks on various government policies; block leaders, who informed their neighbors about various programs such as food conservation; car pools; and preinduction counseling for draftees. There was also a Junior Service Corps for boys and girls under fifteen which assisted in a variety of programs. As the war wore on, these programs undertook a heightened significance.*

By July more than 7,000,000 Americans had volunteered for some form of civilian defense activity, and by mid-1943 more than 12,000,-000 Americans were registered, about a million less than would eventually be in the armed forces. As the wartime rhetoric might have it, America was awakening . . . the people were on the march . . . listen to them Adolf, Tojo, Il Duce! Listen to the mighty tramp of their feet—a nation aroused—ready to wipe the Axis off the face of the earth!

All over the country, in cities large and small, people were engaging in air raid drills and mock bombing raids in which CAP planes dropped flour-filled bombs packed by eager schoolchildren, and Boy Scouts lay about in ghastly poses, covered with ketchup, while workers bustled about, giving mock succor. In Oregon an entire town spent all day Sunday practicing against air raids. In Northport, Alabama, summoned by the mayor riding Paul Revere-like on a horse, 2,000 of the total population of 2,500 turned out for organization of civilian defense. The AFL and CIO locals in San Diego had a brief jurisdictional dispute over who would handle clearing of debris after a bombing raid but in a heartening burst of patriotism squelched their differences and agreed to work together. A recruitment meeting in Hannibal, Missouri, consisting of a parade followed by a town meeting, packed 4,000 people in the armory, and another 15,000 were outside because there was no room for them. The young and old alike were involved. Three ladies all over seventy in a small town in New England did all the plane spotting for their district, dividing up a twenty-four-hour shift.

It was in the small towns that organizational activities reached their zenith. One such model community was Kent, Connecticut, in which only 200 out of a population of 1,240 did not participate. Kent's program had got under way six months before Pearl Harbor, under the

---

* To give a quick idea of the scope of young people's participation in the war effort, herewith the activities over a two-year span of Gary, Indiana, eighth-graders, which may well stand as typical: taught young girls infant care; collected phonograph records; distributed WAR WORKERS SLEEPING signs; sold war stamps at an exhibition of a captured Japanese submarine; discussed curfew law with City Council; distributed anti-black-market pledge cards; took auxiliary fireman and police training courses; collected 500,000 pounds of wastepaper; sold an average of $40,000 worth of war stamps a month; delivered Community Chest material to every home in the city; sponsored a Clean Plate campaign; participated in War Bond and tin can drives; and collected library books for servicemen. Other organizations for youthful war work included the Junior Red Cross, the High School Victory Corps and, of course, the Boy and Girl Scouts.

supervision of a teacher at Kent School named James Humphreys. Like any good general, Humphreys had first ordered a survey of his troops and learned such vital information as that he had people speaking 14 different languages under his command; that there were 256 automobiles; that 80 houses burned gas, 111 wood and 91 coal; that there were 123 horses and 120 people who could ride them; that 44 people owned 974 cows with a daily milk production of 1,255 gallons; that there were 91 rifles, 83 shotguns, 21 revolvers and 12 pairs of crutches. This exhaustive survey was conducted on a face-to-face basis. According to Humphreys, "The questionnaires were delivered personally. We didn't mail them or have someone just leave them there and run. You stayed and told what it was about and then went and got it later on. Reached everybody over 16." Humphreys put in a day that would have given Hitler himself cause for doubt. After five hours of teaching, he coached the school teams, then went straight to the civilian defense office and put in eight hours there, finishing up at 1 A.M. most nights.

The local Ground Observer Corps located its spotters' post in an old bus body converted to a trailer. Air raid warnings were sounded by individual cars, called Paul Revere cars, which went about, sirens wailing, enforcing the blackout. One zealous Kent youth volunteered the services of himself and his horse to replace a Paul Revere car that was temporarily incapacitated. "The horse is black, sir," he urged, "so it would be sort of invisible."

Another model town (and publicized as such in the mass media) was Sheridan, Wyoming, which must have been about number 279 on the famous target list. "Don't think they're scared," one local said. "The emotion out here is the opposite of fright. These people . . . can't fight or build planes, but they can defend their own community and they don't intend to leave the job to somebody else." As for the danger of gas, Sheridan was way ahead of the rest of the country. A class of sixty—double the number needed—was studying decontamination. To eliminate all possibility of error, the blackout chief was also head of the local electric company. And to cap it all, Harold Bryce, a post office worker, and his aides had drawn up a complete evacuation plan by which Sheridan's entire population could head, in an orderly manner, for the nearby hills in the event of a major air raid.

In nonstrategic Rockland County, New York, the OCD was active, although some of the prosperous exurbanites could be choosy. There was the lady who wanted to be an air raid warden. When the local civilian defense head told her that they didn't need any more air raid wardens and suggested that she clean up the Red Cross room in the converted chicken coop that had been designated "Disaster Depot" instead, she exploded: "That's just housework! Why, I do that every day. Besides, I couldn't do cleaning in these clothes."

Even the swank Brearly Nursery School in Manhattan was prepared for an air raid. A notice given to its staff read: "The Nursery School will keep on hand an adequate supply of food, blankets, first-aid equipment, flashlights and lollipops."

Yet progress was far from uniform. As Director Landis said: "There are sections which are relatively unawakened to the imminence of danger." One reporter, to see what was going on out in Kansas, scanned the local papers and found nary a mention of the OCD or civilian defense. In Emporia, five months after Pearl Harbor, the big community activity was the rehearsal of a pageant called "The Unseen Captain." In Gridley, the Happy-Go-Lucky Quilting Club had organized—for sociable quilting, not civilian defense—and in Lawrence, the Kansas University faculty had to dig the dandelions out of the lawn, because this year the students refused to do it. When a mobilization of civilian defense volunteers was called in one town, the local newspaper said the purpose was solely to see how many people would show up—if any. The OCD field offices in other parts of the country were having trouble recruiting full-time personnel, and in some areas already (July, 1942) apathy was creeping in. As one worried CD official summed it up: "A big job is to keep the local defense councils from losing interest. One way is to suggest new activities. Recently in some States we started rumor-exposure groups."

One of the chief eyesores in the civilian defense program was the city of Buffalo. There Mayor Joseph J. Kelly ignored the local defense council and set up his own personal civilian defense organization. His deputy was a political reporter from the local newspaper, "who," one local OCD worker remarked, "knows little about the job but will certainly improve the Mayor's press relations in the *Courier-Express*." The local civilian defense head finally resigned in despair. The town had no auxiliary police, no air raid wardens, no flashlights or helmets, and the stirrup pumps on hand were good only for demonstrations—*i.e.*, they didn't work. One practice blackout was held in December, 1941. The fire engines were brought out and the sirens turned on. The sirens promptly burned out. Yet Buffalo was considered—at least by one magazine writer—"the third likeliest target in the country."

But despite such blemishes as Buffalo, such oases of apathy as

Kansas; despite the hitches and delays and frustrations in other parts of the country; and despite the contradictory commands shouted from distant Washington and the Congressional fan dancers and the bungles and inevitable delays in equipping and getting vital civilian defense equipment out to the workers in the field—despite all these, by June, 1942 the civilian defense ranks had increased more than fivefold from their number at the end of 1941—from 1,200,000 to more than 7,000,000. This turnout represented ordinary people, who simply wanted to do their part in the war in whatever way they could. Certainly, in terms of actual trained personnel, the figure is inflated; still, by the standard of how many people were employed by the extant civilian defense authority it was overwhelming. The people, anxious to "do something," though not terribly clear about what to "do," were spontaneously organizing their own civilian protection, well in advance of coherent state, local or federal leadership. But their mood was a transient one, composed of the fear and wartime enthusiasm of the moment—an enthusiasm that would reach full tide a year later, then, abetted by marked improvement in the fortunes of war and growing indifference in Washington, quickly ebb.

III

THE CHANGING
LANDSCAPE: WAR
TOWNS, WAR BRIDES
AND WASHINGTON

The end of Hard Times was a motley caravan observed on Route 66, near Albuquerque, New Mexico, a road that was both *via doloroso* and passage of hope in John Steinbeck's *Grapes of Wrath*. Now, by the same route, in early 1942 the Okies were returning home. They came in old battered sedans and wheezing trucks and Model T's, sometimes twelve in a car, with all their possessions strapped on the tops and sides—rockers, buckets, shovels, stoves, bedding and springs. A few of the migrants were fleeing what they regarded as the imminent invasion of California by the Japanese, but the attitude of most was summed up by the man who said: "We ain't war-scared or anything like that, but a lot of others were pulling up and cleaning out—not all of 'em understand—and Ma and I figured that if we was going back, now was the time. And, besides, Ed Lou is pretty big now and there ought to be a job for him in the oil fields and maybe for me too."

There were still more than 3,600,000 men unemployed. So the migration had momentum to gain as hillbillies from Appalachia, po' whites and Negroes from the South, farmers from the Midwest, garment workers from New York City picked up stakes and swarmed to the centers of war production.

The factories were rising up out of the raw, graded earth. The year 1942 was a year of frantic construction—more than $12 billion worth of it financed by the federal government, most of that on military camps, factories and installation of heavy machinery.

Near the little town of Starke, Florida, Camp Blanding had been erected in six months of feverish building. The workers turned the little town upside down. "Why, people were sleeping in the streets, in the churches, in the trees," one resident recalled. The local grocer reminisced: "I had two stores and I sold groceries to the construction gangs. Two stores and I couldn't get any help. I worked 18 to 20 hours a day. My weekend profits were unbelievable, but I wouldn't want to go through it again. These fellows from the construction jobs—these carpenters and plumbers—were getting more money than they'd ever had in their lives and they had no place to spend it except in Starke. They were always hungry and they were always buying. It went for five or six months. We all got rich."

This story was being repeated in other little towns around the country—those, that is, lucky enough to attract the construction money. It was a presage of the even better times that would come when the industries got into high gear. Yet the magic wand of federal money touched some and missed others. While a Starke, Florida, might prosper, a Palatka, Florida, would be passed by. Palatka, a town of 7,000, succeeded in attracting a small contract for a few packet boats for the Coast Guard, but that was its only taste of war boom. When gas rationing came, the passing-through tourist trade, which in the past had given the town's hotels and restaurants some business, dried up. Coastal security regulations restricted fishing. Every week, as the year wore on, another store would close, and some folks moved elsewhere in search of work. The local paper, with gallows humor born of desperation, proposed that the federal government build a national cemetery in the town.

Palatka was, of course, a flyspeck on the map; leading the list of have-nots was the nation's largest city. As late as October, 1942, New York had 368,000 unemployed. By mid-November only seven small firms in New York had war contracts, totaling $2,300,000. New York's problem was a magnification of those elsewhere; it was a city of many small businesses, and small business wasn't getting the war contracts. It was the big boys who were getting the gravy—the auto manufacturers of Detroit, and the shipbuilding yards of both coasts, and the airplane factories on the West Coast, and the arms manufacturers of New England, and other areas where new arsenals and the steel and other metal plants had been built.

Even before the war the small businessman was faced with material shortages, for priorities went to those who had defense contracts, and defense contracts, on the whole, went to large companies and their subcontractors. This meant a drop in the new-business birthrate. The U.S. Department of Commerce estimated that 300,000 retailers closed their doors in 1942 alone. *Business Week* said that after two months of war there were 200,000 fewer employers of all kinds—again mostly small business. The magazine termed it the "most severe contraction in the business population that we have ever experienced." More than half a million small businesses of all types failed during the war years.

On the other hand, shortly after Pearl Harbor three large corporations had 17.4 percent of all the defense contracts by dollar volume. One hundred companies were doing 82.6 percent of all the nation's war production in January, 1942. The allocation of government money to private business in connection with the pursuit of the war—ultimately totaling $240 billion—took the form of a giant inverted pyramid; two-thirds of it went to 100 corporations (out of a total of 18,000 that participated in war contracts). The top ten corporations received 30 percent of the total.

Yet this pattern, so worrisome to economic liberals of both the classic and the new schools, was not hatched out of any conscious pro-big-business conspiracy. It was simple, haste-ridden pragmatism—that is to say, a deference to the powers that be. The automotive industry, for example, was the ideal war contractor in terms of business organization. It was concentrated, possessed of a large labor pool and large assembly lines capable of turning out complicated mechanized products, and had long-standing connections with a variety of subcontractors that were able to supply small-part needs. It was *in situ* and a going concern. True, the auto makers sometimes drove a hard bargain in exchange for their wartime services. During 1941, as the defense program picked up momentum, the auto makers were reluctant to convert any of their existing facilities to war production. The year 1941 was a boom year—the first in a long time—in car sales, and with war looming on the horizon, the manufacturers were eager to sell as many cars as they could. The auto makers wanted new plants built at government expense before they would plunge into defense production in any big way. As Congressman John H. Tolan (D., Calif.), chairman of the House committee investigating national defense migration, put it shortly after Pearl Harbor: ". . . aside from truck production, it is questionable whether as much as five percent of the existing automotive facilities of the industry have been used on these contracts [by then totaling $5 billion]. Instead, many new plant facilities are still under construction, a number of which will not come into full production until a year from now." When the industry finally got into full production, its outpouring of war goods was tremendous (it ultimately accounted for 20 percent of total U.S. war production by dollar volume), but when the war came, it was off to a standing, not running, start.

Pearl Harbor did, of course, jar the industry out of its standpat position. At a meeting of auto executives called soon after December 7, Paul Hoffman, head of Studebaker, remarked in the spirit of the times, "Gentlemen, I think the country expects an announcement of a cut in auto production from us this morning." But the manufacturers marked time until a clear-cut order by the War Production Board came, as one of its first official acts, banning all new car production for the duration. On February 10, the last new civilian car, a Ford, Serial Number 30-337 509, came off the assembly line.

The Bureau of the Budget historian was to write after the war, "We built many new factories, and expanded many others which we could not use and did not need. Many of these new factories we could not supply with labor or with raw materials, or if we had, we could not have been able to fly the planes or shoot the ammunition that would come out of them. But in the process we used up critical material which might have gone into something else." After the war the private corporations employing the new factories had the option of buying them from the government at cost less "reasonable depreciation" or less total rentals paid by the corporation to the government, whichever would net the government more. Most corporations exercised this option, for of a total of $26 billion of government and private investment expended on war plants and equipment, an estimated $20 billion worth was adaptable to peacetime production.

To millions who had suffered the Depression years on relief, with occasional spells of odd jobs, this meant a time of opportunity, a time to pick up stakes and head to the war production centers, where there were steady jobs and good money to be had. In times of depression people tend to crawl into their holes and lick their wounds; in good times they head for the money. Estimates of the number of Americans who left their homes to seek work elsewhere—in a different county, a different state or even a different region—ranged as high as 20,000,000. Probably the true number will never be known, but the Census Bureau attempted to capture the figures as best it could, before the time was irretrievably gone. Based on a sample of 30,000 persons, the bureau took a demographic snapshot of the nation in March, 1945, and compared it with the prewar period. The Bureau estimated that by 1945, 15,300,000 persons were living in counties different from those in which they lived at Pearl Harbor; 7,700,000 of these migrants were living in a different state and 3,600,000 in a different part of the country. Comparing these figures with those for migration during the year 1935–40, the bureau found that intercounty migration was down a little, while interstate and interregional were considerably higher.

A major source of this migration was the farm, where, most agrarian economists agreed, there were about 2,000,000 too many people in 1940. Between Pearl Harbor and March, 1945, nearly 5,500,000 people left the farms to live and work in the city (another 1,500,000 went into the armed forces). So effectively did the war siphon off the surplus that there were severe labor shortages on the farms, and in 1943–44, farm deferments were drastically increased by Selective Service. Women, city teen-agers, Axis war prisoners, interned Japanese-Americans and even GI's were pressed into service to help out with the harvest (a time when an additional 3,000,000 laborers are needed). The grip of the agriculture depression, which had held since the early twenties, was at last broken, and farmers' profits soared to record highs. With all this farm prosperity, a reverse migration trend was also operative, for some 2,500,000 people moved from nonfarm to farm areas, presumably to take up farmwork. Still, the farm population suffered a net loss of nearly 17 percent, not counting those in the armed forces. An average of 900,000 yearly headed for the cities—much greater than the 375,000 yearly during the Depression and easily topping the record migration years of the twenties, when 600,000 farmers left the farms every year, never to return, never to be replaced.

Before asking who the migrants were, let us see where they went. According to the Census Bureau, these ten areas were considered most congested as a result of wartime influx: (percentage increase in population between 1940 and 1944 is shown in the right-hand column):

Mobile County, Alabama	64.7%
Hampton Roads, Virginia area (*i.e.*, Norfolk, Hampton Roads, Princess Anne County, etc.)	44.7
San Diego County, California	43.7
Charleston, South Carolina, area	38.1

Portland-Vancouver, Wash.-Ore.	31.8
San Francisco Bay Area	25.0
Puget Sound area, Washington	20.0
Los Angeles area	15.1
Muskegon County, Michigan	14.4
Detroit-Willow Run area	8.2

The combined population increase in these ten areas over the four-year span was 1,782,361, pushing their total population up by 20 per-cent over the 1940 census figure. Note that during this period the civilian population in the continental United States had declined 4 percent be-cause of the excess of troops overseas over natural increase from births and immigration (which dried up to a trickle). Also, the percentage figures are perhaps misleading in some cases, because they do not indi-cate the magnitude of the increase in terms of numbers of humans. Thus, the Detroit-Willow Run area had only an 8.2 percent population increase, but this consisted of more than 200,000 people; similarly, in the Los Angeles area, the added 15 percent population comprised a gain of 440,000 inhabitants. The spectacular percentage increase in the Mobile area was a matter of 92,000 people; in the Hampton Roads, Virginia, area, 153,000—smaller absolute accretions, but still an invasion no matter how you express it.

The greatest percentage of the immigrants settled in the immediate environs of the city or cities, rather than inside the cities. This was re-flected in the mushrooming growth of war worker towns and federal hous-ing projects laid out where there were only rural fields before or, even worse, the ubiquitous "New Hoovervilles"—trailer camps, tent settle-ments, shanty towns, "foxhole houses" and all the other temporary con-glomerations of people which sprang up over the countryside, often as satellites of the new war plants which had been erected on unused land. What this further meant was that these settlements were often located outside the service ambit of city and township governments. They were in a jurisdictional limbo, and there was no local government unit to take responsibility for them; further, many of the small towns to which they were often closest, hence most directly affected, lacked the resources with which to help them, even if they had wished to. Most of the mi-grants were nonvoting, nontaxpaying, nonhomeowning—in effect, politi-cal pariahs.

The geographical flow of the migration was strikingly skewed. Be-tween April, 1940, and November, 1943, thirty-five states showed a net *loss* in total civilian population. The thirteen states that gained did so in numbers varying from California's 1,020,000 to Delaware's 7,240, but the geographical pattern was clear: By far the largest gainer was the Far West—the three coast states of California, Washington and Oregon, in that order, and to a much smaller degree, Arizona, Utah and Nevada. Next to the Pacific coast states, were three South Atlantic states: Maryland, Florida and Virginia. (In a class by itself was the District of Columbia, which gained 162,469 people; the federal government was also a booming war industry.)

The people went to the Far West because the opportunity was there, and the opportunity was there because the war money went West: California alone, with 6.2 percent of the population had by 1944 received war contracts totaling $15.8 billion, or 9.7 percent of the total for the nation. More than half the wartime shipbuilding took place in the three Pacific coast states, and nearly half the airplane manufacture. Because of its location on the sea and the existence of a prewar aircraft industry, California logically helped itself to a large chunk of this production. When the war ended, an estimated 1,000,000 war workers would be out of work, but till then California was truly the Golden State. All told its population increased by almost 2,000,000 between 1940 and 1945. Per capita income rose apace, reaching $1,740 annually, the highest in the nation. Here was the real gold rush in California's colorful history.

In sum the general pattern of the great national migration seemed to be this: Deep South po' whites to the shipyards around the Gulf crescent and in the Hampton Roads–Newport News–Norfolk complex and, farther North, to the Michigan manufacturing complexes.

Southern Negro sharecroppers and tenant farmers to the shipyards and factories of the West Coast; up the East Coast and to the factories of the Middle West.

Arkies, Okies, Tennessee, Kentucky and West-by-God-Virginia hillbillies to Illinois and Indiana and Michigan or to the Southern oilfields and shipyards.

Kansas, Nebraska, Iowa, North and South Dakota plowboys to the great aircraft factories of the West Coast.

New York and other urban small-manufacturing workers to the Mid and Far West.

They came in cars, driving their rubber down to the rims and then paying exorbitant prices for used tires or retreads en route; or, more likely, they sat up or stood in the aisles for days and nights on crowded trains; or they packed their few working clothes into cardboard suitcases, made dust down the red dirt roads of the backwoods South to the crossroads store, and there waited for the bus to take them on the long trip to Pascagoula or Mobile or New Orleans:

> The bus rumbles down the sunny empty highway through the rusty valleys and the bare rainwashed fields and the scraggly woods and the hills the color of oakleaves that are the landscape of winter in the southeast states. Inside, the air is dense with packed bodies and stale cigarette smoke. There's a smell of babies and an occasional sick flavor from the exhaust. The seats are all full. Somewhere in the back a baby is squalling. A line of men and women stands swaying in the aisles. Behind me two men are talking about jobs in singsong voices pitched deep in their chests.
>
> "What's it like down there?" one is asking the other.
>
> "Ain't too bad if you kin stand that bunch of loudmouthed foremen . . . If you look crosseyed at one of them guards he'll reach out and yank off your badge and you're through and that's all there is to it."
>
> "Well, I've worked in about all of em."
>
> "Say, ain't I seen you somewheres before?"
>
> "I dunno. Might have been on this bus. I been on this bus a thousand times."

Everyone, on the move. Young wives with colicky babies, making the long journey to join their husbands at this new war job. Lone men, creased and weathered by work, and pink-cheeked young farm boys, migrating West because they heard there was plenty of work out there, sitting in the dark loneliness of the bus at night, only the glow of the orange spark of their cigarettes for company, their thoughts set free to range back and forth in time and space from regret to hope, over the vast American landscape of shadowy, empty hills and somber forests and little towns, their dark windows staring like empty-skulled eye sockets. In the next seat might be another man, he too sitting staring out at the landscape at night, he too coming from somewhere but off to somewhere else. The low voices hummed in talk of "where-are-you-going?" and "what's-it-like down there?"

> Once I was westbound from St. Paul, in fact, it seemed as if EVERYONE was westbound. With the hum and rhythm of the bus there was an undertone of talk—words—Seattle—Portland—

San Francisco—Seattle—shipyards—Vancouver—how about housing—do you know anyone there? I have an aunt in Olympia—we'll go there first—then we can look around in Tacoma and Seattle. It wouldn't take any imagination at all to think that you were going west on a covered wagon and were a pioneer again. It made me think of "The Grapes of Wrath," minus the poverty and hopelessness.

Men were picking up stakes and moving on. Some left signs on the doors of closed businesses, letting their customers and friends and the whole world (and maybe even God) know that they had vamoosed, flown the coop, skedaddled, made tracks, hit the road, up and went. Signs that read like the one on the door of Joe's Country Lunch in Alabama:

> Maybe you don't know there's a war on. Have gone to see what it's all about. Meanwhile good luck and best wishes until we all come home. (Signed) Joe.

Or that of Lem Ah Toy, Chinese laundryman of Seattle:

> Go to war. Closed duration. Will clean shirts after clean Axis. Thank you.

Signs, signs. Cocky, patriotic signs. The whole country, it seemed, was bursting out in a springtime of patriotism. American flags were displayed everywhere—in front of homes, public buildings, fraternal lodges. Elks, Lions, Kiwanis, Rotary, even trailer camps, gas stations and motor courts had them. Some small towns down South, where, polls showed, support of the war was staunchest, looked as though it were some big holiday, only every day. A hotel in New Mexico had little American flags painted on every one of its windows. Patriotic slogans abounded. Over Main Street in Yuma, Arizona, hung a banner reading:

> TO HELL WITH JAPAN AND ALL HER FRIENDS!

On bar mirrors in small dusty roadside taverns were soap-scrawled fighting slogans, like:

> SLAP THE JAPS OFF THE MAP!
> TO HELL WITH THE JAPS!
> REMEMBER PEARL HARBOR!!!

Roadside billboards blazed with red, white and blue and displayed soldiers, sailors, marines or war workers:

CAMELS ARE FIRST WITH MEN IN THE SERVICE!

Towns with newly risen Army posts nearby lured the GI's to their honky-tonk districts:

SOLDIERS, ATTENTION! COME RIGHT IN! DINE, DANCE, SKATE!

(In Albany, Georgia's red light district, the whores had their names displayed in neon signs.)

Martial posters by second-rate *Saturday Evening Post* illustrators urged citizens to Get in the Scrap or Buy a Share in America. After all: We Lend Our Money—They Give Their Lives. So, Dish It Out with the Navy! Choose Now While You Can. Join the Marines and Begin Firing! And: Back the Attack, Be a WAAC! For America Is Calling. Take Your Place in Civilian Defense.

Young girls sitting in soda fountains adorned themselves with the unit patches of their boyfriends, sergeant's stripes or lieutenant's bars; the soda fountain they were lounging in purveyed such patriotic combinations as: Blackout Sundae, Commando Sundae (War Workers, Get Your Vitamins the Delicious Way), Flying Fortress Sundae, Morale Builder and Paratroops Sundae (Goes Down Easy). In more and more windows hung service flags: red border, surrounding a white rectangle in which were one or more blue stars. Gold ones were making their appearance too ("THE WAR DEPARTMENT REGRETS TO INFORM YOU THAT YOUR SON. . . ." The papers printed names of casualty lists, but never gave total killed and wounded until mid-1942.) Along with the service flags in homes and places of business, small towns had erected Honor Roll signs, with lengthening lists of names and branches of service of their local boys.

Yet behind all this display of patriotism, the American roadside remained constant, with its Burma Shave signs, Bar B-Q's, hot-dog stands, double features and Pal Night, Dish Night and Bank Nights at the movies, chicken dinners or chop suey joints, and roadside zoos and front veranda swings and trailer parks with de-tired, retired trailers up on blocks and the roadside vendors selling hooked rugs and baby chicks, puppies and pottery, goldfish and cactus plants, candy and pecans, antiques and fish hooks, fresh eggs and country hams and cherry cider. And establishments like the Brookside Grill, the Spinning Wheel Diner, Mac's Coke and Malt Shop, Mamie's and the Co-Ed Café still waved their blinking neon signs at passing travelers:

GOOD FOOD IN A COUNTRY TOWN
HOME OF GOOD EATS
COME BACK AND SEE US
NEW BEDS AND GAS HEAT
GOOD MEALS COOKED RIGHT
RUNNING WATER
WE NEVER CLOSE

True, you might see soldiers guarding bridges, but you might also see civilians standing near by, their fishing lines dropped into the water. The jukeboxes were beginning to blare with war songs—"Praise the Lord and Pass the Ammunition," "Remember Pearl Harbor," "Johnny Doughboy Found a Rose in Ireland," "He Wears a Pair of Silver Wings"— but you also heard syrupy escape tunes like "Sleepy Lagoon" ("A sleepy lagoon/A tropical moon/And two on an island"), or Guy Lombardo's version of "Sailboat in the Sky," or love songs like "This Love of Mine (goes on and on)"; or novelties like "Boo Hoo," or Bing Crosby's "We'll Make Hay While the Sun Shines," or "Scatter Brain":

You're as pleasant as the morning
And refreshing as the rain.
Isn't it a pity that you're such a scatter brain?

The rovin' Western mood was rollicking in: "I got spurs that jingle, jangle jingle/As I go ridin' merrily along./Though I'd love to stay forever/This is why I can't remain." The pulse of the times echoed the boisterous, rhythmic clap of:

The stars at night
Are big and bright
(clap, clap, clap, clap)
Deep in the heart of Texas!

The tempo was rudimentary and direct, the words simple, the beat hard. "From Natchez to Mobile/From Memphis to St. Joe/Wherever the four winds blow. . . ."

At last the journey would near its end, and the migrant would catch a glimpse of the city of his destination: "snowy plains where great manufacturing plants jut up among their parking lots like mesas in the desert . . . mills that smear the sky with brown smoke out of tall cylindrical chimneys. . . ."

In green, gently rolling farmland, long, low dull-red brick factories rose up where bulldozers had scraped the land bare. Walter Wiard owned a farm and orchard in an area near Ypsilanti, Michigan, known as Willow Run after a stream that meandered through it on its way to the Huron River. In early 1941, Walter Wiard's land lay next to the site the Ford people had chosen for their new bomber plant, and the Ford people came to him and offered him a nice price for the land. Then Wiard watched as the giant groundbreaking machines went to work. Later he remarked: "It took me twenty-nine years to plant, cultivate and make that fine orchard. It took those tractors and bulldozers just twenty-nine minutes to tear it all down."

Near Chicago, Chrysler Motors and the federal government built the largest plant in the world—larger than Willow Run—and the tough construction workers who built it waded around in mud—mud so deep that the foremen rode around on horses that sometimes sank thigh-deep in it.

Out on the Nevada desert, on the alkaline, white dusty powder rose a magnesium plant, in the steady searchlight glare and heat of the sun.

In Washington, D.C., twenty-seven prefabricated office buildings were erected in less than a year. Tempos they were dubbed, short for temporary. Five hundred workers would assemble at a bare spot of land, and then the posts and crossbeams went up, and the wall sidings made of gray asbestos board were raised like a stage set or a speeded-up film of an old-fashioned pioneer barn raising. Each tempo cost $835,000; altogether they had a total of 3,292,156 square feet of office space— 300,000 more than the RCA Building in New York City, enough for 40,000 workers. They were bare, functional echoing warrens inside, aclatter with the sounds of typing as secretaries and their bosses worked in the same open rooms. In summer they were hot and stifling.

So the workers arrived at the towns and cities where the war plants had risen and got off their crowded buses and walked the streets looking for a job, which was easy to find, and a bed, which was not. They might have landed in LA or San Francisco or Detroit or Pascagoula

or Buffalo or Mobile. In Mobile this was the scene that greeted one
traveler after the bus ride:

> . . . a milling crowd; soldiers, sailors, stout women with
> bundled up babies, lanky backwoodsmen with hats tipped over
> their brows and a cheek full of chewing tobacco, hatless young
> men in light colored sports shirts open at the neck, countrymen
> with creased red necks and well-washed overalls, cigarsmoking
> stocky men in business suits in pastel shades, girls in bright
> dresses with carefully curled hair piled upon their heads and high-
> heeled shoes and bloodred fingernails, withered nutbrown old
> people with glasses, carrying ruptured suitcases, broadshouldered
> men in oilstained khaki with shiny brown helmets on their heads,
> negroes in flappy jackets and pegtop pants and little felt hats with
> turned-up brims, teenage boys in jockey caps, here and there a
> flustered negro woman dragging behind her a string of white-
> eyed children. . . . Out on the streets every other man seems
> to be in work clothes. There are girls in twos and threes in slacks
> and overalls. Waiting for the light at a crossing a pinkfaced
> youth who's dangling a welder's helmet on a strap from the crook
> of his arm turns laughing to the man who hailed him. "I jes' got
> tired an' quit." Ragged families from the hills and piney woods
> stroll staring straight ahead of them along the sidewalks towing
> flocks of little kids with flaxen hair and dirty faces. . . . The
> mouldering old Gulf seaport with its ancient dusty elegance of tall
> shuttered windows under mansard roofs and iron lace overgrown
> with vines and scaling collonnades shaded by great trees, looks
> trampled and battered like a city that's been taken by storm. Side-
> walks are crowded. Gutters are stacked with litter that drifts
> back and forth in the brisk spring wind. Garbage cans are over-
> flowing. Frame houses on treeshaded streets bulge with men in
> shirtsleeves who spill out onto the porches and trample grassplots
> and stand in knots at the streetcorners. . . . The trailer army
> has filled all the open lots with its regular ranks. In cluttered
> backyards people camp out in tents and chickenhouses and shelters
> tacked together out of packingcases. . . . Here and there are
> whole city blocks piled with wreckage and junk as if ancient
> cranky warehouses and super-annuated stores had caved in out of
> their own rottenness under the impact of the violence of the new
> effort. Over it all the Gulf mist, heavy with smoke of soft coal,
> hangs in streaks and glittering the training planes endlessly circle
> above the airfields.

Mobile was "more like a Western mining camp than a Southern
seaport town," another observer said, unconsciously echoing a simile that
many would employ: the raw mining towns of the West in the nine-

teenth century—only now it was wages, not gold, the men were panning.

San Diego, once a quiet coastal town, was inundated with a lusty gang of workers and servicemen. For a new dry dock the Navy dug a hole that seemed as deep as the Grand Canyon, and one old resident described it as "a hole that you could have dumped most of this town [into] when I first saw it 70 years ago." Another graybeard, shaking his head in wonderment, recalled, "We used to go to bed by ten, or anyway, by eleven. Now some theaters and cafes never close! I remember it was like that in the Klondike. Now when boatloads of sailors hurry ashore, and all those soldiers from Fort Rosecrans and Camp Callan swarm in on payday, this town goes crazy. In one day they eat 50,000 hot dogs! Even shoe shine boys get the jitters. Sherman's Cafe has ten bars, and a dance floor so big that 5,000 of 'em can dance at once." Ten years before, exactly 6 men worked in San Diego's one aircraft factory; now there were 50,000. Any innocent tourist who decided to sit for a moment on a park bench would find himself approached by a series of people wanting to hire him to do some kind of job.

The war towns on the receiving end of the sudden influx of workers to man the machines reacted in various ways. Many welcomed with open palms the visitors' money, but not the visitors. Although there was an increasing sentiment of rebellion against federal controls at the municipal government level, there was also a growing demand for federal funds to meet the problems caused by the strain on local services: the crowded schools; the overburdened, underpaid law enforcement agencies, especially those dealing with juveniles; the city hospitals packed to the rafters; the inadequate sewage lines; the pothole-studded streets and crumbling sidewalks and so on. (After the war some localities requested more federal funds to repair the wear and tear—like some farmer who has rented his land at a nice price for a company picnic and the next day submits a bill for damages.) Financially, the towns were better off than they had been in a long time, for while their public works and welfare expenditures decreased (nobody on welfare and no materials available to build anything with), their tax revenues soared—most of it property taxes, but some of it collected directly from the transients in sales tax.

Consider the town of Beaumont, Texas, which needed an incinerator. Next door to the Pennsylvania Shipyards stood a giant garbage dump which exhaled a miasma that could be smelled miles away when the wind was right. With the nauseating smells came flies. An official of the shipyards described what the flies were like: "The flies we get from the dump in the executive offices are so thick that it is almost impossible to concentrate on our duties. Twice a day the rooms are sprayed and the dead swept out with a broom. As soon as it gets warm we have to send people around the yard to spray the men on the job, or they would be eaten up by mosquitoes and flies."

The incinerator had been approved by the Federal Works Administration, and work had been begun. Then the WPB refused the town a priority on a needed bit of equipment worth about $14,000. And so work stopped, and a half-finished incinerator stood in the midst of the stench and rotting garbage, a monument to government shortsightedness, while the stink grew and the danger of typhoid increased apace.

Some war towns met the emergency as best they could by improvising and enlisting the help of local civic groups; others sat back and let things go from bad to worse, and the war workers found themselves living in congested squalor. What was needed was a coordinated effort at the federal, state, municipal, industrial, business and service-organization levels, but this effort was sometimes slow in coming. And many communities where war industries or military bases were suddenly plunked down simply lacked the financial and political resources to do anything and depended entirely upon the actions of agencies of the federal government.

Another factor which made some cities slow in coming to the aid of the newcomers was simply prejudice. If the newcomers had a different skin color or if they came from another part of the country and spoke with different accents and looked like "low life," the conservative townsfolk tended to turn up their noses and erect a screen of rationalizations on the worthlessness of the newcomers, thereby enabling them to avoid any responsibility for helping them. In Mobile the school system was called by the U.S. Office of Education the worst in the nation—a high school built for 2,200 had twice that enrollment; seventy-five new classrooms were needed, but the federal government had provided funds for only eight; average salaries for teachers were only $1,150 per year compared with $1,440 a typist could make with the federal government and the minimum of $2,600 a laborer could make in the shipyards. Even though the cause of these abysmal schools was largely lack of money, teachers and equipment, the attitude of one Mobile teacher toward her new pupils was revealing:

> These are the lowest type of poor whites, these workers who
> are flocking in from the backwoods. They prefer to live in shacks
> and go barefoot, even when two or three workers in a single

family earn as much as $500 a month. Give them a good house
and they wouldn't know what to do with it. . . . I only hope we
can get rid of them after the war.

There was some truth in this picture of the backwoodsmen, of
course; many of these folk were poor workers who changed jobs freely,
who were fiercely suspicious of "the law," and who kept to themselves,
preferring to avoid housing projects in favor of their shacks, lean-tos
and tents. (One man who lived in a tent with his family was offered a
house and refused, saying patriotically: "What's good enough for our
boys in Africa is good enough for me.") Still, there was often little
effort by the local gentry to understand these folk, whose poverty had
scarred them and whose customs were different. Far from not giving a
hoot about what people thought of them, some were acutely sensitive to
the prejudice they met, like the man in Pascagoula living in a trailer who
said, "Those folks in houses think trailer people are vermin."

In Muncie, Indiana—the "Middletown" of the Lynds—they told a
joke about the hillbillies: "Haven't you heard there are only forty-five
states left in the Union? Kentucky and Tennessee have gone to Indiana
and Indiana has gone to hell." Some typical views toward the newcomers:

"They work all week, then lie around drunk on Saturday and Sunday, sleep nine to a room."

"The reason you see so many young fellows on the streets, driving
jalopies all over town on black market gasoline . . . when they ought
to be in the Army, is that the Army won't have them—they're illiterate."

"The hillbillies will work awhile and save $50 in bonds, then go
back home and live on it in the hills for two or three years."

"You want to know what the people are thinking about? Maybe
I'm cynical but I don't think 2% of them are thinking where their next
meal is coming from, let alone about what's going to happen after the
war. Not the hillbillies anyway. And there's plenty others like them."

A popular hillbilly song of the period paid back the Hoosier hospitality in kind. The song was called "Indiana Blues" and the words told
of a homesick hillbilly who longed to "see my folks, hear their jokes."
So desperate was he he'd "even take a train or a plane/Through snow
or through wind and rain," lest he "go insane" from the Indiana blues.
(Another, more popular "homesickness song" was "I Wanna Go Back
to West Virginia," which had a slicker, more commercial tune and a
less doleful mood.)

On the whole, the hillbillies, suspicious of outsiders and the "law," tended to keep to themselves, whether in large or in small cities, frequent their own honky-tonks and cabarets, and demand jukeboxes playing their own sad, lonesome music. During 1942 and 1943, when America was singing such patriotic war songs as "Praise the Lord and Pass the Ammunition" and "Remember Pearl Harbor," the hillbillies, patriotic as the next man, were, typically, singing their own favorite: "There's a Star Spangled Banner Waving Somewhere." This song was considered to be the biggest record and sheet music seller in the country, although its *déclassé* origins kept it off the *Your Hit Parade* radio program, the final arbiter of song popularity. The song was a typical doleful lament, written by Paul Roberts and Shelby Darnell and sung by Elton Britt. It went:

> There's a Star Spangled Banner waving somewhere
> In a distant land, so many miles away,
> Only Uncle Sam's great heroes get to go there
> Where I wish that I could also live some day.
> I'd see Lincoln, Custer, Washington and Perry
> And Nathan Hale and Colin Kelly too!
> There's a Star Spangled Banner waving somewhere,
> Waving o'er the land of heroes brave and true.

Later the hillbillies would give the nation an even more popular song—"Pistol Packin' Mama," which *did* make the Hit Parade, in a slightly bowdlerized version.

On their own home grounds, where they were given a decent shake by the community, the hill people showed themselves in a better light. One such place was the Crab Orchard Lake ordnance plant located in a depressed area in southern Illinois, near the towns of Marion, Herrin and Carbondale—all notorious for labor violence and blood feuds in the twenties. By the 1930's more than half the people might be on relief at a given time. It was the Army that recommended placing an ordnance plant in the area, and Sherwin-Williams, a conservative firm with a good reputation, was given the contract. Within a year, in the fall of 1942, the 500 small buildings making up the plant (ordnance factories were decentralized into small units and scattered about a large area for obvious reasons) occupied 23,000 acres of unused land, creating jobs for more than 12,000 local people. These former coal miners of southern Illinois had their own cultural patterns and outlook on life: The area had one of the highest illegitimacy rates in the country; infidelity was winked at. Further, many of the people had never paid taxes in their lives and had no intention of starting now. The night shift was popular because the men drove unlicensed cars—called night cars because they drove them only under cover of darkness. Nevertheless, Sherwin-Williams had nothing but praise for its people. Plant manager E. E. Ware said, "Never have I met such willing people. The women are particularly enthusiastic. They get after the laggards and are constantly speeding up the work. . . . We expected a wild, restless population, and instead they are the finest people with whom we have ever been associated." The plant was indeed a happy proposition all around and an example of intelligent social planning.

Such foresight was not always forthcoming from Washington. A number of agencies at the federal level were charged with giving aid to distressed war towns—the Office of Defense Health and Welfare, the Federal Works Agency, the National Housing Agency (an administrative organ which oversaw three "action" agencies—the Federal Home Loan Bank, the Federal Housing Administration and the Federal Public Housing Authority) and others. When it came to funds, they all stood at the end of the wartime line, behind the military and the war production effort.

Housing was an immediate and frequently insoluble problem for the migrant war workers. The government and private builders, largely with federally insured mortgage money, built a total of $7 billion of new housing, much of it temporary—barracks, trailers, demountable homes, dormitories and the like. The NHA calculated that it had to provide new or existing housing for 9,000,000 migratory workers and their families. To do this, it built and it scoured up existing vacant rooms and houses with the assistance of local community groups. Existing housing took care of 600,000 workers and their families. Over and above this, private companies built something more than 1,000,000 new units and the federal government 832,000 for a total of 1,800,000 units or housing for about 5,000,000 people: housing for at best 7,000,000 out of 9,000,000 migrants was provided; the remaining 2,000,000 presumably had to scour up their own shelter.

These bare statistics do not of course reflect the flesh and blood of the housing situation—the thousands who had to live in trailers, converted garages, tents, shacks, overpriced rooms, "hot beds," even their own cars during the early part of the war; the rent gouging that went on, even though rents were regulated by the Office of Price Administration; and the difficulties people with children had, especially the wives of servicemen who followed them to their training camps.

Landlord hostility to the newcomers was endemic in this sellers' market. An ad in a Fort Worth, Texas, newspaper revealed it: "Fur. Apt., no street-walkers, home wreckers, drunks wanted; couples must present marriage certificate." On the West Coast, which had had an influx of more than 2,000,000 newcomers, it was chaotic. In San Francisco people lived in tents, basements, refrigerator lockers and automobiles. A city official reported in 1943: "Families are sleeping in garages, with mattresses right on cement floors and three, four, five to one bed." In Richmond, where the Kaiser shipyards were located, people were living under conditions that were worse than the Hoovervilles of the Depression. A trailer camp in San Pablo was crowded with people in trailers, tents and shacks; there was no sewage, and children waded about in a stagnant pond. A family of four adults and seven children lived in an 8-by-10-foot shack with two cots and one full-sized bed. A war housing project at Sausalito offered good living conditions for 4,500 people with self-government, low rentals and health insurance; but when a 90-mile-an-hour gale hit the area in January, 1943, all the tarpaper roofs of the temporary housing blew off.

The housing problem was dramatized when Mrs. Colin Kelly, widow of the war hero, was unable to find a place to live in Los Angeles, where she had gone to seek war work, because most landlords banned children. After the newspapers exposed her plight, she was deluged with offers, but despite her good fortune, she realized her name helped. "I can't help realizing," she said, "that hundreds of other families are having the same difficulties I had."

Not so lucky as Mrs. Kelly were the servicemen's wives in Leesville, Louisiana, a stagnant backwater rudely jostled into wartime by the location of Camp Polk nearby. A reporter discovered young women, some with babies, paying up to $50 a month to live in a warren of sheds, converted chicken coops and ramshackle barns. The places were broken up into cubicles by frail partitions, and three slept in a bed (a separate, evil-looking room was set aside for husbands and wives wanting privacy for consortium). A single toilet and shower served thirty-five people; the local milk disagreed with the babies, many of whom sickened and died, according to the local undertaker, who said he'd buried many of them.

The philosophy underlying the governmental housing program was that "the government doesn't belong in the housing business," which meant that private housing interests were deferred to. In San Francisco, for example, which had a population increase of 200,000, local realtors had initially opposed war housing, saying there were 10,000 vacancies in the area. They were fearful of the competition, of course, but then, when the housing situation reached crisis proportions, they did a turnabout and blamed the federal government for not building enough war housing. And though they had relented on allowing government housing, they were adamant in their demands that only temporary housing, which could be torn down after the war, be built, lest property values suffer. This insistence that war workers be given only temporary or demountable housing was widespread and reflected not only the real estate man's pocketbook talking but also fear that the outsiders would stay after the war. As a result (and also because of the shortage of building materials), much government housing was jerry-built—instant slums they might be called.

The emphasis on temporary structures showed a lack of concern for the nation's future housing needs. Former Administrator of the Federal Housing Authority Nathan Straus warned in 1943: "Temporary houses which have been built recently by the FPHA with a particular view towards saving time and critical material are definitely substandard homes—and we know it. . . . In my opinion, only a straightforward, unequivocal statement is possible; namely, that these houses must come down, or the Federal government will have built a slum of ten years from now."

This view was fine if there was something to replace the wartime housing; but there wasn't, and such was the postwar housing shortage— an estimated 5,000,000 new units needed immediately in 1946 and 12,000,000 in the immediate postwar decade—that the "temporary" structures acquired permanence as stopgap housing. Some are still lived in twenty-five years later and have indeed become slums.

One of the better federal housing projects was that erected near the Willow Run bomber plant. Because of opposition on the part of the townspeople in nearby Ypsilanti and the Ford Motor Company to a planned permanent residential area known as Bomber City (see Chapter IV) and material shortages, construction of alternate, temporary units was proposed and finally got under way in 1943. The first units— a dormitory for single workers called Willow Lodge—were open for occupancy by February, 1943. There followed trailer homes and prefabricated units for families, which were completed in August, 1943. In all there was housing for about 14,000 workers—or one-third the number working at Willow Run plant at peak production.

By wartime housing standards these units were luxury housing, although they were not much to look at, being row upon row of gray, monotonous, flat-roofed buildings. The residents often had difficulty locating their own quarters. One lady always marked her house by a bedspring leaning against the adjoining unit. So much did she come to rely on the bedspring that she forgot the number of her own dwelling, and so one day, when, inevitably, the bedspring was removed, she spent hours searching for her place.

Since the village was located far from gas mains, the residents had to learn to cook on coal stoves, which because of improper drafts were always blowing literally hot and cold. One former resident swore that many a day walking to the bus—the residents called them cattle cars—he kicked a number of hard, black cinderlike objects. When he noticed a woman throwing a pan of them out the door, he realized that the rocks were actually burned biscuits, product of the wayward stove. The flats were sparsely furnished with straight chairs, some labeled "Zero-bedroom" because they were one room, and iceboxes which leaked on the floor were used in lieu of refrigerators. Still, the government was thoughtful enough to erect a nearby shopping center for the Willow Run Village residents—a convenience that many such projects didn't have, forcing wives to drive miles to try to buy food at stores originally designed to serve a prewar population.

Most of the married workers with families overcame these minor hardships at Willow Run and turned it into a stable community. Still there were problems that could have been predicted among such a large and fluid population, many of them unmarried immigrants from the South. One reporter was critical of the "lack of wholesome recreational facilities and the generally drab social environment of Willow Run" which "stimulated private-party types of entertainment, featured by heavy drinking and promiscuous sex relations among fun-starved workers."

The center of the "promiscuous sex" was, not surprisingly, the Willow Lodge dormitory, which the FPHA had opened to unmarried workers of both sexes. The result: "Professional gamblers and fast women quickly moved in for a clean-up." The co-ed policy was quickly dropped, however, and tenant policing, in cooperation with the FPHA, cleaned up the budding Gomorrah.

Contrasting sharply with the housing at Willow Run was what the private market offered on a tract known as the Lay Garden Subdivision —some twenty decrepit farmhouses between Ypsilanti and Willow Run. The only water had to be drawn from wells; sewage disposal was nil, and the outdoor privies stood near the shallow wells, an obvious invitation to typhoid. Crowding was the rule. In one house a family of five lived on the first floor, five people slept in the basement, four more on the second floor, nine people were in the garage, and four families lived in trailers parked in the backyard. But this kind of squalor could be found all over the country, and the inhabitants were not necessarily "white trash."

At Willow Run Village, the federal government did its best to provide standards of health and decency. The people saw themselves as "pioneers"—an anachronistic American euphemism for facing difficulties in common. The government built good, new schools, and the residents formed a variety of community organizations. Still, they were transients at heart, only there for the duration. Once, when the school held a session of group singing, the children were instructed to sing "Michigan, My Michigan," the state anthem. A hush settled over the class, and the children refused to sing. They remembered their *real* homes in other states, and none could think of Michigan as "*my* Michigan."

After the war, signs went up along the expressway linking the Willow Run plant to Detroit reading: WILLOW RUN VILLAGE—TEMPORARY VETERANS HOUSING. The village assumed a new role as housing for young married and single veterans, most of whom were studying on the GI Bill at the University of Michigan. The FPHA continued to run it (but not as a slum) until 1954, when with 7,000 current inhabitants, it was sold—ironically to the town of Ypsilanti, which originally had opposed any permanent worker housing at Willow Run. The town planned ultimately to redevelop the area, but the immediate concern of the local businessmen was that the government might tear it down, thus losing them all those good customers living there.

In all, the government built only $2.6 billion of hasty temporary housing in which people would live after the war, compared to the $20 billion worth of plant facilities subsequently usable by private industry. The shortsightedness of Congress' housing philosophy was expressed in a statement by Representative Fritz Lanham (D., Tex.), author of the Lanham (Community Facilities) Act, under which some of the funds for housing were appropriated. Of his bill, he said: "The real estate business naturally and properly belongs to the real estate men. . . . There is nothing in the Act to do with slum clearance or low-cost housing for low-income groups."

The Lanham Act was the basic legislative vehicle for providing federal aid to war-impacted areas. A total of $343,367,376 had been spent under it as of September, 1944, for a variety of projects: day-care nurseries, sewers, hospitals, garbage incinerators, law enforcement, fire prevention, recreation centers and the like, in communities where existing facilities were cracking under the strain of increased population. Compared with the cost of the war, which was running at the rate of $200,000,000 a day, by 1944 this was not exactly Socialistic largesse. The money, which was granted on a matching basis with the states and localities, was distributed in pork-barrel fashion to communities with the most political clout; there were delays and snarls of red tape, though when the money came through, it was put to good use.

Mrs. Agnes Meyer, wife of the publisher of the Washington *Post*, who traveled throughout the country investigating social conditions in the war towns, wrote, "This brings me to the painful subject of Lanham Act funds. I must in all candor report that their administration is criticized from one end of the country to the other." As an example of the effects of a long delay in requested funds for day-care centers in the Vallejo, California, area, Mrs. Meyer reported how the children of some of the working mothers were faring:

> In the San Fernando Valley, in the city limits of Los Angeles, where several war plants are located, a social worker counted 45 infants locked in cars of a single parking space. In Vallejo, the children sit in the movies, seeing the same film over and over again until mother comes off the swing shift and picks them up. Some children of working parents are locked in their homes, others locked out.

A busybody type of lady with a warm heart described three such locked-out children whom she had noticed roaming around aimlessly in her neighborhood daily. The woman invited them to visit her house when-ever they wanted and offered to read them stories. The oldest girl looked at her unbelievingly. "You mean you really want us?" she said.

A social worker told of seeing a twelve-year-old girl in a beer hall late at night, sitting alone in the corner. Asked what she was doing there, the girl replied, "I'm just waiting for 12 o'clock. My bed isn't empty until then." Another little girl, left in the care of her landlady, confided to a social worker: "I'll tell you a secret. When my mother is away and I don't know where she is I cry. She says she's at work but I don't know where she is and I get scared."

Roving youngsters with nowhere to go were widespread. In Mobile, there were more than 2,000 children who didn't go to school at all, and one high school with an enrollment of 3,650 had a total of 8,217 absences during a single month. One movie theater owner joked with the local lady truant officer: "Miss Bessie, why don't you bring your teachers down here? My place is always full of children."

The role of the movie theater as a parking place for young children was described by a reporter for the Muncie *Press:*

> It's Saturday night—in fact it is early Sunday morning, and the crowded Owl Show at the Rivoli is about out. There is not a vacant seat left in the balcony, it is packed to the roof, and the theater's staff is worn out from its usual problem of playing nurse-maid, truant officer and policeman along with its ordinary job of keeping the routine business of the place in order. The maid in the rest room has had to take care of five teen-aged intoxicated girls, an usher has broken up a race that was being held up and down the aisles. Down in the entrance, sleepy, tired youngsters are awaiting their parents. One little boy, whose small, pinched face already shows signs of age, whose too large coat hangs loosely and whose torn button holes won't hold the varied assortment of buttons, waits. He has picked up a cigarette and has a few puffs while he waits. A little girl, dressed snugly in a warm winter outfit, reads a funny book, her eyes too heavy to see many of the characters blurring before them. . . . "It's much better tonight," Mr. Sowan, the manager, says. "I have had as many as 50 to 60 children left here and sometimes when I leave the closed theater they are still waiting out on the streets, for their family."

Some towns, even without federal assistance, made an effort to set up day-care centers and nursery schools in a variety of ways, and the unions and war industries made an even greater contribution, the latter prodded by the labor shortage and the need to attract women workers, the former by a doctrine of demanding work rights. On the other hand, there was a distinct strain of prejudice against working mothers, who were regarded as selfishly materialistic; forgotten was the desperate need for them in the plants, the fact that many were servicemen's wives who needed to supplement their allotments, and the desire of others to take advantage of an opportunity to save up some money for the future. One of the leaders in the opposition to women working was the Catholic

Church, which in many areas opposed nursery schools and day-care centers.

Just how many children were turned loose while their parents worked was anybody's guess. A survey of working mothers in Detroit, before that city received Lanham Act funds for day-care centers, showed that two out of five working mothers had children under sixteen and half of these were under five. About half the children were cared for in the mother's absence by the father or another relative; the remainder were cared for by domestics, neighbors, friends, nurseries or what was known as self-care or casual care. The latter category consisted of the wanderers; they made up 12 percent of the total.

Lanham Act funds were contributed on a 50–50 basis to a total of 2,892 day-care projects, which affected a total of only 107,000 children. The enlightened localities and industries and unions which provided child-care centers for the most part found that the children adjusted well, even though their mothers were on the swing shift and picked them up in the middle of the night while they were asleep. (The reason the mothers were working on the swing or graveyard shifts was not always by choice; union rules usually awarded the seven to three shift on seniority—and the men had the seniority.)

Not unrelated to the shortage of day care, the overcrowded schools, the entry of youngsters into industry, and the lack of parental supervision was an increase in the incidence of crimes committed by teenagers (a term that came into wide currency during the war, along with juvenile delinquency). Juvenile arrests increased 20 percent in 1943; in some cities it was even higher—San Diego, for example, reported an increase of 55 percent among boys and 355 percent among girls. This was not a reflection of a nationwide crime wave, for crime on the whole—at least according to FBI figures—dropped during the war, with the exception of assault and rape. This was because the young men, who committed the largest percentage of crimes, were off in service. One of the heaviest areas of increase was among girls under seventeen who were arrested not only for various forms of "sex delinquency" such as prostitution, but also for violent crimes. In 1943 alone, the number of girls arrested for prostitution increased by 68 percent over the previous year.

Among the boys, it was largely theft and a striking incidence of acts of vandalism, destruction and violence. Some of these acts seemed a kind of acting-out of war fantasies—such as the thirteen-year-old "thrill saboteur" who put a stick of dynamite under a railroad track,

lit the fuse and ran. The dynamite did not go off because he had attached no cap. He explained his action by saying he was attempting to
close off all roads into the town and set himself up as "dictator."

With the girls, delinquency took the form of an aggressive promis-
cuity, and the lure was the glamor of a uniform. These "khaki-whacky"
teen-agers—some barely thirteen—were known as V (for Victory) girls.
They hung around bus depots, train stations, drugstores or wherever
soldiers and sailors on leave might congregate, flirted with the boys, and
propositioned them for dates. They were amateurs for the most part,
the price of their favors being a movie, a dance, a Coke or some stronger
drink. (A joke of the time ran: Sailor: "I'm going to Walgreen's to
meet a girl." "What's her name?" "How should I know?")

The V-girls were easily recognizable in their Sloppy Joe sweaters,
hair ribbons, anklets or bobby sox and saddle shoes, trying to look older
with heavily made-up faces and blood-red lipstick. In Detroit the Navy
had to build a fence around its armory, located in the city, to keep
out not the enemy, but the bobby-soxers. In Chicago, sailors said it
was worth one's life to try to walk from the Navy Pier to State Street,
where the V-girls swarmed like flies. In Mobile, the girls themselves
bought contraceptives for their dates, and when one druggist refused to
sell them to a group of girls, he was jeered at and called an old fuddy-
duddy.

The V-girls had their similarities all over the country. Some of them
followed their lovers when they were transferred to another post, but
many were left stranded when the boyfriend left. These often ended up
working as waitresses or as barmaids in servicemen's hangouts, passing
from one uniform to another.

There had always been teen-age girls who "did it," of course; war
made them more visible, more independent, more mobile. One estimate
had it that the V-girls represented at most only one in 1,700 out of their
age group. More conservative girls, caught up in the transitoriness of
wartime meetings and the glamor of a uniform, might also "do it,"
but they were more discreet and less promiscuous and conducted their
assignations in more privacy.

The V-girl was next door to being a prostitute, yet there was about
her at least a certain refreshing lack of cold professionalism. She offered
a lonely GI transitory fun and excitement, devoid of the professional's
matter-of-fact indifference. She could also, of course, offer him VD, for
there was a higher incidence among the amateurs than among the professionals. In 1941, Congress, worried about the mother's vote, had

passed the May Act, which forbade houses of prostitution near military bases. The result was that a lot of establishments were closed down and their inmates put out to walk the streets. These and their amateur competitiors were found to inflict VD at a much higher rate than the house-based girls.

In 1943, a study made in the Third Naval District (Texas and the Southwest) found that 80 percent of the cases of VD were attributable to girlfriends or pickups. After San Antonio, Texas, cleaned up its red-light districts, the girls started working in cabs and alleys, causing a public health official to express regret over the cleanup and assert that the girls and madams of the houses had been much more cooperative with authorities and easier to police than their free-lance counterparts. A bill was introduced in the New York State Assembly penalizing "one infected with venereal disease who has had sexual intercourse with a person in the United States military service." The bill's preamble stated that "four times as many soldiers are infected from contact with willing girls in their teens as from prostitutes."

In view of this, it was not surprising that there was a school of thought which advocated supervised, inspected brothels for soldiers, in the ancient tradition of camp followers. The rationale was not only that the risk of VD would be lessened, but also that if soldiers didn't have such outlets, they would turn to seducing—or raping—the "nice" girls of the town. In November, 1941, Winfield Scott Pugh, a naval surgeon, wrote: "What substitute do we offer for prostitution? Like it or not, somebody's daughter." A similar view was expressed by a New York endocrinologist in a monograph entitled, presumably with unconscious irony, *Morals vs. Morale in Wartime.* The doctor wrote:

> The young soldier on leave with healthy instincts is quite likely to seduce a "good girl" if there is no "bad girl" around or if one is too difficult to find. The "good girl" is handicapped by her emotional attachments, is motivated by patriotism or is uniform-mad. Usually, she knows little or nothing of prevention. . . . The "bad girl" is usually wise. Her past experiences protect her as well as the boy.

The guardians of morality—whose view on the subject had been expressed in a 1942 *Reader's Digest* article by Gene Tunney entitled "The Bright Shield of Continence"—of course were against any kind of sex by soldiers with women other than their wives (if that) and would be shocked at the idea of brothels near Army camps where innocent young selectees would be exposed to unholy, irresistible temptation leading to inevitable corruption. (There was a similar logic running through the efforts of temperance groups to ban the distribution of beer to combat troops or its sale at PX's.)

As for the servicemen themselves, the Army traditionally liked to say that 15 percent "won't," 15 percent "will" and the remainder occasionally would succumb to temptation if the serpent insinuated itself (these figures derived from World War I). For that wavering 70 percent, the problems of finding "nice girls" in the camp towns, whether their intent was to deflower them or take them to the Sunday night meeting of the Epworth League, were often insuperable. A GI summed up his difficulties meeting women in a letter to a former professor:

> I never realized it would make so much difference when I was in uniform. You would think I had leprosy. In spite of a lot of patriotic platitudes—it's all different. You have your choice between a low level of sensual women who are always about where men in uniform are and who isn't exactly a prostitute but isn't much better, and the very professional welfare-conscious attaché of the U.S.O. There isn't anything else. My buddy and I got a big laugh out of a newspaper comment that people near army camps were opening their homes to soldiers on Sundays. The truth is that most of them live in mortal fear that one of their "innocent" daughters might be contaminated by a date with one of the boys in uniform.

The professor commented that judging by what he heard from other former students in service, many civilians wanted to be friendly, but as every soldier knows, a soldier "is a category and a category which is not too complimentary."

In conclusion the professor decided: "A number of men who normally are conventional in their behavior and whose verbal beliefs are reasonably consistent with their behavior, have, under war conditions, developed a sort of *schizoid morality*—one moral code for peace time in the home community and another for war time in a strange community." A newlywed GI, he added, was probably in the same moral boat as the unmarried one.

Still, if the number of marriages and families formed is any sort of index to the degree of adherence to the American fundamental belief in marriage, the war period could be looked upon as fostering a salubrious moral climate. Beginning in 1940, as prosperity began to take hold and the Depression receded, the marriage rate began to rise abruptly—one is tempted to say alarmingly. In 1940, the number of marriages was up 13.8 percent over 1939; in 1941, as war became increasingly imminent and the possibility of separation (as well as the possibility of avoiding the draft) added a spur to a young couple's decision, the rise was 7.3 percent. In December, 1941, 10 percent of the year's weddings were consummated—second only to June's 11.5 percent. During the first three months of 1942 the sale of wedding rings rose 300 percent; the popularity of double-ring ceremonies not only quickly depleted jewelers' stocks, it also betokened a highly moral reciprocal promise of fidelity. By 1943, as the ranks of the bachelors were reduced by the draft, the trend was reversed and marriages fell off 10.3 percent. The downward turn continued through 1944; then in 1945, as the boys began coming home, a rise of 9.5 percent was recorded, presaging an even more frantic scrambling into matrimony in 1946.

A bit more surprisingly, the number of families—households—increased during the war by 2,000,000, despite a countertrend toward merging households (as when a wife whose husband was off in the service went to live with her mother and father; by 1945 there were 1,500,000 families living "doubled up"). But this was probably a normal result of population increases and, of course, the rising marriage rate; had there been no war the increase would probably have been greater. More reflective of wartime living was the rise in the number of families with a married woman at the head, the husband absent; the number jumped from 770,000 in 1940 to 2,770,000 in 1945.

The rush to wed was impelled as much by prosperity as it was by the war. A justice of the peace in Yuma, Arizona, a marriage town just over the California border, explained the sudden upswing in business in 1941. Not love but "aircraft did it for us," he said. "The figures began going up as soon as those boys were given employment in those plants at San Diego and Los Angeles and were taken off W.P.A." Aircraft workers had been issued 90 percent of the licenses since the summer of 1941. "You see, when they were on the dole they had girls but no money. Once off the dole and once getting good money they began sending for the girls back home—girls in the Middle Western states, a great many of them. The girls wouldn't waste any time in coming in and then on weekends—we get the great rush on weekends—they'd all come hustling over to Yuma." It was the same story in Cincinnati, where weddings involving defense workers increased 51 percent; in Baltimore, where they were up 47 percent; and in Youngstown and Akron (up 17 percent) and Detroit (up 12 percent).

Of course, at that time a wife would also qualify as a dependent and men with dependents were deferred, until Congress discouraged this by establishing an allotment system in 1942. Under it, a man's wife would receive a minimum of $50 a month, $22 of which was deducted from his pay and $28 contributed by the government. To preserve family life and also perhaps to encourage a population increase to offset anticipated manpower losses in the war, the Selective Service Act deferred fathers until 1943, when manpower needs were so pressing that so-called pre-Pearl Harbor fathers were drafted.

Whether the Selective Service Act's policy was responsible or not (and we must give the parents some credit for initiative), the birthrate did go up during the war in a preview of the postwar baby boom when returning GI's set about forming families as fast as they could. Since the 1920's the birthrate, like the marriage rate, had been declining, but in 1943, it rose to 22 per 1,000—the highest in two decades. Most of these babies were "good-bye babies," conceived before the husband shipped out. Since the wife's allotment check would be increased upon the child's arrival, finances were no longer a major worry. In addition, there were compelling emotional reasons: The father, faced with the possibility of being killed in battle, was depositing a small guarantor to posterity, an assurance that someone would carry on his name, while the wife was given something to hold onto, a living, breathing symbol of their marriage.

Every couple planning marriage had to face the prospect of a long separation, possibly a permanent one. To those young people contemplating a wartime marriage the dilemmas were hard ones; perhaps it was the heart, quickened by unreasoning faith and hope for the future, that decided the issue. Society counseled caution, of course. A typical voice was that of Dr. Galielma F. Alsop, a Barnard College physician, who approved of wartime marriages, provided the couple had known each other "a reasonable length of time and are really in love." This rather obvious advice having been proffered, Dr. Alsop launched into a paean of enthusiasm: "Once assured in your own mind, marry him—the soldier, the sailor, the man in the sky. . . . Rise to the heights of the occasion and make the necessary sacrifices with a woman's traditional high courage. Be your husband's equal. Win the war with him."

So they were married, this courageous young couple; perhaps they did know each other well and were in love, or perhaps they had met on a weekend pass and married in haste. Or perhaps the woman had eyed covetously the allotment check and looked forward to a life of some ease (and if he was killed, there was always the $10,000 to the widow from his life insurance). A $50-a-month allotment was of course not princely, but a GI overseas, with nothing else to spend it on, would usually send part of his regular pay home.

With the going rate only $50 per month per husband, a really ambitious girl might decide she needed four, five, six or more husbands to support her in any kind of style. Inevitably there developed the wartime racket of bigamous marriage for allotment checks. The girls who engaged in it came to be known as Allotment Annies. They posted themselves in bars around military bases and struck up acquaintances with lonely servicemen, otherwise known as shooting fish in a barrel. The men, desirous of the certainty that when they went off to battle, there would be a girl back home waiting for them, writing them V-mail letters, could often be had. So they married, the hero went off to war, and Annie stayed home and collected a lot of those pale blue-green checks from the U.S. Treasury Department.

A representative Allotment Annie was a hustling seventeen-year-old named Elvira Tayloe, who operated out of Norfolk, Virginia, and specialized in sailors shipping out from the large naval base there. Working as a hostess in a nightclub, she managed to snare six live ones and was working on her seventh when caught. This came about because a couple of sailors on liberty had met in an English pub, and as servicemen are wont, as the warm beer flowed, took out wallets and exchanged pictures of their gorgeous wives. Both were surprised, to put it mildly, when their pictures turned out to be identical, both of Elvira. A fight ensued over whose wife was being adulterous with whom. After the shore patrol had cooled them off, the boys joined forces, Elvira was traced and her career of cupidity brought to an end.

At heart Elvira seemed a girl who was simply defrauding the government but in doing so spreading a few moments of happiness along the way; else why would all those boys have married her? Somewhat more macabre was the young lady who combined the allotment-check dodge with the instincts of a born actuary. She specialized in Air Force pilots, whose mortality rate was known to be above average. There was always the possibility, then, that the marriage, in addition to yielding a monthly dividend, might hit the $10,000 jackpot.

Such cases were flagitious examples of the errant ways of the hasty heart in wartime. Other, less larcenous marriages in haste would find postwar repentance in the divorce courts. In 1945, sociologists were already warning about an enormously increased postwar divorce rate—

even higher than the record established following World War I. The sociologists were right; their predictions of one in four marriages ending in a divorce were somewhat conservative. The hasty, immature marriages; the long separations; the delays in the husband's return which the wife couldn't understand; the wives, who had been bravely concealing their gripes so that He Wouldn't Worry and who began to pour out all their troubles on V-mail when the war ended, which to a soldier who had been through a lot seemed distant, plangent chords of feminine self-pity; and the postwar housing shortages and difficulties of setting up a home which exacerbated the feelings between two near strangers trying to recall what they had seen in each other that night at the USO—all these factors conspired to send couples muttering to the divorce courts.

Wartime marriage was hard, and the real miracle was that so many survived it. What the husband did overseas during off-duty hours is beyond our scope, but the girls back here were, largely, brave—and true. Not heroic; but they got by. Some, it is true, cracked up, or fell into dalliance with a representative of the local supply of 4-F's and joyriding war workers. Others suffered in silence.

Florence Hollis, a social worker, described the plight of some of the war brides: how many went through periods of frustration, anger and loss, sometimes bitterly blaming their husband for his absence, then sinking into states of hysterical grief, followed by depression and mourning—the simulacra of the death of a loved one. For such women, war work was truly a godsend, permitting the channeling of festering energies into a cause, providing the sociability of the office or factory, and opening up an avenue of escape from the toils of self-pity, helplessness and loneliness. "Do Your Bit," those garish patriotic posters said, manipulating a fundamental human desire to contribute, *to be a part of something bigger*.

Still, living from day to day is, like fighting in a total war, not a matter of unfurled flags, marching bands and cheering crowds. For the best women of that generation, it was at bottom largely a limbo time, a waiting:

> We must learn to wait. To endure the slow trickle of time from hour to hour, from day to day, for weeks in anguish and suspense. And then wait for some message, a letter sent from far off—a small scrap that tells something of how he was—some time ago when it was sent. We must have a life that's endless fear and doubt. The war work we can do is more than welcome—we work too hard to put off the next returning cycle of thought—is he safe,

is he well, will I hear from him soon? We learn to crowd a life-time of living into a week—or a few days—or hours. War brides, married while he was on furlough, we wait for the next leave, when we can get back. In those brief days, the joy is desperate, underlain by the knowledge of certain separations again—the clock ticks off numbered moments gone. And the train takes him off again—off to unknown places where our love cannot follow, cannot know how he is and we return to the uniform, the long hours of work, and fear and waiting. . . . If we bear children, they may never know their father. . . . We live and fight that our children may have the life that war has taken from us.

Those were the words of a Vassar graduate, revelatory of a life based on sacrificing today to a promissory note drawn on the future. And, in a characteristically American twist, the chief intended bene-ficiaries were to be the children. This was a generation whose chief goal had been security, suddenly plunged into man's most dangerous adven-ture, war; its dream for the future, then, lay in its progeny and the stability of a house, a job and family life.

A variation on this attitude was described by Nancy MacLennan in an article on the service wife in the *New York Times Magazine:*

> Paradoxically her thoughts are of the past and of the future. The present is simply the waiting room to peacetime. She ac-quires an omniscience. The value of money decreases. Her ambi-tions become more homespun. "Life is short, fate uncertain," she reads between the lines of all the nation's war posters. And she reacts accordingly, taking what she wants from life while she can get it and deciding that when her husband returns she will "see to it" that he attains what he is really looking for in life and not that alien yoke to which, as false ambition, he may have enslaved himself. No news is good news. He will come back. The simple credo is universal.

Faith redoubled in the orgiastic future; when the war was over, there would come the strength and will to achieve the things one really wanted. . . .

Life gave another portrait of the typical Army wife. Her husband is a lieutenant in India and her $180-a-month allotment makes her atypical right there, yet she adds some less dramatic hues to the por-trait. She lives in a 3½-room apartment, rent $65 a month; she spends $45 a month on food for her herself and the baby; she doesn't go out on dates, goes to parties unescorted and doesn't have a great deal of fun ("There's always some woman who thinks you're trying to take their man away"); sometimes at night she gets the blues and cries, but her baby son cheers her up a lot; she writes her husband a letter every day; she spends her evenings listening to the radio a lot (Guy Lombardo's is her favorite orchestra); when she hears "Soon"—"their song" in 1935, when they were married—she becomes sad. The current popular song was not so far off then:

> Saturday night is the loneliest night of the week
> 'Cause that's the night that my baby and I
> Used to dance cheek to cheek
> I don't mind Sunday night at all
> 'Cause that's the night friends come to call
> And Monday to Friday go fast
> Then another week is past.

A survey of wives and sweethearts of men in service by *Time* magazine concluded:

> U.S. women have changed. . . . They are more self-reliant. New work in factories and more work at home has given them new responsibilities, and they have met them. But above all, U.S. women are lonely. Some hide it behind cheerfulness or a bright hard face, but the loneliness is there. The women want their men to come home. With a unanimity which would startle oldtime feminists they want to quit their jobs, settle down and have children. Three years of war, much of it spent in furnished rooms or with in-laws or in trailers or small hotels, has put a lovely light around the little white cottage.

One young war wife accounted for her days in this way:

> I work half a day in a bank, while my in-laws take care of my daughter. Herb's letters are full of our little girl: "How is she? Has she stopped wetting the bed? Does she talk about me?" I have to fill my letters with fake stories about her. I'm just living until the day Herb comes back. We used to gripe about our house: the roof leaked, we needed new screens and all that. Well, just give me any old house now. Anything, anything.

Dr. Jacob Sergi Kasanin, chief psychiatrist at Mount Zion Hospital in San Francisco, went so far as to identify a neurotic syndrome characteristic of servicemen's wives in 1945. Like many men who went overseas and cracked up before they reached combat (there were estimates that as high as one-half of the combat-trained troops avoided battle by "psyching out," getting a dishonorable discharge and the like), the wives had their own form of crackup: The physical symptoms included depression, colitis, heart palpitations, diarrhea, frequent headaches. Hardest hit were the recently marrieds who had no children. They often developed "pathological reactions" in the form of resentment against their husband or even inability to recall what he looked like. (This was true even among fairly normal wives. One such wife decided to knit a sweater for her husband. As the months of separation drew on, her idea of her tall husband grew accordingly. He sent a picture of himself in the new sweater; it reached halfway down to his knees.) These women often had followed their husbands to his embarkation point; then in symbolic identity with him, they stayed there, and some couldn't take the loneliness, away from home, and began going to the bars, meeting other servicemen in transit. (The ratio of female alcoholics—defined as those who got into trouble with the police—to male alcoholics in Chicago was one to two, compared to one in five in 1931.)

For the more mature marriages, the ones in which the couple would pick up the pieces of their life and put them back together after long separation, there were still changes to be faced. A Navy doctor took a look at himself in the mirror one day and saw that he had grown bald and fat. He wrote about this to his wife, and she wrote back, sadly, "You will find that three years have done quite a bit to me, too."

The war, then, upset the social topography as it did the physical landscape; people met new places, new situations, new jobs, new living conditions, new ways of life, new temptations, new opportunities. There were social ills aplenty, but for all their novelty, they were perhaps the familiar ones; war simply exaggerated them and made them more visible. A sociologist writing on juvenile delinquency in *Federal Probation Officer* expressed a view that most diagnosticians of society would share:

> . . . many mothers of school-age boys and girls work in normal times; families are "broken" either physically or psychologically in normal times; children are exploited in normal times; some young people have always earned good wages and spent them unwisely; families always have moved from one neighborhood or community to another; some recreational facilities of an undesirable nature can be found in most communities in normal times. . . . Actually war does not create new problems with which we are unfamiliar. It accentuates old problems and in so doing the number of boys and girls affected is increased greatly.

One can only add that, in view of the familiarity of the problems and their increased magnitude, the governmental agencies might have done more to alleviate them. But of course, to Congress, stepped-up programs of social welfare would have smacked of "New Deal social experiments," and besides—don't you know there's a war on?

The citizenry out in the provinces who thought they had problems could take a measure of malicious satisfaction, if they wanted to, over the fact that their nation's capital was perhaps the most mixed-up, down-at-the-heels war town of them all. Its traditional industry was mainly government, of course, but everybody in the provinces knew that Washington's "bit" was doing the war's desk work—paper shuffling, tabulating, enumerating, filing. What people in Washington did was concoct complicated forms and schedules, issue directives, create agencies and, when they had some spare time, which was often, sit around and lobby, trade favors, peddle influence, gossip, boondoggle and, above all, take part in colorful feuds for the delectation of newspaper readers everywhere.

An exaggeration of course, but Washington was easy to poke fun at. It was a sort of sitting lame duck for conservative writers who gleefully pointed to whopping inefficiencies, pullulating paper work, labyrinthine bureaucracies, overlapping jurisdictions and a steady stream of executive directives. (FDR issued more executive orders during his Presidency than all previous Presidents combined.) "Washington Wonderland," they called it; "A red-tape-snarled, swarming, sweating metropolis"; "an insane asylum run by the inmates"; or in the words of a taxi driver: "the greatest goddamn insane asylum of the universe."

Overcrowding was Washington's most obvious physical symptom. Since 1940, more than 280,000 government job seekers had poured into town to hold down jobs as clerks and typists in the burgeoning wartime bureaucracy. Most of them were girls; most came from small towns all across the nation. They were drawn by the lure of higher wages—a girl could make $1,600 a year as a typist—and though they reveled in their newfound affluence, they could never get over the high prices, at which they clucked and shook their heads like tourists.

They were set down into a sort of Dogpatch with monuments, plagued by an acute housing shortage, overburdened and capricious public transportation, a cost of living that gobbled up their salaries (that government typist making $1,600 was lucky if she saved $25 in a year) and temporary office buildings that were as homey to work in as a railroad station.

Washington's housing shortage became an overused comic premise in movies and plays about the city, but to the people who lived there it was not always so funny. People paid $24 or $35 or more a month for glorified cubicles or jammed into shabby boardinghouses. They jostled for bathroom access with a herd of fellow boarders and were lucky if they could get a bath once every ten days. Landladies discouraged women tenants because they were wont to do their own laundry, request kitchen privileges and entertain gentlemen callers in the parlor. "Men, on the other hand," observed one concierge, "don't wash anything but themselves and eat all their meals out."

Hotels limited guests to a three-day stay. Hospitals had reverted to something out of Dickens; it was the practice to induce childbirth, for otherwise a room might not be available at the right time.

Nearly half the city lived in slums; the vilest of these were the "alley houses" inhabited by Negroes. There several families were crowded into single rooms, and twelve-year-old girls sold themselves on the streets, and gangs of eight-year-olds carried knives.

For a family—especially a family with children—it was nearly impossible to find a place. Pathetic want ads appeared in the newspapers: "Won't someone help a refined enlisted Navy man and wife, employed, no children, to obtain an unfurnished room or two with kitchen?" Houses for sale were flagrantly overpriced, and people in Georgetown bought up old, run-down houses for $3,000, renovated them and sold them for five times what they had paid. Renting a house was dearer yet: tiny Georgetown houses rented for a minimum of $250 a month, and some larger houses in other neighborhoods that were by no means mansions were going for $1,000 a month. After President Roosevelt's death, the thought quickly occurred to a lot of people at the same time that the new President would soon be moving out of his two-bedroom, $120-a-month, rent-controlled apartment. The switchboard at Mr. Truman's building was jammed with calls; the operator told each caller that the President had already promised the apartment to at least three people.

Buses were always overcrowded, and their schedules were uncoordinated and irregular. People carrying large packages—the OPA banned deliveries—jammed them into the briskets of badged government workers. To ease the crush, the bus companies took out all the seats and installed "stand-sits"—an apparatus against which one leaned, like a shooting stick.

Daily at five o'clock the exodus of people fleeing the Munitions Building was something to see. Thursday night was shopping night for the government workers, and the downtown streets took on the look of "Times Square on New Year's Eve—without the gaiety," in the words of a reporter. People swarmed into the Safeway stores and pawed over the meager supply of meat; if they were lucky, they might get a bit of veal, never beef. In the great mansions in Chevy Chase, however, the cuisine was always *haute* and ample. People came in their office clothes, and hosts sent out reminder cards of an evening's event—everybody's schedule was so hectic—and included instructions on how to get there by bus or streetcar.

Uniforms were everywhere, representing a rainbow of international military pageantry. At night American soldiers and sailors crowded into the little nightclubs, and Washington night life boomed as it never had before or since. As part of its hospitality to servicemen, Washington offered, in addition to man-starved G-girls ("Washington is the loneliest town," one of them said), the highest VD-contraction rate among servicemen of any city in the country.

Foreign heads of state visited the city with monotonous regularity, to be accorded pomp and parades and cause massive traffic jams. Washington had become a world capital; the British maintained a staff of 5,000 diplomatic and military and civilian liaison personnel in the city. Washington had become a kind of second capital for them.

Everyone shared cabs, when they could get them, and rode on a share-the-fare basis. Laundries and dry-cleaning establishments were so overworked that many turned away civilian business and concentrated on Army and Navy uniforms. A visitor told of his Herculean efforts to get his laundry done. After being turned away from three places, he approached, in a state of rising desperation, still another. The tough-looking proprietor told him abruptly "We don't take no new customers." When the man offered to pay extra, the launderer snarled, "You heard me the first time." A policeman directed him next to a Chinese laundry, which was locked, the man inside deaf to his knocking and a sign in the window which read "No more Cloes until Friday." Finally, after stopping off at a drugstore for a cold drink and finding them out of what he wanted, he met a man carrying a laundry case. "If I were you," he told the other, "I'd wrap that up in brown paper and take it to the nearest post office and mail it home." "I guess you're right," the stranger replied. "No use trying to get anything done in this town. Now maybe you can tell me where I'm going to sleep tonight. I've been in this town four days and I haven't found a room yet."

Like housing, office space was in short supply, even with the ugly new temporary buildings. The government resorted to pressuring businesses and private residents to move out, and the President spoke darkly of "parasites"—useless people occupying vitally needed space. About the only solution to the office shortage was for the government to move out of town. This it did, in part, setting up branch offices in Richmond, New York, Chicago, St. Louis, Cincinnati, Kansas City, Philadelphia and Baltimore. More than 35,000 government employees moved out, too.

Soldiers with steel helmets and fixed bayonets patrolled around the White House. The lawn in back was dug up and a bomb shelter installed for the President and his family. Antiaircraft guns were placed in parks. Congress was shocked to learn, however, that the "guns" on its roof were actually wooden and manned by dummy soldiers.

In 1942 the world's largest office building was completed across the Potomac near Arlington. Called the Pentagon, its labyrinthine corridors and offices housed 35,000 office workers. When people wondered what in the world the War Department would do with such an enormous building in peacetime, the President explained that it would be used to store government records and quartermaster supplies, which seemed to satisfy everybody.

The unpleasantries of Washington living stimulated a fast rate of turnover among government workers. As thousands arrived every month from the sticks, other thousands headed home. In the war's first year there was an enthusiasm and even a gaiety among the government workers, and they worked long hours out of self-transcendant patriotism. But gradually an apathy set in; perhaps it was the sheer strain of wartime living, and perhaps it was that many bureaus had overhired and there was nothing much to do. Patriotic fervor began to ebb; the war job became just a job; War Bond and Red Cross quotas were frequently not met. There was, one man said, a feeling of "living in a fog" which:

> affects even the secretaries and the stenographers, even the people who sweep out the offices. I can see the greatest difference in them now and a year ago. At first everybody came to work on the dot. They stayed on till six or seven in the evening. Nobody minded coming back after supper. They were in a fever to get the work done. They'd come here to work for their country like the rest of us. And now look at 'em. . . . By half past four they are so restless the office is a madhouse. At five o'clock it's a panic. You'd think the building was on fire the way they stampede for the elevator.

The city was also aswarm with lobbyists—representatives they liked to call themselves—the "five-percenters," meaning that was their cut of the contract they negotiated for the business they were representing. They haunted the crowded cocktail lounges at the Shoreham, Mayflower, Carleton, Statler, Willard, Raleigh or Wardman Park hotels, where when heads turned upon his entrance a government man knew he was the star of the moment and when they didn't he knew he was on the way out.

The government men joked about the lobbyists' ways of currying favor: "Well, we have the two eagle club. That's for the men who get lunch and dinner out of the representatives of business interests. . . . The three eagles get cocktails, too. The four eagles get a room at the Mayflower or the Carleton. Board and lodging all complete."

Despite the war-spending largesse flowing out of Washington, this war administration was perhaps the most honest one, by and large, in American history. On Capitol Hill sat the vigilant watchdogs of Senator Harry S Truman's special subcommittee investigating the national defense program, exposing padding, excess profits, waste and bottlenecks.

Still, a man in power in Washington, with businessmen beating down his door for war contracts, could go a long way. One veteran Washingtonian described the process, albeit elliptically:

> Yes there's no money being handed around in satchels. From that point of view there has never been a war administration with such clean hands. But there are other ways. Maybe it would be more accurate to say that there are no more cash transactions in this town. . . . If you've got the power the money comes to you of its own accord. A man who's been in government, even who's made a flop in government, comes out so magnetized with power that the greenbacks fly right to him.

Many of the government officials were businessmen themselves— the "dollar-a-year-men" come to bring business know-how to Washington and often working at jobs in which they dealt with the industry they had come from. Many did not hesitate to use their influence to benefit that industry. Most were not production men or technicians, but rather trade-association types, front men. Their dollar-a-year salaries from Uncle Sam were supplemented by their home companies, which continued to pay them their old salaries all the while they were exiled to Washington, a practice scarcely calculated to encourage impartiality. Yet their jobs were not without sacrifices. They might stay in the best hotels, but in a cubbyhole of a room for which they paid $10 a day. A man who had a family back home might maintain them at a cost of $40,000 of his annual pretax salary of $50,000 a year from his company, which left him only $10,000 a year with which to live the Washington high life.

Washington was where the reins of enormous governmental power had been drawn, theoretically. The war administration was centered there, but sometimes its power got lost up some bureaucratic corridor or misfiled in some office pigeonhole. One government man compared it to the tar baby of the Br'er Rabbit stories: "Christ it's the tar baby. You know the tar baby. . . . You try to give it a kick and your foot gets stuck and you try to give it a punch and your fist gets stuck and you try to back off and butt it with your head and your head gets stuck."

Another man described getting something done in this way:

> You work in a vacuum. Higher up everything seems cloudy and drifting. The clouds form and scatter and reform. It drives you crazy. . . . All down the line I've gotten a group of self-willed men to make concessions to agree to cooperate for getting out this commodity that the war economy needs like hell. I was so worked up at one point I didn't sleep for a week. At last it seems as if everything is smoothed out and everybody is going to be happy. Then at the last moment somewhere in the higher brackets it's no go, a bottleneck, other considerations. It's like trying to work a telephone keyboard with half the wires out and you never know which ones are cut. . . . Now while I'm trying to get a new directive, one that will stick, I'll tell you what's going to happen. The juice will ebb out of the proposition. The guys I've sold on it will start looking out for number one. How can you blame them, goddamit! Self-seeking is so simple.

It was a war government of high-strung individualists right up to the top. Symptomatic were the feuds that raged beneath the benign, distant eyes of the President, who let his men fight it out, then made his own choice of a course of action. Men fought for pet policy like stage mothers at an audition before him; they also connived and leaked and schemed to oust a rival.

The feuds splashed across the front pages as a bemused public looked on. In 1942, Sidney Hillman, labor's man in Washington, fought it out toe to toe with William Knudsen over who should run the Office of Production Management, the government agency charged with running the civilian war production effort. Then Harold Ickes, the Secretary of the Interior and Petroleum Coordinator, among other hats, got into it with Leon Henderson, the egghead chief of the Office of Price Administration, over gasoline rationing. Then it was Charles E. Wilson, formerly of General Motors, deviously raising the issue of civilian control over the military in the War Production Board, in a confrontation with Ferdinand Eberstadt, a brilliant former Wall Street moneyman. Next Vice President Henry A. Wallace, of the high-minded, interminable oratory, tangled out of his league with crusty, shrewd old Jesse Jones, head of the Reconstruction Finance Commission, which dispensed millions daily to build war plants on the strength of a phone call from a needy but patriotic industrialist; Wallace's specially created agency the Bureau of Economic Warfare had run afoul of the RFC, to which it had to go for money to buy up strategic materials overseas, and Wallace accused Jones of "obstructionist tactics." Jones, a wealthy Texan, counterbatteried that Wallace's remarks were "a tirade filled with malice, innuendo, half-truths and no truths at all." Undersecretary of War Robert Patterson then locked horns with William M. Jeffers, the Rubber Coordinator, over how much rubber the Army should get. Magisterial old Cordell Hull and his Undersecretary, Sumner Welles, oozed venom between them, over the latter's attempt to circumvent Hull on foreign policy matters, until Welles was eased out amid the hint of scandal. Other clashes, less spectacular, made the headlines, as leak bred counterleak.

Ultimately the clashes ended up on the desk of the man in the Oval Room, who somehow managed to settle them and go his own way. Then he would turn his attention back to a subject his heart was really in: the conduct of the war. For he was, above all, the Commander in Chief.

NOTE: The Roosevelt Administration spawned wartime agencies in wondrous profusion. Lest the reader have difficulty in digesting this alphabet soup, herewith a rundown of the leading and lesser such agencies:

WPB (War Production Board). Successor to the OPM (Office of Production Management) and SPAB (Supply and Priority Allocation Board). WPB was the civilian agency charged with coordinating the wartime economy, primarily by allocating scarce materials among war producers and civilian goods manufacturers, stopping or limiting production of civilian items, setting production quotas of war goods in consultation with the military, formulating production schedules sufficiently in advance so that all the component parts made by subcontractors would be ready for final assembly, mediating among rival military and civilian claimant agencies and so on.

WLB (War Labor Board). Primarily concerned with settling and adjudicating labor-management disputes in defense industries.

WMC (War Manpower Commission). A superagency composed of representatives of the War Labor Board, War Production Board, Selective Service System, etc., which attempted to foresee the nation's overall manpower needs and allocate available manpower among the military, war industry, agriculture and other essential civilian needs.

WRA (War Relocation Authority). Administered the detention of enemy aliens and was primarily responsible for running the Japanese-American internment camps.

OPA (Office of Price Administration). See Chapter VII.

OWI (Office of War Information). Coordinated release of news by government agencies to the press; acted as liaison between press and government; prepared propaganda for overseas use; supervised the government's "war information program" in all the media, including motion pictures (through the Bureau of Motion Pictures—see Chapter VI) and radio (Domestic Radio Bureau—*ibid.*).

WSA (War Shipping Administration). Responsible for the procurement and supervision of the merchant navy, including recruiting and training crews.

OWM (Office of War Mobilization). Another superagency, presided over by "Assistant President" James F. Byrnes, with jurisdiction over home front affairs (the other "assistant President," Harry Hopkins handled foreign relations as Presidential emissary). Byrnes presided over a council numbering the power elite of wartime officialdom, including the Secretaries of Navy and War, the Director of Economic Stabilization, the chairman of the War Production Board and the War Food Administrator. One of its chief functions was to referee governmental infighting and prevent leaks on same to the press. Byrnes' job was explained by a WPB official in this way: "Suppose you and I have a disagreement in arithmetic; you claim that two and two make four, while I claim that two and two makes six. We take it to Jimmy Byrnes for a decision. He's apt to get us both to agree that two and two make five."

OSRD (Office of Scientific Research and Development). Coordinated and initiated research and development in weaponry and distributed federal funds for scientific projects to industry and universities.

ODT (Office of Defense Transportation). Charged with keeping the trains running on time, allocating transportation space and matériel priorities for building new carriers and curtailing unnecessary civilian travel.

Also: ANMB (Army and Navy Munitions Board), the procurement agency for the military, which let war contracts; BEW (Bureau of Economic Warfare), Henry Wallace's attempt to amalgamate foreign policy and procurement of raw materials abroad, an early casualty; DCB (Defense Communications Board); DPC (Defense Plant Corporation), an arm of the Reconstruction Finance Commission which built defense plants with federal funds; DSC (Defense Supplies Corporation), another RFC arm which purchased machine tools needed for conversion of a plant to war production; ICWI (Interdepartmental Commission on War Information), self-explanatory; JMUSDC (Joint Mexican–U.S. Defense Commission), liaison agency for joint strategic planning; MRC (Metals Reserve Corporation), employed by the RFC to stockpile strategic metals; OADR (Office of Agricultural Defense Relations), pass; OC (Office of Censorship), censored outgoing and incoming foreign mail, movies, radio transmissions, etc.; OCD (Office of Civilian Defense), see Chapter II; OCIAA (Office of the Coordinator of Inter-American Affairs)—the coordinator was named Nelson Rockefeller and his job was mainly to keep the South Americans happy through a steady flow of propaganda; ODHWS (Office of Defense Health and Welfare Services), administered Lanham Act funds to aid war-impacted areas; OEC (Office of Export Control); OEM (Office of Emergency Management), merged into the OWI; OFF (Office of Facts and Figures), ditto; OLLA (Office of Lend-Lease Administration); OPC (Office of the Petroleum Coordinator), planned and administered the allocation of the nation's gasoline, though the OPA handled the rationing program; PJBD (Permanent Joint Board on Defense), a U.S.–Canadian liaison strategic and resources planning agency; RRC (Rubber Reserve Corporation), the RFC agency for stockpiling rubber; SSS (Selective Service System); WIC (War Insurance Corporation), another RFC dummy which underwrote war damage insurance policies for private insurers.

IV

COST-PLUS

The new director of the War Production Board, Donald Nelson, in a speech in January, 1942, said: "We are going to have to rely on our great mass production industries for the bulk of our increase under the war program. Wherever we can we must convert them to war production, and convert them quickly. The only gauge we can apply to this process is: What method will most quickly give us the greatest volume of war production in this particular industry?" In the automotive industry, as in other major industries, the best way was: First, order a complete halt in civilian production, and second, lavish the industry with new facilities and war contracts. The rest was up to the industry (although the government came to recognize it had to play an umpire's role in allocating vital materials that were in short supply and in setting production quotas in terms of military needs). So long as industry delivered the goods in abundance and on time and of sufficient quality, the government, in effect, was getting its money's worth. Eventually this system worked sensationally well in terms of results, but it was bound to exact its social costs.

The history of the conversion process was embodied, in an exaggerated way, by the famed bomber plant at Willow Run, Michigan, which revealed all the faults and virtues of America's conversion from peace to war. Willow Run was first conceived by Ford Motor Company production chief Charles E. Sorensen after a meeting of auto manfacturers called in October, 1940, by William Knudsen, then head of the WPB's prewar predecessor, the Office of Production Management. Knudsen had called the meeting to involve the automotive companies in the production of parts for airplanes under the new defense program, which, prodded by public concern over the fall of France and the British defeat at Dunkirk, was just getting under way. Some of the auto companies did the limited retooling necessary and began turning out the parts, but Ford hung back. Sorensen, however, did tour some of the aircraft plants on the West Coast and was struck by the confusion and wasted motion he saw there. That night in his hotel room he sketched a design for an ideal plant in which bombers could be mass-produced on a continuous assembly line, like cars. The government bought the idea, as did the Ford management, and ground was broken for the new plant in the spring of 1941, with the government underwriting the cost, which ultimately reached $65,000,000. It was grandiosely envisioned as a completely self-contained bomber assembly line, with all operations taking place within a single vast structure. This building was "L"-shaped, one mile in length and a quarter mile wide. When completed, it contained more than 1,600 pieces of heavy machinery, 7,500 jigs and fixtures. Amply publicized, it struck a responsive chord with the American penchant for bigness as an end in itself, and acquired a sort of mechanical folk-hero-*cum*-superman status like the Jeep, the Flying Fortress, the Norden bombsights and other of those products of American ingenuity that were going to win the war. Indeed, it was confidently predicted that Willow Run would disgorge B-24 bombers at the rate of 1,000 a day and employ up to 100,000 workers.

Eleven months after the ground was broken for the Willow Run plant, the first bomber rolled off the assembly line. If Willow Run was in operation, it was also plagued by a series of problems that threatened to transform it from a white hope into a white elephant. For one thing, the location of the plant was dubious. It was set down in rolling farmland 10 miles from the nearest community, which was Ypsilanti, a small college town (population 12,000), and 30 miles from Detroit, where of course the labor supply was concentrated. This location—chosen before Pearl Harbor, when gas rationing and a tire shortage were not foreseen—was decided by Ford upon considerations that worked largely to the benefit of the Ford Motor Company. For one thing, the company was cultivating soybeans in the area, and Ford was thinking about using the plastic made from the soybeans to manufacture planes after the war in the handy Willow Run facilities. More to the point was the plant's location just inside the borders of Washtenaw County (one corner of the plant was a bare 25 feet over the border). This location, critics pointed out, took Ford outside the jurisdiction of neighboring Wayne County, dominated by the city of Detroit and considered prolabor. Further, as the largest landowner in the county, Ford would dominate local politics. Finally, since most workers would have to commute from Detroit, it would be more difficult for the union to be active. To nail down this last advantage, it followed that Ford would oppose any permanent housing for the workers near the plant. When, in fact, a plan for a federal housing project of 6,000 units, containing 30,000 people, was put forward, Ford security men went so far as to rip up government surveying stakes. Local real estate interests also opposed the scheme for selfish reasons, and the Ypsilanti townspeople were frightened by a potential postwar "ghost town" on their doorstep— especially the bonded debt to be incurred in erecting the necessary utilities. (The housing project, popularly known as Bomber City, was no mere stopgap community. The plans were described by *Architectural Forum* as "the most workable and human guide to the [architecturally] integrated community produced to date.") The Federal Public Housing Authority finally backed down on its plans, saying that they would require too many critical materials. Finally, about 10,000 units of temporary housing were built, including 5,000 dormitory units for single persons, 2,500 temporary family units and 2,000 trailers.

The upshot was that more than 50 percent of Willow Run's workers commuted the 30 miles from Detroit, a one-hour drive each way. The many who didn't have a car or couldn't share a car pool took the crowded buses at a cost of 70¢ a day, which was 8 or 9 percent of a day's wages—no small sum. As a result, Willow Run had trouble attracting workers and had a high turnover, as high as 50 percent a month. In one month, the plant hired 2,900 new workers but lost 3,100 old workers. After all, why spend all those hours commuting, when the Detroit factories were crying for men and Detroit papers printed eight pages of help-wanted ads a day? By the end of 1943 only 35,000 workers were on the job, although even Ford estimated that 58,000 were needed; the absentee rate was 17 percent (high for the nation); and production crept along at the rate of barely a bomber a day. People began calling the plant Willit Run? In the twelve months prior to January, 1944, there were about 1,000 "flyaways" from the plant. Compounding the production lag was friction between labor and management. The ordinary workers disliked old Henry Ford's ban on smoking in the plant, the company cafeteria was a gouge, and workers eating there claimed to have found mice in milk bottles and maggots in their sandwiches. On the other hand, plant physical facilities and the excellent medical care were praised by visitors.

Eventually, management, under Sorensen's production genius (until he was forced out in 1944 by Harry Bennett, old Henry's hatchet man), scaled down the grandiosity of the original conception. Instead of a complete bomber factory, the plant was converted to strictly a final assembly line, and half its operations were farmed out to Ford subsidiaries in other parts of the country. By May, 1943, 550 machines were moved out of the plant to other locations; this in turn reduced Willow Run's labor requirements. The work force became more stable, and the longer the men remained on the job, the more experienced they became and the more production increased. As the bombers were turned out in greater regularity, the workers' morale was raised. To augment the labor force, Ford reversed company policy and hired women, even sending agents to Texas and New York to recruit them. (Although ultimately about 40 percent of the total work force was female, the company refused to utilize the local Negro population—particularly Negro women—as much as it could have.) By 1944 most of the production and morale problems had been ironed out, and the great plant was producing 500 B-24's a month in August.

Despite waste, disorganization at all levels, the shortages of raw materials, the speedups and the slowdowns, the bottlenecks and the breakthroughs, it became clear, at Willow Run and elsewhere, that a production miracle was in the making. The government was pumping money into the economy at an average rate of $2.3 billion per month. Such a rosy business climate, in which contracts were awarded, not to the low bidder, but rather with the promise to pay cost-plus (also known as fixed fee), encouraged management to go all out, hell for leather and damn the costs. As Lawrence Bell, head of the Bell Aircraft Corporation, put it when asked how he liked doing business on this basis:

"I don't like it, but for a rush job it's the only thing. Of course it contributes to waste. For maximum economy, go flat price. If you want maximum output, you have to go fixed fee. The volume of our business is more than a hundred times the capital invested. On flat price it would take a small error to wipe us out. The whole staff would be frightened of going broke, and production would be secondary.

"On the flat price I'd want to do a smaller business and watch it to the last detail. In this way [fixed fee], every official can give his whole attention to the volume of the product. Net result—the unit cost may be less in the long run because you divide it between bigger output."

Cost-plus allowed the war-goods producer to overextend himself in expanding production, knowing that his increased costs would be met. He had a guaranteed customer—Uncle Sam—who generously assured him of both his costs and a nice profit. Further, in many cases his plant expansion would be underwritten by either a low-interest loan from the Reconstruction Finance Commission (or guaranteed by the Federal Mortgage Agency) or by direct government handout to build, in return for paying a reasonable rent on the facilities as long as he used them and a further option to buy the facility at war's end for a relatively low price. Moreover, for tax purposes all expansion costs could be amortized over a five-year period when war profits and taxes would be highest, instead of the usual twenty.

In essence, what Roosevelt and his advisers had decided was that business would not be forced to produce but would be given incentives in the form of money impure and simple. As Eliot Janeway put it: "[Roosevelt] was counting on money, not on leadership to prime the production pump."

Not that business wouldn't earn this money—although a few would connive and cheat to get more than their fair share—for it had to deliver the goods or lose future contracts or have imperfectly performed contracts renegotiated. All the government (that is, the military: the procurement divisions of the War Department, the Navy Department, the Maritime Commission and the Aeronautics Board—all of which dealt directly with the war industries under the attempted guidance of the WPB) would do was tell business what it wanted. The question of *how* it would be produced was left up to business, and as long as business delivered the goods, business would be paid its asking price, within some kind of reason (and subject to stringent renegotiation and a wartime excess profits tax, reaching 90 percent of the dollar). So, although there was plenty of grousing about red tape, paper work, favoritism to labor at the expense of management and even government interference in the economy, most big businessmen were happy to do business with government (and after all, the personnel of the WPB were all ex-businessmen— the dollar-a-year men—men who spoke their language, who had their interests at heart). The business-minded *Kiplinger's Newsletter,* in early 1942, quoted "business-minded men within government" as saying that the WPB program represented "the last stand of private enterprise."

But to allow industries to compete free-enterprise style for steel or machine tools or construction lumber would lead to anarchy, inflation and a nationwide black market. In this area, the government had to become regulator, as well as pump primer, and allocate the materials according to need.

The system devised by the War Production Board (after many false starts) was known as the Controlled Materials Plan and was put into full effect in July, 1943. The trouble with earlier priority systems had been that there were more manufacturers with high priorities than there was steel, and having a priority didn't ensure one of getting the steel he needed. As Henry J. Kaiser defined it, "A priority is something which gives you an option to ask for something which you know you're not going to get anyhow." Further, even though the machine-gun maker might get his steel, his subcontractor who produced trigger springs might be unable to get *his* steel, though his priority was as high as the prime contractor's.

There was also inefficiency and red tape in government and bickering between the civilians and the military. For the small business-men the process of getting a war contract was often heartbreaking, for Washington had become a brawling, sprawling boomtown. As one of them described it: "Washington's a funny town. It's got scores of hotels, and you can't get a room. It's got 5,000 restaurants, and you can't get a meal. It's got 50,000 politicians, and nobody will do anything for you. I'm going home."

Most of the businessmen on the other side of the desk—the dollar-a-year men who descended upon Washington to work with the WPB—and their staffs were financial experts rather than production men because private business held onto the latter. The working conditions could also be horrendous. There was the famous case of the Textile Roundtable, which, although it occurred immediately before the war, illustrated the conditions many WPB people had to work under. The WPB's Textile and Fiber Bureau had recruited fourteen executives from the industry. The men arrived on the appointed day and found their headquarters was an office already crammed to the brim with personnel. They did not even have a place to hang their coats. As they arrived, they were seated at a large round table—the only remaining desk space. The table, however, had only twelve chairs; the last two men had to sit outside the circle. An amusing routine developed. It was described by Frank L. Walton, head of the bureau:

". . . the man who got there first and put his brief case on the table in front of a chair and sat down had a seat for the day. If he moved, he did not dare move his brief case. That brief case represented his right to the seat. The two men who had no chairs just sat around or stood around. Surprising as it may seem, this went on for three weeks or more before we could get desks and crowd them in, two or more men to a desk. During this time we could get no more telephones and all were trying to use one telephone sitting on a window sill nearby. Secretaries were difficult to secure but we had nowhere to put them even if we could have gotten them. These men, who had not written a longhand letter in years, were trying to answer urgent letters or telegrams from the industry with a pencil and paper, being careful to make a carbon copy. Or they would go to outside telephones to put in calls in answer to telegrams and letters. They would even pay for the calls themselves."

Under these physical conditions and with inexperienced personnel, the lack of efficiency became scandalous. The Truman Committee uncovered numerous examples of delay caused by mislaid priority orders. The committee told of Lend-Lease procedures calling for shuffling papers around the horn of twenty departments, a process that took six weeks. Rivalry among the various services' procurement agencies explained much of the delay: Each exaggerated its needs and connived to get more than its share. In *Roosevelt and Hopkins* Robert Sherwood describes how such rivalry delayed production of landing craft resulting in a shortage just before the North Africa invasion, late in 1942. The trouble was partly due to the failure of top officials to foresee the need for the craft sufficiently far in advance, but "it was also due to the Navy's reluctance to devote shipbuilding facilities and scarce materials to the construction of vessels to be used for essentially Army operations."

There was no overall program meshing raw-material supply with manufacturer demand. The inadequacies of the Production Requirements Program as a system for coordinating war production with available materials inevitably cried out for reform. This was not long in coming (indeed the debate over an alternative plan was sputtering almost at the PRP's inception). What finally emerged, after much bureaucratic pulling and pushing, was a new plan which, though it had faults, was simpler and at least not a hindrance to war production as PRP was threatening to become.

This new system, the Controlled Materials Plan, was the brainchild of Ferdinand Eberstadt, formerly head of the Army-Navy Munitions Board, a Wall Street banker in civilian life and now vice-chairman of the

WPB in charge of supply. Under the CMP, an *allocation* or dividing-up-the-pie system replaced, in part, the *authorization* system of the PRP. What was allocated were the three most basic metals: steel, copper and aluminum. Prime contractors (that is, manufacturers receiving orders for finished munitions directly from government procurement agencies) using these metals on a war contract would state how much of the materials were needed in making a unit of the goods they were turning out (*i.e.,* General Motors would say how much steel was needed to make one Sherman tank); this estimate included the amount they used plus the amount used by the subcontractors who supplied them with the component parts. They filled out another complicated form reflecting their inventory at present, their schedule of production, the total amount needed to fill future orders and so on. All this information was sent to the WPB. Meanwhile, producers of the three materials sent their estimates of production for the upcoming quarter, giving the WPB an idea of the total supply of that material that would be available. The "claimant" or procurement agencies of the Army, Navy, Aeronautics Board and various essential civilian, Lend-Lease and construction activities would calculate their needs for the calendar quarter in question. The Controlled Materials branches of the WPB dealing with steel, copper and aluminum would then take the total estimated demand of the claimant agencies, translate it into the total amount of the materials needed, and attempt to pare it down to conform it to the total amount of the material that would be available. Finally the Requirements Committee would allot a certain amount of the materials to each claimant agency—say, 20,000,000 tons of steel to the Army for all its various programs. The claimant agency would in turn divide this pie up among its prime contractors, each of which would retain the share of the allotment it needed in its own production and delegate the remainder to its subcontractors. Necessary civilian goods had equal priority to munitions.

This system, if it was that, called for such voluminous paper work that a small manufacturer might find himself too shorthanded to undertake it. Worse, the manufacturers were prone to overestimate their requirements as a hedge against possible future shortages.

Another weakness in the CMP was its limited number of controlled materials. As the war wore on, other types of metals and other materials became scarce (*e.g.,* lumber), yet a manufacturer whose production schedule and controlled material requirements might have been already approved by the WPB would find his request for a noncontrolled material disapproved by the industry branch responsible. Solutions were proposed for this built-in bureaucratic conflict, but none was ever adopted because of opposition to additional government control of materials by the industries involved.

Nevertheless, once it got into gear (by the end of 1943), the CMP worked well enough. Under it war production doubled in 1943, even though the labor force remained about the same as 1942, while total civilian consumption did not fall off. Certainly, there were other factors at work stimulating the economy to such productivity, but the CMP provided an orderly framework for dividing up the most basic raw materials among manufacturers. In addition, by cutting back and rationing allotments to the construction industry, the CMP reversed the trend toward excessive capital construction endemic in 1942.

Hand in hand with government's dramatic expansion of war production through heavy financial pump priming and allocation of key raw materials to manufacturers by need went government's power to order a halt of nonessential production. This power, delegated to the President by Congressional enactment, was exercised early in the war, when the WPB, as one of its first official acts, ordered a halt to auto production. Other such cessations or curtailments following in rapid succession, in the form of L-Orders, usually cut back production to a percentage of the prewar level in that industry or established quotas in other terms. It was the stick accompanying the carrot of cost-plus war contracts.

As the months passed in 1942, businessmen without war contracts saw their output dammed to a trickle or indeed dried up by these orders. During the first three months of 1942, *Business Week* intoned a weekly litany:

Bicycles: sale, shipment and delivery frozen pending rationing. *Electrical appliances:* civilian production will cease May 31, 1942, on some fifty types, including toasters, percolators, griddles, waffle irons, heaters. *Flashlights and batteries:* use of iron and steel curtailed; aluminum, rubber, chromium, nickel, tin (except in solder) and brass and copper (except in electrical fittings) banned entirely. *Metal household furniture:* iron and steel restricted and all other metals banned. *Household utensils:* iron, steel, zinc cut 10–50 percent from 1941 levels in the manufacture of cooking utensils, garbage cans, dishpans, etc. *Plumbing fixtures, radiators:* use of critical materials curtailed. *Razors and blades:* blade production limited to 1940 level, safety razors cut 30 percent across the board, straight razors limited to the 1940 level of production. *Metal signs:* use of metal cut 50 percent from 1941 levels for next three months, then banned entirely. *Tea:* cut back 50 percent from 1941 levels. Packages may not contain more than a quarter pound or fifty teabags each. *Toys and games:* use of metals severely restricted; selected metals and plastics, cork, silk, coloring and oils banned entirely. *Collapsible tubes:* use in packaging nonessential lines prohibited; use of tin in manufacture restricted to 7½ percent for tubes containing medicinal and pharmaceutical ointments; toothpaste and shaving cream tube production pegged at 100 percent of the 1940 level (and another WPB order required purchasers of toothpaste or shaving cream to turn in a used tube at the time of purchase). *Vacuum cleaners:* all civilian production halted. *Vending machines:* all manufacture of cigarette, food, candy, nuts and chewing gum vending machines halted. *Metal windows:* manufacture and sale forbidden. *Caskets:* use of iron and steel in caskets, shipping cases forbidden after July 1; use of all other metals forbidden immediately.

Because most manufacturers had accumulated such large inventories during the boom year of 1941, consumers did not feel the pinch on most goods until well into 1943. Supplementing the L-Order system were the WPB's M-Orders which worked at the other end of the line to allocate raw materials. An early, typical M-Order banned iron and steel in more than 400 products (gold or silver were still permitted, if rather prohibitive in cost). The combined effect of L- and M-Orders was to bring to the end entirely the use of critical metals in the manufacture of civilian goods by July, 1942—seven months after the war began and more than two years after the inception of the defense program.

To the businessman, the alert was clear: Convert, find substitutes —or perish. Many manufacturers did convert to war production, if they could get a contract—an eventuality, as we have seen, that was not always to occur. The big mass-production industries were most vital to the war production program, and they received the bulk of the business. Yet what of the small manufacturers with twenty employees or less? There were 135,000 of them, employing 6 or 7 percent of the labor force and using 5 percent of the raw materials. How were they, without large plants and assembly lines, to produce war goods? Some of them couldn't and went under, but a sizable number of others snagged a broad spectrum of subcontracts.

In November, 1941, red, white and blue trains bearing a wide range of sample parts needed in defense production which small businesses could make had toured the country, informing small businessmen what war production they might convert to. A manufacturer of ladies' compacts converted to delaying mechanisms for shell fuzes and tiny radio parts. A floor waxer plant bored gear housings for antitank guns. A merry-go-round manufacturer turned to making gun mounts, plane gears and jigs and fixtures for tank production. An organ company converted to airplane parts, and a pinball machine maker to 20-mm shell cases and armor-piercing shells. The Kleenex company took another tack entirely, making two-gun and four-gun .50-caliber machine-gun mounts. A manufacturer of animal traps converted to making cores for .30- and .50-caliber bullets. A maker of orange juice squeezers turned to making bullet molds. A casket maker became a producer of airplanes.

Typical of those small and medium-sized businesses able to convert successfully to war production was the Standard Steel Spring Company. In peacetime, Standard had been one of that large network of subcontractors to the big auto manufacturers, supplying bumpers and springs. When it became clear that auto production would be halted for the duration, the Standard management cast about for a wartime product it could make. The company decided that with its equipment and know-how in heat-treating metal, the logical thing would be armor plating. A war contract was obtained, and the conversion to armor plate was carried out. In peacetime the company had grossed $60,000 a month at most; soon it was doing many times this, with a huge backload of orders. So impressed was the Army with Standard's program that it enlisted more small manufacturers to make armor plate with Standard as the prime contractor in charge of letting subcontracts. A variety of manufacturers was assembled, each capable of performing at least part of the armor-making operations. One plant might get steel from the mills, flame-cut the plates to size and ship them to another member of the complex for heat treatment, straightening, sandblasting, drilling, grinding and machining. The plates were then returned to the first plant for painting, stenciling and assembling into sets for shipments to the big tank plants (which were, of course, the same auto manufacturers that had been its prewar customers). This efficient—and preexistent—interlocking arrangement was thus, in addition, another reason for the bestowal of such a large volume of defense contracts on the auto business and its subcontractors.

Other businesses without prewar ties with the big war contractors had to organize their own self-help programs, often at the community level. The most famed of these small-business consortiums was located in York, Pennsylvania. This city of 50,000 had, in 1940, some 110 factories doing an annual business of $70,000,000; only 5 employed more than 500 workers and 70 employed fewer than 100. York's industries turned out a gamut of civilian products, including bank vaults, artificial teeth, refrigeration and air-conditioning equipment, farm equipment, chairs and hydraulic power machinery. When the national defense program began in earnest, York's civic and business leaders, goaded by editorals in the two local papers, formed a defense committee to plan ways of attracting defense contracts, including pooling of labor and equipment by the local factories. By Pearl Harbor nearly all of the town's industries were doing war work, either as prime or subcontractors. The result was a tremendous boost to the York economy, which had been stagnating through the Great Depression, when the demand for bank vaults, among other things, was off. Total sales rose from the prewar $70,000,000 annually to $125,000,000. Employment rose by one-third; at the same time, the town's population increased by only 1,000 persons. When it came to jobs, York was taking care of its own first.

But if York illustrated how a community's businesses, working together, could attract a flow of war dollars, it also illustrated the faults of planning purely by profit-minded businessmen. For one thing, labor was weak in York. Wages were low, and only intervention by the War Labor Board at one plant brought them up to the 40-cents-an-hour minimum. A typical York worker started at that salary, and if, two years later, he was making 48 cents an hour, he was lucky. The CIO called for a 70½-cent basic rate, but management refused to negotiate, and when the union struck, strikebreakers were brought in. Also, under the York system factories would borrow workers with needed skills from each other. Supposedly the borrowed worker would keep the seniority he had acquired at his old job when he returned to it after the war; however, in practice management refused even to make this guarantee. Housing was short, but when the government authorized the building of 960 defense housing units in York, the local Chamber of Commerce, worried about a large surplus population of ex-war workers when peace came, cut the number to 210. The city also remodeled some old rooming houses to make available another 300 rooms, living arrangements not aimed at encouraging immigrant workers to settle permanently in the town, as ownership of a house would have.

York was a kind of showpiece for the War Production Board, illustrating that small business could get war contracts. Its example was emulated in other parts of the country. But the "York plan" did not solve small businesses' problems in any large way. As Donald Nelson wrote after the war: "This movement spread all over the country, and it is too bad that only a relatively small percentage of all small manufacturers were able to take advantage of this effective arrangement."

Manufacturers requiring critical materials and unable to convert to war production were less fortunate. When the M-Orders came, they were confronted with the choice of finding a substitute for the material (or a way to reduce the amount of it used in making the product) or going under. As a result, much ingenuity was exercised in redesigning products to use substitutes—such as making bathroom faucets out of cast iron instead of brass and chrome. Often enough, however, as soon as a substitute metal was found, it too might well go on the critical list.

The earliest manufacturers to undergo this game of falling dominoes were the hosiery makers. Silk, of course, had become scarce in 1941, when the government laid an embargo on the Japanese product. All of the industry's chips were then bet on nylon, which, until the silk embargo, went into about 20 percent of all the hose sold in the United States. But then nylon was drafted to make parachutes (each parachute consumed the equivalent of thirty-six pairs of nylons), and nylon hose became as scarce as silk ones. In addition, a basic ingredient in nylon was phenol, which was used in a number of war industries and in short supply. This left rayon and fine cotton lisle hose, but the rayon producers couldn't keep up with both the demand for heavy-duty rayon for use in tires and that of the hosiery manufacturers, and fine lisle cotton or even the coarser 60- to 80-count cotton was about as scarce as nylon and rayon. Also, although necessity would force their adoption, cotton hose were about as popular among American women as rhinestone engagement rings. As a result, the hosiery business went into rapid decline. As one manufacturer said, hopelessly: "We could figure a way to knit them of grass one day and the next day there would be a priority on grass."

It was so very often the little things. The record industry, for example, was nearly undone. Records were made of shellac, and shellac came from a resinous substance called lac, secreted by a small beetle indigenous to northern India. Shipping from India was undependable, so the record makers were often cut off from this source of resin. Rather than substitutes, however, they turned to salvage for a replacement. In the Philadelphia area, RCA Victor dealers began quietly to post signs offering two cents each for old records, regardless of condition. Soon scrap was making up 10–15 percent of records produced, and it was possible to make an all-scrap record. (This would give off surface noises, but the reproduction of most phonographs of the day was so poor that the public didn't notice it anyway.)

The exigencies of war called a variety of new products and materials into service. Plastics found an increasing number of uses, even in heavy machinery. The infant frozen food industry received a modest boost because of transportation difficulties and the shortage of tin for tin cans. Dehydrated food processing, still somewhat in disgrace because of its production of dubious quality dehydrated foods during World War I that were dubbed sawdust, received a second chance. Improved procedures making possible a more palatable product won it a number of armed forces and Lend-Lease orders. Still, it never achieved any great civilian acceptance. A Brownsville, Texas, processor explained why to John Dos Passos: "The price of vegetables has gone so high that you can ship anything you grow at a profit fresh; so there's no incentive for processing. . . . Isn't that something?"

The Recordak Corporation of New York City, a maker of microfilm and equipment, found the war just what the doctor ordered to improve its business. In the early part of the war, the threat of air raids and sabotage caused a number of governmental departments, businesses, libraries, art galleries and private individuals to have microfilms made of important records, documents, manuscripts and so on, so that the originals could be stored in vaults. University Microfilms in Ann Arbor, Michigan, which in normal times microfilmed rare books for students, received a commission from the American Council of Learned Societies, financed by the Rockefeller Foundation, to film 25,000,000 pages of rare manuscripts in England. The films were deposited in the Library of Congress for future reference in the event of the destruction of the English originals. And of course V-mail letters to overseas troops—microfilms of regular-sized letters that were blown up again after overseas transit— received wide usage because of the government's request to reduce shipping space.

Women's clothes were dealt a series of M- and L-Order blows: L-85 banned full skirts, knife pleats and patch pockets (part of a general "no fabric over fabric" rule). Order M-217, conserving leather, limited shoes to six colors—black, white, navy blue, and three shades of brown. L-Order L-116 placed limitations on laces and embroidery.

Nonetheless, America's fashion designers—now freed from Continental influences—managed to come up with a variety of new styles, and their ingenuity was stimulated rather than crippled by the restrictions.

The wide padded shoulders of the late thirties and forties went out and were replaced by natural shoulders or the bare-armed look, which became popular (and was also softer and more feminine). Long evening dresses vanished, replaced by décolleté ballerina-length gowns. The use of accessories such as hats, gloves, handbags, dickeys, gilets and jabots as wardrobe extenders became popular, as did two-in-one or three-in-one outfits—that is, suits or dresses with interchangeable parts which made one's wardrobe seem larger. Along with padded shoulders, large fancy hats disappeared and were replaced by smaller ones that were more harmonious with natural shoulders. The turban—carried to almost grotesque lengths by the movie star Carmen Miranda—was very popular and practical in factory work. Coats acquired a military cut, in line with the times. The greater simplicity in shoe styles resulted in more low-heel models (for walking comfort) and led to the popularity of the ballet slipper. Latin-American influences on clothes design was also more pronounced than at any other time (e.g., the bolero). Girls tended also toward simple frocks; the pinafore or jumper dress was almost a uniform. Dresses also had to be designed to meet the challenge of the girdle shortage (the use of rubber in girdles was banned), and a variety of tactical plans was worked out to fight the home front's battle of the bulge. *McCall's* Washington newsletter advised the Self-Mortification-for-Victory method: "Just what the lack of girdles will eventually do to styles is anybody's guess, but Washington's experts don't hold out much hope for a return to solid, hefty bulges. Stay slim for healthy beauty and morale —that's their advice. . . . Go slow on fats and sweets. And take exercises." As if on cue, a beauty shop offered a "De-War Figure Control" plan. The dress manufacturers helped out with such designs as the following, advertised in women's magazines:

"No girdle required for this dress of tobacco brown spun rayon, with no fastenings (zippers gone to war), adjustable at waist and bust."

"Duration suit: Both jacket and skirt of this rayon gabardine tailleur are adjustable at the waistline; designed for wear with or without a girdle."

The corset manufacturers also designed rubberless girdles. One, in a regression to grandmother's day, used whalebone, while another employed piano wire, thanks to a ruling by the WPB that girdles were necessary to women's health and could have priorities (piano wire was critical material). As an ad in the *New York Times Magazine* put it: "The corset and brassiere creators of America faced—and met a

challenging situation in the midst of a desperate rubber shortage."
Painted-on stockings, or leg makeup, replaced hose, and some ladies
went to excruciating lengths in painting on a seamline; more practical,
less vain sorts simply went bare-legged.

Indeed, even though hampered at every turn by shortages, the
women's beauty industry shared in the general wartime prosperity. The
reason was simple: More women were working in increasing numbers,
and one of the first liens on their paychecks was their beauty needs.
Women's haircut prices started at 50 cents, but most women wanted a
"styled" haircut from $5 up. The prewar $2–$3 permanent wave soon
receded into memory, and women were paying at least $5 in most
shops. On the male side, barbers, of whom a shortage developed as
they went off to war, were making from $50 to $100 a week. There was
no ceiling price on haircuts, and men's haircuts, which averaged 50 cents
each before the war, averaged upwards of 65 cents with a high of $1.15
in Napa, California, and $1.25 in Alaska. With added money in their
pockets, men were partaking of all the added luxuries the tonsorial
arts could offer, as this scene described by *Time* magazine shows:
"In Ed Massey's barbershop at 3306 Main Street, Kansas City, a big
muscular man eased himself out of a barber's chair. He had just had
'the works.' Time was when the big man, a steamfitter by trade, would
have thought it mad folly to come to Ed Massey's for anything but a
haircut. But last week his pay envelope held $140, and he now frankly
enjoyed these little male luxuries: haircut, shave, shampoo, scalp
massage and shoe shine—everything except a manicure." For the beauty
parlors, business was almost too good, and they had a chronic help
shortage because girls who used to enter beauticians' schools were now
flocking to the defense industries. And these same women war workers
demanded extra services such as oil shampoo, finger waves and mani-
cures, not to mention various therapies designed to soften work-hardened
hands. The shops substituted toothpicks for scarce hairpins, sewed curls
in place with thread, and used parchment in place of aluminum foil
in permanent waves. A lengthy WPB order, based on surveys of
American women in which they were asked what cosmetics were
absolutely vital to their morale, made such fine distinctions as finding bath
oil essential and bath salts nonessential. The women respondents were
agreed, however, that face powder, lipstick, rouge and deodorants were
most crucial, and a WPB spokesman rationalized that not only does a
girl get a lift from a trip to the beauty shop, but "Her resultant
vivacious spirit, self-confidence and geniality, being infectious, are

transmuted directly to the male members of the family." The Hump Hair-
pin Manufacturing Company advertised its Hold-Bob Pins with the
caption "Beauty is her badge of courage." The copy read:

> She wears it proudly—this badge of courage. It helps her face
> a shattered world with calm valor and deep faith.
> It's a tonic to the war-torn nerves of those around her.
> It's a silent eloquent way of saying, "There must be no
> letting down. We will fight on to Victory!"

Small businessmen such as auto dealers and electrical appliance
stores were not fortunate enough to have anything to advertise, since their
basic wares were gone with the war. A spot check of electrical appliance
dealers in Los Angeles showed most of them surviving, mainly by adding
other lines of merchandise such as furniture, giftwares and phonograph
records. There was also a strong demand for repairs of worn-out
appliances or rebuilding discarded ones. With the auto dealers it was
less easy to offer alternate lines of merchandise, and many had to close
down. One Detroit dealer converted several cars on hand into ambulances
for civilian defense work, and there was a brief movement to have the
dealers all over the country act as distributors of civilian defense
equipment, but nothing came of it. Goebbels Beer took a full-page ad
in *Automotive News* offering beer distributorships to "enterprising" auto
dealers. Goebbels pointed out that all that empty showroom space would
be perfect for storing beer. The dealers, however, did not rush to make
this radical transition, preferring to hold onto their franchises as best
they could until the postwar needs. Many expanded their repair businesses
to keep the nation's aging autos and tires in operation. Plenty of spare
parts were on hand, but a shortage of skilled mechanics soon developed,
and salesmen were put into coveralls. Others went into the secondhand
car business and found it highly lucrative—especially with the thriving
black market in used cars that soon developed.

As the war drew on, substitutes for rationed goods were offered,
cloaked in appeals to patriotism, with the retailer saying (in effect):
"Because of the war, I can't get the right materials, so please buy these
inferior substitutes—and help me make a buck." At Christmastime,
1943, the department stores came up with a Victory Line of all-wooden
toys. In New York, Macy's and Gimbels trumpeted the patriotic virtues
of gifting children with them, throwing in drastic price slashes. There were
wooden wagons, scooters and machine guns. But despite the patriotic
appeals and price cuts, shoppers turned up their noses.

On the other hand, during the great whiskey shortage of 1944 (the government had commandeered all the industry's alcohol production and its backlog had finally run out), a whiskey distilled from potatoes was snapped up by thirsty New Yorkers. Booze was booze, no matter what you distilled it from. Connoisseurs deprived of French champagne were advised by the *New Yorker* that "There is, for instance, a considerable stock on hand of the Syspelt champagne from Australia, which seems to be one of the most satisfactory pinchhitters for a good French growth champagne that has yet turned up." Also recommended to ease the oeonophile through the rigors of war were South African champagne; Portuguese, Cypriot and South African brandy; and New York State sherry.

On the other hand, too much consumer patriotism sometimes could also be a cause for alarm. In the early months of the war, *Life* magazine ran a feature in praise of the use of patches to save clothing— just one of the examples of the patriotic masochism so prevalent then. "Instead of pussyfooting around with almost matching material which fools no one, smart patchers are boldly proclaiming their patches by using contrasting materials." This sent shock waves through the garment manufacturers, who worried that nobody would buy any new clothes anymore but that everyone would go around looking like the Scarecrow in *The Wizard of Oz*. This, of course, did not occur, and *Life*'s synthetic fad made little headway.

The average housewife, having plenty of money and few ration points, tended to buy canned goods graded "fancy" rather than "choice"; similarly, she would buy a brand name, with its connotation of quality, rather than the cheaper, unknown brands, except when nothing else was available. Other consumer quirks in the supermarket, as reported by *Time,* were that macaroni sales were down because tomato sauce and cheese were scarce; that when butter was scarce, pancake mix sales dropped; that rather than buy rationed catsup, shoppers bought unrationed pickles or relish for their hamburgers; and that baking powder sales had slumped because so many women had jobs and were too tired to bake when they got home. Because of gas rationing, the little neighborhood ma and pa store received a boost in its battle against the big supermarket chains; people had to patronize a store within walking distance.

The war operated in bizarre ways, in giving heretofore humble materials a sudden boost. As one contemporary historian wrote, it became rather like a Walt Disney educational short with all these various anthropomorphized products enlisting in the war effort—Señorita Coffee

Bean giving her all as a basis for plastic used in fuselages; Chiquita Banana enlisting as a source of high-octane gasoline; Milo Milkweed giving his cuddly down—handpicked by troops of Boy Scouts—for use in life jackets, replacing scarce kapok. Oh, what Walt could have done with the "spider ranch" in Frederickstown, Ohio, where the spider's thread was collected on reels for use as cross hairs in gunsights and bombsights. Even the castor bean, source of the notorious castor oil of boyhood legend, achieved its moment of glory as a lubricant in airplane engines and as a substitute for tung oil, which was used in paint and varnish. So moved by this, no pun intended, was one newspaperman that he wrote in all seriousness in the New Orleans *Times-Picayune:* "Some day after this war is over, we might erect a monument in one of our public parks. On it would be a lovely but humble plant with this inscription: 'To the castor plant which helped us win the war; from a grateful nation.'"

The millions of servicemen had their unique needs, and these stimulated several unusual industries. California tattoo parlors had a small boom, with more customers coming in than at any time within the last twenty years. Contrary to the Popeye tradition, more of the customers were soldiers than sailors; psychiatrists would probably explain this form of self-mutilation as a symbolic achievement of manhood. The greatest demand was for inexpensive, practical designs—names and Social Security numbers led the list (indicating also a concern with death), followed by small daggers, ships, flags, initials surrounded by a heart and eagles with their wings spread. Another business which boomed was the prophylactic industry—although perhaps we should not assume that the product was used "for the prevention of disease only." The greeting card business had a big boost, as families communicated various greetings to their boys in service. The best-selling card was "To my son in the service on Mother's Day."

For the consumer in sum, it was a time of shortages, but not major sacrifices, except in certain places at certain times. True, the mobilized economy could not have more guns without having less butter. (Creamery butter production declined to the lowest point since 1925, as the government ordered milk production be used mainly for cheese, canned or dried milk, for shipment overseas to servicemen and under Lend-Lease. Butter was rationed and frequently unobtainable, and the average annual butter consumption per capita fell to 11 pounds, as opposed to 17 pounds in the late thirties.)

War brought flush times, but the consumer price index rose 47 percent between 1939 and 1945, while wages rose by about the same percentage (consumer price index, 1945: 147; average wages, $44.39, compared with 100 and $23.86 in 1939). Total salaries and wages increased from $52.6 billion in 1939 to $112.8 billion in 1944—when the dollar would buy about 75 percent of what the 1939 dollar would buy. Production of civilian goods dipped to about 80 percent of what it had been in 1939, the biggest decline being in hard goods—autos, refrigerators and so on—but consumer expenditures rose from $61.7 billion to $98.5 billion during the same period. Overall, then—despite higher taxes, notably the 5 percent "Victory Tax" surcharge—consumers had more money in their hands and fewer goods to spend it on. Nevertheless, they spent it liberally, although much of it was used to pay off mortgages and other debts or plowed into War Bonds and other savings; total individual savings rose from $6 billion in 1939 to $38.9 billion in 1944. By the end of 1945, when more consumer goods had begun to appear on the market, this wartime savings figure had already fallen to $35.3 billion, indicating the direct relationship between saving and the availability of goods on which to spend money.

Much of the excess purchasing power went into luxury goods, which often enough were not price-controlled. Thus it was that the diamond industry became a $1-billion-dollar business in the war years.

The nation's clothing business was hit hard by voracious Army demands for worsteds, woolens and other textiles. By 1944 there were serious shortages of men's clothing. One patriotic style change early in the war, designed to conserve materials, was christened the Victory Suit. It would have no lapels, no vest, no patch or bellows pockets, no cuffs, and an adjustable waistband instead of belts or suspenders. This was not widely adopted, but men's suits generally had no cuffs or pleats. (Lord & Taylor, however, did come up with a suit for what the store's ads called the "home front hero"—a modified Ike-jacket style; the advertising promised: "Even if he's a 4-F, he can feel like a hero.")

The Roosevelt government unleashed the energies of war industry by giving the entrepreneurs their heads, with a maximum of incentive, tax write-offs and postwar tax refunds to offset wartime excess profits taxes up to 80 percent, and a minimum of coercion (though with a good deal of regulation, which is another matter but which sometimes has— or seems to have—effects very much like coercion). The stick, though kept under the table, was nonetheless real, for Congress had delegated to the President practically unlimited powers to commandeer any facility of resource for war production by executive order.

The central strength of American industry was its mastery of the application of mass-production techniques to the manufacture of war goods; such application was essential to large-quantity output in a short time. Such techniques were innovated by Eli Whitney while making muskets for the War of 1812.

Because the Army and Navy's between-the-wars program, with a few notable exceptions such as the B-17—although even it had to be substantially modified—and the Norden bombsight, was woefully inadequate, the United States entered the war not only short of arms but employing sometimes obsolete and poorly designed weaponry. An example was the light tank for which the Army placed a large order with Chrysler Motors. In design it harked back to the World War I model used at Flanders, although the armor was thicker. Its air-cooled engine was unsuitable for desert operations, its 37-mm cannon a popgun by German panzer standards and its treads were usable only on concrete roads. Chrysler engineers were particularly intrigued by an exotic type of spring in the chassis that none of them had ever seen before. At last one engineer recalled something similar in an old railroad manual. Upon investigation, it turned out that the spring was the volute type used in freight cars and discarded long ago by the railroads as obsolete. The engineers proceeded to design a new, much-improved model, but it was months before the Army admitted the faults in its own prototype. As the war drew on and American equipment received the acid test of combat, the opposite trend developed—especially in the Army Air Force. Soon the services were demanding immediate modifications to correct every wrinkle that showed up in combat or the addition of new gadgetry in response to new enemy weapons even though such fluidity in design was often incompatible with standardized, quantity production.

Some items of military equipment, of course, such as the Jeep or the M-1 rifle, could be turned out in mass quantities without the constant need for change in order to counter new weapons. But in the aircraft industry it was a different story; experienced manufacturers knew they had to keep their machines and methods flexible so that necessary retooling could quickly be effected. An example of ignoring this truth is provided by Ford's Willow Run plant where the production people, still thinking in terms of hallowed mass-production methods going back to the Model T, employed long-lasting hard-steel dies which were poorly adapted to retooling. Aircraft experts warned Ford's production engineers that what was needed were cheap soft-steel dies that were more easily adapted to the necessary changeovers. Because Ford ignored this advice, it experienced major delays in reaching full production of B-24 bombers.

In other instances superior foreign weapon models such as the Bofors and Oerliken guns were imported and adapted to American mass production. However, American technology soon came into its own under the direction of the Office of Scientific Research and Development, headed by Dr. Vannevar Bush. Governmental, military, industrial and academic scientists, with more than a billion government dollars to spend, perfected a variety of technical innovations for the war effort. (Patents on inventions by private industry reverted to the industry at the war's end, even though financed by federal money—no small windfall.) Among the thousands of these were the myriad improvements of radar, sonar (which played a part in breaking the German submarine blockage), the VT proximity fuze, various specialized types of rocket weaponry, amphibious vehicles such as the DUKW, flamethrowers, medical techniques such as blood plasma and the large-scale production and therapeutic employment of Sir Alexander Fleming's penicillin, synthetic drugs such as Atabrine (a substitute for scarce quinine), jet planes, improvements in flight conditions (the pressurized cabin, the anti-G suit to prevent blackouts during pullouts from steep dives), DDT and the nuclear bomb.

In addition to groundbreaking scientific discoveries were the basic nut-and-bolt improvements and alternations of weapons made by anonymous engineers in the factory. Often enough, their "discoveries" were simply improvements in the production process. Most industries revamped their employee suggestion programs, offering cash awards or glory. During one such campaign at RCA Victor, a long list of prizes was offered, capped by fifteen all-expense trips to Miami; mass meetings were held; and various stunts such as breeches buoy demonstrations and even mock tank and plane attacks were staged to whip up employee enthusiasm and patriotism.

Within a year of Pearl Harbor, American industry was gushing out millions of units of a wide variety of planes, ships, guns and other munitions. For the first time in American industrial history, American manufacture was operating at full blast. There was no worry about overproduction: Production—and production alone—was all that mattered. By wartime dollar values, the total for the entire war came to $186 billion worth of munitions. One historian, attempting to translate production figures into more familiar terms, called it the equivalent of building two Panama Canals every day—and a good deal more. When FDR called for 50,000 planes in 1942, his opponents scoffed. They were right; only 47,000 planes were produced. But in the next year it was 86,000 and the year after that, more than 100,000. Looked at another way, between December 7, 1941, and June 8, 1944, a total of 171,257 planes was produced—an average of 68,500 a year over this two-and-a-half-year period from Pearl Harbor to D Day.

Mass production had other advantages besides its capability of turning out goods in large quantities. For one thing, assembly-line operations could be broken down into simple machine or hand tasks. This meant not only standardization of parts and efficiency of operation, but also the widespread use of semiskilled labor, so that men could be quickly trained and take their places on the assembly line without needing a long period of apprenticeship or schooling. Much of the new labor was unskilled—youths, the aged, women, poor Southern whites and Negroes from the farms, white-collar workers, small businessmen who had lost their businesses because of the war and so on. Most of these people had probably never seen the inside of a factory before; on the whole it was a group from which no high level of skilled craftsmanship could be demanded.

To see this process in action, take the example of the Bofors gun, developed by the Swedes before the war and which the British were producing in quantity. It had two or four barrels capable of firing 40-mm shells rapidly and was an effective naval antiaircraft gun because of the screen of fire it threw up. The Swedish prototype of this complex piece of machinery was entirely hand-crafted, and it took 450 man-hours to produce one gun. The problem then was to break down the gun into a number of standardized parts which could be turned out in quantity by simple machines operated by the semiskilled labor available. The contract for manufacturing the gun was awarded to Chrysler Motors, whose engineers immediately set to work disassembling a prototype model, measuring each part, translating standardized dimensions to blueprints and then designing jigs, dies and other machine tools. This was accomplished in an incredibly few months, and when full production finally got under way, Chrysler workmen, many of whom were unlettered country boys, were taking 10 man-hours to turn out a gun which had taken the Swedes 450.

In the case of the Oerliken antiaircraft gun, a Swiss invention, Pontiac was awarded the contract to adapt it to mass production. By January, 1942, ahead of schedule, Pontiac was tooled up and in full production on orders of 19,100 guns, which it would produce at an estimated rate of 1,250 per month. It was working under a Navy contract under which it would receive $7,000 per gun based on estimated costs plus a fixed fee of $490. By the time it had produced its first 2,000 guns the cost had dropped to $6,377 a gun. By the last 4,000 guns of the original 19,100-gun order, the cost per unit had fallen to $5,355.26, in turn calling for a reduction of the fixed fee to $385 per gun—a 23 percent reduction in total costs. Originally, Pontiac had estimated that it would take a total of 428 man-hours to produce one gun; by January this had been reduced to 346. Other savings were effected by simplifying parts.

Similar economies were effected in other industries and went hand in hand with dramatic, ahead-of-schedule conversion to war production. The Saginaw division of General Motors approached the Army as early as 1937 with a proposition that it mass-produce Browning machine guns, heretofore leisurely handcrafted by veteran artisans in dusky arsenals smelling of cosmoline. As the defense program also worked at a leisurely pace until it came under the goad of actual war, it was not until March, 1941, that production got under way, on a contract that called for 40 guns by January, 1942, and accelerated to a humming 160 by March. In actuality, after Pearl Harbor, Saginaw accelerated mightily and produced 28,728 guns in March. This quantity production lowered the price per gun from $667 to $141.44. In the aircraft industry, during the war the price per pound—which, like steaks or tomatoes, was the way the WPB statisticians evidently calculated those things—of long-range four-engine bombers dropped from $15.18 to $4.82, a saving of around $500,000 dollars a bomber.

By far the most famous and spectacular application of mass production was employed by shipbuilder Henry J. Kaiser, who became something of a folk hero and a frequent reference in radio comics' jokes as a symbol for getting something done fast. Even when it was found he was violating steel priorities, newspaper columnists rose to his defense. He was "old Henry," a shrewd, practical, no-nonsense man, who above all could Get Things Done and Deliver the Goods. He had a simple, pragmatic philosophy for doing this which he expressed to one reporter: "Success in anything depends on three things. First, you must visualize what the need is. Second, you must visualize how and when the need can be met. And third, you must visualize the organization that can meet it." A description of his Richmond, California, yard in operation by a visiting European journalist is worth quoting at length:

> The principle is the same as that employed by a child when it takes building blocks from a box and builds a house. Every single fragment of the hull is prefabricated and numbered. A few minutes

after the vessel has left the slip hundreds of workers swarm over it and scrape away the grease on which it has been launched. The enormous cranes on the quay have been awaiting the signal to move and bring up enormous steel plates to be sunk on the slipway to be welded by hundreds of welders, and in a turn of the hand the keel of the new ship is laid. A great deal of the superstructure has been prepared ashore and is hoisted on deck by giant cranes. There are ten, twelve, or fifteen slipways side by side; cranes come and go; there are lorries and railway wagons behind the welding shops, and depots supply the raw materials and thousands of parts. Four or five days a week a new keel is laid, a new ship is begun. After the launch the vessel is conveyed to the outfitting quay where hundreds of workmen stand waiting for the anchor to drop. At a given signal they rush on board. Every single one has his specialized and limited task . . . anti-aircraft guns are mounted, wireless and refrigerators installed . . . and on the fifth or sixth day the crew goes on board and a new Liberty Ship weighs anchor.

Back in 1941, when the Maritime Commission had preempted the original British design for a merchant ship that would be constructed by mass-production methods and known as the Liberty class, it hoped that under an emergency crash program the shipbuilding industry would be able to produce one ship every six months. By 1943 Kaiser had brought that figure down to twelve days. Such a fair-haired boy was Kaiser that he was able to wrangle a total of $150,000,000 in RFC loans from the government. These he poured into the Fontana steel mill in California, the Permanente magnesium plant, and partnership with Howard Hughes in building a giant wooden cargo plane—from which he hastily withdrew, leaving Hughes to pour millions into the project. The steel mill was sold at a loss after the war; the magnesium plant was a flop. The loans were secured by Kaiser's shipbuilding profits—which in one year totaled $24,000,000 before renegotiation. In 1950 Kaiser still owed the government $44,500,000. Though the most famous shipbuilder, Kaiser was by no means alone; overall, 5,600 merchant ships were built during the war with a deadweight tonnage (*i.e.,* cargo-carrying capacity in terms of tons of 2,240 pounds) of 56,400,000. In the peak year of 1943, 1,949 ships were produced (of which 1,238 were Liberty ships) by the eighty-odd shipyards that had Maritime Commission contracts. The 27,000,000 deadweight tons produced during the first two years of the war were more than enough to offset the serious losses caused by the depredations of Nazi U-boats and helped tip the balance in the Allies' favor in the Battle of the Atlantic.

Other contributions to the success of American war production can be mentioned briefly. Conservation of scarce raw materials was effected by more economical methods of production and by unremitting campaigns against waste. Thousands of tons of scrap steel were recovered in the steel mills after a serious scrap shortage had, in the early months of the war, curtailed production. Substitutes for scarce materials were widely employed. When a shortage of brass developed, to give only one example, a steel cartridge case was designed, something thought impossible by the experts. The synthetic rubber program reached high gear by 1944, when 80 percent of the total of 800,000 tons consumed was synthetic (in 1941, total rubber consumption was 868,000 tons, of which 1 percent was synthetic).

Another factor was cooperation among members of the same industry involving the sharing of trade secrets, patents, know-how, research data, production techniques and parts. This was particularly successful in the aircraft industry. The big West Coast aircraft manufacturers formed an Aircraft War Production Council for purposes of overseeing this cooperation. It was believed at the time that FDR wanted a single czar for the aircraft industry—czars were the cry in 1942. But the manufacturers didn't like the idea; they weren't yet so cooperative that they would subordinate themselves to one of their rivals. Donald Douglas, head of Douglas Aircraft, was supposed to have said, "We looked at each other and knew that any one of us might be picked for the czar. Nobody wanted to be czar and we didn't want anybody else to be czar. We decided to offer the President an eight-president Soviet to regiment our part of the industry." In a single week, early in the war, Nelson noted such exchanges as 16 engine mounts forgings from Consolidated to North American; 1,000 step nuts from Lockheed to Vultee; one-half ton flathead model rivets from Consolidated to Ryan; 300 special aircraft bolts from Consolidated to North American; 1,000 cotter pins from Vultee to Douglas; and the lending of the use of its hydro press by North American to Northrup when the press of the latter broke down. (A similar cooperative arrangement prevailed in the automobile industry. It was directed by the Automotive Council for War Production, under managing director George Romney.)

War unleashed and mobilized the powerful energy of American production; it gave workingmen jobs and made them part of a knightly quest whose goal was the killing of the hydra-headed Fascist monster. There was a hum and throb of industry everywhere in the land; at the big war production centers in smoke and flame and the clang of machinery around the clock, seven days of the week, munitions were being forged. In overwhelming force, industry bent all its efforts toward the single goal of more production—and still more. There were slackers and slow downs and finaglers, but on the final balance sheet, the factories broke every previous production record and poured forth a flood of goods. Gone was the stagnation, the business conservativism, the time and motion study men, the cost cutting, the plowing under of crops, the millions of idle workers of Depression times; unleashed was American productive and technological genius. As Allan Nevins wrote:

> A British observer, D. W. Brogan, remarked during the conflict that "to the Americans war is a business, not an art." He meant that the Americans approached it with business resourcefulness and efficiency, as they had approached the harnessing of the Tennessee Valley or the exploitation of the Mesabi Iron ranges. . . . Never before had war demanded such technological expertness and business organization. . . . The modern American genius, the genius of the country of Whitney, Morse, and Edison, precisely fitted such a war. After our invasion of France, we were told that our armies lurched forward to the Siegfried Line like a vast armed workshop; a congeries of factories on wheels with a bristling screen of troops and a cover of airplanes; the most highly mechanized advance in history.

Of course it was the men in the armed forces who won the victory, who laid their lives on the line for patches of ground in steamy jungles or sunbaked atolls in the Pacific or gutted French farmhouses in Normandy. But if American technology could have found a way to fight war entirely without men, it would have done so; indeed the crowning achievement of that technology, the atomic bomb, was employed in precisely that role. Rather than hurl our men into what was believed—rightly or wrongly—to be an interminable and bloody struggle for Japan itself, Harry S. Truman authorized the use of the bomb in their stead—"to save American lives." It was a fitting, and terrifying symbol, of science and technology harnessed to the destructive ends of war. Though many, when they read of this terrifying new weapon, feared for its future consequences and other men debated the necessity and the morality of its use, most Americans overwhelmingly approved under the inexorable logic of ever more sophisticated—and destructive—weaponry, just as they had indifferently endorsed the bombing of German cities or the fire bombing of Tokyo which took more lives than did Hiroshima and Nagasaki.

Americans, in short, believed in unleashing the sorcerer's apprentice, if that was what it took to end the war. For by 1945 they were weary of war, of the casualty lists in the papers and the shortages and ever-increasing costs; true, they had not suffered as other nations had, but enough was enough—so then end it; blow up the entire Japanese archipelago if necessary, but end it. Of course, there was a good deal of pride in the triumphant advance of American troops, and the production record on the home front, but wartime life was never looked upon as a *way* of life; it was an interlude; make automobiles and refrigerators and stoves, not war, and, above all, as soon as the military men thought it was possible, bring the boys home, let the War Be Over. News of the high cost of the Battle of Iwo Jima wrenched this *cri de coeur* from an American lady who wrote the Navy Department: "Please for God's sake, stop sending our finest youth to be murdered on places like Iwo Jima. It is too much for boys to stand. It is driving some mothers crazy. Why can't objectives be accomplished some other way? It is most inhuman and awful—stop, stop!"

Hers was an extreme outburst of emotion, perhaps, but it said something shared by many, though they had buried it in their hearts. The Army officer in North Africa ordering a sustained barrage against an enemy-held hill who said, "I'm letting the taxpayers take this hill," would have had the approval of the taxpayers, whose dollars pumped into the great corporations, working hand in glove with the military, made possible the awesome production and technological feats of which the atomic bomb was the apotheosis, and the alliance of science, the military, and the war-spawned arms industry, twenty-five years later, the legacy.

V

GIVE US THE TOOLS

By late 1943 industrial America had the machine power for all-out war production. It had adequate raw materials to feed the machines and a reasonably workable system for allocating them, but as military operations flared up on multiple fronts and the casualty lists lengthened, Selective Service grew hungrier for manpower. It was 5,000,000 . . . 7,000,000 . . . 10,500,000 by the end of 1943 . . . 13,000,000 men between eighteen and fifty were called or enlisted.

The U.S. Census Bureau estimated in 1944 that had the normal peacetime growth trend continued, the labor force in that year would have reached 57,360,000. In actuality, the labor force numbered 64,-010,000 in 1944 (including the armed forces). Subtracting 10,000,000 men in service, we have left 54,000,000, or 2,000,000 less than the prewar year 1940 labor force of 56,420,000, which meant, with 8,410,-000 unemployed, 48,000,000 were working. But wartime needs called for practically a doubling of total production; in 1944 the government purchased $90 billion worth of war goods and services, or nearly half of the gross national product of that year of $197.6 billion. Even adjusted for inflation, this government spending alone was equal to about 70 percent of the total GNP for 1939, the last peacetime year, which was $88.6 billion. (Total GNP in 1944 adjusted to 1939 values was $138.32 billion—more than a third again as much as the 1939 level.) In 1944, of course, unemployment was at an all-time low of 800,000 (so that 7,000,000 of the 8,000,000 unemployed in 1940 had been siphoned into the employed). Thus in 1944, 54,000,000 workers—12½ percent more than in 1940—on the farms, in the factories, in retail trades, service industries, nondurable and durable manufactures, were producing 57 percent more goods. In manufacturing alone (where, of course, munitions production was concentrated) productivity rose 25 percent between 1939 and 1944. (In the forty-year period between 1889 and 1939, productivity increased on the average 1.9 percent a year.) The Department of Commerce estimated that output per worker in 1943 was one-third greater than in 1939. However you look at it, the productivity record of American war workers was outstanding.

Nearly all the munitions produced were adapted to mass production, making possible assembly lines, division of labor, machines turning out standardized parts and all the other techniques that multiply the productive power of a single man's hand.

New sources of workers had to be tapped for the labor force, but in wartime this was not enough. People simply had to work longer hours. Obviously, five men working eight hours of overtime every week will add the labor of an extra man working a forty-hour week. Thus, in February, 1943, the President decreed a minimum forty-eight-hour week for munitions industries, with overtime for Sundays and holidays. The average workweek in manufacturing rose to forty-five hours a week—and in some industries it was fifty or even sixty hours. One economist estimated that this overtime was the equivalent of adding 5,000,000 workers to the economy. Of course, as the British had discovered in 1940, too much overtime can be counterproductive, and it is better to limit hours so that the workers have adequate rest and go to their jobs reasonably refreshed and able to work at top efficiency. On the other hand, the unions were jealous of the prerogatives, and blocked extra hours. Be that as it may, most war workers put in long hours at monotonous and grueling tasks, six days a week.

Major strikes in the coal, steel and railroad industries received enormous criticism during the war, requiring strong action by the President and stimulating the passage of antilabor legislation such as the Smith-Connally Act (which ostensibly curbed unions but actually merely provided a cooling-off period, a worker vote as a condition precedent to a strike and gave government power it already had to take over striking factories); nevertheless, another factor in labor's increased productivity was undoubtedly the relative labor peace that prevailed most of the time. A comparison with the peacetime years immediately prior to the war proves that by and large, labor lived up in spirit, if not in letter, to the informal "no-strike" pledge the union leaders gave the President in 1941. During the years 1935 through 1941, an average of 16,000,000 man-days a year were lost because of strikes. During the full war years of 1942 through 1944, however, the average was around 8,600,000 man-days idle during each year. In the crucial conversion year of 1942, only 4,180,000 man-days were lost—an all-time low. And Secretary of Labor Frances Perkins, claiming that wartime strikes were not nearly so threatening to the war effort as they were made out to be by the predominately antiunion press, said the percentage of man hours lost by strikes in proportion to total man-hours worked was only two- to four-tenths of one percent; even in a "bad month" it reached only six-tenths of one percent. Further, many of the strikes were of short duration, wildcat strikes involving only a handful of employees.

An innovation which contributed to harmony at the plant level was the labor-management committee. These committees discussed grievances but were primarily a device to increase efficiency through communication to management of the ideas of workingmen. The program was a mixed success. In some plants they were window dressing, while other employers resisted them as Socialism or encroachment on management's sacred autonomy (for example, Ford, which stated that "in the way of experience, of ability along management lines, labor has nothing much to offer"). On the other hand, some liberals had outsize expectations that the committees were heralding a new era of "industrial democracy," but of course they did nothing of the sort. At any rate, by war's end some 5,000 of them were in existence, widely varying in power and effectiveness. The committees campaigned against absenteeism and for safety, care of tools, etc. By giving the worker a chance to sound off and be heard by management and by improving communication between the two sides, they no doubt increased production, as well as morale.

The last element in labor peace was the more intangible one of *esprit*, patriotism, or what-have-you. Or rather it was a sense, among the war workers—a competitive, excited sense—of being part of a larger effort. Sheer quantity of production became an end in itself, and workingmen could watch with satisfaction as the production figures in their own plant climbed. When this was not the case—as during the first year or so of Willow Run's existence—morale sagged and turnover and absenteeism soared. Also, many of the men and women had sons or brothers or husbands in the services and felt a personal involvement in both pushing themselves to the limit and making certain the parts or weapons they turned out were well made and would not fail in the test of battle. There were several cases in which companies were responsible for faulty munitions that went to the front and perhaps caused the death of GI's. These cases involved a small proportion of businesses in war production, but when they occurred, they were due to the turpitude of management, not labor. The workingman had nothing to gain from cutting corners, unless he was on piecework rates. More typical was the attitude of the worker for one of the big auto companies, who complained to John Dos Passos about his company's lax standards:

> I may be dumb, but I'm a pretty good grinder. I like to do a first rate job. Today I about blew my top trying to get through the work as fast as they wanted. I worked on a camshaft for an airplane motor. I know it's got to be right. Men's lives depend on it. It's not like an automobile that just breaks down. Over there [*i.e.*, in the front office] they just can't get that automobile out of their heads. If it isn't to the right thousandth of an inch, the foreman, he says, put a burr—that's a metal coating—on it and let her go. It'll pass the inspector and what the hell? I may be dumb, but I think of the guys who are going to use that plane. We're in a war, ain't we?

It is unfair but of some educational value to contrast these words with those of Thor S. Johnson, general manager of the notorious Anaconda Wire and Cable Company convicted of defrauding the government of an estimated—the total amount was never known for sure—$6,000,-000 and delivering more than 90 percent defective communications wire to the military. Exhorting his foremen to redouble their efforts to get the defective wire past government inspectors, Johnson was reported to have said on one occasion: "Any employee who is not able to get wire past these jerk inspectors ought not to be working in the plant."

Not that all workers were staunch, patriotic and self-sacrificing. Theft in war plants of tools and parts was a common racket, and in the first six months of 1944 alone, more than 3,000 FBI investigations resulted in 600 convictions. Then there were the two welders working on Liberty ships at the Bethlehem Fairfield Shipyards, who were being paid on a piecework basis and conspired to raise their weekly take by employing "slug" and "bridge" methods of welding, which gave the appearance of proper welding but actually were techniques for concealing faulty joining, which would likely come apart when the ships were subjected to heavy seas. As a result, the two were raking in $200 a week each, while their brothers averaged $60 to $75. The inferiority of their work, coupled with the abnormal amount of money they were making, came to the attention of the FBI, and the two were convicted for war fraud. There were other instances of men seeking to raise their piecework take who bribed company checkers to pass their inferior, speeded-up goods—in at least two cases, entire shifts. There were other kinds of carelessness, practical jokes and malicious (not enemy) sabotage causing plant breakdowns. Nevertheless, such cases were usually the work of a few. Even more important, there were no instances where labor unions were involved in such practices.

Perhaps the best way to illustrate the importance of morale in production is to consider a negative case history. At the Brewster Aeronautical Corporation, with plants in Newark, New Jersey, Long Island City, New York, and Johnsville, Pennsylvania, the pay was good and the union was king—but the workers still weren't happy. During the Depression the union had bargained an advantageous contract from management in exchange for not demanding high wages. Armed with this strong contract and abetted by a succession of management reorganizations, the union gradually increased its power, until it had management by the throat.

When the war came, disproportionate numbers of the portly, slow Brewster Buffaloes were shot down and probably did worse than any other American plane against the Japanese Zeros. In April, 1942, the Navy took the plant over by authority of the President; after reorganization it was returned to the management. But production did not increase. Finally Henry Kaiser was brought in as chairman of the board, and several of his production and labor relations people were sent to Brewster to seek to set things right.

While all this upheaval was taking place at the management level, the union under its hard-nosed, fanatical president, Tom De Lorenzo, consolidated its power. De Lorenzo's stated philosophy was: "Our policy is not to win the war at any cost. The policy of our Local Union is to win the war without sacrificing too many of the rights which we have at the present time. . . . If I had brothers at the front who needed the 10 or 12 planes that were sacrificed [during a recent strike], I'd let them die, if necessary, to preserve our way of life or rights or whatever you want to call it."

The "rights" De Lorenzo sought to preserve included the prerogative of effectively preventing management from firing a worker if the union wished him to be retained and a corresponding power of its own, through its trial board, to fire any union member for such causes as "remaining at work during a stoppage," "using language unbecoming to brother workers," reporting a fellow worker who was sleeping on the job, or "insubordination to department stewards" (quotes taken from actual trial board hearings).

Whenever management tried to rationalize production by shifting men around to balance skilled and unskilled personnel on the various shifts or the assembly line, it had to wrangle interminably with the union. Strikes, slowdowns and walkouts were staged by the union on trivial pretexts (one was held after three probationary employees were fired when caught sleeping in a fuselage); thirteen of them had occurred during the period June, 1942, through September, 1943, costing 719,337 man-hours of work, or the time needed to make sixty-five planes.

Workers' morale was consequently low, but there was no high turnover. Pay was good, and evidently housing was not a problem. The big problems were absenteeism, which ran 12 percent a month for women and eight percent for all employees, and general apathy and loafing.

One worker summed up the underlying malaise at Brewster: "We have good wages now, but the Brewster employees have found out that wages alone cannot make a man happy. We are just as patriotic as any other Americans. We don't like these slow-ups and strikes. Some of us are ashamed of the fact that we work in a factory with such a reputation, but when the shop steward points toward the door with his thumb, we have to go [on strike], or get in Dutch. The worst of it is that hard work and ability count for nothing in this set-up. If you want to stay in this place and get along or be upgraded, you have to stand in with the shop stewards."

Generally, it was the enormous, old-line corporations that were least concerned about their employees' welfare off the job and most jealous of preserving their managerial sovereignty against real or fancied interference. The medium or small dynamic young companies engaged in aircraft or merchant shipping production usually had the most enlightened labor relations.

When an old company looked ahead to the postwar world, it was in a sense looking back to its prewar competitive position; the new wartime industries had practically nothing to look back on. All they could do was exploit their cost-plus situation to the fullest, produce as much as possible as fast as possible so that financial reserves could be built up, and hope that the brave new postwar world might demand something they could make in a related peacetime line. To achieve this production, they had to attract workers and keep them happy, and since the government was paying most of the bill anyway, they did all they could to improve working and living conditions.

In the main, though, such programs as management had for its workers were most successfully applied during working hours and in the field of labor relations. For every Brewster, there was a plant like Grumman, on Long Island. Here there was no housing problem; local labor was sufficient to meet the plant's needs, and these local folk all could live at home. Commuting was necessary for many, but the company worked out share-the-ride plans and even had what was called a Little Green Car service: company cars which serviced broken-down vehicles or ran errands for workers—turning off the gas at home, fetching forgotten glasses and the like. The company emphasized sports and sponsored teams. When Negroes were hired, the management took pains to hire first three Negro basketball stars, whose prowess on the company team so impressed the workers that the subsequent integration of other Negroes was carried out smoothly. No discrimination in advancement was practiced, and Negroes or women received promotions routinely like everyone else.

A big factor in high employee morale was a special incentive pay system authorized as an experiment by the War Labor Board, under which Grumman workers could make above their wage ceilings by producing more. The management also believed in providing a variety of diversions to relieve employee monotony. The rhythm of the plant was not frenetic; people worked at a steady but not panicky pace. Women workers were given two ten-minute rest periods daily, and the management did not permit time and motion studies—the bane of so many workers. Turnover, as a result, was only three percent per month, including draftees, and absenteeism less than 1 percent. Because of all this, production at Grumman was higher than Navy quotas; in 1940 the company was doing only $19,000,000 in business; for the year 1943, it did $390,000,000.

Grumman was run by a partnership that was not uncommon in such medium-sized, new-growth plants: The president, Roy Grumman, was an engineering genius, a postwar pioneer in commercial aviation during the lean Depression years; his vice-president, L. A. Swirbul, was the production genius. Grumman was shy, sensitive, inarticulate; Swirbul, hearty, extroverted, driving and a talker.

None of Grumman's 25,000 workers, it should be added, belonged to a union. Management claimed it was not antiunion in principle; the company had grown so fast from a small factory to its present 25,000

employees that there was no time to organize, Mr. Swirbul told an in-
quiring reporter, adding: "A good union would be a swell thing, if it
were already there, but any transition now would upset the organization
and hurt production." Opinions of the workers were not solicited, but
it was assumed they preferred the enlightened paternalism of Swirbul.

Perhaps the most touted example of the Grumman type of enlightened paternalism was a medium-small Cleveland firm making airplane starters and automatic pilots known as Jack and Heintz, or Jahco
Associates. Here, on a smaller scale, was the Grumman production
genius-engineering genius team. Bill Jack was the dynamic executive
force. A former machinist and union organizer, he had founded several
businesses, which he had sold off when they had become successful,
before starting Jahco with his partner, Ralph Heintz. It grew from a
small firm housed in an old warehouse into a plant of five buildings
employing several thousand men working two twelve-hour shifts a day,
seven days a week, on war contracts. While Heintz remained in the
background, designing the parts Jahco turned out, Jack ran the production line. His men evidently loved him, for his absentee rate was minus
1 percent, his turnover nil, and there was a waiting list of 35,000 to
come work for him.

The main reason was that the workers—Jack called them associates—made big money, working an eighty-four-hour week; even unskilled laborers could make more than $7,600 a year. (Jahco had a
union shop; anything above forty hours was paid time and a half.)
Jack believed in relieving his employees of all worries except production.
The company provided them with medical, life, and accident insurance
and free medical care; the cafeteria doled out free meals and vitamin
pills around the clock; and there were coffee urns and bouillon or fruit
for free snacks, of which the workers could partake whenever they felt
like it. If a man became tired, he could take time off for a steam bath
and a massage, which the plant provided; if a man looked frazzled,
Jack would send him for a two-week Florida vacation at company expense. But the men were expected to work seven days a week, twelve
hours a day.

Jack himself was omnipresent, if genial, Big Brother, working
an eighteen-hour day, sometimes sleeping on a cot in his small office,
talking with anyone who had a problem, dealing personally with most
production snags that arose. Jack had a special passion for the PA system, making a variety of announcements throughout the day, whenever
the spirit moved him ("Attention, Associates . . . Anybody who wants

help in making out his income tax report should find Joe Jones. He's got all the dope . . . He'll be around the shop all afternoon . . . Don't nobody forget now that we are going to the Golden Gloves tonight. Everybody turn out . . .").

His showmanship, togetherness, efficient management, and hard cash worked—and worked so well that the Army no longer inspected his starters: Jack's own inspectors were sufficiently tough and honest, and Jack's workers took such pride in their work that they turned out a good product. Jack and Heintz were also tigers for improving production efficiency; in 1942 the company received national publicity when a Senate investigating committee praised the cut in costs it had made in the performance of a Navy contract. The added profits were shared with all the "associates," a gesture impossible for General Motors or U.S. Steel to make because of obligations to its stockholders. Once when he was an organizer for the International Association of Machinists, Jack wrote the following in an editorial for the union paper: "I believe that the human equation should be the paramount question considered at all times." This was a rule Jack practiced, and it made him and his men plenty of money; it also seemed to make plenty of airplane starters for the Army Air Force.

War industry tapped hitherto-dormant sources of labor in quiet eddies, obscure backwaters, underground springs. From tenant farms, mined-out hill country, farmed-out land, backwoods, piney woods, fishing boats, mill towns, and wide places in the road the war workers came. Or from the humdrum seclusion of retirement or the housewife's kitchen; or from small businesses killed by wartime restriction; or from teaching, law or other white-collar professions. All were people anxious to help the war effort and itchy for the excitement and fat salary envelope of the war plants.

Some of this human tide was the hidden poor of the Depression, emerging above ground at last and holding their heads up in the sun of pride once again; they were also those who had been excluded from the working force by the tight job market of the Depression, who were not needed; and they were young wives or widows whose husbands had been called by war and who needed the money to supplement their allotment checks.

The backbone of the pickup labor force was still the dwindling number of experienced factory workers and craftsmen and the foremen who trained and supervised, but the added impetus of energy was provided by these new workers or those who were not new but whose skills had rusted through years of being unemployed. The number of workers who spent years on relief is hard to estimate, but recall that in 1940 there were more than 5,000,000 unemployed and another 2,000,000 plus doing government make-work with Work Projects Administration and Civilian Conservation Corps and other New Deal projects. Many such people had become inured to relief, resigned to their unemployability. To them the wartime prosperity was a break in the clouds, but with the fatalism of the downtrodden—or the countervailing pugnacity of the union members recalling the labor wars of the thirties—they believed that the clouds would lower again as soon as the war ended and that they would sink back into their economic oblivion.

Others belonged to minority groups that had not been given a fair shake of the job opportunity dice. For the first time, many of them saw an opening in the wall, a chance to move out of their prison and seize jobs and income hitherto not open to them. But many were to find that when they moved out of the safe invisibility of their assigned "place," they drew increased hostility from other competitors, that often their economic betterment merely increased the intensity of the hostility against them. Instead of jogging slowly and safely behind the front runners, they had joined the racing pack, where they found themselves competing for the richer prizes, elbowing past or being elbowed by their competitors.

On the whole, once lack of training and experience had been corrected, it was probably as intelligent, hardworking, reasonably skillful, willing and apt a working force of free men and women as ever assembled in the world's short industrial history. One does not intend to downgrade the workers in the other Allied countries who worked under more trying, even dangerous circumstances—or the Axis countries either, for that matter—but the American workers, given the raw material base, the tools, money and technology, outproduced all the rest of the world combined.

Although genus *War worker* was composed of many species of Americans, he was sometimes lumped together as a class, as a composite stereotype. Stable, middle-class, business-oriented segments of some communities looked on him as a kind of blue-collar parvenu. If he flashed his newly acquired money, he was resented; if he used this money to buy his way into sanctums where he previously was unwelcome, this resentment was compounded. Hence, the story related to John Dos Passos by a Detroiter:

You know there's a restaurant here a gang of us has patronized for some time, a little like "Twenty-One" in New York, the same kind of food, the same atmosphere. Well, I'll be damned if four of them didn't come in there one evening and sit down at a table and ask for a bill of fare. . . . The fellow who runs it, he has a special bill of fare for people he doesn't like, about twice the usual price. Well, these guys never batted an eyelash. They ordered up all the most expensive wines, the guy ran his finger down the card until he found what cost most and paid for it out of a pay check on one of the automotive concerns for a hundred and twenty-six dollars, told the waiter to hurry because he had to go to work . . . but they never did go to work because they got to drinking. . . .

Multiply such scenes by the thousands, and you have the image of the war worker as a fast-spending lout, a "slacker," heedless of the morrow, getting fat on inflated war wages while the boys overseas were dying in the foxholes—in sum: "them." Add to this a nativist strain of antiunionism, which had acquired a defiant strength during the violent sit-down strikes of 1937 and which during the war fed itself on the wave of strikes in 1943 and 1944, and you get a growing hostility among many solid American folk—the Babbitts, the farmers, the great amorphous small-business class (as much a state of mind as a class), the Roosevelt-hating Union Leaguers, and so on—toward these working people, who were in fact the strong backs of American war production.

Although most of the people who worked in the big plants saved their pay or needed it all for necessities, a rowdy minority worked hard and played harder. They were the visible ones who thrust hundred-dollar bills hot from pay envelopes through movie ticket windows and on bars, gambling tables and jewelers' counters. To many—not just the simple folk fresh from the relief rolls—there was something febrile, unnaturally flushed about the times.

One looked back and saw Depression; one looked forward and saw the Victory and the just, peaceful, Four Freedoms world the slogans promised would follow—a world at once impossibly rosy and obscured by uncertainty. More absorbing was the Now of a ten- to twelve-hour day in the factory; home to a trailer or shack; up again the next morning; maybe six days a week on the job. There was little time to think about the present, but when one did, it all seemed temporary, unreal, an in-between time, a break in the normal continuity, a life built on sand that might suddenly be washed away when the war ended, when a vague reckoning might have to be paid—a Depression perhaps or, at a more homely level, a husband returning from overseas to confront a working wife who had become bored with not sitting under the apple tree and Saturday night being the loneliest night of the week. No wonder a small but highly visible minority lived drifting lives, changing jobs at a whim (there was always another one), working but making sure one had a damn good time when one was away from the factory. This frenetic pleasure seeking was most florid in the big war towns, where the motion-picture theaters were open twenty-four hours a day, and war workers attended the swing-shift matinees at one in the morning, and the streets were crowded as if night had been banished and the bars were three-deep with workers coming off work or bracing up to go on. Always there was the unquenchable thirst for pleasure, amusement, gambling games, escape from the drudgery of the assembly line. A reporter for *Daily Variety* described this mood as he observed it in Detroit:

> Detroit . . . where Irving Caesar's "Dear Public" got $32,000 for its opening week, where they stand in line for a glass of beer, where you can't get a good steak, even from Mr. Black [the black market], where The Bowery, a night spot, spends around $10,000 weekly for a floor show; where all night clubs get an admission fee, where more dames wear slacks than in Hollywood, where any kind of act can get good dough playing saloons, where a house can gross upwards of $40,000 weekly with a mediocre stage show, where somebody made a mistake and a race riot resulted, where swing-shift shows birthed, where it takes the reserves to get a vandal out of a theater, where the sidewalk madonnas get too much opposition from home talent, where there are more hill-billies than in Arkansas, and where everybody has two sawbucks to rub against each other. Detroit, the hottest town in America . . . Baghdad on Lake Michigan. . . . If the backwoods improves after the war, Detroit can take a major share of the credit, for there are over 400,000 people here who previously lived in whistle stops, four corners and fur pieces down the road.

More hillbillies than Arkansas? Four hundred thousand hicks from the sticks? Well, an exaggeration. They stuck out so it just seemed there were a lot of them. From the South Atlantic and South-Central states, these poor whites and dirt farmers poured into the cities. Some indeed came all the way North, like the Oklahomans and Texans Henry Ford's men recruited for the defense plant of Willow Run. Most of the others simply moved to a big war industry city closer by.

Down from the hills they swarmed, leaving their families behind un-til they got settled. Those who could not find housing may have returned, even though the money was better; but most of them took whatever housing was available and lived in squalor, earning themselves the reputation of being people who didn't care if they lived like pigs.

Perhaps, in a sense many of them didn't, because they were used to living in poverty—and to a woman who'd lived in a cabin that had unfinished floorboards, with cracks through which you could see the ground, a trailer was a Taj Mahal—or else they regarded the situation as temporary, intending to make a pack of money and return home to their marginal farms after the war was over, like the man in the bus heading for Mobile who told John Dos Passos his whole story in a few spare sentences:

> He wears a thin sunfaded suit of some cottony material worn at the elbows and knees but his white shirt is clean. He has wavy brown hair and deepset eyes in a sallow slightly pockmarked face. Suddenly he begins to talk very low staring down at his cigarette. "Went down an' got me a job down there, 'spector, 'spectin' ammunition before it goes on board ship . . . I got me a certificate that'll find me a job any time I want one . . . Been workin' in a cotton mill up home, not so bad . . . good people to work for, company gives you a nice house, sells you coal cheap, pay was a dollar a day, before transportation got so tight; company's all right but there ain't no money in it. They don't pay no wages. My wife she works there too. I'm goin' to leave her home so that she kin keep the house. I wouldn't carry her down here where I goin'. I'm lucky to git a place to stay. A nephew of mine down there, he's goin' to board me for seven dollars a week. That's cheap but he kinda likes me. I'll git home once a month or fix it so my wife kin come down an' see me. Couldn't do it oftener. This trip wears a man out . . . Company's helped a lot of folks build up homes. They lend 'em money for materials an' some fellers build their houses theirselves . . . One of these days I'm goin' to build me a long house out in the woods. I'd buy me a piece of land an' cut down the trees to build the house with."

Or even more succinct was the old lady living in a tar-paper shack who said: "We may not be around these parts for long. We got a house and a piece of land back home, and we figger to go back there soon's this job's over."

In the boomtown of Mobile men slept the way they worked, in "hot beds" in eight-hour shifts round the clock for 25 cents and up a turn. It was a town where each evening there were lines a block long at every one of the restaurants. Once inside people fought for the waitress,

likely a cute blond trick from East Jesus, Texas, who told you only the
chicken croquettes were left and got 50-cent tips from the sailors and
who had probably run away from home to follow a serviceman boyfriend. There were always lines—lines outside theaters and lines at the
liquor stores and lines at the doctor's office. And too, a sense of being
hemmed in by the throngs of aimless people crowding the sidewalks,
wandering about with no place to go, nothing to do but stand in another
line or gawk at the captured Messerschmitt on display to boost bond
sales.

There was good money to be had in the yards. An unskilled worker
could start at 50 to 60 cents an hour in the big Alabama Drydock and
Shipyard Company or the Gulf Shipyards, whose great cranes towered
starkly against the skyline, dominating the city, and which between them
employed 40,000 of the 65,000 industrial workers in Mobile. Four bits
an hour was pretty good money for the South, and any man who was
worth a lick could raise that to $1.17 an hour in the space of a month
or so by changing jobs and being upgraded each time. Never mind that
in peacetime a man who could not weld 120 feet a day was fired, while
in wartime the average was 32 feet a day. It was the land of opportunity
for the hillbilly, and so they poured in, overtaxing the services of the
city, country and federal government.

Entirely different problems were raised by another large group
whom the demands of war put to work—the women. As was mentioned
earlier, during the period of April, 1940, and August, 1943, an additional
4,400,000 women entered the labor force, or about 3,000,000 more than
would have during normal times. About 1,300,000 of these were employed in agriculture, and the rest in manufacturing, clerical work, the
professions and so on.

These women war workers—that is, these women working because
of the war, women who would not be working in peacetime—who were
they? Contemporary statistical information about them was minimal, so
only a very sketchy profile can be drawn up. The female war worker
was more likely to be married (56 percent of them were) than single.
The husbands of about one-fifth of these married ladies were not present
—presumably mostly away in the services.

Prominent among these servicemen's wives were the women who
entered an industry directly engaged in war production because they
wanted to make their contribution to the war effort while supporting
themselves. In age, a bare majority of the new entrants were between
twenty and forty-four years; however, a sizable proportion was made up

of older married women, whose children were grown up or who were childless. Another sizable proportion—perhaps as high as one-third—consisted of young girls, under twenty, still in school who worked full or part time, often dropping out of school when the strain of a full-time job and the excitement of being on one's own became too great.

Often, especially in smaller cities, the women replaced the men of the town who had gone off to war—even, in many cases, taking over their husband's jobs. These women were hired in preference to importing migrant workers. (For example, in Muncie, Indiana, the population increased by only about 2,500 during the war, but employment increased from 16,000 to 25,000, not counting the 7,500 from the city and surrounding county who had entered the services. More than half the women would quit their jobs, it was found, so one firm preferred to hire Negroes, as "the lesser of two evils.") Among the older women entering the labor force was a numerous body of those who had worked previously but whom the Depression had expelled from their jobs in favor of men. Among these, many were probably mothers of servicemen, who worked to take their minds off worrying about their sons or who had already lost a son in the war and worked to forget their grief. And finally, there were some 10,000,000 women working in 1944 who had also been working at the time of Pearl Harbor—more or less the permanent core of women workers in the labor force.

The flesh-and-blood females who womaned the machines and rivet guns and welding torches were all sizes, shapes, ages and social backgrounds. Some worked under hardships equal in every way to those undergone by men; they showed themselves capable of equaling or bettering the performance of men, and they added both sex and idealism, distraction and enthusiasm to the smoke and grit and flame and sweat of the great factories. They also replaced men in hundreds of job classifications never previously open to them. They even preempted some jobs for themselves permanently because they could do them better. The surprise was not that they could do such jobs but the fact that anyone was surprised they *could* perform so well.

War has a way of sweeping aside old prejudices and habits of thought. With society ostensibly mobilized toward one end, any mores standing in the way of the means best adapted to achieving that end were theoretically stowed away on blocks for the duration, like the family car. During the thirties men resented women competing with them for the few jobs available. When women did have jobs, they were discriminated against flagrantly; "women's jobs," lower pay for equal work, a cutoff of the degree of advancement kept the men happy and un-threatened.

In wartime, however, with the man more likely to be removed from the scene, his woman was left to make out for herself. Further, war work acquires a solid ring of patriotism: It was almost *necessary* to the country's patriotic *amour propre* to see these pictures and newsreels of grimy-faced girls in slacks, handkerchiefs or turbans on their heads, doing unglamorous physical labor beside men, making a V for Victory sign as they drove their tanks off the production line to the testing ground. Working woman became part of the human strength of the nation; she joined the ranks of fighting men and workingmen unified in the steadfast march toward the goal of Victory.

Of course she must remain pretty and feminine For the Boys, to boost their morale and give them Something to Fight For, preserving herself—the Home Front—exactly as he remembered it, for her guy, when he came home (although she might wear her slacks more often than she used to and "nice girls" didn't wear slacks).

In a popular, gushy woman's book of the period, *Since You Went Away* by Margaret Buell Wilder, the heroine gives vent to her wartime feelings in a letter to her husband who is shipping out:

> If only we could have gone with you! To see and hear and feel what you'll find! As it is, the whole thing is real to us only in flashes we're not yet part of the bone and sinew. . . . We go home from a film about Midway or from *The Watch on the Rhine,* temporarily exalted or stirred, then sink back into a sort of sympathetic detachment. . . .
>
> There's a remedy for that yet, of course . . . bombing and starvation—but it probably accounts for the relative apathy of the Middle West . . . and certainly for the restlessness of people like me who can't get closer to the war itself. . . .
>
> As to the latter, my personal dissatisfaction, I've decided that an actual production job is the most likely answer. Not Wright Field, not committee stuff, but a nasty ear splitting greasy over-all job that would make the guns and planes real to me. . . .

To many young girls and war wives, the war plant meant excitement and adventure of an equivalent sort to what their own men or the men of their generation were experiencing. The factory offered good money, emancipation from financial worries (which in a low-paying "women's job" would have been present), and participation in the wartime hot swing tempo and excitement.

For the single girl, the factory or the government job in Washington provided a chance to meet men—although many were sorely disappointed when faced with lonely lives far from home, learning by personal experience the meaning of the phrase "manpower shortage." For indeed there were only 1,700,000 unmarried male civilians between twenty and thirty-four, for whom, on the job, about 4,100,000 bachelor girls were competing (in 1940, unmarried men in this age group outnumbered the unmarried women by a ratio of 3 to 2). There were, of course, in the camp towns and the port cities and Washington, plenty of GI's, but so many were in transit. Quick meetings, quick courtships and maybe marriage—and then once more you were alone again. Further, the job was often wearing and dull, and wartime austerity took the glamor out of life by limiting the fancy things one could buy with what extra money one had after paying high rents and food prices. So with freedom went inevitable, if not insurmountable, grief for the young girl living her own life.

For the married woman, the pressures, practical and social, were rather different. The older woman, whose children had grown and were perhaps in the Army (and her husband as well), had plenty of motivation and excuse, financial and patriotic, for getting a war job. Even if her husband was at home, there was still the incentive of getting a good paycheck. Even the reasonably well-off middle-class wife might be induced to enter war work—most frequently when her husband was off in the service, however, for otherwise the Code of Babbitt exercised a hold, and "committee work" was more acceptable, if less lucrative.

The novel *Since You Went Away* mentioned above, when made into a movie, was drastically altered in several ways, one of which was to make Mrs. Hilton, the mother-heroine, a bit better off financially, so that apparently, unlike the heroine of the book, she does not really need to work, although she does take in boarders. At the end of the picture, she decides to take a job as a welder in a shipyard, but not for the reasons of the heroine in the book (who actually never does take the kind of job she fantasizes about).

In one of the picture's final scenes, she is shown in the war plant sharing lunch with a new friend, an immigrant lady (a social type white, Protestant, middle-class Mrs. Hilton would not meet in the ordinary run of her life), who tells her how she escaped from the old country, quotes Emma Lazarus' poem, and says tearfully "You are what I thought America was." Mrs. Hilton replies humbly, "In my own small way I help in a shipyard. I hope I may be worthy of those words." The propaganda point the film was making was that although a mother with two nice teen-age daughters (not juvenile delinquents, of course) has an important job as a force keeping the home together—the foundation of our life—it is permissible and patriotic for her to want to Do Something More, to do factory work, beneath her class.

The real question was not "Should women work?" but rather a series of questions. What sort of work should women do; would they require pampering and all sorts of frills and extra considerations; what other drawbacks as workers did they have; should they get paid as much as men; would they become "mannish" or disrupt discipline in the factory where they mixed with males; would they be willing to return to the home when war was over; and, if no to the last, would they take a job from some returning GI?

As for the question of what work they could and should not do, the experts thought they could do just about anything that men could, if it did not require too much physical effort or too heavy or highly skilled operations, if it could be broken up into easier machine operations, if special safety precautions could be devised. They could indeed. Women were riveters, spot and torch welders, hydraulic press operators, crane operators, shell loaders, bus drivers, train conductors, bellhops, life-guards, lumberjacks (coyly dubbed "lumberjills"), cowgirls, section hands, coal mine checkers, car washers, filling station operators, taxi drivers, barbers, policemen, ferry command pilots, and football coaches —to toss out a sprinkling.

When women were taken on at the Aberdeen Proving Grounds, after a good deal of traditional resistance, to perform tasks ranging from loading shells to cleaning and firing big guns, the commanding officer, according to a contemporary historian, "had pondered seriously the hazards involved: Would women faint when a big gun went off? Would they be nervous about handling gun-powder? Could they be relied upon to stick to the recipe and not experiment in loading a shell? Would they mind getting very, very dirty and greasy?"

Women's entry into other occupations often drew similar cluckings. Sometimes the newspapers would devote a more than routine story to, say, Curtiss-Wright's sending 400 college girls to engineering school for ten months or the California Shipbuilding Corporation teaching women to read blueprints, hitherto presumably an arcane masculine field of knowledge; actually the development of "exploded" blueprints made them accessible to untrained workers, male or female.

The cartoonists had a field day with the presumed humor inherent in women working—at least early in the war, again reflecting society's uneasiness with the situation. The working girls were sometimes portrayed as typical giddy females, as in the cartoon showing two girls loading shells. One says gaily: "This is a lot better than cooking—you just follow the recipe and hear no crack from your husband about it not being like Mother used to make." The husband became the butt of many jokes, the premise being that while his wife was out winning the war, he naturally was assuming her role at home, as in the drawing of the harassed father on the telephone, children crawling about getting into various mischiefs, saying to his wife: "I know your home defense work is important, dear! But someday will you tell the kids what I did to help win the war?" Even if the husband worked, too, his newly working wife had acquired an added aggressiveness, as in the cartoon showing a wife running to work, carrying a lunch bucket, shouting back at her husband, whom she has just bowled over as he came in: "As long as we're on different shifts, you'd better use the back door so this won't happen every morning."

The working mama's relationship to the kids was also altered, as witnessed the cartoon showing two high school girls at the soda fountain, one sighing: "After a date, I can't confide in Mother any more, now that she's on a night shift—and what I'd have to say sounds awfully silly in the daylight." The changed roles of single girls who worked was also a source for some amusement, as in the cartoon of two young girls on the steps of "Mrs. Snitwich's Finishing School for Girls," one bragging: "I flunked in charm and social composure, but I passed in welding and riveting!" This same young girl on the job would say, as the cartoonist had it: "That new foreman is simply divine—you've no idea how thrilling he is when he takes your hand in his, looks dreamily into your eyes and murmurs: 'Baby you're the best little drill-press operator in town!'"

In the movies, the traditional boy-meets-girl, boy-loses-girl-through-misunderstanding, misunderstanding-cleared-up, boy-gets-girl plot was transplanted to the contemporary scene as in the 1942 musical *Priorities on Parade*. In the end boy gets lady welder—who turns out to be attractive after all, but not before he is put off by her seeming mannishness and she is subjected to kidding by various types who think women workers are creeps.

The "amazon image" of the lady war worker was not confined to movie plots. A Norman Rockwell *Saturday Evening Post* cover showed a lady war worker displaying her bulging biceps. The pundit Max Lerner, writing in the leftist tabloid *PM,* ruminated about what he called "The New Amazons." "The traditional maidenly modesty," Lerner wrote in early 1943, "is showing signs of cracking. A group of girls coming out of a war factory behaves very much like a gang of young fellows." He recalled a dispatch from New London describing lady welders on submarines who "dressed in their working clothes . . . scarcely can be distinguished from men," and a report on the women of Mobile, Alabama, where "there is a new type of tough girl emerging, although still in a minority; she can outdrink, outswear, outswagger the men. Does this mean," ponders Lerner, "we must prepare for the new Amazons? Who knows? Certainly there are signs that the medieval court-of-love woman, whose type still is dominant in our day, is doomed."

If some women war workers' behavior gave rise to comparison with Amazons, what of the idea of women soldiers and sailors? Questions such as how to train, equip, and employ the ladies were debated in Congress when the bill creating the WAAC (Women's Army Auxiliary Corps; later, symbolically, the "Auxiliary" was dropped) was passed. A Washington reporter solemnly printed the protest of a soldier to his girl, who wanted to join the WAC: "I won't have a girl of mine called a WAC." When the girl defended the name, the soldier said firmly: "All right, you can be a WAC, but you won't be mine."

At Fort Des Moines, where the WAC's were to train, there were worries about their care and feeding. The mess sergeant after much thought gulped up this basic truth about the female gender: "My observations are that women are much daintier eaters than men."

When the bill authorizing a Navy equivalent of the WAC, called WAVES, was before the House, Representative Beverly M. Vincent of Kentucky affirmed the old-fashioned Southern view of womanhood as God's creatures "made close to the angels." He scoffed at the theory that the WAVES would release male personnel for sea duty, saying that girls would be more interested in "putting on lipstick and looking in mirrors" than doing any work. He criticized spending the $200 it would cost to provide uniforms for each recruit and pounced on the Navy's suggestion that some WAVES would be used in the culinary services: "Why, bless you, do you not know that they are not going to spend $200 to dress up a girl and then put her in the kitchen?"

In the end these service women performed rather unglamorous and circumscribed tasks, usually far behind the lines. A revised version of a

World War I song, often sung on troop trains at the appearance of a WAC or WAVE, reflected the ambivalent male attitude toward the idea of women as soldiers:

> The WAC's and WAVES will win the war, parley vous
> The WAC's and WAVES will win the war, parley vous.
> The WAC's and WAVES will win the war,
> So what the hell are we fighting for?
> Hinky dinky parley vous.

But the plant manager, faced with a labor shortage, desperately in need of workers, and trying to meet his production schedule, harbored no such ambivalence. There were only a few firms that refused to hire women or were reluctant about it. Even the conservative Ford Motor Company, which in all its history had employed women only in clerical jobs, had a work force made up of 40 percent women at the Willow Run plant. As manpower became scarcer, there were no more worries about whether women could do the job, for the women had proved they could—so well, in fact, that a poll of manufacturing plant managers revealed more than 60 percent of them regarded their women workers as capable of producing as much as or more than their male workers could in the same job.

War plants actively recruited women. In Bridgeport, Connecticut, for example, 5,000 additional women were sought by one ordnance plant in an all-out campaign which featured the slogan "If you can drive a car you can run a machine." The steel industry, which offered some of the toughest jobs of all but which had a tradition of hiring minority groups that other industries would not—hence its high percentage of Negroes—opened its gates to women. Coal mining also drew women, although they worked aboveground. Women made up about 12 percent of the work force in the shipyards and 40 percent in aircraft assembly plants. They were popular workers in ordnance plants; in many they made up more than half the work force. And in other industries the percentages were even higher—such as the barrage balloon factory which employed more than 90 percent women and the Sylvania Electric Company assembly lines for tubes used in the VT proximity fuzes, which depended entirely on women on the theory that the greater dexterity of their smaller fingers were better adapted than men's to assembling the tiny tubes.

The war industries found many jobs in which women could perform better than men. In the aircraft factories, small women could squeeze into the tight places necessary to welding jobs (dwarfs and midgets were also used). Women had always found a place in the canning and other food-processing industries, and they were especially in demand in the powdered egg industry because they were skilled at deftly breaking open an egg and sniffing it for rottenness before allowing it to enter the dehydration process. Women, so the assumption was, were better at a host of repetitious, minute and monotonous tasks which men bridled at and did not perform efficiently.

Even the traditionally feminine skills were sometimes transferable intact to war production. One plant needed some precision filing done on refined instruments. The foreman had the idea of sending out a call for all former manicurists working in the plant; the girls were able to file the delicate instruments just as skillfully as they had their customers' nails.

True, women required some special coddling—special in the sense that management hadn't needed to accord it to male workers—in the form of clean, more attractive rest rooms, added medical facilities, special laborsaving machines adapted to their smaller stature, and day-care facilities for young children.

Although women were probably more conscientious about coming to work than many men, at the same time women workers tended to have a higher rate of absenteeism. Much of this was unavoidable, for the working woman found it difficult to keep house and put in a full day's work. Marketing was a problem because stores might not be open when she came off the swing shift at midnight. Or, especially in war-boom towns with swollen populations, stores would often run out of commodities, especially meat, and if one wasn't there at a certain time, one ended up with no food for the children. So women took days off for shopping, or to clean house, or because a child was sick, or for a variety of reasons related to their domestic responsibilities.

If the exigencies of war demanded women do men's work, it followed, then, that women should receive equal pay for equal work. This indeed became national policy on November 25, 1942, when the War Labor Board issued an order allowing employers to raise women's wages as much as was necessary to bring them in line with men's. In the automotive industry, for example, women's base hourly rates were immediately hiked an average of 20 cents. Nevertheless, the order never penetrated to many smaller concerns, and the average female production worker still made about 40 percent less per week than did her male counterpart. (The average weekly earnings of female production workers in twenty-five manufacturing industries in July, 1946, were $33.70, compared with $50.78 for men; during the war the discrepancy was somewhat less, hence the 40 percent figure above.) This differential was due to a variety of reasons. Women, generally, had accumulated less seniority, so were working in lower pay grades. Their lack of seniority also made it difficult for them to be upgraded and meant that women were in the last-hired, first-fired category. In 1944 twice as many women were laid off as men. Some companies maintained separate seniority lists for women.

Another way to evade the equal-work, equal-pay policy was by classifying certain jobs, normally done by men but now filled by women, as "women's jobs" and paying commensurately less. There were also discriminatory differentials in base rates in incentive systems and in hiring rates; also, where incentive bonuses were in effect, women might continue to be paid on straight hourly rates. The government's implementation of its policy was less than forceful, and the unions often did not insist in their contract demands upon upgrading policies for women. So the contemporary joke—"Remember when women had to get married to get men's wages?"—was not entirely apt.

Contrary to the doomsayers, the woman who did equal work, whether equally paid or not, did not become identical with the man with whom she achieved equality. Some of the girls might tend to dress like men they worked beside, but the majority clung to their femininity in the teeth of the basically antifeminine demands of the factory. Most women war workers dressed practically in slacks or slack suits and low-heeled shoes and wore turbans or bandannas on their heads to tie up their hair.

During the uniform craze of 1942, when the nation was engaged in hectic debate over the design of the uniforms for various women's civilian and armed services organizations, several large factories summoned (with a fanfare of publicity) leading designers to suggest attractive and safe outfits for their girls. Lily Daché whipped up helmets and turbans for Douglas and United Aircraft and Sperry Gyroscope, while another chic designer, Vera Maxwell, was responsible for the coveralls for the Sperry girls. The coveralls were made up according to thirty-one different specifications arrived at after lengthy deliberations among plant officials, safety engineers and the workers.

But such outfits were the exception, and most factories made no effort to provide their girls with glamorous uniforms. Let them interfere, however, in what the girls themselves wanted to wear and they were buying trouble. That was the experience of the Vought-Sikorsky Aircraft Corporation when it sent home fifty-three girls for wearing sweaters on the job. Management explained that sweaters were *verboten* on "moral" grounds, *i.e.,* too sexy, and said the girls should wear slack suits. The United Auto Workers local countered that girls in the office wore sweaters, so why were they immoral in the factory and not in the office?

The bosom question heaved and swelled all out of proportion, and management changed its tack, saying that sweaters were banned for safety reasons and bringing in the National Safety Council to testify that sweaters caught fire easily because they attracted static electricity and also, if snarled in machinery, they did not rip like cloth and hence were more likely to pull the wearer's limb in after them. Ann Sheridan, the "Oomph girl," entered the dispute and said that sweaters per se weren't bad; however, a little girl in a big sweater might be a safety hazard, while a big girl in a small sweater might be a moral hazard. The Conciliation Service of the Labor Department finally had to intervene.

The danger that the long, peekaboo hairstyles popularized by Veronica Lake might be ensnared in the machinery also worried responsible officials. It was estimated somehow that about 20,000 girls in war plants were dangling their peekaboo side dangerously close to machinery every day. An appeal was dispatched to Paramount Pictures, home of Miss Lake, that she make the requisite publicity sacrifice for the war effort. Miss Lake patriotically adopted an upswept hairstyle and watched her career promptly go into an eclipse.

Those Jeremiahs who feared that once war had given her a large foothold into industry, the American woman would stay there had cause for alarm in the poll of lady members of the UAW in which 85 percent of them said they would like to continue working after the war. Similar surveys of West Coast shipyard and aircraft assembly workers elicited identical sentiments. Such intentions gave many thinkers a severe case of the postwar jitters laced with strong doses of Depression psychology. In any event during the second half of 1945 more than 1,320,000 women were given their walking papers, and the number of women employed declined at a rate twice that of men. From August 15 to September 30 alone, 820,000 workers, of whom 320,000 were women, were laid off. Within a year of V-J Day more than 2,160,000 women had been trimmed from the ranks of the gainfully employed, and the percentage of women in the labor force had dipped from 36 percent to 29 percent.

Recall that in 1940, women composed 25.5 percent of the labor force, so there was still a net increase of about 4 percent after the war. And in terms of women actually employed, the increase was from the prewar 12,000,000 to 16,600,000 by November, 1946. About two-thirds of the women who went to work during the war stayed there. In six wartime years the net gain in percentage of women in the labor force was almost equal to the increase that took place between 1900 and 1940. Out of the total female population, however, there were still 69 percent over age fourteen listed as "housewives" or otherwise not gainfully employed.

Because of voracious wartime manpower needs, those women who did work gave up many of their protections under state labor laws. Such limitations as a maximum eight-hour day and forty-eight-hour week were suspended, and the need for workers generally was so desperate that many of the laws won by labor in the dark ages of the Industrial Revolution were set aside for the emergency.

At the war's inception the major unions had divested themselves of their most fundamental right, the right to strike, and accepted severe limitations on the scope of collective bargaining. Strikes, of course, occurred; most were minor wildcat strikes, but others, like the traumatic bituminous coal strike of 1943–44 and the steel and railroad strikes, brought government intervention.

Perhaps the most painful inhibition placed on labor in the name of wartime necessity was the so-called Little Steel Formula of 1942, laid down by the War Labor Board, which limited all wage increases to 15 percent above a 1941 base for the duration. This limitation became increasingly onerous, and labor chafed under it, its information agencies spewing out a stream of statistics proving that the cost of living had risen not 19 percent, as the government said, but 30 percent, at least.

The government yielded a bit on Little Steel by allowing labor advances through the back door, as it were, while holding the main wall unbreached. Thus, such fringe benefits as portal-to-portal pay, health insurance, pensions and so on were permitted to sweeten wage agreement packages. These sugar tits didn't pacify labor completely but quieted it enough to get through the war. And the labor leaders who met with FDR in late 1941 to offer their services like feudal princes meeting with the king had received in exchange several important beneficences.

For one, their participation in government labor policy at the highest level was ratified, and they were given membership on the War Production Board and other offices. Their role in plant management was resisted, however, by a management jealous of its absolute sovereignty, and the plan of dynamic young Walter Reuther of the United Auto Workers for labor's mutual participation in the operation of war plants (under a labor-management committee system) was ignored. Nevertheless, the conditions of service labor extracted included a labor-management committee, defanged of any power other than consultation and advice but at least giving it a voice in plant operations, especially from the production standpoint.

Most important, labor got the right to include a maintenance of membership clause in employment contracts. (This required that workers join the union after a fifteen-day grace period or lose their jobs.) This was a watered-down closed shop, but the latter, which labor really wanted, was impossible in view of public opposition. (Polls showed that only one American in ten favored the closed shop idea, although it was a cornerstone of labor theology; fewer than three of ten favored the milder union shop.)

A further governmental strengthening of labor's right to organize (even while many of its rights were suspended in wartime) occurred during the famous Montgomery Ward incident in 1944. In essence, Montgomery Ward, which had one of the most conservative managements in the nation, denied the power of the War Labor Board to compel it to recognize a union that had been chosen as bargaining unit for its employees in a duly supervised election. Montgomery Ward claimed a variety of defenses to the WLB, but in essence it was denying the union's right collectively to bargain for its members. If Montgomery Ward didn't want to bargain with the United Retail, Wholesale and Department Store Union, Montgomery Ward insisted, it didn't have to. The government said otherwise, and the nation watched as the government asserted its authority and two husky GI's carried chairman of the board Sewell Avery from his office—and with him any illusions that management's prerogatives in dealing with labor were absolute.

On the whole, labor's forbearance was mighty, in view of members' deep-seated fears about their postwar future, of serious food shortages in war-boom areas where the Office of Price Administration's meat quotas had not been calculated in terms of added population, of rising food prices, of the WLB's 17,000-case backlog representing accumulated worker grievances, and the general decline of those social services most directly affecting working people. Such strikes as there were never crippled the war effort. At worst, the coal strike may have held the steel industry from achieving its maximum production in 1943; still, in that year it set all-time records and produced more than the rest of the world combined. The peak number of man-days lost during the war because of strikes, 13,500,000 in 1943, was less than one-fourth of the number lost through industrial accidents in that year.

In sum, organized labor achieved a measure of security and respect during the war and so gained a permanent place both at the bargaining table and in the shop as a responsible authority for handling a volatile working force under terms of the contract. It also gained in membership; total union membership rose from 8,900,000 in 1940 to 14,800,000 at war's end.

Nevertheless, while organized labor as a whole gained, and real wages for the average industrial worker rose from $28.12 weekly in 1941 to $36.72 in 1944, there were setbacks in laws governing the conditions of labor—setbacks which, of course, weren't entirely due to organized labor's sins, whether of omission or commission. Like a great vacuum cleaner, industry sucked workers into it from every crevice and corner of the society, and if the labor laws in any way got in the way of this flow, they toppled like straw men.

Such was the case with child labor laws. With the drafting of eighteen- and nineteen-year-olds by 1943 and the labor shortage in general, war plants had no scruples about hiring youngsters, and many states suspended their laws for the duration. By 1944 an estimated 3,000,000 young people between the ages of fourteen and seventeen were working. The United States child labor laws, part of the Fair Labor Standards Act of 1938, required that no child under sixteen could be employed in manufacturing, and in dangerous industries, none under eighteen. Still, many youngsters flocked to the boomtowns or entered hometown war industries. A goodly number of these must have been under sixteen, for even though enforcement of the law was weak, between June 30, 1944, and June 30, 1945, 13,289 minors were found illegally employed by the Labor Department's Children's Bureau. This figure was 57.5 percent above the same period in 1943–44 and nearly three times that for 1942–43.

Many working youngsters—perhaps most—filled jobs in drugstores or restaurants, clerked in dime stores, or became pinsetters for bowling alleys or cashiers in supermarkets and the like and so were not subjected to the stresses and hazards of war industry. Still, the results could be anticipated: long hours, night work, accidents, interruption of education (high school enrollment fell off by more than 1,000,000 between 1940 and 1943), and lack of parental supervision and increased juvenile delinquency. These youngsters were perhaps the hidden scandal of the war-worker army. People alternately viewed them with alarm or ignored them; hard-pressed personnel officers continued to hire them, even in violation of the law; and parents of many of them continued to look the other way, if indeed they were around to look at all, and sometimes even encouraged the youthful breadwinners to contribute to the family pot.

To another underemployed group in the country, the relaxation of standards in wartime was a boon. The war gave the Negro worker a considerable entrée into industry. Even with defense demands, however, the hiring of Negroes was slow in coming. Instrumental was the threatened march on Washington in 1941 under the direction of A. Philip Randolph, president of the Brotherhood of Pullman Porters, for the purpose of opening up more jobs for Negroes in defense industries. The situation Randolph and his brothers were protesting was indeed scandalous. In a survey of some 300,000 openings for workers created by defense contracts, it was discovered that well over half were closed to Negroes by company policy. Randolph threatened his march, and the President, urged, it was said, by Mrs. Roosevelt, issued an executive order banning discrimination because of race, creed or color in any industry holding defense contracts and establishing a Fair Employment Practices Commission with powers to investigate complaints but not to compel compliance with its orders.

This helped, but even by September, 1941, 51 percent of all defense jobs were still closed to Negroes. Gradually, however, under government prodding but mainly out of the need for workers, the situation opened up. By 1944 Negroes held 7.5 percent of all the jobs in war industries. This was somewhat less than their proportion of the total population (9.8 percent), but it was an improvement.

Within specific industries the hiring policies varied. The iron and steel foundry and secondary smelting and refining industries had long hired Negroes, and the proportion in these two industries grew to 24.8 percent and 33.6 percent respectively. Even in 1941, shipbuilding was reasonably open to Negroes; more than 190,000 eventually were to find jobs in it, and Negroes made up about 12 percent of all the workers. Such fields as industrial machinery, however, employed only 4.7 percent Negroes at the war's peak; and the high-paying aircraft industry had at most 6.4 percent Negroes on its payrolls. Altogether, the number of Negroes employed in manufacturing increased from 500,000 in 1940 to 1,250,000 in 1944.

Many unions, being discriminatory themselves, were not much help to the Negro worker. The CIO and its affiliates generally fostered equal treatment, upgrading and promotion for the Negro worker, and only a few of its Southern locals were *de facto* segregated. The AFL was a different story. More than twenty-five of its affiliates either excluded Negroes from membership entirely, admitted only a token number while practicing tacit discrimination, or maintained segregated locals for Negro members. Two of the most powerful of such unions were the Machinists and the Boilermakers, who between them represented 30–40 percent of all the aircraft frame workers in the nation and better than one-fifth of the nation's shipyard workers. The Machinists excluded Negroes entirely, while the Boilermakers admitted Negroes to segregated locals but denied them any voice in union policies. (In 1945 the California Supreme Court held that Local 6 of the Boilermakers must cease such discrimination or else the closed shop section of its contract be declared null and void. Such discrimination, the California court declared, was "contrary to the public policy of the United States and this state.")

Among the unaffiliated unions, the railway brotherhoods excluded Negroes by a provision written into their constitutions. Of the thirty-one national unions discriminating by either rules or practice against Negroes, nineteen were in the railroad industry. Yet one-fifth of the 1,500,000 railroad workers were Negroes. The FEPC fought this discrimination as best it could, finally, in 1943, issuing a directive to twenty railroads and seven unions in the Southeastern states that were party to a 1941 secret agreement excluding Negroes that they must cease discrimination; however, only four of the railroads complied. The others—and the unions—ignored the order. The Supreme Court, in another case, ruled that under the Railway Labor Act such pacts were null and void.

Aided by the informal efforts of the FEPC, Negro railroad employees made other small gains. For the first time Negro car cleaners became eligible for promotion to carmen's helpers and Negro dining car waiters could be promoted to dining car stewards' jobs.

In other industries, however, upgrading of Negro workers was a festering sore, largely because of the hostility to it by their fellow white workers. When the Philadelphia Transit Company, at the behest of the FEPC, upgraded eight Negro porters to drivers, the company union, which had recently lost a bargaining election to the Transport Workers Union, called a strike, whose main animus was race hate. Holding the strike illegal and that the national interest dictated that Negroes be used as drivers in view of the acute manpower shortage, the President ordered the U.S. Army to take control of the company, and the strikers returned to work. The company union leaders who called the strike were later indicted by a grand jury; the TWU signed a contract giving the members pay raises and other benefits, and the eight Negro operators were kept on.

White workers, especially those in the South, resented upgrading because it would at worst put Negroes over them or bring them into closer association with Negroes. These resentments cropped up in many industries whenever Negroes were given jobs for which they had traditionally not been eligible.

In Washington, in another instance involving a transit system, local Negroes demonstrated against the streetcar company because it would not hire Negro conductors and motormen. The company surveyed its white employees and found that if they did hire them, most of the whites would quit. They didn't mind having colored men in jobs that could be all colored. It was the mixing that whites resented. The streetcar employees were overwhelmingly Virginians or old Washingtonians. This was the Southern Washington, a town where a Negro diplomat couldn't stay at a good hotel and where, on the streetcars, Negroes and whites rode on an equal plane until the cars crossed over into Virginia, at which point all Negroes had to move to the back of the car.

War industry also enabled some Negroes to break free of their semi-indentured condition as sharecroppers in the South. An estimated 700,000 Negroes migrated across state lines in search of work during the war; of these, 400,000 left the South, about half going West to the Coast and the rest to the East Coast and Middle West. The number of Negroes in the South who were tenant farmers dropped from 74.5 percent to 72.4 percent, and the number of sharecroppers dropped from 44 percent to 39.8 percent. Surveys showed that the largest increases in Negro population took place in the war-boom areas off Detroit–Willow Run, Hampton Roads, Los Angeles, San Francisco and Mobile, Alabama. This migration was not nearly as great as that which had taken place during World War I, however.

In wages, too, many Negroes had an upgrading during the war. In 1940 the average Negro urban worker made $457 a year, while his white counterpart made $1,064 per year. A survey of 2,000 industrial workers in 1944 showed that the average Negro worker was making $37.77* a

---

* About the same as the average female worker.

week, or about $1,976 per year, while the average white worker was making nearly $50 a week, or $2,600 a year. These Negro workers, of course, were among the highest paid in their race; still, the figures show they had closed the gap somewhat with white workers. However, their lack of seniority and the discriminatory policies which prevented upgrading kept their wages well below what the average white worker could expect.

The reluctance to hire Negroes in many war industries also indirectly contributed to social problems. For example, in Mobile, the shipyards often discriminated against local Negroes and instead imported Southern whites, swelling the population beyond the capacity of the city to handle it and fueling racial tensions. The Mobile race riots of 1943 were the result of company upgrading of Negro workers, which the Southern whites bitterly resented; labor union circles accused the shipyard management of deliberately fomenting trouble so that it would not have to upgrade its Negro workers.

War gave the Negro woman a chance to get out of the domestic service field to which she had traditionally been confined. Employment of Negro women in manufacturing leaped from 50,000 in 1940 to 300,000 four years later. There was a concomitant opening up of white-collar jobs to the Negro woman, an area from which she had been completely barred in the prewar years. But while eventually 100,000 Negroes secured such jobs, they represented only about 1 out of every 30, compared with the 1 in 3 white girls who held white-collar jobs as secretaries, sales clerks, switchboard operators and the like, As a result of this opening of doors to Negro women, the number of all women in domestic work dropped 20.4 percent between 1940 and 1944—the only category of women's employment so to decrease.

This caused great hardship among Southern ladies used to domestic help for $2 a week. So unhinged did some become that they believed in the existence of so-called Eleanor Clubs. These Eleanor Clubs, whose existence was totally the figment of some rumormonger's imagination, were supposed to be encouraging rebellion among the colored maids. They had been established by Eleanor Roosevelt, who, it was well known, actually entertained Nigras at White House social functions.

So the uprising level of general prosperity elevated the Negro like everyone else—only not so much. Some might point out, too, that in reality it merely restored him to his position before the Depression. In the last boom year of 1929, 1,024,656 Negroes or 7.3 percent of the total, had decent-paying jobs in manufacturing and mechanical occupations. By 1940 this total had fallen to 657,933, or 5.2 percent, meaning 400,000 Negroes had lost industrial jobs. Then came the war, and a peak of 1,350,000—8 percent—was working in this field. Yet in terms of the Negro's percentage share of the total job "pie," the gain was only .7 percent.

And at war's end the "last-hired, first-fired" principle continued to plague the Negro worker. Layoffs were swift and drastic immediately following V-J Day. A spot survey of ten major cities taken by the Urban League revealed that 135,000 Negro workers had been laid off by industry. In the privately owned shipbuilding industry, which had employed nearly 200,000 Negroes in the peak years, only 10,000 remained in 1946. Of course, as peacetime production began to heat up, in certain labor shortage areas—*e.g.,* the Detroit auto industry—Negroes were taken back on, but the great majority—as many as 90 percent—were hired in an unskilled or semiskilled capacity, and the United Auto Workers stated that there was "continued sharp discrimination against Negroes in promotion and upgradings." The postwar era is beyond the scope of this book, but by 1946 discrimination against Negroes (and Mexicans, Nisei and Jews) was on the upswing. Symbolic of this was the assassination of FEPC by the Southern-Republican coalition in Congress. Many Negroes were better off after the war, but discrimination was still widespread and in some areas, absolute.

As for the other new workers added to the labor force, they came in all varieties. There were aged and retired people, some brought back because they had skills that mass production had caused to be forgotten. Such were the retired ship carpenters who had worked on wooden ships and who were needed by a Maine shipyard with a contract for wooden minesweepers. No one in the present generation of workers, accustomed to steel bottoms, knew how to use an adz. So this shipyard found about 100 of the old boys, now working as farmers, lobster fishermen, or simply sitting around, whittling, and brought them back to work. The youngest was in his sixties, and the oldest was eighty-four.

Handicapped workers took a new lease on life in war industries. A War Manpower Commission survey showed that there were nearly 200,000 placements of handicapped workers in 1943, compared with only 27,703 in 1940. These could perform many jobs; blind workers—to give just one example—sorted the sweepings in airplane plants to salvage the rivets and were able to distinguish by touch among the eight kinds used.

Another source was ex-convicts, whom employers were traditionally reluctant to hire. And as the war drew on, another increasing source of labor appeared: disabled veterans discharged from the services. One tool manufacturer, eying his labor shortage, had hired several in the spring of 1943. He told John Dos Passos that "In the long run [he] expected that to be the most important part" of his new worker supply.

VI

WILL THIS
PICTURE HELP
WIN THE WAR?

Following Pearl Harbor one of the first reflexive gestures of Hollywood was a rush to copyright topical titles. Rights were prudently reserved to *Sunday in Hawaii, Wings over the Pacific, Pearl Harbor Pearls, Bombing of Honolulu, Remember Pearl Harbor, Aloha Oe, Yellow Peril, Yellow Menace, Spy Smashers, Spy Swatters* and *The Stolen Bombsight* —not to mention *My Four Years in Japan,* and the greatest trademark of them all, *V for Victory.* MGM, finding itself with *I'll Take Manila,* an Eleanor Powell musical, on its hands, searched wildly for a new title, while Twentieth Century was congratulating itself on having *Secret Agent of Japan* ready for the cameras. Paramount hurriedly canceled *Absent Without Leave,* about an AWOL GI.

The anxiety and gloom in the early months of the war made Pearl Harbor as subject matter something best forgotten. Thus, in the Humphrey Bogart espionage picture *Across the Pacific,* based on a prewar *Saturday Evening Post* story, "Aloha Means Good Bye," about a plot of the Japanese to bomb Pearl Harbor, the locale was changed to the Panama Canal because, as Charles Einfield, director of advertising and publicity at Warner Brothers, said: "we felt it wise to leave Pearl Harbor out of it, for all this can do is remind us of defeat." It was not until March, 1942, in *A Yank on the Burma Road* that an actor first denounced Japanese perfidy at Pearl Harbor.

"Because of the war," reported the New York *Times* in early

1942, "prospects for the coming year are thoroughly confused and predictions by film executives consist of tentative and often contradictory generalities. On the one hand studios have feverishly announced pictures about conflict, on the other, studios have abandoned war stories and decided that pure escapism will be the only acceptable alternative. As a third alternative [*sic*]—and one which has emerged in England during the last year—factual treatment of war scenes and activities in documentary presents a new avenue of endeavor." Even as Paramount shelved production of Somerset Maugham's novel *The Hour Before Dawn* because of its war theme, it was rushing into production *Wake Island*.

Along with the rest of the West Coast, Hollywood was swept by rumors of imminent Japanese bombing raids. World premieres with flashing searchlights were banned, but one resourceful showman had Grauman's Chinese covered with translucent paint that glowed discreetly under ultraviolet light and provided a tent at the entrance to shield reporters' flashbulbs. Along Wilshire Boulevard stood a row of odd-looking concrete igloos of various shapes and sizes, with a sign announcing BOMB SHELTERS FOR SALE. The resemblance of several of the studios to nearby aircraft plants was an immediate cause for anxiety, and to forestall a fleet of Jap planes from mistaking the Warner Brothers lot in Burbank for the Lockheed plant nearby, Jack Warner had his set painters inscribe a 20-foot arrow on the roof of a sound stage pointing toward Lockheed and in large letters: LOCKHEED—THATAWAY.

Most of the studios erected sandbag air raid shelters on the lot, equipped with playing cards, dominoes, dart games, pianos and jukeboxes. At some studios there were separate but unequal shelters for executives and stars and technicians and extras. And all these civil defense preparations did not reach such proportions that the really important things were forgotten. A Warner Brothers executive, when asked about an early air raid drill at the studio, replied: "Oh, it was a big success. The *Life* photographers were there and got swell pictures."

Hollywood's yachtsmen turned over the entire Hollywood fleet to the Coast Guard while the Army commandeered an arsenal of guns used in Western pictures. Because of the vulnerability of the Los Angeles water supply system, with its shallow mains and exposed aqueducts leading down from the mountains, owners of swimming pools were required to keep them filled at all times as reservoirs. Air raid spotting was popular, and some of the more elegant wardens entertained their friends on their roofs, keeping an eye cocked for enemy planes while spending a convivial evening. Studio wives and starlets alike signed up for war work, especially with the Red Cross and American Women's Voluntary Service, whose uniforms were considered the most attractive. And when the Hollywood Canteen was started under its hard-driving president Bette Davis, stars and studio executives alike donated their time as hostesses and dishwashers.

As Hollywood's citizens fanned out on the home front, others were volunteering more directly for the fight, and milestones began appearing in *Variety* and the fan magazines:

"Aged 37, Henry Fonda enlisted on the sly, not even notifying his press agent."

"Jimmy Stewart a year ago quietly fattened himself to meet Army physical requirements, and when he had put on 10 pounds bade farewell to Louis B. Mayer and without any fanfare became Private (now Second Lieutenant) James Stewart."

"Bob Cummings' own glorious story of why he's leaving the screen. . . . He wants to get going. He wants to have a hand in beating the living daylights out of the Nazis and the Japs and all the rest of the gang who because Uncle Sam is at heart a peace-loving old gent have had the effrontery to go to war against him. He is a typical American, Bob is, easy going, careless of his privileges until he finds them threatened; tolerant of the other fellow's vices until he is hit below the belt. And when he is mad, he knows how to fight."

Clark Gable went in in early 1942, still mourning the death of his wife, Carole Lombard, in a plane crash while returning from a bond tour, and a solemn debate was touched off whether or not actors were more valuable acting (and paying big taxes) or going to war. Wrote one reporter: "Clark Gable shouldn't be *allowed* to be a soldier. War is too serious for us to be playing sentimental games. He has a duty and Hollywood has a duty and they should be made to stick to it." The Selective Service System ruled that motion pictures were an essential industry (provoking the Screen Actors Guild to announce it wanted no such favored status). In any case, by October, 1942, 2,700 men and women from the motion-picture industry, or 12 percent of the total number employed at the start of the year, had entered the armed forces.

The first inkling that movies could also do their part came with President Roosevelt's statement in December, 1941, that "The American motion picture is one of our most effective mediums in informing and entertaining our citizens." He also laid to rest the question of censorship, at least in broad terms, saying: "The motion picture must remain free insofar as national security will permit. I want no censorship of the motion picture."

In mid-January, 1942, Lowell Mellett, newly appointed by the President as Coordinator of Motion Pictures, arrived in Hollywood for a meeting with the industry's War Activities Committee, which had been formed to mesh the industry's production with government requests. His office was directly empowered by the President to serve as a sort of clearinghouse through which all films produced by government agencies for civilian distribution were to pass. It was also instructed to produce and distribute films of its own designed to inform the public about the war and to consult with other government agencies about their films. Finally, his office was to act as liaison between the federal government and Hollywood, consulting and advising with motion-picture producers on the best ways in which they could serve the war effort.

If FDR had affirmed the principle of freedom of the screen, the beast of some kind of government control of the motion pictures was still omnipresent. But the wolf, if wolf it was, came in lamb's clothing in the gray, wispy, frail-looking person of Mr. Mellett, whose speech to the executive royalty of Hollywood was mildly admonitory and mostly conciliatory. Stating that he believed "freedom of the screen is as important as freedom of press or of speech," he threw the film makers a nice bouquet: "We are hoping that most of you and your fellow workers will stay right here in Hollywood and keep on doing what you're doing because your motion pictures are a vital contribution to the total defense effort."

Mellett also bestowed a belated garland of praise on those film makers who had made anti-Nazi pictures before the war: "Whether it was foresight, intuition or instinct, you saw what was happening in the world. You couldn't have done more in your efforts to educate people. The government, of course, was pleased but we were unable to advertise what you were doing. Some misguided people in the Senate advertised the job you did, however. . . . Now nobody is concerned if the government frankly engages in such cooperation. Now we can help you in your work."

Mellett's allusion to the "misguided people in the Senate" referred to Senators Gerald P. Nye of North Dakota and Burton K. Wheeler of Montana, the isolationist Republican and Democrat who conducted an investigation in 1941 into what they branded as the prowar, prointerventionist, pro-British propaganda in Hollywood movies. Warned Senator

Nye darkly in one speech: "At least 20 pictures have been produced in the last year all designed to drug the reason of the American people, set aflame their emotions, turn their hatred into a blaze, fill them with fear that Hitler will come over here and capture them, that he will steal their trade. . . . [The movies] have become the most gigantic engines of propaganda in existence to rouse war fever in America and plunge the Nation to her destruction." The Senator went on to list the heads of the film companies, many of whom bore Jewish names, saying that "in each of these companies there are a number of production directors, many of whom have come from Russia, Hungary, Germany, and the Balkan countries. . . . Why do they do this? Well, because they are interested in foreign causes. . . . Go to Hollywood. It is a raging volcano of war fever. The place swarms with refugees. It also swarms with British actors."

One of these British actors, Douglas Fairbanks, Jr., who was indeed interested in furthering his country's cause in the United States, had written a letter to the President, whom he knew, complaining about pressure from another source. Joseph P. Kennedy, the ambassador to the Court of St. James's, had met with a group of studio heads for three hours, in December, 1940, and, as a former movie executive as well as a political figure, expressed his views on anti-German movies. (Fairbanks admitted he was not at the meeting but said he got identical reports of what was said from four people who were present.)

"[Joseph Kennedy] apparently threw the fear of God into many of our producers and executives by telling them that the Jews were on the spot, and that they should stop making anti-Nazi pictures or using the film medium to promote or show sympathy to the cause of the 'democracies' versus the 'dictators.' He said that anti-semitism was growing in Britain and that the Jews were being blamed for the war. . . . He went on to state definitely that the Catholic Church wanted peace at any cost as the only means of bringing people back to the churches. . . . He repeated very forcefully that there was no reason for our ever becoming involved in *any way.*" Fairbanks protested strongly against this pressure and reiterated his own feeling that the United States should give all possible aid to his homeland.

Though Nye and Wheeler were able to find any movie that had war and British characters in it (*e.g., That Hamilton Woman,* a film about Lord Nelson) to be automatically in favor of the United States' declaring war on Hitler at once, there were, of course, some openly anti-Nazi films made during the period, of which the most trenchant and angry was *Confessions of a Nazi Spy,* produced by Warner Brothers and released in 1939. The movie left no doubt of Hitler's blueprint for conquest and posited an unholy alliance of German Bundists and spies working to undermine this country. The isolationists' vendetta culminated in hearings before a Senate subcommittee, with Wendell Willkie ably defending the movie industry by making free speech the issue.

Actually, belligerently anti-Nazi films such as *Confessions of a Nazi Spy, The Mortal Storm,* and *Escape* did not do too well at the box office. "Preparedness" pictures such as *Flight Command* and *I Wanted Wings* did a little better. But Universal hit the jackpot in February, 1941, by treating the whole peacetime draft as a laughing matter. Two comics named Bud Abbott and Lou Costello were a smash in *Buck Privates,* which they quickly followed with *In the Navy,* becoming the leading box-office attraction of that year.

Certainly Nazi propaganda was not unrepresented in this country. A German film called *Sieg im Westen* ("Victory in the West") was playing in the Yorkville district of Manhattan in May, 1941. Arch Mercey, Mellett's assistant at his then post as head of the Office of Government Reports, wrote to his chief that "the applause in the theatre is amazing. Hitler naturally enough draws the most applause, but there is plenty for the parachutists, dive bomb pilots and advance guards."

The government's own prowar film program was practically nonexistent. A total of twenty-five government films were made in all 1941. Reluctant to give up valuable screen time to government films, the movie industry refused to distribute any Office of Government Reports films on national defense that were more than three minutes in length. Although it promised it would not interfere in the content of these shorts, the Motion Picture Committee Cooperating for National Defense insisted on seeing the outline and the narration of each picture before completion and on setting up its judgment on what should or should not be released. Reported Mercey to his chief: "The Committee is exercising a censorial power over the government at the moment."

Now, in wartime, the roles were reversed. The government was assuming new powers over the entire country, and the movie business was just another war industry eager to cooperate out of fear that it would be considered "non-essential" and strangled by lack of priorities. FDR's promise of no censorship was not given cynically, but never in our history was the government to assume, albeit temporarily, such tacit power over a medium of mass communication.

Immediately after Pearl Harbor, movie attendance took a rollercoaster ride downward. People preferred to stay at home, especially during the anxious days immediately following December 7, when blackouts were in effect, when air raids seemed imminent and when everybody sat around his radio listening for news or reassurance from Washington. But by Christmas business was picking up again. When *Mrs. Miniver* appeared in early 1942, with its message of direct involvement in the war by the home folks, it become the leading box-office grosser of the year.

Hollywood slowly settled into a wartime routine. The dimout came to Hollywood—and brought out a host of walkers come to gape at the darkened streets. Hollywood Boulevard, dimmed out, was deserted between twelve and four in the morning. The Brown Derby had brown blackout paint on its windows. After four, the swing shift workers were on the streets window-shopping or patronizing the few all-night movies and restaurants.

Photoplay magazine reported: "Guess what the Hollywood girls are doing these evenings with so many eligible men at the wars? They are banding in little groups and doing the night spots together. T'other eve, Phyllis Brooks, Carole Landis and Arline Judge made the rounds as a threesome and had a grand time!" Liquor shortage? "If you were privileged to be behind the bar after ordering a highball," noted a *Daily Variety* observer, "you'd see the spirits come pouring out of a thimble."

The patriotic necessity for a star to be seen in deglamorized dress doing war work quickly communicated itself to the public relations profession. *Daily Variety* reported the new technique for building up a female star:

> No longer are actresses pictured as leisurely, luxury loving dolls. Today's femme star or player is as virile as the men—shown washing dishes in canteens, sweeping, hefting five-gallon coffee cans, doing hundreds of other things to prove she can take it, that she's doing her share in the war effort. Jewels, clothes, luxury are out—screenlady today is war conscious . . . minimize theatrical qualities, magnify human attributes. Factual publicity comes into its own.

How factual it would be remained open to question; but certainly the style had changed. Jane Russell, after being selected with much fanfare for the female lead in Howard Hughes' *The Outlaw,* was kept amply in the public eye for two years by PR genius Russell Birdwell, even though she had never been seen on the screen before, while the movie was shot and reshot, at the behest of the Hays Office. In addition to a famous photo of busty Jane lolling against a haystack, which was one of the most popular GI pinups, a typical spread in a national magazine would show her in the following *mise-en-scènes:*

Falling asleep after a day at the Navy recruiting station.

Artist James Montgomery Flagg sketching her.

Her selection as "the girl that parachutists prefer to be up in the air with."

"A training school plane unit is named Russell's Raiders."

"She gives a demonstration of what not to do in traffic."

"Five sailors tell Jane she's their favorite in any port."

"Jane is a pinup girl in dozens of Army camps. Here Private Albert Goertz, attached to a San Francisco anti-aircraft unit, knits a sweater for her. His progress is slow, as his tentmates have jealously been hiding his needles."

With male stars the publicity problem was more elemental. It boiled down to: Why ain't he in the Army? Or, as *Daily Variety* put it: "No more he-man build up of young men as in the past, for these might kick back unpleasant reverberations. If the build up is too mighty, public may want to know if he's that good why he isn't in the Army shooting Japs and Nazis. This is a particularly touchy phase and p-r has to be subtle about it."

The principal war work in Hollywood beyond making movies was still show business as usual: entertaining troops and defense workers, selling War Bonds, and appearing gratis in government or industry film trailers and radio shows and exhorting people to do a large variety of things deemed necessary to winning the war, ranging from saving fats to paying their income taxes.

Dorothy Lamour, whether clad in her sarong or in mufti, played a starring role in the various bond drives. She was credited with selling $350,000,000 in bonds. Hedy Lamarr dispensed kisses to buyers of $25,000 bonds; one man was so emotionally overwrought when his actual moment of ecstasy came that he fainted before he could collect.

In the first big War Bond drive in September, 1942, Hollywood went all out with a Stars over America "bond blitz." Three hundred and thirty-seven actors and actresses participated, working eighteen hours a day and taking punishment from the mobs that greeted them. There were casualties. Carole Lombard had been lost in a plane crash in

January, 1942, on an earlier tour. Greer Garson collapsed from nervous exhaustion; Bette Davis had to convalesce when it was over; Rita Hayworth quit in the middle from exhaustion. The 1942 drive sold $838,540,000 worth of bonds, against a quota of $775,000,000 for the industry, representing one-sixth of the total sold. In all, Hollywood stars made a total of seven tours, covering 300 cities and towns. Free movie days were held, the admission price a bond.

Entertainers were sent out to camps in the United States and lonely outposts all over the globe and right up to the front line. Under the direction of the Hollywood Victory Committee, 6,810 artists from Hollywood traveled 5,237,000 miles to entertain GI's. At least two commercial movies, *Follow the Boys* and *Three Jills in a Jeep,* told Americans about this in considerable and heartwarming detail, lest they forget.

By mid-1942, the governmental machinery for regulating the movies was getting into high gear. On May 6 the War Production Board issued an order setting a maximum limit of $5,000 per picture on new materials used in building sets. The WPB's Order L-178 froze raw stock (unprocessed film). Thenceforth, the basic stuff of Hollywood, the film used in the camera, was subject to WPB allocation. Although cellulose, the basic component of raw stock, was needed to make gunpowder, the real cause of the shortage was the increased needs of the Army and Navy and the other branches of the government, which had stepped up their filmmaking enormously and which, of course, took priority.

On October 27, legislation freezing wages was announced to take effect on January 1, 1943. Economic Director James F. Byrnes issued an order to limit salaries to $25,000 a year beginning January 1, 1943. With allowable expenses, this meant a gross salary maximum of $67,000. Hollywood was thrown into a panic, and loud noises reverberated in Holmby Hills. That national institution Louis B. Mayer's salary, always admiringly reported annually ($949,766 for 1941), was threatened, as well as the earnings of most of the top stars, directors, producers and writers. The battle cry became "Why work?" After you reached the limit, the studio couldn't pay you, and the profits therefrom, upon which the company paid a 40 percent corporate profits tax, were retained by it. So you had the choice of either working for nothing with the fruits of your labors divided among the studio, the stockholders and the United States—fat chance—or laying off, or, in the case of males, going into the service and postponing all taxes for the duration. No longer could a star work lucratively in both radio and films; he had to choose one or the other, and little of that. Fortunately, however, Congress soon repealed the measure. (In 1944, 250 Hollywood employees were making more than $100,000 a year, and 50 were in the $200,000-plus bracket.)

The cut in film stock meant in practice that Hollywood would be getting about 25 percent less film than in prewar days. Samuel Goldwyn predicted that a motion-picture shortage was definitely in the offing, and he advised studios to make pictures as fast as possible while film—and actors—lasted. From other quarters, there was a cry for fewer pictures, and specifically the end of the double feature system which had been under fire for years from theater owners who felt they were being bludgeoned into taking inferior B pictures in order to stay in business—*i.e.,* they had to run double features in order to compete with other theaters that did so, whether they liked it or not. A Gallup Poll showed that 71 percent of the people asked would gladly give up double features for the duration, but a hard core of moviegoers concentrated among teen-agers and people in the lower economic classes favored them, and this group bought a disproportionate number of tickets. Ultimately nobody had the courage to deny good Americans, especially those of voting age, the right to set their minds adrift for a few hours in a movie house.

The predicted film shortage did not develop, however. Although the total number of films released declined from 533 in 1942 to 377 in 1945, there was never any want of them. Much credit for this goes to the conservation measures the industry put into effect and adhered to. Scenes were rehearsed before shooting was done, cutting down the number of retakes. Credits prior to the film were reduced and advertising trailers eliminated. Single takes were the rule for rushes, stills instead of movies were used for wardrobe and other tests, and reprinting of approved takes was eliminated.

Set restrictions were met by the infinite ingenuity of the Hollywood technicians. Scriptwriters included as few different backgrounds as possible. Since the expenditure limitations applied only to new materials, savings were effected by reusing reclaimed materials. Even nails were straightened and used again, for the 8- and 18-penny sizes were needed for war plant construction. Wood was conserved by substituting sets made of canvas painted to resemble wood. Signs warning employees to save materials in order to preserve their jobs became commonplace. (Film scripts were often stamped with the exhortation SAVE PAPER. SAVE YOUR JOB.) The customary use of aluminum and metal was out. Certain paints, including pigments used in makeup, were scarce. Underwater photography was banned because the rubber cables used for the cameras were not to be had. (To help the war effort, Cecil B. De Mille even donated the much-publicized rubber squid used in *Reap the Wild Wind.*)

Shortages of other materials also caused problems. Scarcity of razor blades was a major annoyance because they were used in cutting films. Sugar rationing meant that sugar composition windows through which the hero could safely dive could no longer be made. Breakaway chairs, made of balsa and used for crashing over a villain's head, went the way of priorities because the fall of the Philippines cut off the main balsa supply. And bottles for breaking over heads were also *hors de combat,* because they were made of resin and resin was needed for a large number of war jobs.

Because of set-building restrictions, location shooting enjoyed a minor vogue. Alfred Hitchcock filmed *Shadow of a Doubt* entirely on location. Scenes that took place in New Jersey were actually shot in New Jersey, and Santa Rosa, California, served as the typical American city in which most of the story took place. (It was also used to stand in for an Iowa town in *Happy Land.*) *Commandos Strike at Dawn* was shot in Canada with real commandos in the cast, and many another war film employed real troops and training camp scenery for their battle scenes, with the gratis cooperation of the U.S. government. Location filming was restricted from another quarter, however; gas rationing and tire shortages sometimes created insuperable transportation problems.

The set and the sound stage became the sites of many of the battles fought in Hollywood's make-believe war. Blackout restrictions on the West Coast ruled out exterior night filming, and security regulations curtailed the use of beaches and, of course, the open sea. Even reservoirs were out for security reasons. Finally, the noise of military planes passing overhead made out-of-doors filming in the Hollywood area chancy.

The result was those slightly-phony-if-you-looked-closely scenes in which toy planes zoomed about the skies on wires, toy submarines sank to the bottom with a tinny clunk, and toy ships rocked and pitched in storm-tossed studio tanks. Of course, real combat footage was increasingly made available by the Bureau of Motion Pictures, and this could be spliced in from time to time. The danger in doing this was that reality might well steal the picture. Howard Barnes' review of a British film called *The Avengers* in the New York *Herald Tribune* applauded the "thrilling newsreels of a British raid on the Lofoten Isles (Norway) . . .

inspiring . . . on-the-spot glimpses of a systematic Commando assault on a Nazi Norwegian base." Barnes concluded: "And so their inclusion in *The Avengers* lends at least a touch of authenticity to a film which is otherwise mainly a lot of very obvious fiction."

The steady drainage of manpower into the services was always a major problem. The loss of skilled technicians was keenly felt, and it was not uncommon for a studio ready to start a picture to find that it had no electricians available. As their name suggests, extras were most expendable. In 1942 alone, 1,200 of them transferred into war work because their Screen Actors Guild files listed skills that could be employed in defense plants. When MGM sought to rent two dozen babies at $75 each for *The North Star,* it found mothers no longer in need of money and hence loath to loan out their children.

More seriously regarded was the loss of leading men. Many of the stars served with distinction. Robert Montgomery drove a French ambulance before the United States was involved and later commanded a destroyer at Normandy. Jimmy Stewart was a colonel in the Air Force by war's end. Henry Fonda served in the South Pacific. Wayne Morris shot down seven Japanese planes (well, one in the air and six on the ground). Sabu was in the Air Force and flew fifty missions as a tail gunner. Bob Cummings was a lieutenant in the Air Force. Tony Martin got into trouble for bribing a recruiting officer to station him in a cushy job on Treasure Island. When Clark Gable went in, the women of America were heartbroken. In the words of one fan magazine in an "Open Letter" to Clark: "In the movies you have represented a man that every woman—at least practically every American woman—could love as a son, as a brother—or as a man. And that's what you mean now that you're in Uncle Sam's Army—You are Everyman, every American man who is the center of Everywoman's thoughts today, her prayers, her hopes."

According to *Daily Variety* the opportunities for the untried young man with a deferment were unlimited: "The war-year of 1943 will go down in motion picture history as the year in which studios scoured the country with a fine-toothed comb in an attempt to uncover able young men who could be elevated to high prominence almost overnight." Elsewhere, the trade paper observed: "Old process of long drawn-out build-up has been junked. Producers realize that quick, effective and imaginative blurb campaigns are the proper recipe for actors who prove themselves capable of being catapulted into stardom by being cast in top roles."

One such anointed neophyte was Bowen Charleton "Sonny" Tufts III. Tufts, 4-F with a football trick knee, simply walked up to a casting director, accompanied by a friend who said, "This is my friend Sonny Tufts, and he'd like to be in movies." A screen test followed, and before he knew it, he was playing the male lead (albeit a small part) in *So Proudly We Hail*. That agent summed up the ideal male discovery best who told a producer: "I've got a great prospect for you—a young guy with a double hernia."

Early in the war, things looked so bleak that retired actors were being eyed as romantic leads. HOLLYWOOD RECLAIMS ITS VETS was the headline in a trade paper. The story went on to predict bright futures for such as Creighton Hale, Frank Mayo, Tom Wilson, H. B. Warner, Maurice Costello and Monte Blue. Makeup men could work miracles, but there was a hitch to retreading these old tires. Adolphe Menjou, when told he was being sought after again, said: "That may be, but if I play romantic starring roles again it will be the first time in a long while that some of these feminine stars have played opposite actors their own age." (Indeed, there was something slightly incestuous about the mature Irene Dunne playing Peter Lawford's mother in *The White Cliffs of Dover* and Van Johnson's sweetheart in *A Guy Named Joe*.)

Western B movies, traditionally a sagebrush ghetto where male stars were content with a comfortable livelihood and their coterie of loyal fans, provided another source of manpower. But it proved to be difficult to pry the rugged heroes out of their chaps. Republic's Don "Red" Barry dismounted long enough to star in *Pearl Harbor,* but in the course of this sortie among the dudes, he was required to smoke a cigarette, a clear violation of the Code of the Western (cowboy heroes never smoke). The New York *Times* reported: "Don 'Red' Barry has dispatched letters to all his fan clubs saying . . . [his smoking] in *Pearl Harbor* is an abhorrent professional necessity and that he never touches tobacco in real life." Charles Starrett, thirty-nine, father of twins and the fourth-ranking player in the oater field, was importuned with romantic roles but resisted, being content with his cowpoke's earnings. Johnny Mack Brown, it was said, "has the polish to carry off a white-tie-and-tail role" but stuck to his six-guns. The studios continued to grind out the Westerns, and the male stars of the war years emerged from other territory.

One shortage requiring top priority action was that of Japanese villains, Japanese-Americans having been taken out of circulation by the federal government. The onus of villainy fell on those of Chinese descent. To Hollywood's filmmakers all Orientals looked alike (they had obviously not read the little guide in *Time* magazine of December 22, 1941, which told how to distinguish Chinese from Japanese: "HOW TO TELL YOUR FRIENDS FROM THE JAPS: Virtually all Japanese are short. Japanese are seldom fat; they often dry up as they age. Most Chinese avoid horn-rimmed spectacles. Japanese walk stiffly erect, hard-heeled. Chinese, more relaxed, have an easy gait. The Chinese expression is likely to be more kindly, placid, open; the Japanese more positive, dogmatic, arrogant. Japanese are hesitant, nervous in conversation, laugh loudly at the wrong time"). When a movie such as *Dragon Seed* was made, in which all the characters were lovable, heroic Chinese, Occidental players were used in the roles. China became Katharine Hepburn striding around in elegantly tailored pajamas and speaking Pearl Buck's Biblical prose ("But Ah cahn't stay alwahys in the courtyahrd. These ahren't ancient times"). An exception to this was *30 Seconds over Tokyo,* in which Chinese actors, some of whom were amateurs, had fairly substantial parts and performed with dignity and appeal.

The sudden demand for Chinese Japanese villains, experienced or not, meant that just about anybody could make a movie if he was Chinese. Among the new stars was Richard Loo, a beer salesman, who upped his earnings to $1,500 a week for making *The Purple Heart;* H. T. Tshiang, a poet by trade, who had starved for years in New York peddling his poems in pamphlet form, suddenly found himself making $800 a week in the same picture; and Harold Fong, the bartender at cameraman James Wong Howe's Ching How Restaurant, moved into the $1,700 a week category.

The leading Oriental villains (if we exclude J. Carrol Naish) were Sen Yung, Chester Gan and Philip Ahn. Gan specialized in portraying stolid brutal Japs. Sen Yung was the treacherous, English-speaking Japanese, whose mastery of American slang he turned back on the Americans in such films as *Across the Pacific* and *God Is My Co-Pilot.* ("OK, you Yankee Doodle Dandy, come and get us. Where are you, gangsters? Come on up and get a load of that scrap metal you sold us.") Sneeringly, he epitomized Japanese treachery at Pearl Harbor—at first he was victorious, but in the end he always got his. Philip Ahn, a Korean, was perhaps the most sought-after villain of all, with his nasal, flat voice and his masklike face that looked as if it had been carved out of India rubber. Ahn eventually tired of his typecasting and refused any more Japanese roles, saying he wanted to play romantic Chinese leads. Although he did play a heroic Chinese doctor in *The Story of Dr. Wassell,* there were no romantic Chinese leads, Turhan Bey having been cast in the only available one, opposite Hepburn in *Dragon Seed*.

When Japanese characters had roles broader in scope than simple villainy, Caucasian actors were often used. In *Behind the Rising Sun*, Tom Neal played a young Japanese student who studies in America, then returns home, where he is gradually transformed into a fanatical militarist. The Japanese statesmen in *Blood on the Sun*, again, were played by American actors.

The demand for Nazi villains was more easily met. A variety of actors, some of German or *Mittel Europa* origin, did stints as beastly Nazis; they included Raymond Massey, Helmut Dantine, Conrad Veidt, Peter Lorre, Cedric Hardwicke, Martin Kosleck, Paul Cavanaugh and John Abbott. Lorre was so nefarious a personality that he carried off a tour de force of sorts by playing both Nazi and Japanese villains. Veidt, a favorite Nazi officer, managed to make amends before his death in 1943 by playing a good German in *Above Suspicion*.

But these war-ascribable novelties in actors' opportunities aside, the brunt of the manpower needs was borne by the veteran male stars who were deferred because of age, children, health, etc., and the young "discoveries" who were thrown into the breach as replacements. After all, though Gable, Fonda and Stewart were gone, Gary Cooper, Spencer Tracy, Bob Hope, Bing Crosby, Cary Grant, Fred MacMurray, John Garfield, James Cagney and Humphrey Bogart, among others, remained—experienced, mature actors and box-office attractions. An ample supply of newcomers provided the fresh attractive faces, the acting potential and the youth necessary to lure teen-agers to the theaters. Among the new stars who came to prominence during the war were Frank Sinatra, Gene Kelly, Danny Kaye, Van Johnson, Robert Walker, Gregory Peck, James Craig, Gig Young, John Payne, Guy Madison, John Hodiak, Peter Lawford, William Eythe, Dana Andrews, Richard Conti, George Montgomery, Sonny Tufts and Alan Ladd. On the female side, Ginger Rogers, Claudette Colbert, Myrna Loy, Paulette Goddard, Irene Dunne, Hedy Lamarr, Betty Grable, Rita Hayworth, Dorothy Lamour, Veronica Lake, Judy Garland, Jennifer Jones, Dorothy McGuire, Ingrid Bergman, Greer Garson, Lauren Bacall, Donna Reed, Joan Leslie, Esther Williams, June Haver, Lucille Bremer, Margaret O'Brien, Betty Russell and Jane Russell maintained or blazed into first- or second-degree brilliance.

Between July and October, 1942, there were thirty-eight war pictures in production out of a total of eighty-six, and of those thirty-eight, twenty-four dealt with espionage and sabotage. The Office of War Information and its newly acquired Bureau of Motion Pictures were con-

cerned at this imbalance. It was bad for morale to have these scare
pictures, based on purest fantasy, and the Department of Justice in the
fall of 1942 felt called upon to state that no major acts of sabotage or
espionage had been uncovered. Also, the OWI was concerned lest the
monopoly of this type of picture might vitiate the impact of the quality
war pictures that made real contributions to its "war information program." The British experience had been that too many war pictures
(especially those concerned with combat heroics) set up a law of di-
minishing returns in the form of audience apathy to all pictures with a
war message. It was better to limit their number.

The efforts of the Bureau of Motion Pictures seemed to have some
effect, for the glut of spy derring-do dried up by 1943. In early 1942 the
bureau was organized and placed, nominally, under the Domestic Branch
of the Office of War Information. The bureau had three offices: a main
Washington office, under the ever-reshuffled Lowell Mellett, for liaison
with the government; a New York production unit under playwright
Sam Spewack and William Montague, Jr., which made propaganda films;
and the Hollywood office under Nelson Poynter, which affected the
on-the-spot liaison with the movie companies. Armed with a budget of
$1,300,000 for the fiscal year and 140 employees, the BMP entered
the celluloid war in earnest.

The Hollywood office was opened the first week in May. By August
13, 1942, Poynter's assistant Fred Polangin, in a memo to his chief in
Washington, reported satisfactory progress. They had set up a tiny office
with a staff consisting of himself, Poynter and a few researchers and were
working in close cooperation with the film companies. They had made it
plain, Polangin said, that the BMP wanted no control over the industry,
that it was to be regarded merely as a Washington liaison office. "It
was not long before we were accepted as such," said Polangin, "and
the cooperation was overwhelming."

Their beachhead secured, the American flag planted in Hollywood,
the BMP proceeded in good bureacratic order to compile a manual.
Called *The Government Information Manual for the Motion Picture,* the
thick book set down official government policy on a variety of issues
for the guidance of the moviemaker. Particularly advocated was the
casual insertion of a constructive "war message" in a picture whenever
possible:

> At every opportunity, naturally and inconspicuously, show
> people making small sacrifices for victory—making them volun-

tarily, cheerfully and because of the people's own sense of responsibility, not because of any laws. For example, show people bringing their own sugar when invited out to dinner, carrying their own parcels when shopping, travelling on planes or trains with light luggage, uncomplainingly giving up seats for servicemen or others travelling on war priorities; show persons accepting dimout restrictions, tire and gas rationing cheerfully, show well-dressed persons, obviously car owners riding in crowded buses and streetcars.

To bring home the grim realities of war, the director advised: "In crowds unostentatiously show a few wounded men. Prepare people but do not alarm them against the casualties to come." And show them that this is a democratic war: "Show colored soldiers in crowd scenes; occasionally colored officers. Stress our national unity by using names of foreign extraction, showing foreign types in the services."

The bureau also suggested that each filmmaker ask himself seven questions before undertaking a movie, most soul-stirring of which was: "Will this picture help win the war?" Filmmakers were also urged to ascertain if their film clarified, dramatized or interpreted a "war information problem"; to contribute something new to our understanding of the world conflict; not to make use of the war purely as a basis for a profitable picture; to be sure the film would not be outdated by current conditions when it was released, and, if they were thinking of making an "escape" picture, not to "create a false picture of America, her allies or the world we live in." In addition the moviemaker was summoned to account for himself before the bar of posterity: "Does the picture tell the truth or will the young people of today scorn it a few years hence, when they are running the world, and say they were misled by propaganda?"

Besides seeking these high standards, the BMP's overworked staff was viewing films and scripts and placing those containing any "war content" into one of six categories of "war information" set down by the OWI: The Issues (why we fight; the peace); The Enemy (his nature); United Nations and United Peoples (our brothers-in-arms); Work and Production; the Home Front (sacrifice); and the Fighting Forces (the job of the fighting man at the front).

By December, 1942, the BMP was circulating among Hollywood executives a letter signed by Mellett requesting that as a "routine procedure" studio treatment and synopses be sent to the BMP for review. "This will enable us to make suggestions as to the war content of motion pictures at a stage when it is easy and inexpensive to make any changes which might be recommended." A reasonable request, once the principle of review had been established, but it had on the face of it, war or no war, the look of prior restraint. Wrote H. R. Wilkerson in the *Hollywood Reporter:* "Our producers and their company heads should know that control of our screens, first through control of our scripts is being talked of and planned." To pacify recalcitrant producers, the BMP reemphasized that it was not attempting to control the screen, cooperation by the studios was strictly voluntary, and so on.

The upshot was that the studio heads met and agreed to cooperate fully with the bureau. Mellett's tiny agency had won a tiny victory against the Hollywood titans, but the fact persisted that the bureau was a buzzing fly that could be brushed off at any time.

Certainly, the studios did not have to cooperate; certainly, in practice some of them cooperated a lot, some of them cooperated a little, and some of them cooperated not at all. When Hollywood chief Poynter asked to see a rough cut of Paramount's *Miracle of Morgan's Creek,* an irreverent comedy by the independent-minded Preston Sturges poking fun at the flag, motherhood and heroism, among other things, his request was ignored. He shot off an angry telegram to Mellett in January, 1943: "This is the only studio which has ever refused specifically request of this nature. It is only studio not fully cooperating and it is not cooperating one iota." (The film was so daring that James Agee wrote in the *Nation:* "the Hays Office has been either hypnotized into a liberality for which it should be thanked, or has been raped in its sleep." Agee also reported that the second time he saw the movie a line was deleted. The line, spoken by the father of the heroine who has been impregnated by a soldier unknown and is expecting her baby on Christmas Eve, went: "You may be expecting the President of the United States.")

A more representative case history is to be found in the interplay that went on between the BMP and MGM, the makers of *The White Cliffs of Dover.* The plot concerned the saga of an American girl who marries a wealthy English lord just prior to the First World War. The lord is killed in the war, but not before presenting Miss Dunne with a son (Roddy McDowall). Embittered at the loss of her husband, Miss Dunne vows she'll never let her boy grow up to be a soldier. Storm clouds gather, however, and soon her son, now grown and played by Peter Lawford, goes off to fight "just as his English sires had done."

Miss Dunne had wanted to spirit him back to America, where he would be safe, but his sense of familial duty—transmitted genetically from his "English sires" as with racehorses, one presumes—is unswerving. Miss Dunne reconciles herself to the war; son is wounded in the commando raid on Dieppe; she holds him in her arms as once again the Americans enter the war; and we fade out upon thousands of marching American troops demonstrating Anglo-American cooperation and Miss Dunne rhapsodizing, "I see them. Your people and my people. Only the uniforms are different. How well they march. How well they march together."

Lest anyone think that Miss Dunne harbors any latent anti-Saxonism because once again America has been drawn into the war to save England, she promises her son that this time "all those proud and beautiful young men. They'll help bring peace again, a peace that will stick," adding: "God will never forgive us if we break faith with our dead again."

All the qualities of such a picture would seem to satisfy any demands for pro-British propaganda. But no, the BMP's reviewer complained about the "presentation of wartime England in terms of an outdated feudal society and the constant emphasis on Anglo-British antagonisms" which "could be gravely detrimental to the war program." MGM for the most part stuck by its guns. However, one scene was added: a love scene between the young master and the tenant farmer's daughter, both now grown up and in uniform, their class differences thus erased. The affair is shown as more serious than just a brief dalliance, and Miss Dunne is made to comment upon it: "There was a different England in the air. I liked the girl."

Whatever failures it had, the BMP proceeded to machine-gun a steady stream of suggested changes in scripts:

> Don't make blanket condemnation of all Germans and all Japanese as this country does not regard the German and Japanese people as our enemies, only their leaders.

> In an adaptation of a novel about a farm boy, the hero should not enlist in the Army despite all the criticism of him as a 4-F; rather he should come to realize how important food production is to the war effort and stay home to fight the battle of the farm front. An actual case, where the car of a young man who had a farm deferment was painted yellow, is suggested to the scriptwriters for inclusion.

> A little horror picture called *The Revenge of the Zombies* was totally disapproved for foreign release (but released domes-

tically anyway) because it depicted Negroes as inferior beings.
A picture preliminarily titled *America* had a sit-down strike in it,
    and the reviewer suggested the strike be omitted or, if it were
    absolutely necessary for dramatic purposes, be made another
    kind because sit-down strikes suggested the capital-labor vio-
    lence of the thirties and the War Labor Board was trying
    to foster harmony between the two.
A movie implying Germany was threatened by internal dissension
    was disapproved, lest it foster overconfidence on the home
    front.
Don't show Chinese in menial, servant positions.
Don't show Englishmen at a lavish banquet, since a theme of Axis
    propaganda is that US Lend-Lease food is being squandered
    by our Allies, while people at home tighten their belts.
Don't show American heroes as "cocky, bumptious and undis-
    ciplined" because such screen heroics are resented overseas.
And so it went. Hollywood could always use a civics lesson. Many
other suggestions, however, seemed more niggling and of questionable
practicality in terms of the realities of motion-picture making.

Back in Washington, Lowell Mellett was walking an increasingly
precarious tightrope. Jiggling it at one end was Congress, in which
the Republican-Southern reactionary coalition directed a steady fusilade
of criticism against FDR and his programs. They were especially
suspicious that the OWI's domestic operations would become a
"Roosevelt propaganda agency." In February, 1943, for example, Senator Rufus Holman, an Oregon Republican, attacked the OWI *Victory*
magazine as "window dressing for a [Roosevelt] personal political
campaign." He was also critical of Frank Capra's *Prelude to War*
(not an OWI production), saying: "At the conclusion of the picture
I was convinced that Mr. Roosevelt intended to seek a fourth term in
the presidency." At the other end of Mellett's tightrope was the movie
industry, always conformist and willing to cooperate but anxious about
censorship and possible disruption of its profits through too much
government interference.

The issues of government censorship and propaganda, Hollywood's
responsibility to society and freedom of the screen never came to a clear-
cut head, however. Rather, as is the rule in America, a congeries
of forces, possessed of a variety of motives often different from those
they professed, combined to gang up on the BMP and eradicate it. The
BMP's real sin was its weakness in the bureaucratic jungle of Washington

as it began acquiring influential enemies. First, there was the War Department. Frank Capra, the director, had volunteered his services to make indoctrination films for the Army and had turned out several, including an hour-long feature called *Prelude to War*. For whatever reasons, certain brass hats liked the film so well that they wanted the civilian population to see it. (The film was made from captured enemy films and newsreels depicting atrocities, thus showing the true "nature of the enemy.") Bypassing Mellett, the War Department gave 150 prints of the sixty-minute film to the OWI's Domestic Branch in Washington for release through the War Activities Committee. By May 23 it was definite that *Prelude to War* would be released without charge to the distributors. Drew Pearson reported dire threats that the government would take over 25 percent of the screen time unless the industry complied. There was resistance among the distributors, but finally, they reluctantly agreed to circulate the film.

Then, on May 18, the OWI received a shock. The House of Representatives, ignoring the recommendations of the Appropriations Committee, in a fit of pique authorized absolutely not one cent for the entire Domestic Branch. On July 15, meeting in joint conferences, the House and Senate compromised on a $2,750,000 appropriation for the Domestic Branch, but the Bureau of Motion Pictures was wiped out. Its appropriation was cut from $1,300,000 to $50,000, and its job henceforth limited to liaison work with only a Washington office. Its film reviewing and production were at an end.

On the same day, Mellett, now the sacrificial lamb, handed in his resignation to FDR, who appointed him to a special mission to the Middle East, a favorite form of Coventry for retired administrators in those days.

Actually during the BMP's existence a well-coordinated public war information program had been worked out with the cooperation of the War Activities Committee. The propaganda shorts were written either by the OWI or by a Hollywood studio, with the Bureau of Motion Pictures providing guidance and research assistance. Shooting was done either in Hollywood or at the OWI's New York unit. In all, fifty-two propaganda shorts were distributed through 352 film exchanges in thirty-one cities that would handle the films without cost. Twenty-six of the films were to be made by the studios on a voluntary basis and for profit (which was to be donated to charity). These were known as the *America Speaks* series. Twenty-six were to be made by the OWI's Production Unit and were known as *Victory Films*. These were distributed for nothing, and the exhibitors were pledged to play them. It is impossible to say, however, how many theater owners actually ran the films. For example, in Chicago area, 645 out of 728 theaters pledged to play the *Victory Films,* but actual play dates on all the reels released up to June 1, 1942, ranged from 81 to 378, depending on the film.

Through its Educational Division the OWI also distributed 16-mm films for nontheatrical showings in churches, schools, fraternal organizations and the like.

There were, throughout the country, an estimated 20,000 16-mm projectors and a large potential audience of information-hungry adults and children. Indeed, it was believed that the production of the OWI's film section reached a greater audience in those nontheatrical showings than they did in the movie theaters through War Activities Committee distribution. A survey in January, 1943, revealed that OWI films had a total of 31,500 showings to an audience estimated at 4,700,000. Combat films were the most popular (and for some there was a long waiting line); English documentaries distributed through the British Information Service were also in demand. Perhaps never before had the potential of the movies as an educational medium been so widely realized; whereas before the war the use of films as teaching aids in the classroom was a rarity, after the war it was to become commonplace. And many of the films used would be productions of the OWI's Overseas Branch, originally designed to give foreigners a lesson in democracy.

Indeed, here, as in England, the documentary film, which had had an honorable but limited history in the twenties and thirties in the hands of such pioneers as Robert Flaherty and Pare Lorentz, took a new lease on life. There were, of course, the combat documentaries which achieved new heights of realism in showing the horrors of war and even achieved a kind of terrible beauty. Films such as Leland Hayward's *Marines on Tarawa,* John Ford's *The Battle of Midway,* John Huston's *Report from the Aleutians* and *San Pietro,* William Wyler's *Memphis Belle,* and Louis De Rochemont's *Fighting Lady* brought war home to Americans, and audiences welcomed their authenticity and honesty. Some of these products, however, were less successful. Darryl Zanuck's documentary on the North African invasion was scored by reviewers as a shoddy job of filmmaking that showed little of interest about the fighting there.

A surefire way to appeal to the home folks, or so it seemed to the scriptwriters, was the guilt approach. That is, our boys are out there fighting and dying, so what are *you* doing about it, back in nice cushy civilian life? Such a film was *Letter from Bataan,* a short made in 1942 by Paramount. An actor representing a wounded GI in a Corregidor hospital is shown writing a letter home to his folks: "For one thing tell the folks not to hoard food. We haven't had anything but a little horse meat and rice for days. . . . Tell that friend of yours, Mrs. Jackson, to stop bragging about all the coffee and sugar she's got stored up in her cellar. And kitchen fats, Mom. Don't waste any. Kitchen fats make glycerine and glycerine makes explosives. Two pounds of fat can fire five anti-tank shells. And pass this along to that brother-in-law of mine, Ray, who won't use a razor blade twice. It takes 12,000 razor blades for one 2000-lb bomb." The film ends with the announcement that this was the boy's last letter; he died in the hospital.

The "for the want of a nail the battle was lost" theme was a popular one. As usually developed, the leading character, the one who is held up as an object lesson, omits through laziness or carelessness to do some seemingly small act and, through a chain of circumstances, practically causes the loss of the war, or at least delays D Day by six months. *Conquer by the Clock* was one such film. Made by Phil Resiman, Jr., Frederic Ullman, Jr., and Slavko Vorkapich, the team which made the highly praised *Private Smith of the USA* and *Women in Arms,* for RKO's *This Is America* series, it was about time and the consequences of wasting it. A girl defense worker leaves the assembly line to sneak a smoke in the ladies'. Because of her dereliction, some cartridges without primers are sent out, and a soldier loses his life because his gun won't fire. (As James Agee observed mischievously, but with impeccable logic, *Conquer by the Clock* "fails to suggest that the same thing might have happened if her visit to the toilet had been sincere.")

Still, many people were moved by the Hollywood fictional jobs. A short called *It's Everybody's War,* narrated by Henry Fonda, told the story of a National Guard regiment from the fictional town of Jefferson, U.S.A., which meets its doom in the Philippines. The shocked townspeople devote themselves to war work in memory of "their boys." When it was shown at the Ohio Theater in Columbus, "many in the audience cried," reported an observer.

Yet perhaps inevitably a reaction set in, and people tired of too much propaganda from the screen. When the controversial *Prelude to War* was shown in Schenectady, one man in the audience reported that the reaction was one of indifference. "I was rather shocked at this," he wrote the OWI, "and several times my wife and I led the applause to see if we could stir it up. . . . My wife heard rather caustic comments in the ladies' room." *Prelude to War* was not a "crying" film; still, the attitude in Schenectady was perhaps symptomatic of a wider, growing apathy to the routine propaganda film.

Was the Bureau of Motion Pictures really necessary? The hidebound reactionary and Roosevelt hater in Congress had, up to a point, a valid doubt about its worth, but, alas, for the wrong reasons. It is probable that Hollywood would have staggered along without it. Certainly in the most sensitive areas—avoidance of films that depicted an ally in a manner offensive to the people in that country—a case could be made for the BMP's advisory functions. A picture like *Iceland,* which portrayed an Icelandic character as a stupid clod who loses the girl to a handsome American GI, provides an example. Turning that country into a kind of lavish skating rink whose sole *raison d'être* was to display the talents of Miss Sonja Henie, it caused an uproar of protests in that country. By the same token the bureau was able to persuade the studios not to reissue *Kim, The True Glory* or *The General Died at Dawn. Kim,* with its pro-Empire, white-man's-burden mentality, was thought to give aid and comfort to those who were criticizing the British for fighting the war solely to keep their colonies (a favorite theme of German propaganda, as well as of editorials in the Chicago *Tribune* and *Life* magazine). *The True Glory* was an attempt to exploit people's interest in the Philippines, although actually it was about the Huk rebellion and showed Americans fighting Filipinos. As for *The General Died at Dawn,* the Nationalist Chinese government had been implacably opposed to it ever since its release in 1936, because it was thought to embody Chiang Kai-shek in the character of a cruel warlord who is opposed by Gary Cooper, man of the people and implied Communist.

On the other hand, there is some question of just how effective the BMP's don't-offend-our-allies-policy was. The bureau's obvious weakness was, of course, that its role was advisory, so for every *Kim* it stopped, there was a *White Cargo,* which the producer, hungrily eying the box-office potential of a dusky, underdressed Hedy Lamarr slithering around seducing white colonials, refused to halt.

Then too, the question of what is offensive to a given foreign country is often a murky one. Such was the hold of Hollywood on movie audiences everywhere that it could, paradoxically, get away with certain falsifications of reality. In a way, people abroad had been conditioned to accept a certain quotient of fantasy in the Hollywood product—and indeed, amid wartime austerity, welcomed it. A case in point would be

Mrs. Miniver. Among the British intelligentsia (and any objective observer would concur) the picture was held to be a distortion of British
middle-class life and British life in general. A critic writing in the British
Film Centre's *Documentary Newsletter* called it the "phoniest war film
ever made" and thought that "many . . . will be disgusted by its gross
misinterpretation of character and types . . . a world which seems to
consist of giggling housemaids with their bucolic young men; doddering
servile station masters; glee singers in their feather boas; duchesses and
their granddaughters, black-mailing comic grocers and truculent, ever-
leaving cooks. . . . The Minivers or people like them, were under the
bombing . . . but the Minivers were in the minority. The cooks and
housemaids, grocers and station masters, bargers and tugmen were certainly there in the middle of it and overwhelmingly in the majority." Yet
the same critic admitted that London audiences were brought to tears
by the movie, swallowing the film's sentimentality whole and accepting
it as an American pat on the back for their sacrifices.

At the same time, the British showed themselves as not completely
docile to Hollywood. When *Objective Burma* was exhibited there, a great
tide of resentment welled up because the film seemed to present Errol
Flynn winning the Battle of Burma—primarily a British operation, in
fact—single-handed. In one theater people rioted and threw their seat
cushions at the screen. The protest was so great that Warner Brothers
had to withdraw the film from overseas distribution. Probably the real
culprit was Jerry Wald, the executive at Warner Brothers who suggested
that the movie be made in the first place. Alvah Bessie, who wrote the
original story, recalls that when Wald suggested the film to him, he had
replied, "But Jerry, there *are* no American troops in Burma." To which
Wald countered, "Oh, that's all right. It's just a movie." The movie won
Bessie an Academy Award nomination for his story.

On the whole, Hollywood trod the sometimes dizzying suspension
bridge of foreign policy warily. Where foreign pressure or OWI influence
failed to stop an offending item, the Office of Censorship was still waiting to head it off at the gateway by denying an export license. The Office
of Censorship's standards were strict. Forbidden for export were movies
held to be in the following categories:

> Gangster and other action films which do not reflect true American
> life and conditions or that might give the impression to for-
> eigners that the United States is not a nation of law-abiding
> people.

> Scenes showing racial discrimination.

Scenes showing Americans living off the fat of the land amid lavish
surroundings and unconscious of their obligations to their
fellowman.

Films which paint Americans as supermen winning battles single-
handedly or assuming a general air of nationalistic superiority.

Pictures treating with imperialistic desires on the part of any of the
United Nations.

Pictures that would discredit the war effort of any of the Allies.

Subjects that would show the United States oblivious of war and its
conditions or, in reverse, being apparently the only nation
involved in the war against the Axis.

The loss of foreign business might not be fatal to a given picture,
but by the end of 1944, when the Allies had pushed the Germans and
Japanese out of most of their occupied territory, 40 percent of Hollywood's gross receipts were from foreign countries. The largest market,
at least in the early war years, was South America, which was also
strategically important. Because of the delicacy of inter-American relations, the office of the coordinator of Inter-American Affairs kept a
watchful eye on movies dealing with the area.

More, it suggested movies for Hollywood to make and undertook
some of its own. Thus, when the Rubber Development Corporation
sought to stimulate Brazilian rubber production, the OCIAA made a short
called *Rubber for Victory,* which was shown in Brazil through Hollywood distribution outlets. The OCIAA also asked Walt Disney to make
an animated cartoon pitched at South American audiences. The result
was *Saludos Amigos* embodying ideas set down by the OCIAA; it was
guaranteed against financial loss by the government. The guarantee was
unnecessary, for the movie was a hit in South America. Indeed, whenever South America could be dragged into a film, it was. Often it was a
musical number sung by Carmen Miranda as she danced one of the
Latin-American dances that were in vogue. Always, South Americans
were referred to as our "good neighbors." (There was even a propaganda love song called "Good Night, Good Neighbor," in the movie
presentation of which Alexis Smith as a languorous señorita was sere-
naded by Dennis Morgan.)

The first months of the war and the time immediately prior to it
brought a wave of spy pictures. Cheap to make, they also could be
rushed out quickly to capitalize on the wartime mood. Besides, established, continuing characters could often be employed in them, and
presumably appeal to a ready-made public. Thus, such screen detectives

as the Falcon, Ellery Queen and even Sherlock Holmes, who made a sudden time-machine jump into the twentieth century to match ratiocinations with the Axis, were immediately enmeshed in enemy intrigue, at home and abroad. Cowboy favorites were similarly employed in several movies, and even Tarzan swung into action against the foe.

These spy melodramas probably mirrored the general anxiety in the air, for intrigue implies a shadowy world, where identities are not what they seem and the enemy lurks in his secret hideaway doing his damage. They had no lesson to teach and certainly did not mirror any real menace, for the FBI was repeatedly denying that subversion was a serious threat, and most reasonable men agreed that Axis undercover activities in this country were not a matter of serious national peril.

Yet to look at those movies you would have thought that America was swarming with spies. They all had a curious childishness about them, a regression into hysteria and simplistic heroism, a world of comic-strip heroes and villains.

These films also served as an outlet for aggressive fantasies about the enemy. If at first these sneering villains triumphed, in the end the cocky, all-American hero gave them the beating of their lives. A kind of elemental satire was employed in depicting the Axis agents. They were crude caricatures who ranted of the New Order and shouted *Heil Hitlah!* automatically like robots. Sometimes, however, a dash of comedy was added to their characterizations (sometimes the comedy was unintentional). A recurring motif was the quarrel between the Japanese spy and the Nazi spy who would inevitably betray each other.

These themes—childish aggression, caricatures of the enemy and the wishful belief that the Axis partners will have an inevitable falling out—occur in *Invisible Agent,* a B-grade melodrama of this period which can well stand as typical.

Early in the action of *Invisible Agent,* Jon Hall, who will become the title character, identifies himself as the grandson of "Frank Griffin," the inventor of the drug that makes people invisible (thus establishing a lineage with the thirties movie *Invisible Man,* starring Claude Rains). Hall is called to Washington before Pearl Harbor by high government officials, who ask him to revive his grandfather's formula. Hall refuses; he does not think the world is ready for it.

Then comes the news of the attack on Pearl Harbor, and once again the government begs Hall for the secret formula. "The enemy is planning a nationwide sabotage attempt," warns one official. "We must know when Germany is going to strike." Hall agrees that the formula must be used and embarks on a preposterous mission whereby, now invisible, he is parachuted into Berlin and makes contact with a spy ring headed by Ilona Massey, as a glamorous wealthy German courtesan (with a Hungarian accent) who wheedles military secrets out of German officers. After various escapades, Hall and Miss Massey escape to England in a captured Nazi plane, but not before he has destroyed on the ground a squadron of Nazi bombers that were about to take off to bomb New York. With the foiling of this raid, which was to have set off a wave of sabotage by Nazi agents throughout the country, the Nazi plan completely crumbles.

The enemy was delivered a crushing blow in *Invisible Agent,* but even this enemy was depicted as stupid and ultimately ineffectual. Cedric Hardwicke, as the Nazi, vaunts the superiority of "German logic" and is a man given to saying things like: "There's no place in our New Order for sentimentalists" and "It's good to see your friends arrested. It hardens you." His villainy is expressed by Hall when he says "You Nazis, I pity the devil when you arrive in bunches." There is also, of course, a Japanese spy (Peter Lorre) who is appropriately sinister and treacherous and given to such dialogue as "The Rising Sun never sets, so her spies never sleep." Hall insults him with a racial stereotype: "I can't tell you Japs apart," he says at one point. Inevitably, the Nazi-Japanese collaboration breaks down, as Lorre and Hardwicke each seek the invisibility formula for his own government. Treachery among the enemy is rife. At one point a Nazi, who has fallen out of favor, but who knows where the Invisible Agent is hiding, demands of Hardwicke: "Will you give me your word as a National Socialist that you'll reinstate me if I tell you where he is?" The Nazis, then, are like Boy Scouts; there is always an ultimate oath necessary, rather like "Scout's honor" or "cross my heart and hope to die."

At the movie's climax, Hardwicke and Lorre struggle, and Lorre, through the use of jujitsu, defeats Hardwicke, then kills him and rips off his Nazi insignia. "We've failed, Schaeffer. I'm going to make an honorable man out of even you." Then Lorre commits hara-kiri. Not only do the villains get a comeuppance from the hero, but so dastardly are they that they destroy each other. It is the expression of a sort of magical belief that evil will destroy itself. Why? Because it is so evil.

Another type of spy film enlisted that 1930's American movie hero the gangster against the Axis. Representative of this trend were *All Through the Night, Lucky Jordan,* and *Hitler, Dead or Alive.* In *Lucky Jordan,* the conversion of a gangster to a good citizenship through serving his country is the central motif. Lucky Jordan, who "controls all the rackets in town," receives his draft notice. As played by the petulant, stone-faced Alan Ladd, Lucky is totally cynical about the war, and he orders his lawyer to find a way for him to evade the draft. "There's a war on," says the lawyer. "Yeah, Santa Anita is closed," Lucky retorts. The lawyer tries to fix Lucky up with a phony dependent, but the scheme doesn't work. Once in, Lucky is the spoiled individualist who refuses to subordinate himself to discipline.

Through convolutions of plot, Lucky comes to be pitted against the Nazi spy ring. Its leader tries to convince Lucky to play ball. "I've met a lot of American gangsters," he tells Lucky, "and their viewpoint and ours are very similar. When they want something they take it. . . . Why do you want to work for a country that considers you an enemy of society?" But Lucky has learned firsthand, through physical confrontation, how evil the Nazis are. (And the love of a USO hostess has also redeemed him.) As he puts it: "Maybe because I don't wanna see this country run by guys who beat up old ladies." Lucky returns to the Army; at last his toughness is enlisted in the cause, and he is a worthy citizen. But he has not lost his cockiness. In the last scene, wearing fatigues, Lucky is digging a latrine. He throws dirt on the sergeant's foot, saying: "Sorry, I thought it was your face." The rebel has been tamed, but the swagger, toughness and bravery of the criminal, which makes him such a good man to have on our side, are not.

As the first six months of the real war progressed and our troops suffered a series of defeats unprecedented in our history, the tough individualist was abandoned; now it was time to depict the American fighting man. Hollywood tried to radiate a grim seriousness from the screen in its combat pictures which would awaken the slumbering American public to its responsibilities while bolstering its morale and puncturing complacency and overconfidence.

A series of pictures ensued which might be called Last Stands. They glorified American defeats and yielded to the temptation to provide crumbs of comfort by depicting glorious, isolated and totally fictitious victories. They also looked backward, summoning up the past as evidence that we were a nation with a glorious military tradition, that what "we did before, we could do again."

The first war picture rushed to completion was *Wake Island,* which achieved substantial critical and box-office success, including an Academy Award for its director, John Farrow. The events in the movie were a fairly close approximation of what actually took place—probably as much as was known at the time. For dramatic purposes a feud is carried on between the marine commandant of the island (Brian Donlevy) and the foreman of the civilian construction battalion (MacDonald Carey), who contends that Donlevy's prewar air raid drills are unnecessarily interfering with his men's work, thereby pitting Preparedness against Civilian Apathy. After the Japanese attack, Carey and his civilian crew join in wholeheartedly, of course, though Major Devereux—Donlevy— advises them against it, lest they jeopardize their status as noncombatants.

Along the way, there is pause for a little philosophizing. Talking to a marine pilot whose wife was killed at Pearl Harbor, Donlevy sermonizes about what they are fighting for. The enemy with his "stinking bombs" killing women and children is sheer mindless destruction, and "We've got to destroy destruction. That's our job." A religious note is injected when a corporal comes upon a young marine praying. The young marine is embarrassed, but the corporal dismisses his embarrassment: "That's all right. Nothing wrong with praying. There are no atheists in foxholes." That famous phrase had already become a national cliché through a *Reader's Digest* article, and it was grafted onto *Wake Island* as a kind of familiar patriotic piety. Similarly, when a wave of Japanese invasion barges approaches, Donlevy is made to say, "Don't fire until you see the whites of their eyes," invoking a famous martial phrase from the armamentarium of history.

At the end of the picture, the surrender of the island is not shown; instead we see featured players William Bendix and Robert Preston making a last stand in their foxhole; an explosion covers them with smoke, and in the last frame a grinning Japanese runs up and fires his machine gun down in the foxhole. Never to show Americans surrendering became a tradition in the war film, the Last Stands always ending in a blaze of defiant gunfire. The OWI is alleged to have forbidden an opening shot in *Bataan* which showed the American flag being lowered and the Japanese flag replacing it. (However, in *Back to Bataan,* released in 1945, about the reconquest of the Philippines, there is a scene in which the Japanese lower the American flag at a Filipino school. The Japanese officer orders the Filipino principal to haul it down, but, to symbolize how much the Filipino people love us, he refuses and the Japanese shoot him.)

The real Battle of Wake Island had little strategic importance and represented no major American defeat. At the same time the resourceful defense of the garrison caught the public's imagination, and the alleged statement of Major Devereux—"Send us more Japs" (which he actually did not make)—was still another of those crumbs of PR heroism the public so eagerly devoured.

The fall of the Philippines was a different story. Here was a major defeat for America, occurring at a time when Allied fortunes all over the globe had reached their nadir. *Wake Island* depicted the jaunty but hopeless courage of American fighting men against overwhelming odds and left it at that. But the Last Stand pictures about Bataan tended to preach that Bataan was a delaying action which had won America time to rearm by tying up thousands of Japanese troops in the Philippines. In other words, a tactical defeat but a strategic victory.

The idea is stated by Clark Gable playing a cocky, lady-killing war correspondent in *Somewhere I'll Find You*. Gable is a Cassandra figure, similar to Joel McCrea in *Foreign Correspondent* (1939), who warned of the Axis menace before U.S. involvement and told America to "ring yourself around with steel." Gable, while in Berlin, "slipped the Japanese ambassador a mickey in his sake" and learned of Japan's plans to attack the Unites States. But his newspaper employer is an appeaser who "thinks he can keep things he wants by giving away things he doesn't need"—*i.e.,* Hitler's aggression can be stopped by giving him Czechoslovakia. Gable's wanderings, interspersed with a love affair with Lana Turner, land him finally in the Philippines, after Pearl Harbor. There he plays the Voice of Truth Speaking to America. Between posting himself behind some studio rocks with the other defenders and shooting Japanese, he busies himself dictating his Big Story. He tells the American people of heroic sacrifice ("They turned soldier Davis into a gold star on his high school service flag"); Japanese atrocities ("The Nippos bombed Field Hospital Number 3 last night. All hands lost"); triumphs ("a Jap flyer went hunting his ancestors in the jungle"); and U.S.–Filipino cooperation ("brown men and white men fighting together and when they bled their blood was the same color"). Gable ends his story on a note of optimism. "Three hundred thousand Japanese were tied in knots long enough for America to get off her Sunday clothes." (At that time the number of Japanese troops in the Bataan Peninsula was considerably less than 100,000.) "This story isn't finished," he concludes; "the punchline's yet to come."

In *So Proudly We Hail,* a story of Army nurses on Bataan released in 1943, Bataan becomes both a scourge to the American conscience and a buyer of time. One of the nurses agonizes about the shortage of medical supplies and the failure of the rumored convoy's arrival. "Why

aren't there any supplies? . . . I'll tell you why. It's our own fault.
. . . Because we believed we were the world. That the United States of
America was the whole world. Those outlandish places—Bataan, Corregidor, Mindanao—those aren't American names. No—they're just
American graveyards." But while isolationist America has let them
down, the defenders know that their stand has meaning. "We've become
what they call a delaying action. We are saving time and I hope to God
the people back home aren't losing it for us. . . . It's our present.
We're giving them time."

In *Cry Havoc* (1943), also a story about nurses in the Philippines,
a somber message for the home front again occurs. One of the girls turns
off the radio broadcasting a program from the States. "We don't listen to
it," she explains sarcastically. "We're tired of being told there's a war
on." "I'll bet most of the people in the States are scared to death they'll
have to do something," adds another nurse. They too expect a convoy
with supplies to come to their relief, but the convoy is sunk. In a
moment of despair, one of the girls says, "We can't win," meaning the
war. But the tough head nurse (Margaret Sullavan) contradicts her:
"We can't lose!" She then pulls down a map and demonstrates the big
picture. "What the Japs intended to do is walk down through the Philippines," she explains. "They'd just walk right through. . . . California
was their next step. They didn't think we could hold out in Bataan more
than two weeks. . . . But our boys didn't like the idea of their walking
through and they dug in and held out. . . . We're winning the war.
That's all that's important."

At the end of the picture, the nurses are trapped in their dugout,
with escape impossible. After a Japanese voice is heard calling down from
the entrance, "Come out with your hands over your head," the women
slowly march up the steps, and the movie ends. To spell out their fate
more explicitly would probably have been considered too brutal. For
some reason, perhaps racial, the rape of white women by Japanese was
never presented on the screen. The rapes were always of Chinese
women. From the standpoint of civilian morale, the nurses' surrender,
since it was by helpless women, rather than American fighting men, was
acceptable, and by very faintly implying what could happen to these
women in the hands of the Japanese, it would serve to arouse anger and
hate in the audience.

The movie was based on a play by Allan R. Kenward which contained so many gross inaccuracies that it drew an angry letter of complaint from Captain Florence MacDonald, who had been in charge of

the Army nurses in the Philippines. To the playwright she wrote: "You have managed to include horror, war, birth, death, destruction, horror, Lesbianism, insanity, hysteria, horror, smut, murder, spies, sex, horror, and even a little nobility. . . . It should bring wonderful box office."

Even before the release of *Cry Havoc* the Bureau of Motion Pictures' reviewer objected to the impression given by Margaret Sullavan's speech that the delaying action on Bataan was singlehandedly winning the war. He tried to have dialogue changed so that the idea was that it was "helping" win it. Further, he suggested that the map used in the scene be a world map, so that our Allies' contribution could also be mentioned. The role of the Filipino troops in the defense of Bataan was also scanted. There were some 50,000 of them on Bataan, as against 20,000 Americans giving the impression that the Americans were doing all the fighting. In addition, the Filipinos were referred to (offensively said the reviewer) as "natives."

The best of the Last Stand pictures was *Bataan,* released in 1943. This story of a pickup squad of thirteen men who delay the Japanese long enough to permit the main body of forces to retreat was grimmer and less pretentious in style. Inexorably, sometimes horribly, the little band is killed off. There is a minimum of Hollywood hokum, and director Tay Garnett employed the advancing Japanese as a sort of creeping terror. At one point they glide silently through swirls of milky fog toward the Americans in their foxholes, and at another point, suddenly the trees and bushes start moving and are revealed as camouflaged Japanese. The American cause becomes hopeless, and it is then that the wounded pilot (George Murphy) manages to take off in his battered plane filled with dynamite and crash it into the bridge that the Japanese must cross. But this delays them only a little more; in the end the tough sergeant in command (Robert Taylor) is overwhelmed.

Bataan is terse in its articulation of the meaning of the Last Stand. At one point, Robert Taylor cries out to the advancing Japanese defiantly: "Come on, suckers! What are you waiting for? . . . We'll be here. We'll always be here. Why don't you come and get us?" Rather than elevate the lost cause in the Philippines to a strategic victory, the picture makes it a lonely, grim defeat on a foreign soil. "It doesn't matter where a man dies," says Taylor, "so long as he dies for freedom." They are fighting in a good cause; the temptation to make something more of it is resisted.

But in all Last Stand pictures war became a histrionic event calculated to arouse sympathy. There was always the young kid whom the audience identifies with and who is killed—*e.g.,* Robert Walker in *Bataan,* whom a critic described lovingly as "a garrulous youngster, as green and pliant as a sapling branch, whose emotions rush unguardedly at the surface and send wistful signals to your heart." There was the Japanese atrocity and the defiant curse laid on the perpetrators, as in *So Proudly We Hail:* "They're machine gunning! They're strafing [the hospital]! The beasts! The slimy beasts!" There is the act of redemption through supreme sacrifice, as when Veronica Lake in *So Proudly We Hail* blows up herself and the advancing Japs with a hand grenade so that the other nurses can escape. There is hysteria, as when a character in *Manila Calling* (1942) goes berserk under the strain, as does the nurse's aide in *Cry Havoc.* And there is terror, as in *Bataan* when the silent enemy creeps up on the beleaguered defenders.

And of course there was the presentation of the enemy as, in the approving words of the BMP reviewer writing of *Cry Havoc,* "formidable, and ruthless." He was never directly confronted however; invariably referred to as a monkey, a Nippo, Mr. Moto or an ape, he is subhuman evil and does not ever speak.

The home front was preached to, and there was an implied question whether the people enjoying soft comfortable lives in America were worthy of the sacrifices being made for them. In *Eve of St. Mark,* adapted from Maxwell Anderson's poetic, stilted and milksoppy 1942 play, GI's holding a small, strategic island debate whether they should go or stay. One says that there are millions of people safe in America who have never done anything for the war effort. The hero (William Eythe) counters: "But we are here." "What difference does a rock make?" asks the cynic. "What's the good of savin' the whole world if you lose your life in the process?" Two million was bet on horse racing last year; how little people are aware of the war! Then the Depression is recalled. People had gone hungry then. Who was to say it wouldn't happen again? "How do we know that the whole thing's worth fighting for?" But another advances the triumphant reasoning that they are fighting for a Depression-free world of tomorrow, or, as he puts it: "We're not fighting Japs. We're fighting so that 1950 kids won't have to steal potatoes from boxcars," as *he* had to do during the Depression. All this philosophizing leads them to magnanimously forgive the dereliction on the home front, and they vote to stay on their rock.

It need hardly be said that these lectures from the screen were garbled echoes of the American collective conscience speaking to itself. Their origin was in civilian Hollywood; the words were written by civilians seeking to project some punchy, simple message they thought Americans wanted, and needed, to hear as long as it was consonant with the political, social and commercial values of their studio. The Last Stand picture, then, functioned as a kind of catharsis for its audiences by providing a bit of masochistic scourging of their complacent souls.

Historian Allan Nevins described the national mood so strikingly reflected in these movies:

> Many millions of reflective people were troubled by a feeling for which no counterpart had existed in the First World War; a feeling that the nation was partly to blame for the catastrophe. The origins of the first war were not our affair. It had flared up in the Old World as a result of purely Old World forces. We were dragged into it or so we believed. But not so with this far greater collision. It was our affair, because we had been given a chance in 1918–20 to help stop all future conflicts, and had turned our back on the opportunity. When we might have furnished mankind continued leadership, we had failed it. We were paying the penalty. Beyond question this sense of a partial responsibility, this troubled conscience, imparted to tens of millions of Americans a feeling of moral obligation. Never had we been more acutely conscious of both past failures and future opportunity. We had been given a second chance, in which we could rectify our errors, atone for our failure, and write a better page. The feeling that the war was to some extent an atonement could not be translated into Sousa marches and hiphooray oratory. . . .

Not all was gloom on the Hollywood screen, however, but the main problem of the realistic script was to set the hero in a position where he could win. In China the Flying Tigers had been successfully fighting the Japanese Air Force before the war had begun for America. Consequently, *Flying Tigers* (1942) was made, and hero John Wayne, overcoming various vicissitudes, shoots down a number of Japanese planes and heroically blows up a Japanese bridge by flying dangerously close and dropping nitroglycerin. In *The Navy Comes Through* (1943), Robert Taylor masterfully pilots an old four-stacker destroyer behind a smoke screen and sinks an enormous Japanese battleship. His admiral (Charles Laughton) is watching, and jumps up and down on his bridge with childish glee, chortling, "A destroyer sunk a battleship! A destroyer sunk a battleship!"

One popular story was the *Behind the Lines* picture, in which a small band of Allied heroes is plunked down in Germany (never Japan) and proceeds to fight its way back to safety, playing merry havoc with the Germans while in transit.

In *Dangerous Journey* (1942), Errol Flynn leads a group of British soldiers disguised as Nazis. On their train ride to Berlin one of the soldiers exults: "We're going to be the first invasion to hit Germany since Napoleon." And that seemed to be a function of these pictures, to raise audience morale by showing attacks against the enemy heartland, thus embodying the widespread longings for an invasion of Europe. After committing considerable sabotage, the group evades its pursuers and proceeds to a small German airstrip where the Germans are readying a bomber with British insignia for a heinous attack on a waterworks "that provides half of London's supply." Flynn successfully gets the plane in the air, while Ronald Reagan mows down seemingly hundreds of Germans from the turret guns. As a sample of the spirit of those intrepid invaders, Flynn, when England is sighted, says: "Now for Australia and a crack at those Japs."

It was such prototypical American fighting men as Flynn that caused the *New Republic*'s movie critic, Manny Farber, to write exasperatedly:

> The central character . . . has by the end of the picture become a hero of the war no matter how he started—as a sulker, the brother of the captain's hated rival, or an idiot. These heroes are treated in groups rather than as individuals, and though they are given a democratic texture of names . . . they are given only one personality . . . a man of average looks, on the handsome side, very friendly, short on ideas and emotions . . . and capable of trading you a wisecrack.
>
> The only conflicts in the picture arise out of someone's discontent with the way things are going. . . . This conflict is resolved during the first battle, when the unruly one awakens to the fact that the Germans or the Japs are bestial, that he would rather be fighting than leave for a good shore job. . . . The tolerance of this American is exhibited by his love and care for a dog which he finds or is given . . . and which he often calls Tojo or Hirohito.

The real United States armed forces may have had its share of prima donnas in the upper echelons and gold bricks in the lower, but if they had been present to the degree they were in the movies, it is doubtful they could have taken Phoenix City, let alone Tokyo. Sometimes this type was simply an individualist, a surly loner, as was John Garfield in *Air Force*. This 1943 film, an epic of the adventures of a Flying Fortress crew, had Garfield as Winockie, a turret gunner who was browned off because he had been flunked out of pilot's school. Told by the Old Sarge (Harry Carey) that he is needed, Garfield gradually becomes a member of the crew; his moment of truth comes when he watches a parachuting American flier riddled by Jap bullets. Picking up his machine gun (the plane is grounded at the time), he shoots down the Japanese and empties his gun into the flaming wreckage.

A variant of the loner is the spoiled rich kid, epitomized by Robert Taylor in *The Navy Comes Through* or John Payne in *To the Shores of Tripoli.* Both are sons of famous fathers, and an old salt who served under their fathers is put over them. They feud with him, but in the end they become good fighting men, learning to do things the Navy or Marine way. (A twist on this is provided in *Destroyer,* where the old salt—Edward G. Robinson—stubbornly clings to command, until Glenn Ford as the man of the new Navy takes over.)

Rivalries were also common; here there was perhaps a distant bow to that post–World War I classic *What Price Glory;* mainly, however, the feud served to propel the plot in the interludes between fighting scenes. The rivalry is often over a girl and in the classic romantic triangle mold, as in *Fighting Seabees,* a John Wayne epic, or *Alaskan Highway,* a story of the construction gangs that built the Alcan Highway. The triangle is generally resolved by the heroic self-immolation of one of the rivals. In *Destroyer,* the old salt-new Navy rivalry of Robinson and Ford includes Ford's courting of Robinson's daughter (Marguerite Chapman), who remains loyal to Pop until the last reel.

In a different kind of rivalry film, *We've Never Been Licked* (1943), there is the black sheep who proves himself a hero. Richard Quine and Noah Beery, Jr., play cadets at Texas A & M just before the war who are both after the same girl, with Quine somewhat in the lead. Quine has spent time in Japan and grows friendly with suspicious-sounding Japanese—who later turn out to be spies after the secret poison gas formula invented by the school's twinkly old chem prof. Wrongly accused of helping the Japanese steal the formula because of his past chumminess, Quine is cashiered from the school and ROTC and goes off to Japan to broadcast anti-American propaganda with his Japanese buddies. But of course he is just playing possum, waiting for his chance to meet up with old comrade Noah Beery in the Pacific skies and direct him to the Japanese fleet, thus winning the Battle of the Coral Sea or whatever it was. In the end, Beery gets the girl and Quine gets the hero's medal plus his face superimposed over marching A & M cadets.

The thing all these heroes had in common was that they couldn't really get going in the war because of some personal problems, whether age, love, bitterness or whatever. None of them was fighting for money or to stay alive or because they were drafted. Those Axis movie straw men who accused the democracies of being "soft" and "individualistic" seemed to be right; however, the truth was that the scriptwriters simply couldn't write a war story about real GI's, so they had to engraft upon the cinematic war "plots" and "characters" hot out of the Story Department's time-tested files. Only *Guadalcanal Diary* (1943) managed to show a wartime engagement without resorting to histrionics, and it was based on a book written by a reporter who had been there.

Aside from the documentaries, the best and truest war movie to be made was *The Story of GI Joe* (1945), an extremely able and dignified adaptation of the low-key reportage of Ernie Pyle, filmed by William Wellman. Here, though there are actors playing roles, we have an artful accumulation of incidents in the life of a platoon of ordinary GI's fighting their way from North Africa up through Italy. Aided as they were by Pyle's eyewitness accounts and humane view of the ordinary footslogger (plus documentary footage from John Huston's *San Pietro*), the scriptwriters freed themselves from the need for a "plot," gaining thereby in truth and artistry. War was seen as a series of episodes, some brutal, some boring, some comic, which happened to a group of ordinary men. There was no propaganda or preaching in *The Story of GI Joe,* only the moments of anguish of Pyle (played by Burgess Meredith) and his expression of hope at the end: "That is our war and we will carry it with us. I hope we can rejoice in victory but humbly reassemble our world in a form so firm and so fair that it will never happen again. For those under our crosses we can only murmur, 'Thanks, pal.' "

If *The Story of GI Joe* revealed a rare Hollywood maturity, it also reflected a national mood of war-weariness, of "let's just get it over with." The soldiers became skilled professionals, men doing a job, trying only to survive. This was no lament that wars had to be fought, only that men had to die fighting them.

In quantity, if not quality, Hollywood's "war production" was impressive. According to the Bureau of Motion Picture's statistician, Dorothy Jones, out of a total of 1,313 features made during the full war years 1942-43-44, 28 percent were concerned with the war. As did other war industries, Hollywood reached its peak production year in 1943, when fully one-third of its features dealt with the war directly or indirectly. The falloff in 1944 was due to over production, an event re-corded by this *Daily Variety* headline of July 7, 1943, which said it all: STUDIOS SHELVE WAR STORIES AS THEY SHOW 40% BOX OFFICE DECLINE. "Send us more entertainment" rather than "Send us more Japs" became the distributors' ignoble cry; even the Bureau of Motion Pictures recom-mended fewer but better war pictures. Those glorious, naïve days of 1942, when audiences cheered the American flag on the screen or sobbed their hearts out over poor, brave Kay Miniver, were passing, although quality war films continued to do good business. The heyday of Holly-wood patriotism was fast fading and coincided with the demise of the Bureau of Motion Pictures. Also, war had become more real, even to the home front, and audiences were increasingly more sophisticated; with a daily diet of extensive war reporting in the newspapers, magazines and on the radio, they became skeptical of fictional heroism. Instead of ap-plauding the propaganda shorts, people snickered, and in Strands and Gems and RKO Palaces around the country, a new balcony sitter made his voice heard, his audible wisecracks at the expense of screen heroics splitting the popcorn-smelling dimness.

Audiences no longer watched movies with the silent reverence and gratitude for escape from their troubles that had been so characteristic during the Depression. Also, with money about and a shortage of other amenities, theaters became social centers, for parking kids, for necking in relative privacy and for footloose teen-agers—all of which, made the movie on the screen sometimes incidental. Theater owners reported an ominous wave of vandalism—mostly by young people. Seats were ripped, even burned; fights started and some theaters had security men patroling the aisles. With money in their pockets people talked back to Hollywood (while continuing to patronize its product for want of anything better to do) and, as the wave of vandalism indicates, even vented their hostility on it while in the theaters. Still, more than 90,000,000 people went to the movies every week, and yearly grosses soared to an all-time high well over a billion dollars, even though admissions rose an average of 33 percent. Despite the distributors' complaints about the plethora of war movies, just about anything filmed would pay for the negatives.

Morale was the excuse for Hollywood's wartime product—an elu-sive word if there ever was one. Probably, the morale most frequently energized was that of small boys and teen-age girls who sat in darkened theaters, their hearts quickening to the phony war on the silver screen. There was ecstatic release in watching John Wayne driving a steam shovel at an enemy tank, picking it up and dropping it over a cliff. Or

Andy Devine shooting down an enemy plane with a shotgun. Or the insouciant fastidiousness with which Errol Flynn spat out a hand-grenade pin, like spitting out grape seeds.

For the girls there were those heart-tugging, cute young heroes—Robert Walker in *Bataan* and *Since You Went Away;* Sonny Tufts in *So Proudly We Hail;* and Van Johnson in *A Guy Named Joe,* eating in a Chinese restaurant and spinning out a long shaggy story about a man with a false leg in a burning house. The girls they left behind them were all sweet, well-scrubbed and mildly sexy in the bunny sweaters—Joan Leslie typified them all. Gee, their hearts almost broke to think that those guys would go off to war without being kissed—and most of the boys, who usually had states for names, like Jersey, Texas, California *et al.,* were more often than not virgin in the kissing department, not to mention—heaven forbid!—the s - - department. Often these war-crossed youngsters would debate whether or not to marry before he goes off to war. Either he or she has a hang-up because of knowing someone whose spouse was killed in the war and doesn't want to marry and regret. But then one will come through, like Eileen in *This Is the Army:* "Open your heart, Johnny! We're all in this fight together—women as well as men. Let's share our responsibilities—our love—our faith in the future of our country." So they would get married, and if ever a wife, sweetheart or mom had moments of worry about her boy meeting up with an enemy bullet overseas, there was always someone to say the reassuring, magical words: "He'll come back." That was always the moral, the magic talisman—"He'll come back."

And America was not alone in the struggle. There were the heroic Allies—the Chinese, the Free or Fighting French and, yes, the Russians. The Russians were jolly, twinkling people (when not fiercely engaged in guerrilla warfare and earth-scorching), who always seemed to be smirking a jolly smirk and setting straight the record about their jolly country. Their apotheosis was reached in *Mission to Moscow,* in which a faceless FDR (a full-view FDR, in the Hollywood protocol, was *lèse-majesté;* only Jesus had been previously accorded such reverence) sends Walter Huston off to Moscow to make friends with the Russians. There he has many interesting adventures, such as being followed by two jolly secret police men and finding out the truth about the Moscow trials, which, it turned out, were necessary to save Russia from a prewar Fascist plot. Through the picture pass those eternal Hollywood Russians, with Weber and Fields accents, as James Agee observed, their fingers always symbolically beside their noses as they explain, with amused patience, why women drive streetcars or proclaim the Soviet Union's great accomplishments under Stalin in simple words—as in this exchange between two commissars:

1ST COMMISSAR: We are entering a new era, don't you think so?
2ND COMMISSAR: *I* think we have done *remarkably* well!

But the subtleties of international politics were mostly confined to the thoughts of heroic underground members in between blowing up bridges. There was always great optimism among their ranks, and given time, they would have probably won the war themselves, thus stealing the credit from Errol Flynn. Stunned by defeat, they rallied and woke up to their new destinies; as the excited Maquis in *Cross of Lorraine* says: "De Gaulle is in the mountains with five—eight—ten thousand men!"

Occasionally there was a tip of the hat to the American Negro soldier, most often in the form of a production number full of jiving, tap-dancing Negro boys and girls, featuring good old Eddie "Rochester" Anderson as a slack-lipped Negro GI. *This Is the Army* saw fit to bring out Joe Louis and ask him: "Hello, Joe. Nervous?" To which Joe with his natural simplicity replied: "Mr. Jones, I just quit worrying the day I got into uniform. All I know is I'm in Uncle Sam's Army and God's on our side." "I don't know who could have said it better," says Mr. Jones, ushering Joe out to make way for the Harlem production number.

Your ordinary, plain, garden-variety GI Joe always knew what he was fighting for, although he couldn't define it in fancy words. He was fighting for the smell of fried chicken, or a stack of Dinah Shore records on the phonograph, or the right to throw pop bottles at the umpire at Ebbets Field. He was most frequently represented by a character invariably called Brooklyn who was sometimes vaguely Jewish, but not too obviously so.

And, as the more articulate characters told us, it was a People's War; that was why we were fighting it:

It's the people's war because they have taken it over now and are going on to win it and end it with a purpose—like men with dignity, in freedom. [*North Star*]

All people will learn that and come to see that wars do not have to be. We will make this the last war; we will make a free world for all men. "The earth belongs to us the people." If we fight for it. [*So Proudly We Hail*]

. . . this is the war of all the people. It must be fought in factories, fought in the hearts of every man and child who loves freedom. This is the people's war. This is our war. [*Mrs. Miniver*]

The people knew that they were fighting for "a peace that will stick." They knew that "This time is the last time"—in the words of Irving Berlin:

This time we will all make certain
that this time is the last time!
******
For this time we are out to finish
the job we started then.
Clean it up for all time this time
so we won't have to do it again!*

As with the ringing optimism of Berlin's words, time was unkind to most of the Hollywood war movies as their one urgent sentiment quickly faded into tinnily echoing nothingness. Still, a few memorable phrases came out of them—words that will not go down in history with "Don't give up the ship," yet that still have the capacity to cause a tear of nostalgia or two:

Well, looks like this is it.
We'll give those little yellow mustard-colored monkeys a dose
    of their own surprise!
Those sons of—heaven.
Anything I can do to hasten the establishment of the New Order
    and to destroy the decaying democracies, I will amply be re-
    warded for.
Grateful acknowledgment is given to the Army Air Force without
    whose assistance this picture could not have been made.
It's Ramirez! . . . what's left of him.
I'm gettin' corns for my country/At the Hollywood Canteen/I'm
    a patriotic jitterbug.
Dear Sis: They can talk all they want about the Japs' jujitsu, but
    a Marine will tell you it doesn't work against a roundhouse
    right to the jaw.
Now go, darling, and don't even look back.
Have you ever seen the look on a man's face when you tell him he
    can't fly anymore?
I don't want any dead heroes in this outfit.
Synchronize your watches, gentlemen.
My legs! Where are my legs?

---

* "This Time" by Irving Berlin. © Copyright 1942 Irving Berlin. © Copyright re-newed 1969 Irving Berlin. Reprinted by permission of Irving Berlin Music Corporation.

Don't try to win the war by yourself, kid.
I'm not much good at prayin'. There are no atheists in foxholes,
son.

THE END
Buy War Bonds and Stamps at This Theater

While Hollywood sent its celluloid heroes into battle, the song-writers quested after a patriotic grail. In the patch of Manhattan real estate bounded by Lindy's and Forty-second Street whose capitol was the Brill Building, inhabited by a colorful tribe of pluggers, tunesmiths and cleffers, the stock civilian question—"What can I do?"—seemed to have a clear, almost mystical answer: "Write the Great American War Song." Memories jerked backward in one united reflex to the First World War and George M. Cohan, whose "Over There," local legend had it, inspired an entire nation to victory. That Cohan's rousing martial air also garnered lush green (as *Variety* might have put it) and became the leading sheet music seller was a fact of life upon which the writers did not necessarily turn their backs. And when superpatriot Representative J. Parnell Thomas led the public hue and cry with his ringing words— "What America needs today is a good five cent war song"—the songsmiths were already at work pounding out march tempi on the Brill Building's public pianos. The kind of song Thomas had in mind, however, also harked back to the Big War: ". . . a good, peppy marching song, something with plenty of zip, ginger and fire." As it turned out, the nation was massively lukewarm to the old-fashioned rousing march type of song, patterned after "Over There."

Heeding the clear call in the first months of the war, the songwriters strained—and produced such highly perishables as "Goodbye, Momma, I'm Off to Yokohama," "The Japs Haven't Got a Chinaman's Chance," "The Japs Haven't Got a Ghost of a Chance," "They're Going to Be Playing Taps on the Japs," "We Are the Sons of the Rising Guns," "Oh, You Little Son of an Oriental," "Slap the Jap Right Off the Map," "To Be Specific, It's Our Pacific" and "When Those Little Yellow Bellies Meet the Cohens and the Kelleys." None of these stirred, none aroused, none caught on, even though their titles achieved immortality of a kind. As in Hollywood, the early mood was precipitous outrage mixed with chauvinism and hatred for the enemy. The treacherous Japanese not surprisingly bore the brunt of the songwriter's righteous wrath, but the rest of the Axis was not omitted, witnesseth: "Put the Heat on Hitler, Muss Up Mussolini and Tie a Can to Japan," "Let's Put the Axe to the Axis" and "Let's Knock the Hit out of Hitler." Such songs were written in a white heat and rushed out to the public, each bearing its writer's frantic bid for fame as the man who first wrote the song that inspired a nation. The fastest such song, introduced by Burt Wheeler on the night of December 7, in a nightclub, was "We'll Knock the Japs Right into the Laps of the Nazis."

> Oh, we didn't want to do it but they're asking for it now
> So, we'll knock the Japs right into the laps of the Nazis,
> When they hop on Honolulu, that's a thing we won't allow
> So we'll knock the Japs right into the laps of the Nazis!
> Chins up, Yankees, let's see it through
> And show them there's no yellow in the red, white and blue.
> I'd hate to be in Yokohama when our brothers make their bow,
> For we'll knock the Japs right into the laps of the Nazis!

By 6 A.M. on December 8 songwriter Max Lerner ("Is It True What They Say About Dixie") had put the final polish on "The Sun Will Soon Be Setting on the Land of the Rising Sun," which made its nationwide debut Tuesday night on the radio program *The Treasury Hour*. Almost as quick was the song copyrighted "You're a Sap, Mr. Jap," three hours before Congress declared war. A gloomy nation was no doubt cheered by "You're a sap, Mr. Jap, to make a Yankee cranky . . . Uncle Sam' is gonna spanky" and "The A.B.C. and D. will sink your rising sun . . . You don't know Uncle Sammy—when he fights for his rights you'll take it on the lamee."

One of the few productions of the hydrophobia school that achieved any popularity was introduced by Eddie Cantor on his Wednesday night show and called "We Did It Before and We Can Do It Again." With its promise to "take the nip out of Nipponese and chase 'em back to their cherry trees," plus a rousing tune (with a slight resemblance to "Over There"), it offered a message which bolstered confidence by reminding Americans of past martial glories and exhorted "We're one for all and we're all for one, we've got a job to be done." Another, savingly leavened by satire, was "Der Fuehrer's Face," first sung in a Donald Duck short. Its employment of the Bronx cheer in turn suggesting breaking wind made it too vulgar for radio play, however.

But the title of the first nationally successful war song was already in the air, waiting to be grabbed by a quick-thinking songwriter. The phrase "Remember Pearl Harbor" is supposed to have appeared first at the top of mimeographed orders of the Office of Production Management in December, 1941. The phrase passed into the language, and soon a song appeared under that title. Its simple lyrics, set to a martial tune, called on an aroused citizenry to "go on to victory."

An even greater success, though, was Frank Loesser's "Praise the Lord and Pass the Ammunition." In racy, colloquial language this told the supposedly true story of a Navy chaplain—or sky pilot—who, when the bombs started falling on his ship at Pearl Harbor, took over an anti-aircraft gun after his gunner and gunner's mate had fallen, crying, "Praise the Lord and pass the ammunition!" The supposed real-life chaplain, Captain William A. McGuire, later was unable to recall saying the words and wrote to *Life,* "If I said it, nobody could have heard me in the din of battle. But I certainly felt what the statement expresses." It also turned out that Captain McGuire did not fire a gun at all but rather helped out by carrying ammunition. It was one of those early myths of the war, like Captain Colin Kelly's heroic sinking of a Jap battleship. No one wanted to deny it because everybody vaguely believed American morale would crumble without such incidents of heroism to inspire them. Further, the song caught perfectly that puritanical strain in the American temperament summed up in Cromwell's phrase "Trust in God, but keep your powder dry."

Besides, the OWI was solidly behind the song—even to the point of forbidding that it be played too frequently on radio lest it be plugged to death, an attempt to breathe life into it beyond the usual span of a hit song. From there, Loesser went on to write another popular war tune, a heroic ballad to the forgotten sloggers of the infantry, "Ballad of Rodger Young," based on the exploits of a real GI who won a posthumous Medal of Honor, and, incidentally, a good march tune, "What Do You Do in the Infantry." Loesser later deprecated his efforts to *Variety*'s Abel Green. Saying he didn't think this war would produce a great war song, Loesser described the type that actually was being written:

> You stay in the middle sort of. You give her [the housewife] hope without facts; glory without blood. You give her a legend with the rough edges neatly trimmed. . . . If you want to sell a housewife Jell-o you don't tell her: "Madam, it is highly probable that your son is coming home a basket case, or at least totally blind. But cheer up, tonight choose one of the six delicious flavors and be happy with America's finest dessert." Nor on the other hand do you tell her a deliberate lie like this: "Madam, our army is so smart and so well equipped that all your son does is sit in an impregnable tank and shoot down Japs like flies, and you can expect him for Christmas, in better health than ever." . . . the radio public may be made to forget that by this time the handsome fel-

low with the silver wings has had half his face burned off in a crash, and that Joe is all drawn and skinny from malaria, and has some very unattractive jungle lice in his beard.

Loesser's remarks were accurate; the war songs of the Second World War not only skirted the unpleasant facts of death, but only rarely achieved a level much above the juvenile (Loesser's "Ballad of Rodger Young" being one of the exceptions).

There were also mundane reasons why Tin Pan Alley produced no outstanding war songs, a simple one being that unlike World War I, this was not a marching war. Troop movements were usually shrouded in secrecy, devoid of patriotic fanfare. Many of the World War I favorites were written in both 2/4 (march) and 6/8 (dance) tempo, so they were played for the public by dance bands, as well as marched to. The popularity of swing during the Second World War made this cross-fertilization difficult if not impossible (although a "swing-march"—the "St. Louis Blues March"—was arranged by Glenn Miller). Further, according to *Variety,* bandleaders became shy about playing strongly militant songs, because audiences were prone to come up to the stand and ask them why they weren't passing the ammunition instead of playing about it. Finally, the new breed of soldier was rather embarrassed by old-fashioned patriotism, and he tuned out any overflamboyant expressions of it, preferring "sweet" dance tunes. And the girls they left behind—especially the teen-agers who were the biggest market for popular sheet music and records—wanted ballads, not bullets.

The public taste in songs passed through several phases, generally so slightly different one from another, that *shadings* might be the better word. Initially came the patriotic phase. Some of the ballads of this phase, along with such war-horses as "God Bless America," "Battle Hymn of the Republic," "Anchors Aweigh" *et al.,* were "I Am an American," "Say a Prayer for the Boys Over There" (a World War I number), "We Did It Before," "Let's Put New Glory in Old Glory," "There's a Star Spangled Banner Waving Somewhere," "American Patrol" (which was given a bouncing rhythm arrangement by Glenn Miller that caught the fancy of swing fans), "Me and My Uncle Sam," "Ballad for Americans," and "This Is Worth Fighting For."

After 1942, though, Tin Pan Alley patriotism gave way to more sentimental songs with a love interest. Such was Irving Berlin's "I Left My Heart at the Stage Door Canteen," from his musical *This Is the Army.* About all the song said was that a soldier had met a nice girl at New York's servicemen's center run by the American Theatre Wing and was so stirred he forgot his heart when he left. Others in this sentimental mode were "The Shrine of St. Cecilia," "Rose Ann of Charing Cross," "He Wears a Pair of Silver Wings," "A Boy in Khaki, A Girl in Lace," and "When the Lights Go On Again All Over the World" (an imitation "The White Cliffs of Dover"). Perhaps in this mood, but in a class by itself, was the biggest selling hit of the war, Berlin's "White Christmas." The song, introduced in the movie *Holiday Inn* by Bing Crosby, appeared in October in good time for the Christmas season. It went on to sell more than 1,000,000 copies in sheet music alone—the first such 1,000,000 sale in a decade—and to top the Hit Parade nine times, repeating this dominance during the Christmases of 1943 and 1944. It was indeed a song in the wartime mood, a bit sad and yearning—an emotion with which both homesick soldiers and civilians could identify.

In contrast with the sentimental songs, several more energetic ditties had popularity. The 1940 hit "Deep in the Heart of Texas," was five times number one on the Hit Parade, while "I Got Spurs That Jingle Jangle Jingle," which was actually a burlesque of the traditional cowboy song, caught the civilian imagination with its theme of picking up stakes, of ever moving on, reflecting defense workers migrating to the war production centers and soldiers boarding troop trains. An obvious favorite with the GI's was the cautionary "Don't Sit Under the Apple Tree," in which the absent soldier warns his girlfriend back home not to fool around after hearing a buddy describe a girl "who loves to pet," which description fits her "to a T."

The boy in the service, of course, had been getting attention in popular music since the peacetime draft. When the draft extension was passed, the matter was duly recorded in the song "I Won't Be Back in a Year, Little Darling" (an amendment of its original title "I'll Be Back in a Year"; the man had been drafted for a year's service). Then came war and a wave of Soldier Boy songs, most of which (with the notable exception of Berlin's hectoring "This Is the Army, Mr. Jones") were either sentimental or in a jocular mood. "Till Reveille," "Last Call for Love" and "After Taps" depicted the soldier dreaming about his girl before he went to sleep. "I'll Be Marching to a Love Song," "Cleaning My Rifle (and Dreaming of You)" and "Sweetheart's Manual of Arms" conjured up Freudian symbols, as well as Graustarkian operetta armies, while "If He Can Fight Like He Can Love" and "Wait Till the Girls Get in the Army, Boys" put war in boy-girl terms. What would happen when the girls got in the Army? Why—

Imagine what the enemy will do when they appear
They'll throw away their arms and holler "I surrender, dear."

When the girls soon did get in the Army, it was commemorated by "Tillie the Toiler (The WAAC)," "The Girl of the Year Is a SPAR" and several other "service" songs.

Most popular of the Soldier Boy songs, perhaps because they were, for one thing, intrinsically better and, for another, in a more contemporary musical idiom, were the "hot" numbers like "GI Jive" and "The Boogie-Woogie Bugle Boy of Company B." While "Boogie-Woogie Bugle Boy" was in the standard Hollywood production number mode, "GI Jive" had a fast, driving syncopation and clever lyrics by Johnny Mercer in the traditional American voice of colloquial satire, laced with slang:

After you wash and dress
More or less,
You go get your breakfast in a beautiful little cafe
They call the mess.
Jack when you convalesce
Out of your seat
Into the street
Make with the feet—reet!

By 1943 the Soldier Boy had given way to the Fighting Man, as revealed in "Ballad of Rodger Young," "Comin' In on a Wing and a Prayer," "A Guy 24 in a B-29," "Johnny Got a Zero" (in which the schoolboys' taunts at a poor student are thrown back into their faces when he enlists in the Air Corps and shoots down a Japanese *Zero*) and "The U.S.A. by Day and the R.A.F. by Night," which was noteworthy as the first song ever written about a bombing pattern.

The success of "Don't Sit Under the Apple Tree" was followed by a similar "Three Little Sisters," in which each of the eponymous sisters loves a boy in a different branch of the service. They promise to "stay home and read their magazines," although the song's last line—"You can tell it to the soldier, tell it to the sailor and tell it to the Marines"— with its use of the idiom for bunk, cast some doubts on the girls' fidelity. "I Came Here to Talk for Joe" was premised on a Miles Standish situation in which an absent GI sends his buddy to tell his girl how much he loves her. Out of step with the others were "Johnny Doughboy Found a Rose in Ireland" and "Somebody Else Is Taking My Place," with their implications that Johnny Doughboy would make it with the colleens or would find somebody else taking his place back home.

The trend rather was toward a dialogue between the Soldier Boy and The Girl Back Home. Following Pearl Harbor, the Soldier Boy would tell his girl not to sit under the apple tree or would vow "I'm In Love with the Girl I Left Behind Me" and tell her to "Stick to Your Knittin', Kitten" or "Be Brave, My Beloved." Then he was awarded his pair of silver wings, while his girl watched adoringly, and went overseas. But strangely, except for occasional word that he had got a Zero, he was heard from only infrequently again. Evidently he took up with Dirtie Gertie from Bizerte (of which a bowdlerized version appeared back home) and Lili Marlene (which was banned on the radio until late in the war); he rarely wrote, and it was up to the poor girl he left behind to suffer the pangs of wartime loneliness: "I'll Pray for You," "I'll Be a Good Soldier Too," "I'll Keep the Love Light Burning," "My Devotion (is endless and deep as the ocean)"—the most popular of this genre—"Always in My Heart," "I'll Wait for You," "Miss You," and extravagantly, "I'll Never Smile Again," a revival of a 1941 Frank Sinatra hit.

The 1943 song "They're Either Too Young or Too Old" continued the dialogue more hardheadedly. In it, the girl gives her boyfriend some practical, down-to-earth reasons why she won't sit under the apple tree: "What's good is in the Army/What's left will never harm me."

In 1943, however, the loneliness songs began to appear as frustration, as in "Don't Get Around Much Any More." The girl in that song has been invited on dates and says (as if in a letter to her serviceman) "could have gone, but what for/It's so different without you/Don't get around much anymore." Similar sentiments were found in the hit songs "You'll Never Know (just how much I miss you)" "No Love, No Nothin' (until my baby comes home)," "Saturday Night Is the Loneliest Night of the Week," "A Little on the Lonely Side," "I Don't Want to Walk Without You" and, probably the most popular of all, "I'll Walk Alone (because to tell you the truth I am lonely)," which led the Hit Parade eight times in 1944. The home front girl had no equivalent of her boyfriend's bawdy songs; if ever she were tempted, the ideal of conduct expressed by popular songs would brook no mention of it.

There were a few risqué songs written during the period, but they seemed to be about another kind of girl, and the farthest they went was a little innocuous double entendre. Most of the risqué numbers appeared in movies. There was "You Can't Say No to a Soldier," "He Loved Me Till the All-Clear Came," "I'm Doin' It for Defense," "Love Isn't Born, It's Made" and "The Bigger the Army and Navy Is, the Better the Loving Will Be," which Sophie Tucker sang in *Follow the Boys.* These songs perhaps reflected the other side of the endless vows of faithfulness; they joke that it was all right for a girl to bestow her favors—out of patriotism. None of these songs had wide popularity. Their lyrics were innocent as the driven snow (although people who knew winked knowingly at their *sub rosa* message, for example, "Love won't exist/If you constantly slap his wrist").

Anything even remotely suggestive could not get radio play, for radio's standards were even more strict than those of Hollywood. Radio was a medium in which "hell" or "damn" were beyond the pale and in which one could not even say "My God," unless directly petitioning the Divinity. "Pistol Packin' Mama," the hillbilly song which became a national hit, had to be considerably laundered before it could be sung on *Your Hit Parade.* It would not do, the censors said, for the man in the song to be "drinkin' beer in a cabaret"; he had to be "singing songs" (the ban on alcoholic beverages on the air was also applied to the song "Rum and Coca-Cola," which became "Lime and Coca-Cola"). Even the cause of mama's wielding her pistol (papa was dancing with a blonde) had to be changed to eliminate any connotation of adultery.

Almost any song about sailors seemed to have ribald connotations, perhaps for a good reason; hence, "As Mabel Goes—So Goes the Navy" was forbidden by the Office of War Information. But "Bell Bottom Trousers," a bawdy chantey, was successfully cleaned up and went on to make the Hit Parade in 1945. "It Can't Be Wrong," "Take Me," and "All or Nothing at All" were more than usually urgent about the need for a physical affirmation of love. And in 1945, when the boys began to come home, there were several songs celebrating how the separated lovers would make up for lost time. "It's Been a Long, Long Time" and "I'm Going to Love That Gal (Guy) (like she's never been loved before)" were in this vein. Of Perry Como's frankly sexy reading of the latter, *Variety* wrote: "none of his squealing admirers was under any misapprehension as to what those lyrics suggested." So there was no reason for concern that sex had been entirely removed from love songs; it had just joined the underground.

But these risqué or subtly carnal songs were for the most part off the Main Street of official popular taste. When the lonely girls of 1944 had had enough of stiff-upper-lip renunciation and V-mail passion, a new cycle slipped in—the Dream Songs. The dream songs were not new, of course, but the wave of them crested at the end of 1944 and through 1945. They had a simple plot: Love (or happiness) denied by the real or waking world is achieved in a dream. The songwriters rang many variations of this idea, but it always boiled down to that. Beginning with 1942's "I'm Getting Tired So I Can Sleep" (actually a soldier dreaming of his girl), the dream became a popular trysting place:

> I'm getting tired so I can sleep
> I want to sleep so I can dream
> I want to dream so I can be with you.*

The following year brought "I Had the Craziest Dream" ("There you were in love with me/When I'm awake such a break never happens") and "Thanks for the Dream" ("Thanks for the dream, it was sweet;/There were your arms wrapped around me . . . Then I awoke, calling your name/Crying for you, wondering who put out the flame"); 1944 saw the popularity of "Long Ago and Far Away" and "I'm Making Believe," but in 1945 there were "I Dream of You," "I'll Buy that Dream," "Sweet Dreams, Sweetheart," "My Dreams Are Gettin' Better All the Time," "Linda" ("When I go to sleep/ I never count sheep/ I count all the charms about Linda/ And lately it seems/ In all of my dreams/ I just put my arms around Linda"), "Laura" ("That was Laura, but she's only a dream") and one of the most popular songs of the year (five times first on the Hit Parade): "Dream." The last was unabashed fantasy; no longer did the dream provide consolation by supplying an absent or indifferent loved one, but in "Dream" it was total opiate:

> Dream when you're feelin' blue
> Dream, that's the thing to do
> Things never are as bad as they seem
> So dream, dream, dream.†

A similar escapism gripped the movies in the form of frequent "dream sequences" in musicals, fantasy and opulent period melodramas. By

---

* "I'm Getting Tired So I Can Sleep" by Irving Berlin. © Copyright 1942 Irving Berlin. © Copyright renewed 1969 Irving Berlin. Reprinted by permission of Irving Berlin Music Corporation.

† "Dream" words and music by Johnny Mercer. © 1944-45. Michael S. Goldsen, Inc. Used by permission.

1945 the nation was tired of war and dreaming of the better, though un-defined, future that peacetime promised.

Expressing a related emotion of war-weariness were the wave of Homecoming and Victory songs that began to appear. The trend of nostalgic longing for a rosy peacetime world had actually begun in 1941 with "The White Cliffs of Dover," followed in 1942 by "When the Lights Go On Again." But the OWI killjoys discouraged such songs as "overly optimistic," "escapist" and corrupted by wishful thinking, and they faded out. But if the irrepressibly optimistic songwriters eschewed peaceful valleys and bluebirds, they were soon back with more rousing, less sentimental numbers such as "Hot Time in the Town of Berlin" ("When the Brooklyn boys begin/To take the joint apart and tear it down") and 1944's "Victory Polka." One of the most successful of the Homecoming songs was "It's Been a Long, Long Time (You'll never know how many dreams I dreamed about you/Or just how empty they all seemed without you)."

The most popular song of 1944, the haunting "I'll Be Seeing You," held a tantalizing promise of future reunification, although the lyrics did not stress wartime separation. The lovers also began to be reunited temporarily through a furlough as in "Fellow on a Furlough" and "He's Home for a Little While." In the former the Dream Song idea was merged with reality, as the song urged the girl to be nice to the lonely GI who'd been dreaming of a girl just like her:

"He's just a fellow on a furlough, out looking for a dream . . ."

More songs of optimism and homecoming followed in steady succession: "When You Put On That Blue Suit Again," "When I Get Back to My Home Town," "My Guy's Come Back," "I'm Gonna See My Baby," "Welcome Home," "There'll Be a Jubilee," and "I'll Be Walking with My Honey Soon, Soon, Soon."

Although a 1945 song addressed a cautionary (and familiar) mes-sage to the new United Nations Organization meeting in San Francisco —"Don't Let It Happen Again"—the general view of the postwar world was painted in glowing terms of prosperity and creature comforts— "There'll be strawberries floatin' in cream," as one song had it. In "Shoo Shoo Baby," the mother sings a swing lullaby to her baby, whose "papa's off to the seven seas," promising that "when he gets back we'll live a life of ease."

Perhaps in part the songwriters' sanguine visions of postwar milk and honey reflected their own growing wartime prosperity. The music business shared handsomely in the increasing amount of money Americans spent on amusements during the war. Sheet music sales were never better; whereas the average hit before the war could be expected to sell 400,000 copies, during the war 600,000-copy sales were common. In 1944 sheet music royalties to the American Society of Composers and Publishers were more than $6,000,000, an increase of 25 percent over 1943. An all time record for sheet music sales was achieved by the score of *Oklahoma!*—1,300,000 copies. People bought all kinds of sheet music, from saxophone folios to old standards. Radio royalties totaled $7,000,000 in 1945. The record business was plagued by shellac shortages and the ban on records for public performance (radio, jukeboxes) by James C. Petrillo's American Federation of Musicians in 1942. But leading artists such as Bing Crosby, Perry Como, Frank Sinatra, Vaughn Monroe, the Andrew Sisters, the Mills Brothers, the Ink Spots, Margaret Whiting and Spike Jones continued to record, either *a cappella,* with nonunion musicians or for home consumption until the dispute was settled.

Whether owing primarily to the shortage of new records or a mood of longing for times past, revivals had great popularity. Some meshed with the wartime mood through identification with movies that had a war theme, notably "As Time Goes By," resurrected for the romantic *Casablanca;* "I'll Get By," hymning the immortal love of Irene Dunne and Spencer Tracy in *A Guy Named Joe;* and "Together," evoking the prewar happiness of Claudette Colbert and her absent husband in *Since You Went Away.*

Purely nonsense or fantasy songs had a certain popularity, although perhaps less so than in the thirties. Particularly annoying in this genre were "The Hut Sut Song," purporting to be in Swedish lovers' talk; "Mairzy Doats," in baby talk; and "Chickery Chick," in gibberish. Cole Porter's "Don't Fence Me In," the big hit of 1945, was another mock cowboy song in the vein of "I Got Spurs That Jingle Jangle Jingle," although its tune went back even farther, popular musicologist Sigmund Spaeth pointed out, to "Polly Wolly Doodle." "Mr. Five by Five" by Don Raye, who previously gave the world "Beat Me Daddy Eight to the Bar," was a popular novelty in the swing idiom, while a rewrite of another old song "The Lone Fish Ball" was popular as "One Meat Ball" and reflected wartime food shortages.

A whole parade of Latin titles marched through the public ear during the war, including "Tico Tico," "Amor," "Brazil," "Besame Mucho,"

"Frenesi," "Poinciana," and "Magic in the Moonlight"; late in the war the traditional Latin rhythms were spiced with a dash of calypso with the quick succession in popularity of "Sing a Tropical Song," "Rum and Coca-Cola" and "Come with Me My Honey."

A musical genre that remained almost entirely contained in its own parochial world was Hillbilly. Few of its songs made the Hit Parade ("There's a Star Spangled Banner Waving Somewhere" did it once; "Pistol Packin' Mama," however, had many appearances), but it was a multimillion-dollar business with some 25,000,000 fans.

The most successful composers of the war, in terms of dollars-and-cents sales figures, were the Broadway and Tin Pan Alley giants of many years' standing—Irving Berlin, Cole Porter and the newly formed team of Richard Rodgers and Oscar Hammerstein II. The latter's music for *Oklahoma!* and *Carousel* and the movie *State Fair* dominated the popular field; at one point in 1945 they had three songs represented on a single *Your Hit Parade* program: "If I Loved You," "It Might as Well Be Spring" and "That's for Me"—an unprecedented feat.

If any one composer could be said to be the great war songwriter, it was Berlin. His "God Bless America" became synonomous with patriotism; the tunes for his show *This Is the Army*—"This Is the Army, Mr. Jones," "I Left My Heart at the Stage Door Canteen," "The Army's Made a Man out of Me," "I'm Getting Tired So I Can Sleep," "Oh How I Hate to Get Up in the Morning" (from his World War I show *Yip Yip Yaphank*)—achieved wide currency; and his patriotic numbers written in support of various government drives were above the run of such songs, though none of them memorable. The best of these was "Any Bonds Today," but there were also "Arms for the Love of America," "Angels of Mercy," "I Paid My Income Tax Today," and "There Are No Wings on a Foxhole" (for the forgotten infantry).

Other songwriters channeled their frustrated patriotism into propaganda songs written at the behest of the OWI or the Songwriters War Committee, with highly forgettable results. Bond drives brought forth a plethora of sales pitches such as "One More Mile," "Swing the Quota," "Get Aboard the Bond Wagon" and "Unconditional Surrender." If it was a scrap drive song you needed, the songwriters immediately obliged with "While Melting All Our Memories," "Cash for Your Trash" or "Junk Ain't Junk No More (cause junk will win the war)." Victory gardens? There was "Get Out and Dig, Dig, Dig" and "Harvey the Victory Garden Man." War dogs? "The K-9 Corps" and "I'd Like to Give My Dog to Uncle Sam." Loose talk? Try "Rumor Man," "A Slip of the Lip Can Sink a Ship" or "Shhh! It's a Military Secret." A song to remind the women of the home front that they're in the fight, too? How about "Knit One, Purl Two," "The Woman Behind the Man Behind the Gun" or "Fighting on the Home Front WINS" (the "official war song of the American housewife"). Air raid drills were reflected in "When the Air Raid Siren Sounds" and "Cooperate with Your Air Raid Warden."

To commemorate our British allies, the writers produced "Who Are the British" and "My British Buddy." And to foster Pan-American union there were "Hands Across the Border" and "Good Night, Good Neighbor." Our Soviet allies came in for laudatory treatment with such paeans as "And Russia Is Her Name," "Song of the Guerrillas," "You Can't Brush Off a Russian," "Stalin Wasn't Stallin'," "And Still the Volga Flows," and "That Russian Winter" (ugh!).

A veritable barrage of musical exhortation was directed at the war workers back home, including "Arms for the Love of America," "We Build 'em, You Sail 'em," "Give Us the Tools," "Over Here," and "On the Swing Shift." Women war workers weren't exempt from this musical flattery, witness: "The Lady at Lockheed," "We're the Janes Who Make the Planes" and "Rosie the Riveter." And the temptations, dislocations and strain of the war workers' life found a place in "Don't Steal the Sweetheart of a Soldier," "Annie Doesn't Live Here Any More" and "Milkman, Keep Those Bottles Quiet" ("Been workin' on the Swing shift all night/Turning out my quota all right"). A superior plea for harmony on a home front torn by race riots was "The House I Live In."

The enduring songs that came out of the war were basically standard peacetime songs. The ballads, like the girls, seemed a little sweeter, a little more poignant. People wanted their popular music for humming, for mental chewing gum, for a backdrop to their work, as low-level poetry to articulate the chaotic emotions of adolescent love, to dance to, to cheer them up and to color their romantic reveries.

Still, a tear or two of regret should be produced in behalf of all these songs of patriotic fervor destined to be almost immediately forgotten. Who can forget "Remember Pearl Harbor," a nagging tune that still sticks in the brain, but who can remember "We'll Remember Pearl Harbor," a song that came out too soon? Nor did "Remember Hawaii," in the same vein, make it, let alone "Cheer Up, Blue Hawaii." In general, the public spurned chauvinistic claptrap such as "Go Back Where You Belong If You Can't Be True to the Red, White and Blue"; sentimental "Mom" songs such as "Ma, I Miss Your Apple Pie" "Don't

Worry, Mom" and "From Baby Shoes to Silver Wings"; corny virtuous songs such as "Let Your Mother Be Your Sweetheart"; religious songs such as "Look, God, I Have Never Spoken to You," "This Is God's War" and "A Tiny Little Voice (in a tiny little prayer)"; and war mother songs such as "Show Your Medals, Mother Malone" and "There's a Blue Star Shinin' Bright in the Window Tonight"—though all were presumably written with great sincerity. The names of heroes and heroic battles celebrated in songs likewise had short lives, for who remembers "The Man of the Hour Is General Eisenhower," "A Prayer for General Eisenhower and His Men," "Hats Off to MacArthur! and Our Boys Down There," "Here's to You, MacArthur," "Stars and Stripes on Iwo Jima" and "There's a New Flag on Iwo Jima"?

To millions of Americans the radio became a primary source of information about the war. In a commercial medium, news was a commercial success. By 1944 NBC alone was devoting 20 percent of its air time to news, compared with 3.6 percent in 1939; 30 percent of Columbia Broadcasting System's programming was devoted to war news; and networks worried about a drastic postwar slump in advertising revenues when there would be no war news to exploit.

Americans had acquired the habit of attending to the radio for news in 1938 during the Czechoslovakian crisis, events of which were reported on the spot, as they happened, by William L. Shirer. As the engine of war roared with increasing speed in Europe, radio reporters were abroad describing the action. Disembodied voices, they became glamorous figures, modern-day Richard Harding Davises. War came, and Americans heard the sounds of the London blitz, the booming chimes of Big Ben and wailing sirens as background to the solemn tones of Edward R. Murrow. Already accustomed to using his imagination to add pictures to what radio dramas and comedy supplied his ears, the listener actively contributed his own vivid impressions to the descriptions of the commentators.

Radio's foreign correspondents went with the newspapermen and combat newsreel teams into the very maw of war. In their descriptions to the people back home, the use of their own words and voices added a note of authenticity and directness to their first-person accounts. Especially memorable were Murrow's broadcast on board a Flying Fortress over Berlin; Larry Tighe's coverage of the invasion of Okinawa from a B-29 under heavy enemy attack; Cecil Brown's recollections of the sinking of the *Repulse,* an ordeal he experienced; Richard Hottelet's description, a few hours later, of parachuting from a burning bomber; Eric Sevareid's account of bailing out of a transport plane and trekking through the jungles of Burma; the eyewitness description by William Shirer of Hitler's grotesqueries at Compiègne; and the voice of George Hicks broadcasting from a warship on D Day ("The platform on which I am standing is vibrating to concussion of the guns and the exploding shells"). Tighe's account was the first of an invasion from an airplane; a Navy radio on Guam picked it up and relayed it to the States. Where —as it often was—instantaneous transmission was impossible, wire recorders were employed for the first time by correspondents to tape their on-the-spot observations amid the heat of battle. The recordings were then flown to the nearest transmitter and relayed to the network back in the States.

Most radio news, of course, was read by commentators in the studio and came from the same wire services the newspapers patronized. Though some commentators lived up to their name by adding intelligent interpretations to their reports, others employed the techniques of radio show biz to keep their listeners on tenterhooks. Some used the voice "signature"—the repeated catchphrase designed to give them public identity (employed by entertainers since radio's early days), in the manner of a commercial for cigarettes or chewing gum—*e.g.,* Gabriel Heatter's "Ah, there's good (bad) news tonight."

Nor were commentators bashful about editorializing or slanting the news. Their biases covered a political spectrum from virulently anti-New Deal and as isolationist as one could get without paralleling Radio Berlin to heatedly pro-Democrat, large *d*. Censorship of such military information as troop movements or production figures was voluntary and effective. Censorship of opinion, however, either by the government or the networks themselves was infrequent with the large exception of CBS. Perhaps the most famous example was the firing of the ultra-right-wing Upton Close by the American network when his criticism of the government and the war effort became too extreme—a move hailed by *Variety,* who compared Close to the demagogic "radio priest" Father Coughlin (who had also been fired for his views).

The listener rarely went unreminded of the war during the average four and a half hours a day he spent before the set. If his radio received shortwave, he could even sample the snide, Oxonian tones of a German propagandist or BBC's code broadcasts to the underground in Europe.

For the imaginative listener it was possible to feel a world at war Out There in a way that newspapers could only faintly provoke.

Hardly had the war begun when broadcasters and government officials were worrying about radio's unique potency as a communications medium—especially about radio news reports triggering public hysteria. The National Association of Broadcasters laid down a code in December, 1941, banning programs "which might unduly affect the listener's peace of mind," and "livid news dramatizations," and "frenzied flashes and hysterical mannerisms" by the news commentators.

Playing of request numbers on record shows was dropped on the theory that agents might employ them to send code messages; weather reports were also discontinued until the fall of 1943, for fear Axis fliers would be tuned in. Stations beefed up their security guards to prevent saboteurs from commandeering them. Man-in-the-street interview programs were halted to prevent some citizen from blurting out a military secret before he could be censored.

In February a series of programs called *This Is War,* suggested by the White House and created by the networks, was launched. These were broadcast simulanteously by all four networks for a half hour weekly over a period of thirteen weeks and were directed by the prolific and protean Norman Corwin, who also wrote several of them. On the first, called "How It Was with Us," the audience heard Robert Montgomery's calm voice sketching reassuringly America's essential goodness (and innocence): "Ordinarily, we Americans are affable enough. We've never made killing a career, although we happened to be pretty good with a gun. . . . We've been concerned not with owning everybody, but with everybody owning. We tried to make our strip of earth a good place to be born on and to live on, and to have some children on."

Subsequent programs saluted the Army, Navy, Air Corps and War Production Board, evoked the nature of the enemy or encouraged young men that their peers all over the world were united with them in the fight against Fascism. The language avoided complexities: The Russians were the good guys maligned by certain unnamed American newspapers (Corwin, the writer, later said he meant 'the Washington-New York-Chicago newspaper axis and Hearst"). Occasionally nuggets of patriotic eloquence glinted in the scripts, such as the line in Stephen Vincent Benét's *Your Army:* "They're going to die in the jungles for the shape of a Virginia field and the crossroads store back home—they're going to die in the cold, for the clear air of Montana and the smell of a New York street." (Benét himself died the next year—of overwork, it was said, writing scripts in support of the war effort.) The Office of Facts and Figures estimated that the programs, which were highly praised, were heard by 20,000,000 listeners.

After the formation of the OWI in mid-1942, radio's war programming effort fell under the advisory jurisdiction of the OWI's Domestic Radio Bureau headed by Donald Stauffer (propaganda beamed overseas was under the Foreign Radio Bureau). This motley collection of "dollar-a-year men, former time salesmen, copy-writers and account executives" spent their busywork days thinking up ways to get "war messages" to the people via radio. Suggested topics at a typical brainstorming session ran the gamut from What Makes the Soviet People Tick to the Logistics of the K Ration. The material was then incorporated into shows or in spot announcements. The DRB also created programs which were distributed to all the stations, to be run at times of the station's choosing —it was hoped, when somebody was listening. Typical was the *Uncle Sam Speaks* series, in which the old gentleman lectured his nieces and nephews accompanied by a dramatization of the topic discussed.

The DRB did not neglect entertainment values, and some of its critics detected a strong adman influence in its prose. The OWI's war was derisively called "the war that refreshes—in six delicious flavors." There may be some exaggeration to this accusation, yet one of the bureau's memos called for more radio "names" and "familiar radio appeals" to chocolate-coat, like Ex-Lax, the unpleasant medicine of its message. The DRB also inherited some of the sponsors' traditional timidity. It long debated whether the term "Fascist" should be applied to anyone other than a card-carrying follower of Benito Mussolini.

A suggestion of another kind of timidity is found in a bureau memo stating the message to be enunciated in one of its campaigns. The original read: "Our soldiers don't care if the hands who made his gun are black or white, male or female, old or young, immigrant or native stock." The phrase "black or white" was deleted by hands unknown.

With its policy of emphasizing entertainment values, sidestepping controversial program matter and gelding writers with a political point of view, the OWI—harassed by Congress—avoided both passion and effrontery. One program issued under the DRB's aegis, however, *did* call for Negro opportunities albeit rather stammeringly:

GUY: [The Negro] gets that way very simple. He gets that way from being kicked around. He gets that way 'cause you want him to die for you and you aren't willing to die for him. He's no sucker.

NEGRO: 'course I ain't. Sometimes . . . readin' in the paper about the war . . . I can't see no difference 'tween whut happens to the people in Europe and whut happen to me over here. Makes you feel like an occupied country. (LAUGHS SELF-CONSCIOUSLY) Funny thing to say, ain't it?

GUY: Not so funny when you consider there are more than one million Negroes possessing varying degrees of skill that is yet untapped by our war industry.

And a DRB know-your-ally program on Russia made Communism into a sort of Slavic REA:

PEASANT: This dam has become a symbol to me . . . of the things my country has done for me. I worked on this dam—comrade— for three years I worked building it. I helped it grow from bank to bank. I saw electric power lines spinning out over the country. I'll never forget my father's face when he saw the electric lights first go on in our little house. He cried for joy. We had as much as the richest man in the old days under the Tzar.
SECOND PEASANT: It was the same with my father too—when our collective got its first tractor.

Needless to say, there was no Communist conspiracy behind this (our other Allies received similar treatment); it simply reflected a philosophy of avoiding all complex issues, a feeling of why bring those things up anyhow at a time when they're fighting side by side with us against a common enemy? The DRB sold the Russians like soap or Pepsi-Cola (Soviet Union hits the spot/Twelve million soldiers that's a lot/Timoshenko and Stalin too/Soviet Union is Red White and Blue), and over them loomed the kindly, twinkling, pipe-smoking visage of Uncle Joe:

We're marching on—the soldiers, the workers, the farmers, the planners, the women! Our banners are waving and our hearts are brave and gay and our eyes are fixed on the coming world of peace and plenty! We are the people of Russia—200 million strong—all fighting for the future of man. You cannot stop our march. We are irresistable as the tides—we are unconquerable as the truth!

And if his facts tended to be oversimple, the dialogue of the radio writer *engagé* often tumbled over into self-parody, as it did in this DRB script:

ANNOUNCER: (FORCEFUL) Woman power!
WOMAN: (POETICALLY) Woman power! . . . The power to create, and sustain life. The power to inspire men to bravery, to give
security to little children. A limitless, ever-flowing source of moral
and physical energy—working—for victory! *That* is woman power!

Critics of radio's propaganda efforts deplored the overemphasis on
dramatization at the expense of factual material. But even the most respected radio script men defended dramatization as the best way of arous-
ing the populace. An extreme expression of this viewpoint was made by
Arch Oboler, the author of the fantasy-horror series *Lights Out* and one
of radio's best-known writers:

> Stating the simple honest fact that a tank a minute or a plane
> a minute is what the country needs will not arouse the man in the
> street to as great a will to do as would the same thesis presented
> dramatically in terms of a Gestapo officer dragging off a son or a
> daughter to enforced labor for the profit of a victorious Master
> Race.

These fictionalizations reflected the general tough-talking, wake-up-
America mood pervading the popular arts. On radio the mood was expressed in the title of one such show, *It Can Happen Here,* which
included this fiery speech calculated to jolt the listener out of his easy
chair:

> . . . but you, America . . . you feel safe . . . smug . . .
> and self-corrected! Yeah . . . you grumble because sugar must be
> rationed and because there are practice blackouts . . . because
> you can't waste all the gasoline you want and because you can't
> buy new automobiles and tires with the money you are earning on
> increased wages and overtime on a better job! . . . Do you think
> the boys that are out in the front lines, who are fighting to keep
> America free for your kids and mine are worrying about a ride in
> the country on Sunday?

As time went on, however, the writing improved; scripts became
better researched, less melodramatic, and the best writers gave their war
messages some personal eloquence. Indeed, this period was one of the
most fertile in radio drama. One of the highlights was a moving script by
Arch Oboler called *The House I Live In,* a fantasy about a man who
has lost his son in the war and wanders the streets of the inevitable
American small town trying to find meaning to justify his loss. It con-

tained a first-class song, of the same title, later sung by Frank Sinatra in a movie short as a plea for brotherhood:

> The house I live in,
> A plot of earth, a street,
> The grocer and the butcher
> And the people that I meet;
> The children in the playground,
> The faces that I see;
> All races, all religions,
> That's America to me.

The acknowledged dean of radio writers was Norman Corwin, whose plays, though their superficiality sometimes betrayed the haste with which they were written, often achieved a poetry in language. Corwin, who pioneered many dramatic devices for radio—sound effects, music, the use of choral voices—had the ability to make the ordinary Joe articulate the war in Common Man Talk. Another able practitioner of what might be dubbed the "fictional documentary" was Ranald Mac-Dougall, who wrote a series called *The Man Behind the Gun*. Mac-Dougall's strength lay in the authenticity with which he reproduced the conditions of war after meticulous, on-the-spot research. In one program he had the listener eavesdropping on a Flying Fortress intercom. This device was so successful that he repeated it on a sub, an aircraft carrier and a tank. He also employed the second-person narration to make the listener a participant in the action, combining both methods in this script about the cruiser *Boise:*

> NARRATOR: You're a chief bosun's mate aboard the *Boise*—a gun pointer—the guy that points and fires the fifteen big guns of the cruiser. Right now you're standing by for action—off Savo Island—in the Solomons—it's nearly midnight on October 11, 1942. Your guns are manned, ready, loaded and laid. You've sighted the enemy, and your eye is jammed into the telescopic gun sight, searching for a target. And now, very dimly, you see a light gray spot on the lens . . . then another . . . and another —five of them. It's them! You can see them plainly.
> BOSUN: (SHOUTING) Target sighted bearing one eight oh! There they are, Scotty . . . pick 'em up . . . pick 'em up—you farmer . . . right-right-right . . . steady, steady now . . . left-left-left . . . There—you're on! On target! Mark-mark-mark!

GI dialogue was also rendered with an ear for slang, but here Mac-Dougall collided with radio's excessive puritanism. He was able to get away with "snafu" until the censors discovered that it did not mean "Situation normal—all *fouled* up"; the locution "She was stacked like a brick courthouse" was created to stand in for the well-known GI simile.

Another technique that Corwin introduced was the voice documentary, in which the voices of ordinary people all over the country were woven together in a single program on themes such as the kickoff of the 1944 War Bond Drive or the United Nations San Francisco Conference. When it was used in a Democratic political broadcast in 1944, Corwin claimed the program swung upwards of 2,000,000 votes to Roosevelt.

Programs such as these were radio's highpoints. For the most part the government's sales pitch, whether it was a campaign to save kitchen fats, buy bonds, use V-mail to save cargo space, be true to your husband overseas, stay on your job, or whatever, was delivered as a spot announcement, as a special program featuring a famed entertainer (such as Kate Smith's marathon for bonds, which sold so many that social psychologists rushed to do studies of radio's influence over the mass audience), as part of the story in a dramatic show (or a comedy too; Don Quinn, scriptwriter for *Fibber McGee and Molly* was particularly adept at weaving his plot line to impart some worthy thought beyond Molly's eternal "Heavenly days" such as not patronizing the black market or signing up for nurse's aides), or as the closing plea of a favorite comic or singer. Eddie Cantor might wheedle blood from his audience before singing "I love to spend each Wednesday with you." Others like Phil Baker, MC of the popular *Take It or Leave It,* altered their sign-off lines for the duration into a patriotic appeal—Baker's was "Bye-bye, buy bonds." And it seemed that Bob Hope's familiar sign-off always found him at some military installation—"This is Bob-broadcasting-to-you-from-Camp-Roberts-Hope, saying . . ."

Many comedy-variety shows traveled to bases, and their writers threw in a sprinkling of local gags for the GI audience, along with the standard fare of endless quips on various comedians' physical characteristics (*e.g.*, Hope's nose and chin, Charlie McCarthy's woodenness, Edgar Bergen's baldness), Crosby's horses and boys, Cantor's Ida and numerous daughters, Lana Turner's sweaters and Dorothy Lamour's sarongs, plus topical jokes revolving around Mrs. Roosevelt's ubiquitousness, Henry Kaiser's productivity, the rubber shortage or the meat shortage (*e.g.*, "So you're in love again. Boy, that love bug must use up all his red points on you!").

Even the kiddies' afternoon serials enlisted their heroes in the war effort. "Almost every chapter of all serials," a radio critic wrote, "contains a war message direct or implied. Millions of young listeners have pledged themselves to save fuel, clothing, collect scrap and otherwise aid the war effort." On a typical day you might find Dick Tracy involved in underground activity in France; Terry, of Terry and the Pirates, fighting Japanese in Burma; Nick Carter tracking down Nazi agents in the United States; Superman fighting domestic saboteurs; Captain Midnight and the Secret Squadron in the South Pacific; Hop Harrigan in Italy; and Jack Armstrong cementing Pan-American relations in South America. Only the Lone Ranger, eternally doomed to ride the range of the Old West with his faithful sidekick Tonto, was not fighting the Axis. The evening adventure dramas were also heavily involved in the war. *Mr. District Attorney* gave weekly sermons on national unity; *The Man from G-2, Alias John Freedom* (a sort of Scarlet Pimpernel of the French underground), *The Whistler, The Man Called X, David Harding—Counterspy, The FBI in Peace and War* and others of this breed did weekly battle with saboteurs and black marketeers.

Despite some reining in by the networks, commercials exploited the war in their messages. Advertising slogans such as American Tobacco's "Lucky Strike Green has gone to war!" tried to tie together patriotism and product. However, the producer of *Information Please* dropped Lucky as sponsor because of complaints about the annoying slogan. The depths that it was possible for the unfettered copywriter to plumb are suggested by the New York cemetery firm which sponsored a news program and inserted the following between flashes of battles and casualty figures: "You never know when to expect bad news, so be prepared. Buy a lot." Still, Pall Mall's "On the land, in the air, on the sea" with appropriate warlike sound effects continued (though one network banned it).

The increased din of commercials amid the usual radio cacophony sounded the note that, despite its coverage of the war and its incessant war messages, for radio it was still business as usual. Companies clamored to advertise whether they had products to sell or not, in order to keep their names before the public and to siphon off swollen war profits on which they would otherwise have to pay high excess profits taxes. Advertisers naturally favored popular entertainment programs, and the broadcasters managed to shunt the more educational and culturally worthwhile (*i.e.,* unsponsored) programs either off the air or into lowlistenership time periods. They reaped their reward: Total advertising revenues jumped 85 percent during the war, and profits before taxes soared to a level 120 percent above 1940.

A few worthwhile shows such as *Cavalcade of America* and *Town Meeting of the Air* continued to be sponsored, but radio's critics complained that the news and propaganda *cum* entertainment diet was deficient in the nutriments necessary to an informed public. When a Princeton Public Opinion survey in 1944 revealed that a majority of Americans had never heard of the Atlantic Charter, did not know what a price subsidy was and were ignorant of how treaties were ratified, radio (and the press) was held at least partially culpable. Congressmen and even executives in the industry itself raised an outcry that radio was becoming too greedily commercial; by 1945, when the gluttony was at its height, Federal Communications Commission Chairman Paul Porter warned against "an alarming trend toward excessive commercialism" to the detriment of radio's public service functions. But these were voices crying out in the electronic wilderness; more representative was the voice of the president of the National Association of Broadcasters:

> After twenty-five years, if the legend still persists that a radio station is some kind of an art center, a technical museum or a little piece of Hollywood transplanted strangely to your home town, then the first official act of the second quarter century should be to list it along with the local dairies, laundries, banks, restaurants and filling stations as a member of the town's business family.

In other words, a radio station had as much obligation to elevate and inform as did the local A&P.

Yet radio entertained, and in moments of crisis such as D Day or the death of FDR it demonstrated that it could be an eloquent participant-observer of contemporary history. When Roosevelt died, it suspended commercial programming for three days, playing somber music or, frequently, a moving program by Millard Lampell, *The Lonesome Train* (about the death and funeral of Lincoln), as the President's body was carried from Hot Springs to Washington to its final resting place. And when V-E Day came, radio celebrated the event with a panegyric—*On a Note of Triumph*—by Norman Corwin:

> Lord God of fresh bread and tranquil mornings,
> Who walks in the circuit of heaven among the worthy,
> Deliver notice to the fallen young men

That tokens of orange juice and a whole egg appear now before the
    hungry children;
That night again falls cooling on the earth as quietly as when it
    leaves your hands;
That freedom has withstood the tyrant like a Malta in a hostile
    sea,
And that the soul of man is surely a Sevastopol that goes down
    hard and leaps from ruin quickly.

VII

SHORTAGES
AND MR. BLACK

Roses are red, Violets are Blue,
Sugar is sweet. Remember?

—WALTER WINCHELL

The effort in the factories and the mines to mobilize for war at first gradually, then rapidly made itself felt on civilian shelves. The pre- and post-Pearl Harbor flush of prosperity ate up the nation's inventory of refrigerators, automobiles, stoves, irons and other durable goods. As the steel, aluminum and other mineral-processing industries strained to expand their capacities to meet the insatiable demands of war, acute metal shortages resulted. Even in 1942, as the American public dabbled its feet in war and went about consumption pretty much as usual, a series of serious shortages loomed upon the horizon, each followed by the disappearance of another amenity of civilian life that long habit had converted into near necessities.

The Office of Price Administration began its stormy and arduous career as inflation fighter and food rationer in April, 1941, when it was created as the Office of Price Administration and Civilian Supply by executive order. Its mission was to prevent "price spiraling, rising costs of living, profiteering and inflation," but its powers were largely "jawbone." Leon Henderson, the veteran New Deal economist who was its first director, labored strenuously but with little effect—concentrating on raw materials rather than finished goods—as the defense-stimulated economy heated up and prices rose 10 percent during the year. With the coming of war, the government moved in vigorously, if erratically, to regulate the economy, pouncing first on groceries, clothing and other commodity prices and rents, while leaving farm prices and wages alone. The Emergency Price Control Act of January 30, 1942, gave the OPA teeth; the General Maximum Price Regulation of April 28, 1942, brought about 60 percent of all civilian food items under a form of control which froze prices at their store-by-store March levels. In January the OPA already had got itself into the rationing business by issuing, on its own initiative, a tire-rationing plan; it never relinquished the rationing territory. Ration boards were set up in every county in the forty-eight states, and more than 30,000 volunteers were recruited to handle the vast paper work involved in controlling prices on 90 percent of the goods sold in more than 600,000 retail stores and issuing a series of ration books to every man, woman and child in the United States. As the war drew on, nearly every item Americans ate, wore, used or lived in was rationed or otherwise regulated. It was the most concerted attack on wartime inflation and scarcity in the nation's history, and by and large it worked.

Rubber was first to go to war—a national crisis for the Japanese conquests in the Far East had gobbled up 97 percent of the nation's crude rubber supply. Only 660,000 tons had been stockpiled—versus an annual civilian consumption of 600,000 to 700,000 tons. The government quickly clamped a freeze on tires, followed by a ban on recapping tires. Only a few could get a certificate to buy a new tire or a recapped one. Anyone who owned more than five tires per car was supposed to turn in the extras to their local filling station. A nation of some 30,000,-000 automobile owners reeled from the shock. Some seemed bent on driving their tires down to the rims; others paid exorbitant prices—$25, $50 each for new ones. Others put their cars away for the duration. One journalistic traveler on America's highways found tires the sole topic of conversation among travelers at wayside stops: "For one thing, [tire rationing] is giving the layman-driver a weird lingo. He now . . . talks of such things as the fabric of a tire and the carcass, of recapping and retreading, as if they were things he learned as a tiny tot, and of the potential yield of rubber plants on the great alkali deserts."

While the experts debated and the government from Roosevelt on down procrastinated about what measures to take beyond tire rationing, practically everyone had ideas on just how to solve the rubber shortage and restore every American's sacred right to drive an automobile as fast and as far as he liked. Suggestions poured into the War Production Board and to the OPA. Many were ingenious, if offbeat; others were from the realm of science fiction and even political satire—*viz.*, the suggestion that all the government had to do was reclaim all the tires on WPA wheelbarrows.

Substitutes for rubber ranging from plastic, white duck, cornsilk and studded rawhide shoes over the rubber were proposed by America's ingenious inventors. One man sketched out a wheel with steel springs for spokes, covered with cornsilk paper. Various types of wooden wheels were put into service—usually on delivery trucks. The WPB was plagued by a man who suggested extracting an oil from garbage and soaking crude rubber in it. In the oil, the rubber would expand—doubling in two days and growing four times after a week's immersion. All that the WPB need do, then, was construct an enormous vat, fill it with garbage oil and dump in the nation's rubber stockpile; in a week, it would be quadrupled. Rubber did indeed swell up when immersed in the oil; the trouble was, after the swollen rubber was put through a dehydrator, an essential step in its processing, it returned to its normal size. The inventor departed, muttering about inventing a fixative, never to return.

More down-to-earth, though still pie in the sky as far as production was concerned, were synthetics and plants such as the desert shrub guayule, whose sap was chemically the same as the rubber tree's (indeed in 1910 when rubber prices were high, guayule rubber had been produced in the United States, making up 19 percent of the domestic supply), goldenrod, rabbit brush (a relative of guayule), milkweed and a Russian variety of dandelion called *kok-sagyz*. None of these turned out to be the panacea. Synthetic rubber derived from either petroleum or natural gas by-products or industrial alcohol was considered most promising. Congress, at the behest of the farm bloc, naturally urged grain alcohol, even though it cost more. FDR courageously vetoed the bill, and petroleum was adopted.

But until the necessary synthetic plants could be built (1941 production was only 12,000 tons) and the Brazilian plantations put into production (Far Eastern competition had beaten out the Brazilian rubber industry in the early 1900's), the nation would have to live off its stockpile supplemented by reclaimed and scrap rubber, and of course 75 percent of this would have to go to the military—and would probably be inadequate. Meantime, what of the war workers who drove to work—

not to mention truckers, buses, taxis and essential drivers like doctors? Of course reclaimed rubber was relatively plentiful—a total of 85,000 tons would be produced during the time period—but it was unsuitable for many military needs, and besides, after being reclaimed three times, it lost its bounce. What was needed, simply, was $700,000,000 worth of new synthetic rubber plants capable of turning out 800,000 tons annually. The civilian faced a bleak future.

His government did little of note for several months to impose any order on the rubber chaos. The obvious answer was a rigidly enforced conservation policy for civilian drivers, a policy that would literally save the driver from himself—in short, gas rationing, for no other limitations would be enforceable. But FDR dawdled, lacking the political courage to deprive the American citizen of his cherished freedom of the road. At one point, the President seemed to have placed his hopes on a massive scrap rubber drive to solve the nation's problems. This took place in June with Petroleum Coordinator Ickes' enthusiastic support. Suggesting darkly that "we suspect that there are people hoarding rubber, and there may even be people in official life who are doing a little hoarding," Ickes ordered all the rubber floor mats in his Interior Department building donated to the cause. This brought a bristling reply from the Buildings Department, which pointed out that it owned the mats, so they were not Ickes' to donate; besides, they were needed to keep people from slipping on the marble floors. The next time Ickes was at the White House, he spied a rubber floor mat, rolled it up and gave it to his chauffeur with instructions to drop it off at the nearest rubber salvage depot.

Millions of Americans followed Ickes' lead and ransacked closets and attics and cellars for old overshoes, hot-water bottles and beach balls and hauled them to the nearest gas station collection point. Like Ickes' floor mat, much of this material was already made of reclaimed rubber and hence only good for making more floor mats; still, a total of 335,000 tons was collected.

But the rubber shortage was not solved, and the President continued to shilly-shally. According to Bruce Catton, who was employed by the WPB at the time, Roosevelt told a meeting of his chief production advisers, "Personally I'm not worried about the rubber shortage." At a press conference he was asked about gas rationing and allowed he could understand why a man in Texas, say, living next door to an oil well with four good tires on his car would be opposed to any limitations on his freedom to use his car as he saw fit. (Shortly before that performance, Roosevelt had said he was considering a proposal to requisition every tire in the United States.) The remark was perhaps a bow to his Southern coalition, as well as the Western states, all of whose representatives opposed gas rationing.

Gas rationing was announced for the East Coast beginning in May. This was not aimed at cutting down on driving and saving tires; it was because of a real fuel shortage resulting from the large number of tankers sunk by German subs in the Atlantic. The Eastern seaboard depended on tanker shipments for 95 percent of its oil, prewar; a pipeline, known as the Big Inch, was being built to link the Texas oilfields with the Northeastern states, but this would not be completed until early 1943. The overburdened railroads would help, but not enough to alleviate the shortage. When Henderson announced his plan to allocate each motorist from two and a half to five gallons a week, the oil industry and its good friend in Washington, Ickes, let out a wounded bellow, Ickes calling Henderson's program "half-baked, ill-advised, hit or miss." A propaganda barrage accused Henderson of maliciously trying to make the American people unhappy and labeled gas rationing an exercise in official sadomasochism whose only purpose was to instill in the American people a proper mood of wartime self-abnegation. The rationing in the East was seen merely as a stepping-stone to nationwide rationing. Be that as it may, Easterners took to rationing with reasonable calm and a probably normal amount of chicanery. On the May 10 weekend, the last before rationing began, traffic was below normal, contrary to predictions of a last-minute spree of madcap pleasure driving. More than 200 members of Congress asked for and were given X cards allowing unlimited gasoline, causing some raised eyebrows.

The President, under the pressure of his advisers, finally appointed a commission headed by the universally respected Bernard Baruch to look into the rubber situation. The commission reported back that the only way to save tires was to limit mileage for the entire nation, and the only way to do that was to ration gasoline, curtail nonessential driving and cut down on speeds. Armed with this holy writ from the sage of Wall Street, Roosevelt ordered nationwide gas rationing, a ban on pleasure driving and a 35-mile speed limit on all of the nation's highways. Gas rationing went into effect on December 1, 1942; it had taken Americans nearly a year to tighten their belts this mere one notch; hardly anyone, from Roosevelt on down, was blameless for this procrastination. Leon Henderson, who, as he himself predicted, had become the most unpopular man in America, resigned, and was replaced by former Senator Prentiss M. Brown, a Michigan New Dealer.

The basis of the ration system was the A, B and C sticker system. An A sticker owner received the lowest gas allocation, four (later three) gallons a week, which the government estimated, at 15 miles to the gallon, would permit 60 miles of driving. The B sticker holder had essential driving to do—such as a war worker who drove his car in a car pool—and received a supplementary allowance. The C card holder needed his car for essential activities—a doctor, for example—and was given additional allocations. Obviously, if you were an A card holder, you were a nobody—a nonessential who puttered about in his car on insignificant little errands while cars packed to the roof with joyriding war workers or large sedans driven by powerful men with mysterious connections blew carbon monoxide in your face. It, is of course, the American Way of Life to Get Ahead, and everybody who could find the flimsiest pretext of essentiality tried to convince his local OPA board that he deserved better of them. One OPA estimate had it that nearly half of all American drivers had B or C stickers (there was also a T sticker for truckers, who could get all the gas they needed) meaning an army of 15,000,000 drivers going about essential occupations, even though a Gallup Poll had shown that of the 45 percent of American workers who drove their cars to work, three-fourths said they could get to work some other way if necessary.

Gas rationing and attendant regulations aimed at cutting down on driving did bring a noticeable decline in cars on the streets. In big cities one could ply the unpopulated boulevards with rarely a start or stop for traffic. Deliveries were curtailed by department stores, and the slogan was "Don't delay, buy it today, carry it away." In the East, milk deliveries were cut to every other day, while newspapers (some using horse-drawn wagons) made only one daily delivery of editions to each news-stand. The decline in driving was accurately reflected in gasoline tax revenues; in New York State revenues for the first three months of 1943 were $6,600,000 compared to $13,500,000 for the same period in 1942. Most significant of all, the auto death rate fell dramatically: on Labor Day, 1942 (before nationwide rationing), there were 169 deaths in auto accidents; in 1941, there had been 423. It was estimated that the highways were being used at only about 20 percent of capacity.

So gas rationing has its salutary results—or so a group of professional cheerer-uppers had it. One of these was Donald Culross Peattie, the naturalist, who extolled the joys of walking, presumably restored to the land by the advent of gas rationing.

> I came back to my desk with blood tingling, with every stale, mundane concern washed out of my head. I had heard the titmouse calling his merry song of *peet-o, peet-o* and song sparrows tuning up on the adder branches where the catkins were hanging out all pollen-dusty and fertile. I had heard the brook gurgling.

Theoretically, if a car owner wanted to travel for pleasure, he had to use his feet—or take the train. In January, 1943, the OPA banned all pleasure driving; even the nonessential A card holder could not use his niggardly three gallons except in pursuit of "essential" business which the OPA defined as "necessary" shopping; attending church services or funerals; getting medical attention; meeting emergencies involving a "threat to life, health or property"; or trips for family or occupational necessities. The OPA ruled that a driver might sample nonessential pleasures on an essential trip (such as stopping for a soft drink) as long as he did not "add as much as one foot to the distance traveled in his car for such a purpose." This came as a shock to the A's; they had thought their sacrifice entitled them to burn up their paltry share in any way they wanted. Of course, such a ban was difficult to enforce, and OPA men took to hanging around racetracks and athletic stadiums, copying down license numbers of out-of-county cars on the theory that just getting to the athletic spectacle was per se pleasure driving. In Rochester, New York, those who had driven to a symphony concert had their books taken away by OPA sleuths; in New York City owners of cars parked in front of nightclubs and restaurants were similarly penalized. Miscreants could lose their gas ration if caught. The ban was finally revoked in September, 1943. Petroleum Coordinator Ickes said it had been necessary because of a gasoline shortage in the East; however, he added cryptically that although the crisis had passed, there was still not enough gasoline to permit any pleasure driving. (For a period during the next year enormous military demands lowered the basic gas allotment to two gallons a week.)

The auto tourist trade vanished. The only way to get to Florida was by train. To get an airplane ticket, you had to have a priority, steamships had been commandeered by the government, and all express buses had been discontinued by order of the Office of Defense Transportation. Still the people flocked South, encouraged by ads persuading them that vacations in Florida were essential to the weary war worker ("Like a soldier YOU need a civilian furlough," said an advertisement of the Daytona Chamber of Commerce; Miami's slogan was "Rest faster here"). Even though the Army had commandeered all but ninety-one hotels in Miami Beach, tourist business there was up 20 percent in 1943 over the previous year. Traces of war were everywhere in lotus land by the Atlantic. Air Corps cadets drilled near the hotels where they were bivouacked; the beaches were patrolled by Coast Guardsmen on horseback. While the dimout was in force, cars had to cover the top half of their headlights and blackout curtains were hung in windows facing the ocean. Practice blackouts were frequently held, and ships were being sunk within a few miles of shore. A family vacationing in Florida might find themselves giving the traditional Sunday dinner for a soldier.

Getting there was hardly a pleasure. The trains were packed with people—tourists, soldiers returning from furloughs to Southern camps and soldiers' wives ignoring government advice by joining their husbands. There was a brisk black market in Pullman reservations. Men circulated among the long lines at ticket windows waving fistfuls of tickets at $10 to $50 markups; tourist agencies added $20 "service charges" to reservations. Hotel reservations had to be made six weeks in advance, and the visitor would be paying rates that ranged upwards of $27 a day. But most of the visitors didn't care what they paid, their wallets were fat with war-stimulated greenbacks. Gambling boomed, and on opening day, 1944, 12,726 customers at Hialeah racetrack bet a record $635,758 —$200,000 more than the previous record high, even though attendance was 4,000 fewer. Floridians welcomed this healthy slice of the national prosperity, but the overburdened railroads decided they would just as soon not have the business. In contrast with the eupeptic Chamber of Commerce ads urging live ones from the North to untangle their war-knotted nerves in the sunshine, the railroad ads told people to stay home. The Atlantic Coast Line's ad went: "It's only fair to tell you trains are crowded these days. You'll be more comfortable at home."

Gas and tire rationing inevitably gave rise to a black market. Correctly sizing up the opportunities for illegal gain in this area, professional criminals moved in, and their operations harked back to Prohibition days. The favored *modus operandi* was to counterfeit ration coupons. The forged coupons (most of which were C coupons, the most generous ration) might be sold to individual drivers by the packet at prices as high as 50 cents a coupon. More frequently, however, the mob's "salesmen" sold them to filling-station operators, who were thereby enabled to sell gasoline at prices ranging from 10- to 25-cents a gallon higher than the ceiling and account for these illegal sales, by turning in the counterfeit coupons to the OPA. Some of the filling station operators were willing accomplices, but in some areas the mobs threatened honest operators with physical violence if they did not join the scheme. There was a case in New Jersey where a woman operator, who refused to take the mob salesman's coupons, was tortured with a burning paper torch. When she fainted, the gang departed but not before they had taken her money and burned all her legitimately collected coupons.

Some gangs employed excellent counterfeiters, old pros who could turn out superior work and exactly imitate the great seal that formed the background. The government employed treated paper for its stamps, which, when immersed in chlorine, changed color and glowed a different hue under ultraviolet rays, a hurdle that was surmounted by theft of the government's paper from its own warehouse. Coupons were brazenly stolen from OPA offices—sometimes with the complicity of the OPA's employees. In Cleveland there was a theft of coupons worth 5,000,000 gallons of gas; in Washington, D.C., 20,000,000 gallons' worth was heisted. The understaffed OPA, aided by the FBI, took extensive measures to detect counterfeit coupons (the dealers turned them in in envelopes which were weighed to obtain a count) and did succeed in bringing a number of the culprits to justice. By summer, 1944, 1,300 persons had been convicted of gasoline black-market activities, 4,000 service stations had lost their licenses for being accomplices, and 32,500 motorists had lost their ration books because of using counterfeit or stolen coupons.

Truck drivers were another source of illegal coupons; those who had more than ample gasoline for their own driving sold their excess to filling station owners, who in turn sold gas to old customers without collecting coupons from them. A transaction uncovered in Cheyenne demonstrated graphically wartime values: A trucker gave a dealer 120 T coupons in exchange for four quarts of scarce whiskey. And there was the case of a McKeesport, Pennsylvania, policeman named Tom Faxon who had decided to run for city councilman and devised a brilliant strategy to win the gratitude of potential voters. Every day he hung around a local gas station and asked each motorist who stopped by if he would care to donate his spare coupons to enable him to use his car for campaigning. Most people were generous, and he daily accumulated a fair number of coupons. That night he went about in his election district, distributing the coupons to voters.

Despite the OPA's efforts, estimates of illegally purchased gasoline ranged from 1,000,000 gallons a week to as high as 2,500,000 gallons a *day*. The OPA itself said that 5 percent of the gasoline sold in the nation was purchased with counterfeit coupons; 15 percent of all C ration coupons in circulation were said to be fakes. In some cities the amounts were even higher: In New York City it was 30 percent, in Baltimore 45 percent, in Newark, 40 percent, and in Chicago, 35 percent. When a flood of bogus coupons hit San Francisco, some 3,000,000 gallons of gasoline were sold illegally in the space of a few days. As is traditional to say regarding these matters, the large majority of American drivers were honest and conscientious, but few Americans were entirely innocent of a little harmless chicanery, such as giving extra coupons to friends (detached coupons were supposed to be invalid).

In some areas of the country, especially the East Coast, there were times when you couldn't get any gas at all. In the summer of 1942 the pumps literally went dry; most stations closed, and motorists and truckers were stranded. Some stations remained "closed" or "out of gas" to all save old customers. In New York, drivers would sometimes tail a gasoline tank truck until, like a pied piper, the truck had collected a string of cars following it to its destined delivery point. Cars would line up for blocks—as many as 350 of them—when word spread that a filling station had received a gasoline shipment.

There were alternatives, of course. New York suburbanites and California war workers alike resorted to bicycles, but bicycles were rationed, too, and people had to have a certificate of necessity from their local ration boards before they could purchase a new one. Walking was possible—even enjoyable to some—but because of a shortage of hides and increased Army demands, shoe rationing for civilians was put into effect in February, 1943. Three pairs of shoes a year was not exactly hardship rations—in 1941 the average American bought 3.43 pairs of shoes. In England the wartime ration was about one pair per year. But by 1944 large military demands had squeezed the civilian supply down to two pairs per person. One of the side effects of shoe rationing was another hoarding spree—this time of clothing, which, rumor had it, was next on the list. In New York, clothing stores experienced a 53 percent jump in business during the first week of shoe rationing. Lord & Taylor finally took a full-page ad in the New York *Times* to announce: "We wager $5,000 that clothes will NOT be rationed this year." At least one bride received a Number 17 (shoe) stamp as a wedding present.

Of greater impact on American life than gas rationing was the rationing of food. People coped with gasoline rationing by curtailing unnecessary trips, forming car pools and share-the-ride clubs, and eking out the life-span of their worn prewar cars and tires (after all, one did not really *need* a new car every year or two). But except for those with the money and elastic consciences for black-market patronage, food rationing hit everyone alike. The first table item to become scarce was sugar, rationing of which began in April, 1942. Scarcities presaging some kind of rationing had occurred in some areas as early as December, 1941. Everyone knew in advance that sugar was going to be rationed, however novel the idea of rationing anything in America was to many people. There was a wave of buying that began immediately after Pearl Harbor. Everyone from bootleggers to housewives who had long memories of the World War I sugar shortage rushed to buy 100-pound bags, and grocers were forced to limit purchasers to 10 pounds each. This artificial shortage quickly became a real one in early 1942, after imports from the Philippines ceased and the shortage of shipping made transportation of the Cuban and Puerto Rican crops difficult. And even though the entire yearly crops of these and other Caribbean sugar producers would be acquired by the United States, there was never enough to meet the increased demands of military and civilian needs. Sugar rationing was never eased and indeed continued without surcease through 1946. In 1945, a bad crop year, civilians consumed 70 percent of the prewar level.

So it was that on balmy nights in early May, 1942, Americans trooped to their local schools, where teachers issued War Ration Book One for each member of the family. Many submitted jovially to this first wartime sacrifice; it seemed little enough price to pay for the privilege of "doing something" for the war effort. For the hoarders it was a moment of truth; they had to make depositions of how much sugar they had on hand; stamps equivalent to this stockpile would be torn from their books. Some carried it off with aplomb: "Poor little mixed up me—only one teensy little cup of sugar in the house. I'm just too scatter-brained to think ahead, I guess." But others caved in under the stern eye of the local schoolmarm, confessed their supplies and took their loss of stamps gamely. And after all, the ration, which averaged out to 8 (later 12) ounces per person per week, was not all that catastrophic.

A lot of jokes circulated about the practice of hoarding, indicating a need for guilty laughter. People perhaps felt secret sympathy with the housewife in the story whose husband decided to play a prank on her. Disguising his voice over the phone, he announced that he was an OPA inspector, knew about the 100-pound bag of sugar she hadn't declared and was coming right over to arrest her. She panicked and immediately poured the contents down the drain. And then there was the fellow who went up to the attic to stash his hoard. He tripped over a big lumpy thing in the darkness—a bag of sugar he had hidden there during the First World War.

A goodly number of people never did understand the need for sugar rationing; after all, they said, only one-sixth of our supply came from the Philippines. The papers told of warehouses piled high with sugar—the Gulf Coast refinery that was turning away sugarcane because it had no storage space, the bags of sugar piled high out-of-doors in Texas. Explanations that there was a shipping shortage didn't help; to some people it was just another government boondoggle. The farm bloc in Congress investigated the sugar shortage but was really worried about Cuban molasses being used to make industrial alcohol, being, as always, eager to protect the exclusivity of good old American grain alcohol.

Others did their bit by cutting back on the sugar they put into drinks and foods. Housewives baked less and used substitutes such as saccharin and corn syrup. They also patronized bakeries more, to save their own ration. Bakeries, in turn, used all the substitutes they could get; Schrafft's revived the honey-molasses coconut kisses it had created during the sugar shortage of World War I. Because of increased home and bakery consumption, honey and molasses became scarce; there were instances of stolen beehives in California, and apiarists branded their hives so they could be reclaimed. Housewives canned fewer preserves, while unscrupulous storeowners took advantage of the sugar shortage by requiring that customers purchase a number of other grocery odds and ends in oversupply before they could buy sugar, thus innovating the tie-in sale, a practice that would spread to every level of merchandising where scarce goods were involved. The Justice Department cracked down on, but never stopped, the practice.

Restaurants lowered the level of their sugar bowls or posted signs urging patrons to be patriotic and not take too much. The patrons surreptitiously slipped a few lumps into their pockets before they paid the check, leading to a cartoon of a wife remonstrating with her husband as they leave a dinner party: "I only hope the hostess didn't see you pocketing those cubes of sugar! You know I didn't ask you to do that—except in restaurants." The first burglar jokes appeared, revolving around the theme of the burglars taking sugar, rather than money (*e.g.,* the thief with his hand in the sugar bowl saying, "Aw shucks, nothin' but money in it!"). Such jokes would later become reality: cases of thieves taking the family butter while scorning the family jewels were reported after butter became scarce.

The subsequent rationing of coffee in November, 1942, proved, among other things, that the hoarding psychology was deeply ingrained in the American character. As did sugar, coffee became scarce several months before rationing was put into effect. As early as June, railroad dining cars started serving it only at breakfast, hotels cut out refills, and coffee ads urged voluntary rationing: "Now we're all sharing coffee —by drinking three cups instead of four." Warning of rationing was officially given a month in advance; housewives responded by cleaning out most of the stocks on hand. A week before the beginning of rationing the government froze sales, announcing the freeze on a Sunday, when stores were closed—a practice that became OPA tradition.

Consumers met the shortage by an increasingly familiar pattern of behavior. Most made do on the ration of one pound per person every five weeks. Those who couldn't patronized the black market, tried stretchers like chicory or followed FDR's tongue-in-cheek advice to re-brew used grounds. The latter piece of advice got the President in hot water with the National Coffee Association, who feared that consumers might learn to like this economical practice and continue it after the war. "We respectfully suggest," it wrote him piously, "that it is harmful to imply even in a spirit of levity that the little coffee we do have should be spoiled in the brewing, and that such waste of good coffee should be practiced to help win the war . . . the American people rightly prefer to have fewer cups of pure, fresh, stimulating coffee properly brewed, rather than more cups of recooked dregs of a watery or adulterated brew." Meanwhile, out in Kansas City, librarians reported a rush on books about soybeans—somebody or other had said that you could brew a good cup of ersatz from them. The mania for substitutes contributed to a tidy little door-to-door salesmen racket in which housewives were offered a so-called powdered coffee, which was actually cracked wheat (it tasted awful).

Scarcity gave coffee an aura of luxury it had never had before. Noncoffee users started drinking it to use up their stamps or gave their ration as wedding presents. When the girls got together for luncheon, the noncoffee drinkers might trade their cup for the dessert of a coffee-starved lady.

When rationing was taken off in July, 1943 (they had, after all, a lot of coffee in Brazil; lack of cargo space had caused the shortage), a funny thing happened: Coffee sales dropped temporarily. Apparently, rationing had increased its desirability. A postscript to the coffee crisis was provided when the OPA issued War Ration Book Four in the fall of 1943. Housewives noticed there was a stamp in the book labeled "coffee" and another coffee rush began. The OPA had to undertake a newspaper and radio campaign to convince the ladies that it would never, never again ration coffee.

"Hoarding" was evil but never very precisely defined. Was buying a single extra can of condensed milk hoarding? An Office of War Information radio program implied that it was. There was definitely a stigma attached to someone who acquired more than his share. The First Lady tried to capitalize on this by implanting the subtle thought that "It's wonderful what your neighbors know about you." Sometimes this community pressure degenerated into gossip compounded of a good deal of envy. In some communities rich people became the butt of rumors that they had vast stores concealed in underground vaults. One little girl got up in school to tell her classmates proudly about the old Colonial house they lived in, which had a secret room. Now, she went on, Daddy used it to keep all his extra tires!

The traditional homemaking virtues were made obsolete by the new rationing ethos. This moral shift was expressed in a contemporary book called *Consumer Problems in Wartime:*

> What was right for the consumer yesterday, even a virtue, is wrong today. The woman who rails at strikes in industry or red tape and incompetence in public officials may have closets stored with canned goods or sugar and coffee. Once that would have meant foresight and good management. Today, it means that ugly thing—*hoarding.*

There was a popular phrase which went: "I'm just stocking up before the hoarders get there."

At the same time the patriotic homemaker, forbidden to hoard, was exhorted to save. She was a soldier and her kitchen a combination frontline bunker and rear-echelon miniature war plant. She saved kitchen fats and took them to her butcher (where she exchanged them for red points); her tin cans underwent a standard processing, which called for washing the labels off, removal of both ends, insertion of the extracted tops and bottoms into the can and flattening it all with one's foot. Government propaganda sought to educate the lady in the kitchen by examples showing the war-conversion values of conservation in the home. One pound of fat, she was told, contained enough glycerin to make a pound of black powder—enough for six 75-mm shells or fifty 30-caliber bullets. If every family in America would forgo buying one can a week, this would save 2,500 tons of tin and 190,000 tons of steel—the equivalent of 5,000 tanks or 38 Liberty ships. Thirty thousand razor blades contained enough steel to make fifty 30-caliber machine guns; 2,300 pairs of old nylon stockings went into one parachute, while 15 pairs could make one powder bag. Thirty old lipstick tubes contained enough brass to make 20 cartridges. The amount of electricity it took to light up the average home fifteen months could make a ton of armor. And so on.

She was urged to "Use it up, wear it out, make it do or do without." This admonition translated into more sewing and repair of her family's garments. Thrift became fashionable in some areas; the Highland School in Rockford, Illinois, organized a Patriotic Patches Club. To join, the children had to wear either a patched garment or one handed down from an older brother or sister. The Homemakers' Club of Harlan County, Kentucky, specialized in converting suits belonging to their husbands in service into clothing for themselves. In New York City cleaners noted a marked decrease in the number of garments arriving with missing buttons and credited it to the increased sewing the ladies were doing for the Red Cross and other wartime charities. What old clothes could not be salvaged were donated to Bundles for Britain, Bundles for America and Bundles for the Starving Hottentots. And when patriotic ladies were not repairing for their own, they were knitting scarves, vests and sweaters for servicemen.

In New York City there was a drive for old furs, which were taken to cooperating furriers, who made them into fur-lined vests for the merchant marine. Used nylon and silk stockings were also begged by the government. And when a housewife wasn't collecting things to donate to the government, she was supposed to be hoarding scarce items for her own use—little things like bobby pins, needles and buttons, all of which had become scarce.

The many service industries devoted to lightening the housewife's load had also been cut off by war. Laundry and dry-cleaning establishments were understaffed, short of fuel, and their service was slow, careless and brusque. The tire shortage and gasoline rationing sounded a death knell to store deliveries, and the days when a woman could do her grocery shopping by phone were as extinct as a mastodon. Department-store deliveries were infrequent or nonexistent; customers were urged to carry all small packages. Charge-account shopping was governed by strict regulation; bills had to be paid within two months or the charge account was frozen. Installment buying was drastically limited. Milk deliveries in most cities were every other day, with the reappearance in some cities of the horse-drawn milk wagon, another of those reversions to a gentler way of life brought on by war.

The domestic servant and the once-a-week cleaning lady virtually disappeared from the wealthier middle- and upper-class homes, where, during the Depression years, they had become a fixture. The reason, of course, was the availability of jobs for women, paying more and offering more independence than did domestic service. Suddenly, the "servant shortage" became a cliché topic at ladies' luncheons all over the country. In keeping with their wartime sleeves-rolled-up, pitching-in image, movie stars were shown doing their own housework, and it was reported that Alice Faye, out of whose prewar retinue only the nurse remained, had offered to merge households with Mrs. Henry Fonda and Mrs. Tyrone Power, who still had their cook and gardener respectively. If evidence was needed that the former maids were going into war jobs, a New York employment agency reported that in the fall of 1942, twenty-three domestics on its listings had taken jobs in industries. Ten of these preferred night shift work washing airplanes at $18 a week to being a live-in maid. The New York State Employment Service said that it had 667 requests for sleep-in maids in one month, and only 118 takers. Indeed, the available maids became choosy; most rejected twenty-four-hour service and demanded nine-to-five hours. The classifieds were full of attractive offers. One Newark lady offered "room, radio, good salary and nice home" and the privilege of wearing her mink coat on days off. The mink coat must have been a potent lure, for she received 100 replies. In general, maids could get just about any concession within reason, and fringe benefits were piled on as lagniappes. In a *New Yorker* cartoon a woman about to interview a prospective maid at an employment agency is interrupted by the servant: "Just a moment. *I'll* ask the questions." During the Depression, girls who had to take maids' jobs to live had jumped at the chance of factory work on the infrequent occasions it was available. In wartime, higher salaries were a lure, but not the main one, which was getting out on one's own, out from under the thumb of a mistress. The ladies, Negro and white, were seeking dignity and status as much as they were seeking money; the ones who replied to the ad offering mink-coat privileges asked the size of the coat first, salary second.

In Washington, a city of private entertaining, the servant shortage curbed somewhat the big formal dinner party. Hostesses were frequently forced to hold their soirees at the Chevy Chase Country Club or other private facilities. Only the *grandes dames* of Washington society could afford to employ sufficient staffs of servants for lavish entertaining.

In addition to her duties around the home, the housewife had her war work, should she desire to give the time to it—and millions did. One day a week might be spent rolling bandages for the Red Cross. Nurse's aides, under the aegis of the same organization, were also in demand because of the shortage of nurses in hospitals all over the country; the U.S. Cadet Nurse Corps also attracted young girls into nursing. The Red Cross Motor Corps trained women to act as drivers in emergencies; since few emergencies arose, much of their actual work consisted of ferrying blood donors to and from the donation points. The American Women's Voluntary Services also contributed to a variety of activities; in its ranks socialites and commoners rubbed elbows. There was canteen work for the USO; the Office of Civilian Defense recruited women for a variety of tasks. Housewives were especially valued for the block system, which envisioned each block in large cities as a unit, commanded by a block leader who acted as an explainer of various government programs, salesman of war stamps, surveyor of housing needs, recruiter of women for local war industries and distributor of anti-black-market pledges. Each block service leader received a kit of instructions on how to perform his or her job. Among the instructions was a suggested speech for a house call which went:

> Good afternoon, Mrs. Smith. I am Mary Jones of 142 East 72nd Street, one of your neighbors, and a member of your local War Council's Block Leader Service. I am called a Block Service Leader. My official job is to carry to every home of the twenty families assigned to me the information on community projects approved by our local War Council. I am calling upon you today particularly in reference to the Food Rationing project about which you probably have read. Is there any information about this project or any other matter that I can give you that will be helpful?

The block service leader was permitted to rephrase this mouthful "in your own words of course" and strongly cautioned to "make it very plain to your neighbors that the information you are bringing to them about a project is in NO sense an 'order.'"

The block system was not an unalloyed success. In a few cities, such as Chicago and Syracuse, New York, there were active block systems, but elsewhere participation was desultory. In New York State, for example, only about 20,000 citizens participated; New Yorkers resented strangers who rang their doorbells and politely asked why they weren't canning more preserves. The block service also fell under Congressional fire; some of the gentlemen were convinced it was a Communist-inspired program whose goal was to Sovietize the entire United States. And in Chicago, charges that the system was a tool of the Kelly machine caused Mayor Kelly to resign from the directorship of civilian defense in 1943.

Less controversial was the Victory garden program, which was probably the most popular of all the civilian war effort tasks. At its peak, there were nearly 20,000,000 Victory gardens in the United States, producing 40 percent of all the vegetables grown in the country. The gardens ranged from farms of several hundred acres managed by war plants and growing food for employee cafeterias down to 8- by 10-foot backyards in Brooklyn, where the natives found to their delight that more than a tree would grow. (One observer reported that "every backyard and vacant lot with a fence" had a Victory garden.) The Department of Agriculture tried to discourage the city farmers to some extent, but such was the enthusiasm of the urban dwellers and the novelty of growing one's own vegetables that the small plots abounded in every city backyard and vacant lot. Many cities had communal plots in parks and other vacant land. Total production was in excess of 1,000,000 tons of vegetables valued at $85,000,000.

Victory gardening combined recreation and patriotism; whole families would journey forth on Saturdays to work in their gardens. Mothers revived nearly lost arts of canning that their grandmothers had practiced by putting up part of the family crop at harvesttime. Community pressure cookers were employed in many states. Children became acquainted with exotic new vegetables such as Swiss chard and kohlrabi, introduced because of the seed shortage.

Garden clubs fought to prevent the replanting of flower gardens into Victory gardens, citing their morale value or, in the case of shade trees (which there was early patriotic talk of cutting down for their wood), their use as camouflage. *House & Garden* assigned the American gardener a dual role in the war effort; first, to plant a Victory garden, but also "to keep the flower garden going—grow annuals for immediate cheerful effects and maintain perennials and flowering shrubs and trees so that their beauty will be a relief to wartime tenseness."

But much as Americans rediscovered the joy of fresh vegetables on their tables, most people quickly gave up the gardening habit after the war and found the convenience of the supermarket preferable. Even before the war's end, the apathy which caused a drop-off in civilian defense participation was also noticeable on the Victory garden front. To stimulate flagging interest, state war councils sponsored harvest fairs at which the amateur gardeners could exhibit their best produce. Even New York City had its equivalent of the county fair. The 1943 Harvest Show was held in the lobbies of RKO theaters throughout the five boroughs; the 1944 and 1945 shows were held in Pershing Square Center. Chicago gardeners exhibited at a festival sponsored by the Chicago *Sun* and held in Soldier Field, complete with barn dancing. There were also nationwide contests for gardeners under the sponsorship of the National Victory Gardens Institute, with prizes in various age groups from elementary school children to adults and also for industrial gardens.

After these maiden paddlings, Americans soon found themselves swimming in a sea of shortages, with only the occasional rationing life preservers tossed them by the OPA to keep them afloat. New typewriters, bicycles and rubber footwear were early casualties; the remaining supply was doled out on a certificate of necessity basis. The requisitioning of copper and brass had, as one of its by-products, an acute shortage of alarm clocks—and a plenitude of tardy war workers. Thefts of clocks became such a problem in rooming houses that many workers took theirs to work. Telephone wake-up services flourished, but so serious was the problem the WPB had to design a Victory model alarm clock for civilian production.

Fuel oil rationing came in time for the icy winter of 1942–43. Shortages had been generated by the huge demands of the North African invasion, launched in November, chronic transportation bottlenecks, stepped-up use of petroleum-coke in war industries and the diversion of oil to the railroads for diesel fuel. Homeowners burning oil were issued a sheet of coupons; they figured their allotment on a complicated formula based on square feet—which was a hell of a way to heat a three-dimensional house. The formula was later simplified so that the consumer received about two-thirds of what he used in 1941—an amount arbitrarily established as sufficient to keep his quarters at 65 degrees. The Pacific Northwest was hit hardest; firewood and later coal were rationed there in 1943. Secretary of the Interior Harold Ickes had, in 1942, advised homeowners to convert to coal and became the butt of hostility when coal had to be rationed. Still, only about 10 percent of all homeowners with *oil* heat had converted.

Other, less vital consumer goods became scarce but were not rationed. Whiskey all but disappeared in 1944, as increased wartime thirsts (consumption rose from 140,000,000 gallons a year prewar to 190,000,000 in 1942) drank up the five-year stock distillers were supposed to have had on hand before they converted totally to industrial alcohol production. The distillers were permitted to devote a month to whiskey production in August, 1944.

Canned beer disappeared because of the tin shortage. Hijackers and bootleggers flourished; racketeers specialized in retrieving empties and filling them with four-to-five-times watered stuff and reselling them (pure water did nicely for counterfeit gin). Liquor stores kept the good stuff back for old customers—often a polite euphemism for charging black-market prices to people they trusted to keep their lips zipped. Some employed the tie-in sale, requiring you to buy several bottles of whatever awful stuff was left around in order to get a single bottle of real whiskey. Moonshiners worked overtime on their traditional night shift, but like everybody else, they were handicapped by the sugar and gasoline shortages. Saloons frequently ran out of beer.

Evil-tasting nondescript brands of Mexican and Cuban rums and gins were drunk when nothing else was available. A foreign concoction called "Imitation Whiskey," containing water, flavoring, inferior cane spirits and sediments from whiskey casks, was peddled as "Colored Distilled Spirits." One bootleg formula, sold under counterfeit labels, consisted of one-half whiskey, one-quarter orange juice and one-quarter antifreeze. In Brooklyn fourteen people died from drinking wood alcohol provided by their friendly neighborhood grocer.

Cigarettes fell scarce in 1944 owing to lowered production after a record high year in 1943. By December nearly every tobacco store sported a NO CIGARETTES sign—although most had them under the counter for favored customers—and in New York queues formed and cigarettes were put on sale only at a set time. Thirty percent of all cigarettes made went to the armed forces, though they were less than 10 percent of the population. Ads such as the following didn't help:

STOP WORRYING ABOUT OVERSMOKING
If you love to smoke, if you hate even to *think* of cutting down . . . especially now when war worries and defense activities keep nerves tense . . . then new Julep Cigarettes are meant for you! Even if you smoke 20, 40, 60, Juleps a day, the last puff tastes as good as the first.

The lack of small pleasures hit children, too. Not a few candy-store owners kept their goodies back for tots who could afford to pay more, and young hustlers did a thriving business in black-market bubble gum. Ice cream was limited to eight wartime flavors and was often scarce because of milk shortages. Chewing gum was short because the Army and the defense plants were hungry for it; also, some of the natural flavorings and gum bases came from the Far East, and no more could be imported. Budding young basketball players, finding rubber sneakers impossible to buy, were reduced to shoes with reclaim rubber soles that left ugly black marks.

The little things could sometimes cause the biggest flaps. When Secretary of Agriculture Claude Wickard announced a ban on sales of sliced bread, ostensibly to hold the price down, housewives sent up a wail of protest. Hardware stores sold out their stocks of bread knives overnight; in Washington all the ladies could talk about was "Do you know where I can buy a bread knife?" They adjusted, though, and tried to follow the recommended procedure for slicing bread (lay the loaf on its side, bottom away from you; start slicing at the bottom). "The greatest thing since sliced bread" became a slangy superlative. Bakers, noting a drop-off of bread sales, lobbied for repeal of the measure, saying they would slice bread without raising the price. The order was eventually rescinded, and relieved housewives stuck their new bread knives in the back of the drawer and forgot about them.

Minor deprivations such as these could be borne, though not cheerfully; of more pervasive impact was the rationing of meats, butter and other fats, and canned goods. Even though America's farms, orchards, pastures, and ranges were producing record amounts of vegetables and meats, Lend-Lease and armed forces demands added an increment of 25 to 50 percent to a civilian demand already swollen by increased purchasing power. The Army and Navy and Lend-Lease needed 6 billion pounds of meat of a total of 25 billion (GI's were fed 4½ pounds of meat each per week; Navy men, 7 pounds). This, added in with a potential annual civilian demand estimated at 164 pounds per person meant a deficit of more than 3 billion pounds. Civilians, of course, went without and actually consumed an average of 140 pounds per capita during the year.

Even bigger demands were made upon canned goods. These were needed for shipping overseas in amounts approaching one-half the entire production for 1943. Accordingly, canned goods underwent rationing. The OPA announced a freeze on sales of canned meats and fish, beginning on February 2, 1943. There followed a hoarding spree that made the coffee and sugar rushes look like a rehearsal of the Bryn Mawr baccalaureate procession. Housewives swarmed into stores towing wagons, perambulators, go-carts—anything with wheels—and ravaged the canned goods shelves and loaded their carts as high as possible with whatever looked shiny and had a label on it. The grand champion hoarder was the California lady who declared 8,400 cans to her ration board at the moment of truth. Canned goods hoarding somehow did not acquire quite the stigma of earlier hoarding—perhaps because canned goods are traditional items for stocking up. At any rate, while the OPA's publicity organs were condemning hoarding, the newsletter of the Government Printing Office was praising the office's dietitian for her coup in laying in an ample supply of cans.

War Ration Book Two was issued in February; on March 1 rationing of other kinds of canned goods and dried beans and peas (later rescinded) was set in motion. Each book contained rows of blue and red stamps, marked A, B, C, D, etc.; the blue stamps or points were for processed foods, the red ones would be for meats, cheese and fats.

Up to this time, rationing had been on a single-item basis: a coupon was good for so many pounds of sugar or one pair of shoes or whatever; quality, grade or kind of product was irrelevant. A $7 pair of Boy Scout shoes cost one coupon, the same as $70 alligator shoes (assuming you could find them). Under the point system, different point values were assigned to different products, enabling the OPA to bring supply more or less in line with demand by making scarce items more expensive in points and lowering the point value of goods temporarily in plenitude. Meats were valued according to Department of Agriculture grades, the relative scarcity of, say, beef in relation to pork and the varying demands for various cuts (lungs, tripe and other organ meats were point-cheap). Each man, woman and child had 48 blue points to spend a month, which would bring him roughly 20–25 pounds of canned vegetables a year. A 1-pound can of beans in 1943 cost 8 points; a 1-pound can of fish, 7. Fresh fruits and vegetables were unrationed. Hoarders were rewarded by a misconceived system which, for each can they declared, deducted half the number of stamps that it would cost them to buy the same item under rationing. Baby foods, which were given low point values, were snapped up by adults for their own use. Most severely inconvenienced by canned goods rationing were the women war workers with families, who depended on canned goods for fast, easily prepared meals.

Meat rationing took effect on March 29. There had already been serious shortages in some parts of the country as early as the winter of 1942. Farmers held back their stock waiting for higher prices; demand was up. Whatever the reasons, the meat situation was teetering toward chaos, and the OPA decided that rationing was the only fair way of allocation. Price controls alone might price the lower incomes out of the market. Initially, each person's share was 28 ounces a week, plus 4 ounces of cheese. During the prewar years, per capita consumption was 2½ pounds; but home economists estimated that the wealthiest third actually ate about 5 pounds, while poor people were lucky if they could afford 1.

In administering meat rationing—perhaps the sorest point of the entire austerity program—the OPA frequently, publicly fell flat on its face. Overzealous in issuing regulations, it was often underzealous in enforcement. At the same time, it was a constant target of the Congressmen of the farm bloc, who wanted no rationing at all, really, just higher and higher prices for farmers. Needing a good deal of public cooperation to succeed, it often met a wide array of chicanery, elaborate evasiveness or just plain passive noncompliance all along the chain of distribution. It did its job as best it could, and the men of integrity who administered it—men like Leon Henderson, Chester Bowles, John K. Galbraith, Thomas Emerson—worked long hours in behalf of the consumer—only to see themselves described in the paper as boondoggling, impractical college-professor bureaucrats. Perhaps the OPA might be compared to a temporary, hasty dam erected against floodwaters of human need—and greed. Though riddled with leaks, it held.

For the housewife, the rationing system meant the mastery of a constantly changing system of point values in the papers; while shopping, she kept one eye peeled on the monetary price and the other on the little red numerals posted on the shelf below products indicating their point price. She practiced double budgeting: money and points. She had to keep track of which stamps were valid during a certain time period, which were outdated, and what they might buy. Announcements in the newspapers gave a running commentary:

Tomorrow—*Coffee* coupon No. 25 expires. Last day to use No. 4 "A" coupon, good for four gallons of *gasoline*.
March 22—Coupon No. 26 in Ration Book No. 1 becomes valid for 1 pound of *coffee* until April 25.
March 25—*Processed food* stamps for April, D, E and F in Ration Book No. 2 become valid. The monthly quota of 48 points re-

mains unchanged. Budget these through April 30.
March 31—Last day to use A, B, and C point coupons for proc-
essed foods in Ration Book No. 2. Deadline for first *tire inspec-
tion* for "A" cards.
April 12—Last day for period 4 *fuel oil* coupons.
June 15—Last day for coupon No. 17 good for one pair of *shoes*.

In his turn, the butcher found himself inundated with OPA directives on how to cut meat, describing every last cut with surgical precision. The purpose of these directives was to ensure uniformity among
the various standard cuts and to force the butcher to give the housewife
fair value. If a T-bone steak was to be given a certain regulated price
and red point costs, then the housewife should be guaranteed, the OPA
reasoned, that she received precisely a T-bone steak, as defined by its
lawyers, and that overcharges be prevented by specifications of exactly
how much fat and bone could be attached to this *de jure* cut of meat.
An excerpt from the Draconian code known as the wholesale beef
regulation—40,000 words in all—shows the length the OPA went to
guide the butcher's hand every step of the way:

> The excess loin (lumbar) and pelvic (sacral) fat shall be
> trimmed from the inside of the full loin by placing the full loin
> upon a flat surface, with no other support to change its position,
> meat side down, and removing all fat which extends above a flat
> plane parallel with the flat surface supporting the full loin and on
> a level with the full length of the protruding edge of the lumbar
> section of the chin bone.

Butchers complained they had to cut by ruler and claimed the OPA
methods resulted in waste; housewives' eyes glazed over as they tried
to figure out point values from charts referring to such arcane criteria
as "yoke, rattle, or triangle bone in." The conservative press rushed to
the defense of the small businessman beleaguered by smart-pants young
Washington lawyers who didn't know their rumps from their chin bones.
Senator Hugh Butler of Nebraska charged that the OPA's pamphlet on
meat cutting (twenty-four pages; with three columns of fine print on
each of the first twenty pages) was so "specific as to be incomprehensi-
ble. . . . The whole thing is nutty. It just shows what a bunch of young
lawyers do when they meet up with a beef chart." OPA director Prentiss M. Brown, smarting under such criticism, stripped many of his
young lawyers of their powers and reduced their number from 2,700 to
100. The OPA's critics had an obviously juicy case, and they flaunted

it to the full, bringing about necessary reforms in the agency and a lessening of red tape.

The winter crisis of 1942–43 saw butchers' display cases gradually emptied of meat. Steak was first to go; soon there was not even hamburger in the East. Housewives trekked from one market to another seeking meat for tonight's supper; some days they were lucky to get frankfurters. So in demand were the latter that OPA told meat-packers to stretch them with various fillers such as soybeans, potatoes or cracker meal. The packers, caught in a price squeeze between regulated retail prices and the unregulated on-the-hoof prices they paid to the livestockmen, were in a state of near rebellion. The farm bloc in Congress refused to pass a subsidies measure that would set an artificial price for meat on the hoof. The cattlemen preferred free market prices, complained their costs were going up, too, and, with the farmer's traditional independence, disliked the "handout" connotations as well as the red tape connected with subsidy payments. Much precious beef flowed into what was christened the black market—a term first used in occupied France in 1940.

Butchers took to keeping back choice cuts for old customers; this made new customers angry. Denials were not always effective, for even if the butcher didn't do it, the emptyhanded customers believed he did. Signs such as this one appeared:

PLEASE BE NICE TO OUR EMPLOYEES!
THEY ARE HARDER TO GET THAN CUSTOMERS AND MEAT
IS HARDER TO GET THAN EITHER ONE.

In March horsemeat made its debut; 60,000 pounds of it went on sale in St. Louis. In Milwaukee the Man O'War Meat Market sold 8,000 pounds of the slightly sweetish meat in a day and a half. A Chicago meat broker predicted a nationwide market for 6,000,000 pounds of muskrat and shipped 200,000 pounds of it to San Francisco, where, one hopes, it was sold as muskrat. Rabbit was esteemed as never before; game was another alternative, and despite limited quantities of gun shells, hunters were out in large numbers in hunting states like Wyoming. Poultry was often scarce; butchers reported that in order to get any from the farmers, they had to buy several dozen eggs too.

In the week prior to rationing, panic buying reached a crescendo. Big-city butcher shops were mobbed. In Columbus, Ohio, eighteen policemen had to be called in to control a punching, shoving crowd. A mob of 50,000 people milled around three big markets in Cleveland; in Chicago policemen stationed in stores admitted only one customer at a time as long as the supply lasted. A store in New York had some smoked meat for sale; immediately a line formed stretching around the block and the police were called. Some stores simply hung up signs reading CLOSED—NO MORE MEAT and stayed shut the remainder of the week. At least one butcher closed for good, leaving a sign that said: NOTICE NO MEAT, NO BUTTER, NO SUGAR. WILL CLOSE FOR GOOD WEDNESDAY. THANK YOU.

The week prior to meat rationing, butter sales were also frozen. Per custom the OPA announced the freeze on Sunday. Still, in some communities, people who heard the news on the radio cajoled their storekeepers into opening up their stores. Some did and sold out their stocks in a short time.

The tumult died with the beginning of rationing on March 29. With meat in the fold, the rationing system was complete, except for a few odds and ends (*e.g.,* preserves and jellies) which came under the ration umbrella later in the year. Except for a short honeymoon during the summer and fall of 1944, Americans endured rationing for the rest of the war—grumbling, conniving, sacrificing, and for the most part complying. Compared to the other belligerents, Americans were relatively well off (the British ration, for example, was about two-thirds of the United States'), although there were times when items like butter, beef, pork and bacon disappeared entirely. But compared to the average level of peacetime living that most were used to, they underwent hardships.

Cattlemen voiced a continuing hostility to the subsidy system when it was put into effect by FDR's rollback order of 1943, which restored prices to September, 1942, levels. Most complied with the law but some remained unreconstructed free enterprisers and sold their meat for the higher going prices on the black market. Feeders—the stockmen who bought range cattle and fattened them for market—were caught in the squeeze of high labor and feed costs and complained of dwindling profits and ruinous marketing restrictions. Independent slaughterers and farmers who did their own slaughtering were able to divert a significant amount of meat by selling it to friends or local butchers at above-ceiling prices. A reflection of this activity was the 75 percent increase in cowhide shipments from unlicensed or uninspected slaughterhouses after rationing began. Much farm-slaughtered meat, which accounted for nearly 12 percent of the total civilian supply, wound up in frozen food lockers without any points being exchanged. The 35 percent of American slaughterers who were not federally inspected handled nearly one-half of the country's total meat supply.

Discontent on the West Coast was exacerbated by a shortage of fresh vegetables. In an area which grew much of the nation's vegetables, people rightly wondered why cabbages were 65 cents a head in Seattle, oranges $1 a dozen in 1943. Transportation bottlenecks and a labor shortage in California gardens were to blame; the sight of unpicked crops rotting on the vine was not uncommon. Ironically, the shortage was in part due to the deportation of Japanese-Americans in 1942. They had specialized in vegetable farming, raising more than one-third of the total California crop. Yet in the Congressional hearings preceding their deportation witnesses had sworn that no labor shortage would follow their removal from the land. Now people remembered how important Japanese farm labor was and told one another: "You'll never get a white farmer to work from sunup to sundown as the Japanese did, with his whole family helping him in the fields."

Food shortages flared up in other parts of the nation. Down in Pascagoula, Mississippi, where the war worker force was composed largely of ignorant backwoods folk, butchers received infrequent shipments and ran out within an hour of receiving what they called display meat, *i.e.,* just enough to liven up their display cases. A chronic milk shortage developed; milk was imported from as far away as Minnesota. The shipyard cafeteria needed 10,000 quarts a day but was able to get only 3,000. Adults were urged not to buy milk for themselves and save it for the children. Many workers were actually going hungry. These simple people had difficulty understanding the rationing system; the backwoods lady who said, "I'm goin' back to Arkansas where they ain't got rationing," reflected the view of many.

Around Beaumont and Port Arthur, Texas, there was a critical milk shortage. Here, too, dairymen were faced with the high price of feed and labor. Twenty percent of them simply went out of business; the remaining ones stayed on as much out of patriotism as anything.

In the soft-coal-mining regions of southwestern Pennsylvania, the shortage of meat was one of the miners' big gripes. Before the 1943 strike a visiting reporter noted: "The most conservative miners as well as the most radical ones anticipate a slow-up, serious disturbances or possibly a rapidly spreading general strike unless positive and reliable assurances as to the food supply are given them at once." These were men used to packing three cold pork chops in their lunch boxes; now a typical lunch consisted of an ear of corn, two slices of unbuttered bread.

The miners, of course, were also angry about wages, which they felt lagged behind other war industries, and the rise in the cost of living (absolutely essential rubber boots were up to $6.20 a pair, or a day's pay). They wanted portal-to-portal pay to make up for the average of three hours' waiting time they spent going to and fro between the mine entrance and their working point underground. Food made up nearly 40 percent of the miner's budget, and with food prices up 44 percent the miner was worse off than in 1941 when he received his last raise of $1 a day. While the company stores observed price ceilings, the small privately owned groceries were more erratic about compliance. But the men worried more about the food shortage than prices. "A man couldn't do the work if he only had lettuce sandwiches in his lunch pail," John Dos Passos was told.

Out in Rock Creek, Wyoming, miners threatened to go on strike unless they were guaranteed seven pounds of meat a week each. Some token measures were taken to supplement their rations, but the shortages continued and the union claimed that absenteeism was running 25 percent because of them. Finally in June, 1945, the miners' ration was increased to twice the standard amount—belated recognition that men doing heavy labor should have more meat than civilians working at desk jobs. (More successful in gaining increased rations were the Wyoming sheepherders, whose lonely jobs took them far from stores where fresh fruits and vegetables could be purchased and who, accordingly, packed a lot of canned goods along. The basic civilian ration of 48 blue points, or about four pounds of canned goods a month, was inadequate, so the shepherds had their ration hiked to 288 points.)

Miners weren't the only heavy laborers complaining. In Washington State, lumberjacks struck for higher meat rations in 1943. Dissatisfaction among lumbermen over food and their low wages caused many to heed the lure of defense industries and leave their jobs. The resultant labor shortage in the forests, coupled with enormously increased wartime demands for lumber, gave rise to serious shortages in 1944. The scarcity of wood pulp caused a serious paper shortage, and conservation measures and salvage campaigns had to be instituted. Magazines, newspapers and book publishers curtailed their number of pages and print runs. Books were printed on thin paper with the narrowest possible margins. Even then, publishers found themselves exhausting their paper allocations.

After Lillian Smith's *Strange Fruit* became a best seller, its publishers, Reynal and Hitchcock, found they simply did not have enough paper to fill orders. They were forced to sell the book to a rival house, which was in a better paper situation. The Boy Scouts trudged house to house, trundling wagons behind them, collecting bundles of paper, inspired by the General Eisenhower Waste Paper Campaign of 1945, which awarded to Scouts who collected 1,000 pounds of paper the General Eisenhower War Service Medal for Extraordinary Patriotic Achievement bearing the general's likeness. In lieu of the medal, however, Scouts received a certificate (paper) explaining there was a medal shortage, too: "The necessity for rushing the manufacture of Military Awards for Heroism delayed your General Eisenhower Medal. You will receive it just as soon as it arrives."

Unable to control the channels of distribution sufficiently to keep food flowing to war plant areas, the OPA urged that plant managements shoulder part of the burden of seeing that workers got adequate diets—a measure made doubly necessary because many workers' lodgings had no cooking facilities and restaurants were overcrowded. This scheme was dubbed in-plant feeding—in other words, employee cafeterias. It worked with widely mixed results, depending on how zealously the plant tackled the job. In Britain, war plants were required by law to give their employees meals, and though the fare was necessarily more austere than in America, each workingman was guaranteed an adequate level of nutrition. In America, feeding of workers was left up to corporate initiative. The more progressive concerns, anxious in a time of severe labor shortage to keep employees happy, did well by their people. At the big Douglas aircraft plant near Santa Monica, the employee cafeteria served 100,000 meals a day. Meals were cheap—running 30 to 40 cents—and the cafeteria operated at a slight loss. The food was good, the atmosphere pleasant. There were picnic tables outdoors and entertainment was provided during lunch hours—bands, singers, boxing and wrestling matches and patriotic speeches by returned war heroes. The cafeteria's buyers scoured the state procuring entire crops at a discount from farmers who were unable to get them to market. Local packers, one of whom complained that he had been ordered by the OPA to ship beef to a Japanese relocation center, did their best to supply meat.

Families who had not been uprooted by war, fared from poor to good, depending on where they lived and the adequacy of their distribution channels. Beef, they had little of, unless Mom had an in with the butcher or patronized Mr. Black (the two were often one and the same).

The government took 60 percent of the prime and choice cuts and 80 percent of the utility grades; an estimated 20 percent of the total, nationwide, found its way into black-market channels. People saved points by eating in restaurants (which were issued their own point allotments; many of the fancier restaurants leaned heavily on Mr. B. or served game). In most large cities meatless days, a hangover from World War I, were observed usually on Tuesdays and Fridays. In the home, the housewives reverted to the stretchers and meatless dishes of the Depression; cheese, an old standby, was rationed, however. Eggs became one of the most abundant meat substitutes; indeed the government so encouraged production that a glut threatened in 1944. As *Time* put it: "389,469,000 patriotic U.S. hens squawked but then settled down loyally to do their stuff."

The butter situation lay at the opposite pole. Butterfat was needed in making cheese for Lend-Lease, and most of the supply was diverted to this purpose. So butter became precious—virtually unobtainable in some areas. To buy even ½ pound of butter took an individual's red point ration for the week. Civilians got about 12 pounds a year—or 25 percent less than they used in the prewar period. Because of the butter shortage, margarine consumption increased, but artificially colored margarine was still subject to a federal tax of 10 cents a pound (the uncolored, enabling the customer to do it himself, had a tax of only ¼ cents a pound). The tax, object of a widely publicized crusade for its repeal by Eleanor Roosevelt, was of course the baby of Congressmen from the butter-producing states. The Minnesota delegation at least had the good taste, when butter rationing went into effect, to remove the "Eat More Butter" slogan from its letterheads; the discriminatory tax remained, however.

Pork was plentiful and a boon to meat eaters, but late in the war it too became scarce; bacon became a memory. One group of Americans weathered all meat shortages very nicely, however—the nation's 2,800,-000 vegetarians. In war, there is always someone who profits.

During the palmy days of the summer of 1944, when the war news was good and Eisenhower's armies raced toward Paris, shortages eased. The end of the war seemed nigh; already the War Production Board was talking of "reconversion" and actually authorized the production of some civilian items such as irons, stoves and refrigerators. (Indeed, Eliot Janeway flatly states that the production war—certain crucial items excepted —was won by the end of 1943; October was the peak war production month, and cutbacks began in December.) Businessmen maneuvered to get a head start on their competitors in civilian goods production; workers began leaving their war jobs to search for a job with a postwar future; war contracts were terminated, sometimes abruptly, causing unemployment. *Time* described the euphoria:

> "Yep," said the man in the second [barber] chair, "I got a $10 bet that this little show will be over by Labor Day." "Well, boys," the big man said, "I guess it's all over now but the shouting. I wouldn't be surprised to see those Heinies fold up tomorrow."
>
> In varying forms, this scene was repeated all over the U.S. last week. The signs were not only in the headlines. Whole communities sniffed the new optimism and reasoned that this would be the last summer for at least the European war.
>
> In some ways it seemed almost like a prewar summer. After two and a half years of war the hardest things to get were Kleenex, Camel cigarettes, and shirts from the laundry.

The OPA lifted the rationing of canned goods and meat, except for beef steaks and roasts. Shortages soon set in, however, and rationing of pork loin, ham and canned fish was restored in August. December brought a temporary halt to the allied advance, as the Germans unleashed their Ardennes counteroffensive. Optimism quickly faded, and rationing was fully restored. Unspent ration points were invalidated so that everyone would start off 1945 on an equal footing. Disappointing production on the farms lowered civilian per capita consumption of meat from the 1944 high of 140 pounds. The black market became more blatant; Congress, faced with another food crisis, grudgingly extended the OPA's life until June 1946. Office of War Mobilization head James Byrnes—who bore the sobriquet of Assistant President because of his large responsibilities in coordinating the war effort—called for a modified form of the civilian labor draft, which had been first proposed by the President in 1944. In its final form the bill would have empowered Byrnes to set manpower quotas for various regions and to order workers in vital industries to stay at their jobs, unless it was determined that they were no longer needed; violation could bring a prison sentence of one year and a $10,000 fine. Its chief backers seemed to be the military and a President whose absorption in his role as Commander in Chief had caused him to lose touch with the home front. In a speech in February, Secretary of War Henry Stimson excoriated soft-living civilians and irresponsible unions. Citing "industrial unrest" and the resentment among GI's, Stimson said in testimony before Congress the home front was "on the point of going sour. I say we have a situation of anarchy and this National Service is a step to cure that situation of anarchy and to restore law and order." Other anticomplacency statements came from

General George C. Marshall (who as an "unidentified spokesman" called the railroad walkout of December, 1944, "the damndest crime ever committed against America") and the President, who formally called for a national service act in his State of the Union message of January 11, under which all men between eighteen and fifty could be drafted into any job for which they were needed and qualified. Those who refused would be sent to the Army—hence, the bill was popularly known as the "work or fight bill." Said the President: "Disunity at home—bickering, self-seeking partisanship, stoppage of work, inflation, business as usual, politics as usual, luxury as usual—these are the influences which can undermine the morale of the brave men ready to die at the front for us." Indeed, the effect on the men's morale was given as the main reason for the bill. However, Generals Marshall, MacArthur and Eisenhower had been raising the roof since July about shortages of certain items, including bomber tires, heavy shells and tents. They felt the need for the labor freeze bill that finally emerged from committee, giving the Director of War Mobilization unlimited powers to freeze anyone to any job any time anywhere for any reason—or no reason—whatsoever.

The House and the administration were solidly behind the bill, but in the Senate opposition built up swiftly. Senator Joseph O'Mahoney of Wyoming called it "the repudiation of democracy. . . . the adoption of the principle by which Hitler regimented the people of Germany and by which Joseph Stalin and his predecessor, Lenin, regimented the people of Russia." Senator Wayne Morse called it a smoke screen, shielding the administration's real motive: fear of postwar unemployment. Having no plans to meet the crisis, Morse said, the government took refuge in the untrammeled power to move men about from job to job. Although the bill's defenders in the Senate—Warren Austin, Alben Barkley, Elbert Thomas and others—vaguely guaranteed that it was strictly a wartime measure and would be enforced "spottily," Byrnes himself seemed to attribute wider scope to it when he said that it was needed "not only for war production but also for the production of essential civilian goods; *and later to facilitate reconversion* [my italics]." This statement, ominously smacking of regimentation of the civilian economy after the war's end, plus the vaguely drawn, broad delegation of powers to the director were sufficient to tip the balance against the bill; on April 3 the Senate voted 46 to 29 to kill it.

The proponents of the bill were no doubt sincere, and the manpower crisis of 1944–45—made worse by higher draft quotas necessitated by increased casualties—was the biggest strain on the war economy since mobilization had begun. Nevertheless, here was a badly drawn bill imposing no limitations on people administering it. Although the NAM and the U.S. Chamber of Commerce opposed it, it did receive the eager support of the military and some in industry who saw it as a way to break the power of labor. In Europe, the men in Eisenhower's army, which had been bloodied by 77,000 casualties in the Battle of the Bulge and was suffering a chronic shortage of infantrymen, could be forgiven if they were indifferent to the fine constitutional issues involved and saw no reason why civilians shouldn't be compelled to serve just as they were.

Still, if the winter of 1944–45 did not bring discipline on the home front, it did see a strain of unprecedented austerity. Not only was rationing restored (and food scarcer than ever), but a number of other conservation measures were taken. For no real reason that people could see, Byrnes ordered the closing of horse and dog tracks by January 3. Ostensibly this politically courageous act was to ease the strain on transportation—owners were forbidden to move their horses from their racetrack stalls; but since other sports, such as baseball, were not similarly regulated, the average person could only conclude that the government was seeking to strike a blow against gambling. The ban lasted five months. When racing was resumed, bettors flocked to the tracks and put down their money at an even more frantic rate, so that during the foreshortened 1945 season the 1944 betting high was surpassed.

In the bitterest winter in years an acute fuel shortage had Americans in the eastern half of the country shivering in their homes. Overburdened railroads (carrying twice the freight load of 1939 with only 20 percent additional freight cars and subject to an alarming number of wrecks because of worn-out equipment), manpower shortages and blizzards were to blame. To save fuel, Byrnes ordered a brownout throughout the nation; all neon signs were forbidden, and stores closed at dusk. Thus did the heartland citizen join the coastal cities that had been observing a dimout since mid-1942. Schools were closed for lack of fuel, and businesses went on short weeks. In New York fuel dipped so low that the Army and Navy donated 5,000 tons of coal and 400,000 barrels of oil for emergency civilian use. Downtown shopping centers in Detroit, Chicago's Loop and other places were empty and dark at night; a few pedestrians, bundled up like refugees, scuttled along the lonely streets, hurrying home to meatless meals. A midnight curfew was imposed on bars and nightclubs and was promptly defied by Mayor LaGuardia, who said the measure primarily hurt on-the-town servicemen who needed the fun. And Admiral Jonas H. Ingram, commander in chief of the Atlantic fleet, alerted deactivated air raid wardens back to their posts, saying that V-bomb attacks on the United States delivered from ships or planes were not only "possible but probable" in the near future. From across the ocean the distant war, in its dying throes, had sent a few last waves lapping against the shores of the United States.

As shortages increased, the law-evading transactions in scarce goods lumped together under the rubric "black market" also increased. The term was a rather romantic one. Actually, the black market was not a clandestine place like a speakeasy or brothel, through whose doors slunk furtive citizens. Nor was it a little man saying "Pssst" from a doorway and opening his shabby coat to reveal pendant steaks, butter, canned pineapple and other precious items. A good deal of the black marketeers were, in fact, "legitimate" businessmen who connived in numerous ways to evade price and rationing regulations. For, as OPA Administrator Chester Bowles defined it, the black market was "really any transaction where a sale is made over a ceiling price; or where there is a transaction of a rationed product without passing of rationing currency." In a sociological study made after the war, Marshall Clinard tabulated that one in fifteen businesses—wholesale, retail, service and so on—was charged with illicit transactions. Further, one in five of all establishments in the country received some kind of warning short of criminal prosecution. In January, 1945, Bowles stated in a letter to his regional administrators:

> We have relied on the assumption that 95% of businessmen will comply voluntarily; that enforcement is necessary against only a reluctant 5%. This has proven too optimistic. We know now that, in many an industry, considerably larger proportions of hitherto reputable businessmen are in substantial violation.

Black-market activity was most egregious in meat, but the food black market in general operated through a rich profusion of finaglings. Out-and-out criminality took the form of hijacking and was mostly in inedibles: Liquor, rayon and shoes led the list, J. Edgar Hoover announced. Cattle rustling was revived in the West. Unlike the rustlers immortalized in hundreds of cowboy movies, this new breed did not pick off on-the-hoof beef from the herds; rather they operated with surgical precision in the manner of mobile slaughterhouses killing, dressing the beef clandestinely, then selling it to a packer.

Rifles with silencers or heavy sledge-hammers quickly slaughter the cattle he has selected, the dead animals are deftly skinned and hides buried in hastily dug holes, and the stolen beef is loaded on trucks for quick disposal by prearrangement with racketeering packers and butchers in nearby cities.

One rancher awoke to discover these efficient latter-day badmen had decimated his herd, leaving only scattered clumps of hide, hooves and heads. Sometimes ranchers caught the rustlers in the act, and gun battles ensued in the tradition of the wild West.

The scarcity of meat brought about a chain reaction shortage of poultry. So much poultry was being siphoned off by the black market in Delaware that the Army couldn't get any for its training camps. Squads of armed soldiers were stationed along the highways with orders to stop any trucks carrying chickens. If it was determined that the cargo was headed for the black market, the soldiers commandeered the shipment, paying ceiling prices for it. The situation in the New York–New Jersey area grew so scandalous that a group of law-abiding poultry raisers held anti-black-market demonstrations at the Newark markets in April, 1944.

Normal commercial channels adopted many techniques to evade OPA regulations. These might take the form of a simple unrecorded payment on the side from a dealer to a farmer. Another common method was for the retailer to accept short weights from a wholesaler. The ceiling price was paid, of course, and the transaction recorded in his books looked perfectly legitimate. Naturally, the retailer passed along his short-weighted meat to his customers, who presumably didn't complain, although the Price Control Act allowed a customer who had been over-charged to sue the merchant for three times the overcharge or $50— whichever was larger. A Washington, D.C., housewife who was over-charged one cent on a can of soup brought suit and won; the U.S. Court of Appeals upheld the law, giving the OPA a much-needed weapon in its fight against the black market.

Another practice—dubbed the red market—was upgrading or sell-ing a low grade of meat at the ceiling and point price of a top-grade cut. Upgrading was also accomplished by ignoring the OPA's detailed meat-cutting regulations in order to sell beef with excess fat, suet or bone. Still another technique employed by wholesalers was the familiar tie-in sale. The retailer, in order to get good cuts of meat, would be re-quired to buy hearts, kidneys and tripe.

Some wholesalers did not bother with such complicated dodges and simply sold meat to the high bidder, ignoring ceiling prices and not collecting ration points. A reporter for the Pittsburgh *Post-Gazette,* armed with $2,000 in cash, made the rounds of the local wholesalers and was able to purchase one ton of meat within three weeks without having to produce any ration stamps. And just in case he did need ration stamps, the ever-accommodating Mr. Black had those for sale too—at the going price of $6 per thousand.

Often price and rationing violations became the standard practice. When the OPA investigated some 1,000 sugar wholesalers, it found 750 violating regulations; prosecutions were undertaken against all of them.

Arrayed against the black marketeers were the OPA's 3,100 investigators and 250,000 volunteers serving on the local boards, plus the Justice Department and other national and local agencies. The OPA drew criticism both from businessmen who thought it was too strict and consumer groups and labor unions that thought it was too lax in its enforcement. Since an investigator's territory averaged out to 1,000 businesses per man, enforcement was at best spotty. Some attempt was made to enlist housewives as price checkers, but cries of "snooping" limited their use.

The courts were not generally helpful, meting out light sentences for the distinct minority of violators who were prosecuted.* Fines were the rule, and prison sentences were obtained in only 1.5 percent of the OPA's criminal cases up to January 1, 1944. One group of cases involving dealers who had made overcharges totaling $400,000 resulted in combined fines of $30,000. In another case a merchant who had bought 70,000 counterfeit ration stamps received a one-month suspension of his license.

Where the OPA could claim its greatest success was in the area of price control. Here there was ample public support; Gallup Polls showed more than 90 percent of Americans favoring some kind of price control, perhaps because so many had painful memories of the inflation of World War I, when prices rose 62 percent between 1914 and 1918 and another 40 percent in the immediate postwar years.

The government also had some success in enlisting the cooperation of the individual citizen in enforcing OPA regulations. More than 15,-000,000 housewives signed—and presumably adhered to—a consumer pledge that went: "I pay no more than ceiling prices. I accept no rationed goods without giving up ration stamps." Whole communities mo-

---

* In England such activities could bring sentences of as much as two years and fines as high as $2,000. Because the English rationing laws were strictly enforced, the black market there was practically eliminated.

bilized anti-black-market drives. In New Orleans, 5,000 civilian defense block leaders carried the message to 150,000 housewives and got them to sign the pledge. Within a month, retail food prices had dropped by 5 percent.

Suffice to say, there was a strong body of public opinion against the black market, and probably most Americans did not knowingly or regularly patronize it. At least that was the conclusion of a Gallup Poll which asked: "Do you think that buying at black market prices is sometimes justified?" Seventy-four percent of the respondents said "No," while 25 percent condoned occasional patronage of Mr. B. It may have been that some of the no's were lying, but probably the percentages roughly followed the lines of actual practice.

VIII

PLEASURES, PASTIMES, FADS AND FOLLIES

Under the most iron and rigid considerations, the only pleasures that should be allowed in war are those fleeting moments snatched from (a) the jaws of death or (b) the coils of duty. In home front America pleasure continued on a somewhat straiter, narrower path than before but continued nonetheless. Although the demands of war work, the constrictions of shortages, the inhibitions of gas rationing, travel bans and overcrowded public transportation and the government exhortations toward puritanical thrift and sacrifice for the boys over there cast a pall upon leisure-time activities, civilians managed to pursue a variety of amusements during the war years, some wholesome, others not so.

Upon occasion when one of the latter (so considered) was seen to have gotten out of hand, a bluestockinged government would intervene and forbid it. But such suppressions were exceptional, and always, it seemed, the stern father would eventually relent. Bans were imposed, then lifted; prohibitive taxes were levied, then rescinded; curfews were tolled, then, well, untolled; and in the main those in charge of the war effort let civilians enjoy themselves as they pleased and contented themselves with levying essential wartime measures aimed at increasing production, conserving scarce materials and preventing undue waste. Indeed, a cardinal tenet of governmental policy toward its workers, repeatedly enunciated by the President with regard to a variety of public amusements, was that off-duty recreation was a salubrious thing, so long as it did not cut into efficiency. There were sporadic, spontaneous exercises in puritanism and self-discipline—notably a resurgence of Prohibition sentiment in some Bible-belt backwaters and a crackdown on houses of prostitution near army bases—but overall, the government encouraged traditional entertainments and spectacles such as the movies, radio, popular music, baseball, football and so on. All that was asked was that the amusement in question pay its governmental tithes, make do amid shortages and not patronize the black market, contribute those of its personnel who were draft-eligible to the armed forces and participate in the various patriotic drives and spectacles. This done, the people were free to patronize, the managers to siphon off as much as they could of the rapidly rising waters of national prosperity.

As for the ordinary person, one effect on him of gas rationing, blackouts, dimouts, help shortages, food shortages and so on was that he probably spent more time at home amusing himself than he ordinarily would have. True, record attendance at the movies, nightclubs and bowling allies showed that people still sought entertainment downtown or at least in the immediate neighborhood. But there was a concomitant rise in home recreational activities. Forced, as it were, a bit more upon one another's company, husbands, wives and children often renewed old, frayed ties; teen-agers, their vehicular mobility thwarted by gas rationing, found themselves returning to the sheltered precincts of the girl's parlor for courtship, instead of the parked car. It was in some ways a simpler way of life, for all the new affluence.

Radio listening, an entirely home-centered entertainment medium, increased 20 percent in the war's first year and remained at high levels. Initially, of course, people were anxious for war news, Presidential speeches and the like, but the family ritual of assembling around the radio for news or a symphony or, more probably, the popular comedy-variety programs such as Jack Benny, Eddie Cantor, Bob Hope, Fibber McGee and Mollie and Edgar Bergen and Charlie McCarthy grew stronger.

Parlor games also rose in popularity; sales of checkers and chess sets zoomed in some areas, and playing card sales were up 1,000 percent. (A 1942 survey showed that cards were played in 87 percent of American homes.) In addition to chess, checkers and such standard card games as bridge and hearts, people played Finch, Rook, Chinese checkers, croquignole and other varieties of indoor games. Keeping up-to-date battle maps with flags on pins was a popular activity, especially among the youngsters, as was, of course, playing "war" in every conceivable form that their histrionic abilities could devise, with an assist to their imaginations from the latest war movie at their local theater. Girls played nurse and learned to sew and knit things for soldiers, as their mothers were doing.

Despite severe paper shortages necessitating smaller margins, thinner paper, smaller type and fewer titles, the sale of books shot up. That people were reading more was reflected in a variety of figures. Total-copy sales rose each year and each year broke an all-time record for the industry. The Book-of-the-Month Club, a leading purveyor of popular titles to the masses, saw its membership double during the war. Paper-back books, introduced in 1939 by the Pocket Book Company, were also snapped up; they had the added virtue, to their publishers, of not using up as much of the precious paper quota. Mysteries were especially popular, selling at the rate of 150,000 copies a week.

In the area of trade book publishing, trends in reading provided an acute barometer of the public mood. Nonfiction books, especially in the technical and history categories—the latter included most topical matter such as war correspondents' accounts—outsold fiction by far. In fiction, the emphasis was on escape, with historical romances and religious-theme books being among the more successful genres, though it was difficult to delineate any clear-cut, overriding trends.

Even before Pearl Harbor, the reading public, to judge from the best-seller lists, was uniformly anti-isolationist: not a single isolationist title ever made the top ten, nor, needless to say, were there any of the pro-German books that had appeared before the First World War. Symbolically, first on the best-seller list on December 7 was William L. Shirer's *Berlin Diary,* which warned in sober, unsensational prose of the Nazi menace as seen by Shirer while a radio correspondent in the German capital.

One fervently pro-English book that did catch people's imagination was a long poem by Alice Duer Miller, "The White Cliffs of Dover." This was a paean to Anglo-American cultural ties, in emotional language, which carried this stirring declaration: "In a world where England is finished and dead I do not wish to live."

With the coming of war, Americans turned to nonfiction even more, and a spate of books out of Europe describing the war ensued. Most of these books told of hairsbreadth escapes, of valiant retreats, of defeat on every front—such books as Robert St. John's *From the Land of Silent People,* about a group of correspondents in Yugoslavia who get out of the country after watching in despair as Yugoslav peasants with wooden carts attempt to fight the Nazi panzers. Thoughts turned to our Allies, and understandably people were most curious (and most ambivalent) about Russia. They rushed to buy Ambassador Joseph Davies' *Mission to Moscow,* a rather naïve, turgid account of his experiences in the Soviet Union, which bolstered confidence in the Reds' capacity to resist and whitewashed the notorious Moscow trials of the thirties. Here was a solid, successful American businessman saying the Reds weren't so evil after all.

Not surprisingly, in those jittery times, the real best seller—although it did not make any of the lists because it was a pamphlet—was the *Red Cross First Aid Manual.* Its sales attested to both a concern about What to Do in an Air Raid and a desire to make a contribution to the war effort. A couple of Big Picture strategy books also caught on with the public, more for the implicit optimism of their message than the accuracy of their conclusions. The ringing title *Defense Will Not Win the War,* by Colonel W. F. Kernan, fueled people's desires to hit out at the Axis on its own grounds; Kernan confidently touted the feasibility of an invasion of southern France by the spring of 1942. *Victory Through Air Power* by Major Alexander de Seversky, on the other hand, saw precision bombing of the Nazi heartland as the surefire strategy—an early job of Air Force propaganda that left an understandably bad taste in the mouths of the other services.

Other popular titles of the day offered humor and nostalgia: Marjorie Kinnan Rawlings' *Cross Creek,* an account of her Florida girlhood; Ilka Chase's lighthearted memoir *Past Imperfect;* and Elliot Paul's remembrances of some raffish Left Bank types, *The Last Time I Saw Paris.*

It was not until later in 1942 that books about American fighting men began to appear. The first to catch the public eye was something of a publishing phenomenon. It was *See Here, Private Hargrove,* by Marion Hargrove, and told of the misadventures of a civilian-soldier basically sincere in his desire to serve his country but perpetually at odds with military authority. The book was actually a collection of sketches Hargrove had contributed to his hometown paper, but their warmth and humor and, above all, their report on the life of American—rather than foreign—soldiers struck a chord with the public; by 1945 more than 2,500,000 copies had been sold.

As American troops became involved more deeply in the fighting, the training camp stage was quickly left behind, and the war correspondents returned with eyewitness accounts of GI's in action. The public snapped them up. Most popular were William L. White's *They Were Expendable,* about PT boats fighting last-ditch actions off the Philippines, and books by Richard Tregaskis (*Guadalcanal Diary*), John Hersey (*Into the Valley*) and Ira Wolfert (*Battle for the Solomons*) on the Guadalcanal campaign. All the latter were heavily censored and conveyed only glimpses—some quite graphic—of the real trials of combat; nonetheless, they were better than nothing, and the public hungered for news. Here books were competing successfully with magazines in informing the reader of the war.

The year 1943 saw another publishing phenomenon that outstripped *See Here, Private Hargrove,* and indeed most best sellers of the past. This was Wendell L. Willkie's *One World,* a log of his journey around the world on a Presidential mission, containing his thoughts on and hopes for the postwar world. It became the fastest seller in publishing history, selling 1,000,000 copies—both paper and clothbound—in a little more than two months and 2,000,000 in two years. It was brought out in several foreign countries, including Denmark, where a handsome edition was published by the underground press.

Whereas in the First World War there had been a rash of books setting out blueprints for the postwar world, this was not true in the Second to any great degree, with the notable exception of Willkie's book, which was in part a heartening report on the friendship for Americans which existed among her Allies and a ringing plea for internationalism. Only two other prolegomena for the peace achieved any wide readership: Walter Lippmann's *U.S. Foreign Policy* and Sumner Welles' *The Time for Decision.*

With the exception of the aforementioned *Red Cross First Aid Manual,* books dealing with home front problems were not popular— perhaps because their writers lacked perspective, and people, caught up in the rush of events and the wartime tempo, sensed this. Only *Under Cover,* an angry blast at domestic Fascist organizations by John Roy Carlson, an Armenian immigrant who had served as a secret agent, achieved best sellerdom.

War correspondents' books continued to sell well, but a certain blaséness set in, and they were not bought up with the same fervor as before. (Also overproduction—more than 100 "I-seen-it" books had been written by April, 1943.) The favorite—overwhelmingly—was Ernie Pyle, who wrote of the ordinary soldier in a fatherly, sympathetic way. His *Here Is Your War* sold nearly 2,000,000 in all editions, and his *Brave Men* which came out after his death in 1945 did well, too. Bill

Mauldin's *Up Front,* which combined cartoons with added prose on what GI's life was really like, was also a big favorite. And in the area of GI humor, Bob Hope's *I Never Left Home,* an account of his tours entertaining troops, sold in excess of 1,000,000 copies.

In the fiction field there were few war novels—the men who would write them were too busy with the war, and most of the established writers not in service steered away from the subject or turned to journalism. Ernest Hemingway became a war correspondent, then quickly switched to fighting as an irregular with a group of French Maquis. John Dos Passos concentrated on reporting and produced a fine impressionistic account of life in the United States in *State of the Nation.* Louis Bromfield wrote mostly about his farm and the food problem, while Theodore Dreiser remained silent. Only Pearl Buck with *Dragon Seed* and John Steinbeck in *The Moon Is Down* dealt with people at war in fictional terms. Steinbeck's book, which presented the German occupiers of Norway in a sympathetic light as little men doing their duty, become something of a *cause célèbre,* as reviewers lashed out against it for its alleged unawareness of the menace of Nazi ideology. The play and the movie made from the book elicited similar reactions.

Several fiction best sellers had religious themes, nothing new in the publishing world but perhaps reflecting people's need for reassurance in tumultuous times. Most read was Lloyd C. Douglas' *The Robe,* followed by Franz Werfel's *Song of Bernadette* and Sholem Asch's *The Apostle.*

Two books that were heavy on sex—to move abruptly from the sacred to the profane—also became best sellers. They were Adria Locke Langley's *A Lion Is in the Streets* and Kathleen Winsor's *Forever Amber.* The former had to do with a lusty Southern politician, obviously patterned after Huey Long, who had a huge appetite for the pleasures of the flesh, as well as power. *Forever Amber* was one of those books that crop up from time to time, written by previously unheard-of authors, that are earnestly bad but that the public devours. Its author claimed to have been writing a serious history of the era of King Charles II, but the result was a floridly sexy (for the times), hard-breathing account of her busty heroine's bed-to-bed progress up in the world.

Forever Amber helped usher in a lushly romantic school of historical fiction, however—a late-in-the-war trend that was emulated, or paralleled, in the movies. Perhaps it was a sign of war-weariness—people seeking to escape to more lavishly costumed times. At any rate, along with *Forever Amber* came Samuel Shellabarger's *Captain from*

Castile and Thomas B. Costain's *The Black Rose*. Yet again, the trend was not an overpowering one. Also on the list in 1945 were *The Robe* (with total sales of 2,000,000 copies by this time); *The White Tower,* by James Ramsey Ullman (man against mountain); *Cass Timberlane,* by Sinclair Lewis (Sinclair Lewis on sex); *A Lion Is in the Streets; So Well Remembered,* by James Hilton (sentiment); *Earth and High Heaven,* by Gwethalyn Graham; and *Immortal Wife,* by Irving Stone.

The nonfiction leader was Ernie Pyle's *Brave Men,* with sales of 687,450 copies for the year (it was number two in 1944). War humor was represented by Bill Mauldin's *Up Front* (which, of course, wasn't, in the text part, all that funny) and *Dear Sir* by Juliet Lowell. Civilian books on the light side included *Try and Stop Me* by Bennett Cerf, *Anything Can Happen* by George and Helen Papashvily, *The Egg and I* by Betty MacDonald and *The Thurber Carnival* by James Thurber. (Compare the war-heavy 1943 nonfiction list which included *One World, Under Cover, Journey Among Warriors* by Eve Curie, *Guadalcanal Diary, Burma Surgeon* by Lieutenant Colonel Gordon Seagrave, and *See Here, Private Hargrove.*)

With people buying books in numbers greater than ever before, publishers' profits were limited only by their paper quotas and taxes; instead of cutting down on the total number of copies printed, they cut back on the number of titles and kept their lists limited to more or less proved sellers. Thus, in 1941, a total of 11,112 titles were published; by 1945 this number had shrunk to 5,564. Although this cutback meant, perhaps, a curtailment in the variety of expression, the publisher's wartime diet was on the whole a sensibly nourishing one, albeit no intellectual feast. As the New York *Herald Tribune*'s critic Lewis Gannett summed it up:

> . . . the publishers, while counting their profits, did a bit less
> flamboyant flag-waving than most of their business confreres.
> Their advertising, generally apeaking, would bear a tolerant G.I.
> scrutiny. None of the successful war novels matched in bathos
> the conventional Hollywood war story; and . . . the books
> were soberer than newspaper headlines or radio thrills. If the
> wartime book output includes little which seems likely to rank
> as enduring world literature, a shelf of World War II books is
> likely to look more sensible, as well as more readable, in 1975
> than a shelf of World War I books does today.

Like other industry groups, the publishing community duly enlisted its war services. Writers organized the Writers War Board under Rex

Stout, the detective story writer, and wrote slogans, jingles, scripts and articles at the behest of various government agencies. Writers such as Harry Emerson Fosdick, Gypsy Rose Lee, Alexander Woollcott and John P. Marquand (whose Japanese detective Mr. Moto was an early wartime casualty) contributed their prose for propaganda purposes at sometimes less than going rates. An estimated 2,000 authors participated, and somebody, he didn't say how, estimated that, in all, three tons of manuscript were produced—enough words surely to inundate the Axis.

The publishers formed the Council of Books on Wartime with the slogan "Books are bullets." In addition to turning out these paper projectiles, they set up a committee composed of three critics, a colonel and an admiral to pick books that were "Imperatives"—*i.e.,* so crucial to the war effort that they should be promoted to the utmost. Among the titles selected were *They Were Expendable, Into the Valley, One World, U.S. Foreign Policy, A Bell for Adano* and Edgar Snow's *People on Our Side.*

One of publishing's most direct and welcome contributions was the Armed Service Edition program. This involved publishing cheap paperback editions—wider than they were high and of a size that would fit into a man's pocket—of current best sellers, classics and perennially popular titles. This program was a huge success; at its peak 40 titles a month were sent out, 130,000 of each to the Army, 25,000 to the Navy. In all, around 100,000,000 copies were distributed free to servicemen, with the publishers taking a small profit from bulk sales and the author receiving royalties of one-half cent a copy. The titles involved— more than 2,000 in all—did not create any great cultural revolution. The men were given what they wanted, and Westerns, mysteries and ribald humor were the most popular. The author most in demand was Ernest Haycox, represented by eight Western titles, followed by Max Brand, Thorne Smith and C. S. Forester. A ban on "political" books imposed by Congress resulted in the supercautious outlawing of such books as Catherine Drinker Bowen's biography of Justice Oliver Wendell Holmes, *Yankee from Olympus,* and Charles Beard's *The Republic,* but the prohibition was later rescinded. The services imposed their own censorship, which was sometimes capricious. The Army, for example, passed *A Bell for Adano,* which was controversial because one of the characters was a crude general who reminded a lot of people of General George Patton (the book had come out about the time of the famous slapping incident), but the Navy vetoed it.

The Armed Service Editions, besides providing men with portable reading material—the ubiquitous books turned up everywhere, invasion barge, submarine, foxhole—may also have converted some comic book readers into readers of books. At the least, they introduced many to the paperback format, paving the way for the greater acceptance of them in the postwar years.

Among the group participation sports, dancing—whether ballroom, square or folk—was a popular way to expend energy, socialize or pursue the courtship ritual. At ballrooms and nightclubs orchestras wafted strains of "hot" or "sweet" music over packed dance floors nightly; USO's and teen canteens shook to the blare of swing from the jukebox. The popularity of jitterbugging, first asserted in the thirties, continued unabated, especially among the younger people, to whom it was a separate world with a life-style and language all its own—as, at the extreme, the zoot-suiters demonstrated. The basic jitterbug step was codified in the lindy hop, but there were many strenuous variations, such as the Balboa, Jersey Bounce, Jig Walk and Flea Hop. Shagging, trucking, Susy Q-ing, spinning one's partner out and pulling her back, spinning her under one's arched arm, a little like ring-around-the-rosy—all those were basic components of the dance as performed by saddle-shoed, bobby-soxed, peg-panted youths out to "cut a rug." Aside from the regional variations, however, perhaps the only change in basic jitterbugging was that by 1944 it had become less wild and acrobatic than in its early days, when the man threw his partner over his shoulder like a judo expert.

But jitterbugging had a limited and mostly youthful number of adherents. If one style of dancing could be cited as the most popular during the war, it would have to be the traditional fox-trot. The waltz, surprisingly enough, enjoyed a distinct revival, and the polka spread beyond its largely ethnic and working-class following with the popular success of such songs as "The Beer Barrel Polka."

Like jitterbugging, the fox-trot evolved into simpler forms. Those swooping "dips" when the man pushed one leg forward and bowed toward his partner who bent back low and "conversation dancing," in which the clasped hands of the dancers were allowed to dangle at the side, lost favor somewhat by 1944. The popularity of tunes with a hot beat such as "Is You Is Or Is You Ain't My Baby," "Milkman, Keep Those Bottles Quiet," and even "Mairzy Doats" also forced non-jitterbuggers to jog along at a faster tempo in a sort of hemidemisemi-jitter.

The rumba, once considered the province of effete café society, achieved a greater mass acceptance through the popularity of Latin-American tunes such as "Brazil" and "Amor"; dance instructor Arthur Murray reported that it was the most eagerly sought-after dance at his schools. The samba gained, too, but never achieved wide acceptance.

Several factors contributed to the popularity of ballroom dancing. Prosperity, of course, meant people could patronize night spots, and they seemed eager to get up on their feet when there was no lavish floor show to engage their attention. On the other hand, the increase in radio listening in the home, reinforced by gas rationing, seemed to make people more *au courant* with popular music, which in turn fostered an interest in dancing to it and experimenting with new steps, as in the case of the rumba. Then, too, dancing was employed as a form of recreation by war workers, who flocked to dance halls, roadhouses and juke joints around the plants during their off hours. So popular was dancing that more than 2,000 war plants provided facilities on the premises for dancing during breaks or lunch hour. Finally, among the young, there was the sociability factor. Countless towns near Army bases provided off-duty recreational facilities for soldiers, mainly through the USO, but churches, YMCA's, and civic groups also offered a variety of services to the soldier—game rooms, coffee and doughnuts, letter-writing equipment and, most popular of all, regular dances at which lonely GI's might meet a local belle—at least on the dance floor. Though conservative parents might bridle at the idea of their daughters fraternizing with strange servicemen, patriotism urged that they swallow their snobbery, although they did insist on strict chaperonage and rules forbidding dating of the hostesses. For the girls it was a flattering rush, this being surrounded by available young men in uniform, and they participated eagerly—to the disgruntlement of the local boys. (The author, who grew up in a small college town in the Middle West, remembers the swath cut by the Navy V-12 students stationed there among the local high school girls and the jealousy among their male peers. A girl was considered a bit "fast" if she spent too much time at the local USO, but a few romances, most of them short-lived, budded between the local girls and the sailors.) Another popular meeting—or pickup if you will—place was the local roller-skating rink, which had similarities to the dance floor in that one could choose a partner and skate around to music. As a result, roller skating achieved an unparalleled following during the war.

As the juvenile delinquency rate rose significantly and pillars of the community responded with alarm, imposing ten o'clock curfews and experimenting with punishing parents of teen-age wrongdoers, teen-age recreation centers or teen canteens sprang up all over the county, designed to keep the kids off the street and in a chaperoned environment. The chief lure of these places—which bore names like Jive Inn, El Canteeno, Juke Box, Hi-Spot and Teen Can—was dancing to a jukebox well stocked with the latest records of Glenn Miller, Tommy and Jimmy Dorsey, Frank Sinatra, the Andrews Sisters, the Ink Spots, Vaughn Monroe, Woody Herman, Skinnay Ennis, Benny Goodman, Perry Como *et al.* Cokes and other refreshments were available, and there were card tables, ping-pong and pool tables and the like, but dancing was the main activity.

For the kids it was a cheap evening out and a chance to practice new steps. Funds for the canteen were often supplied by local civic organizations, and the kids themselves would fix the place up to their liking. Often there was a teen-age board of directors in charge, although adult supervision was ever in the wings, and lively, tolerant young married couples were at a premium as chaperons. There was also a vogue in the larger cities for privately owned teen-age "nightclubs" which maintained a nightclub atmosphere while dispensing nonalcoholic beverages.

Adult nightclubs, after a slump in early 1942, resumed the boom they had begun to enjoy in late 1941. During the entire year New York's fifty-odd night spots grossed $85,000,000, and this trend continued to rise. By 1945 the Copacabana was grossing up to $55,000 weekly, the Latin Quarter, $40,000–$45,000, Billy Rose's Diamond Horseshoe and the Zanzibar, $40,000 each. Business was up 40 percent over the 1941 boom period to $250,000,000 annually nationwide, despite food and gas rationing, liquor shortages and a 20 percent federal amusement tax. Prices were up too, of course, and patrons working on $3–$5 minimums paid $1.25 a drink without blinking an eye (a thriving black market in scotch developed because *nouveau riche* patrons demanded the twelve-year old stuff—or fifteen- to eighteen-year-old rye or bourbon), and the average check was $4.25 per person. Hundred-dollar tips were not uncommon, and *Variety*, looking back on the wartime period, was to write in 1946: "It's no gag that many a waiter . . . was on his second apartment house, and quite a few maitres can retire to Lake Como without worrying whether their Escoffier sheepskin is in jeopardy." In New Jersey, a vast pleasure dome called Ben Marden's Riviera, which Maurice Zolotow dubbed "the Kohinoor of the cafes . . . a movie night club set come to life," was grossing upwards of $1,000,000 annually, and there seemed to be no ceiling.

Decor was plush and garish—pile carpets, velvet on the walls, satin draperies, fountains gurgling colored water, mirrors. As Latin Quarter owner Lou Walters put it: "You gotta keep in mind you are selling them luxury and waste." The trend in entertainment was, said *Variety,* toward "flashy, elaborate floor shows, and hoked-up gaiety," and away from the *boîtes* that merely provided a lavish background to the patrons' do-it-yourself funmaking. One night spot in San Francisco advertised "See Tommy Harris' Nude All-Girl Orchestra"; when the vice squad quickly descended, they discovered that the "orchestra" was a painting. The patrons continued to flock in, painting or no painting.

In New York, big entertainment "names" pulled in the customers, and for the performers it was a busy time. Young Frank Sinatra, fresh from the bobby-sox mania at the Paramount, proved he could draw the carriage trade too, as he broke records at the Waldorf-Astoria's Wedgwood Room; his counterpart, Carl Brisson, who was known as "the older girls' Sinatra," titillated the matronly set at the Club Versailles. The Persian Room belonged to Hildegarde, the Milwaukee-born chanteuse, and the dance team of Paul and Grace Hartman proved popular anywhere. (The dance-team phenomenon, though going back at least as far as Vernon and Irene Castle, had a revival during the war, perhaps reflecting the greater interest in ballroom dancing.)

Sinatra having made "crooner" a household word, other spots looked for imitations. Such stars as Dick Haymes, Perry Como and Dean Martin soon moved on to Hollywood, so The Coq Rouge ran a Sinatra sing-alike contest, which was won by one Martin Kent, whose career turned out to be a short, fast sprint into obscurity. At La Martinique, you could see Danny Thomas; Joe E. Lewis and Jimmy Durante were the Copa's mainstays; the Hurricane might have both Ted Lewis and Duke Ellington; and the Latin Quarter had Georgie Price as headliner, plus a vaudeville type bill of jugglers, acrobats and dancing midgets. Other popular spots in New York included the Stork Club, Dempsey's, Lindy's, 21, Toots Shor's, Leon and Eddie's, the Village Vanguard, Cafe Society, Nick's, El Gaucho, Fife's Monte Carlo and the Rainbow Room (the last was shut down in 1944 owing to high costs and labor troubles).

In the eerily blacked-out Broadway district, patrons queued up outside the clubs, waiting for a table; headwaiters would prowl the line, telling strange faces bluntly that there were no tables and beckoning to old patrons to jump the line and come in. Still, the GI's and their dates out on a farewell spree and the newly prosperous war workers crammed themselves in where they could. The appearance of these new big spenders, coupled with the help shortage, caused one café owner to lament: "It's getting so I don't even know 5 percent of my customers and 25 percent of my waiters." At 21 a sign over the bar warned: BE COURTE-OUS TO OUR HELP; CUSTOMERS WE CAN ALWAYS GET.

One characteristic of nightclub customers, however, was noted by writer Maurice Zolotow: when the war news was bad, people stayed home and, contrarily, when the news was good, people came out to celebrate. Thus the nightclub was not an escape mechanism, but "a mechanism for social and community celebration," said Zolotow. A nightclub owner put it less sociologically: "Every time them Nazis win a battle my business goes down. Don't people want to get away from their troubles any more?"

So frenetic was the spending that Washington began to look askance. At least part of the reason for the withholding tax was the fear that if people had the money in their hands, they would spend it as fast as they could in the cause of *carpe diem*. As *Variety* observed: "It's a certainty many of these saloonatics have little concern about the morrow. When mama goes back to washing the dishes and the $110-a-week driller returns to his $30 white-collar job, they will have memories and a terrific hangover, no doubt but seemingly, as of right now, that seems to be all right all around."

The government further cracked down on the "saloonatics" by increasing the cabaret tax to 30 percent. This measure, at last, hurt. Nightclubs were failing right and left, and 20,000 people were put out of work. So severe were the repercussions that the government backed down and restored the tax to 20 percent, with business quickly returning to abnormal. Early in 1945 the government struck again in the form of War Mobilization Director James Byrnes with his order for a midnight curfew for all nightclubs, theaters and other places of entertainment. The official reason given for what a Detroit bartender christened "the Byrne-out" was to save fuel, manpower and transportation, but citizens—and especially swing shift workers who got off work at midnight and sought their relaxation thereafter—thought it was a form of childish punishment since the war was going badly. As one barfly put it: "So turn off the heat and let us drink in our overcoats." And boniface Toots Shor was moved to utter his now-classic crack: "Any crum-bum what can't get plastered by midnight just ain't tryin'."

Mayor LaGuardia, who was up for relection that year, fought back. Citing the large number of servicemen who would be deprived of their leave-time fun and asserting, "New York is still New York; I don't like

the curfew law," he imposed his own curfew: 1 A.M. The Army re-
taliated by sending in MP's to clear the joints at the stroke of midnight,
but LaGuardia's ruling stuck. Speakeasies and bottle clubs sprang up,
theaters advanced their curtain times, and the nightclubs held their last
or "midnight" show an hour earlier to avoid losing any revenues. As
Variety historians Abel Green and Joe Laurie, Jr., wrote: "Anyway 1
A.M. was OK—it meant that you didn't have to go home on the same
day!"

Elsewhere on the entertainment front, vaudeville made a mild comeback, with performers finding work not only in the clubs but on stage.
The USO camp shows also turned out to be a valuable proving ground
for young talent, but many of these were lured away by lucrative movie,
radio or nightclub offers. Talent costs soared, and this acted to price
vaudeville out of the market, so to speak. A bill at the Roxy featuring
Danny Kaye, Beatrice Kaye and Tommy Tucker's band cost management $37,000 a week; still it showed a profit and other big theaters
such as the Capitol, Paramount and the Strand engaged in fierce competitive bidding for big bands and top entertainers. Grace Moore was
paid $20,000 for a solo at the Roxy, and Jack Benny and Milton
Berle, Bob Hope and Martin and Lewis jacked their prices up to twice
that amount for appearances at the New York Paramount. The De-
Marcos, a dance team, were paid a record—for that form of entertainment—$5,000 a week at the Roxy. But by 1945 the bloom was off the
rose. Two top theaters, the Earle in Washington and the Cleveland
Palace, dropped stage shows, and other theaters followed suit.

The hottest "live" attractions continued to be the big bands and
the crooners, who packed in the teen-agers at stage shows usually run
in between showings of a feature movie. A skinny young singer with
Tommy Dorsey named Frank Sinatra launched the "swooner-crooner"
craze during an engagement at the Paramount in 1942. With the mass
hysteria of lemmings driven to the sea, young teen-age girls wearing their
trademark, rolled anklet socks, which gave them their name—bobby-
soxers—swarmed into the theater and wept, screamed, peed in their
panties and, yes, even swooned when their idol sang in his soft, throbbing
voice, while engaging in discreet foreplay with the microphone. What
matter if the swooning began as a publicity stunt and the girls were hired
by Sinatra's shrewd manager; a pattern of mass hysteria had been established, and other girls at least *thought* they were going to swoon. So
startling was the bobby-sox phenomenon that psychiatrists and other
social thinkers were called in to diagnose the patient. Their conclusions

varied from a mass trauma induced by the absence of men in the armed forces bringing female hysteria to the surface to an orgy of pubescent war nerves. Of course, many of Sinatra's fans were too young even to have lost boyfriends to Uncle Sam; they were merely participating vicariously in a wave of loneliness and bereftness. The sight of the skinny Sinatra, hardly a virile hero along the lines of Clark Gable, seemed also to stimulate an upwelling of pubescent maternal instincts. The poor masculine guys in real life who went off to the Army were gone, perhaps never to return; so the girls reverted back to this premature male symbol, forever fixated in a kind of limp, sexy, draft-free teenhood—someone who, Peter Pan-like, offered escape from the *Sturm und Drang* of adolescence into a never-never land of yearning, unrequited love.

A similar idol, though not a singer, was Harry James, a slender, pencil-mustached trumpeter. James was an excellent horn player, but kept his repertoire in a groove of flashy, romantic tunes or yearning ballads. His first hit, "Ciribiribin," came in 1939, when he was still a member of Benny Goodman's orchestra. With that success he formed a band on his own, which featured singer Helen Forrest, Cork Corcoran on tenor sax and the arrangements of Jack Mathias. By 1942, at age twenty-six, he was atop the pop heap, and his sinuous, seductive trumpet notes blared from every jukebox. Of course, James played for the jitter-buggers too, but he believed in blending hot and sweet. He explained his formula to an interviewer: "I'd get tired of playing jump numbers all the time. My idea of how to play something pretty and artistic is our version of 'Sleepy Lagoon.' I like to mix up our material so that even the dancers will want to listen, and enjoy the melody as well as the rhythm." Part of his appeal lay in his showmanship and technical virtuosity on his instrument, with triple-tonguing, high notes and other flashy tricks. "It has to *sound* hard to kill 'em," James said.

In 1943, James killed 'em at an engagement at the Paramount. Long before the show, lines of teen-agers formed. A riot ensued with fights and broken windows, and the police were called out. Eventually, 5,500 howling fans got in the theater, where they set up a continuous uproar —so loud that the music couldn't be heard. There was jitterbugging in the aisles, and some danced on stage until dragged off. No one left after the first performance, which was followed by a showing of *China* starring Alan Ladd; most stayed through the second performance too. Finally, to clear the house, James announced he would distribute auto-graphed pictures at the stage door. This gambit was successful in clearing the theater, but another riot ensued at the stage door.

Hollywood quickly signed up teen-age idols such as Sinatra and James in hopes of shoring up box-office clout, zeroed by the departure of many male stars to the services, with the female set. Indeed a number of bandleaders, including Tommy and Jimmy Dorsey, Benny Goodman, Vaughn Monroe and Bob Crosby were signed up for one-picture deals. But only James had sufficient authority as an actor to hold his own in speaking, as opposed to baton-waving, roles. The appeal of the others lay in their music, the arrangements and sound they projected on records or from the bandstand; they themselves were not sex symbols. (In 1945, one of the most popular of the big band men in the thirties and forties, Glenn Miller, was lost and presumed dead in a plane crash while on his way to entertain troops.) Most of them, like James, abandoned the frenetic rhythms of swing and concentrated on producing a smooth, slick "jivey" sound or those slow, sweet fox-trots that seemed reluctant to end and sever the clinging partners.

While the kids were letting off steam in the movie houses, the legitimate theaters in New York and on the road enjoyed unprecedented prosperity. Until gas rationing forced a halt to one-night stands, stars who went on tours to the hinterlands cleaned up. Even *Tobacco Road,* which closed on Broadway in 1942 after a record seven-and-a-half-year run, tripled its New York receipts for the past year when it sent out a touring company. In 1941, the road's golden year, Helen Hayes in *Victoria Regina* grossed a record $2,000,000; Katharine Hepburn in *The Philadelphia Story* took in $750,000 in 32 weeks; Tallulah Bankhead in *The Little Foxes* drew $650,000, or $25,000 more than during the play's Broadway run; Lynn Fontanne and Alfred Lunt gathered $800,000 with the Pulitzer Prizewinning *There Shall Be No Night* (an anti-Russian melodrama about the Russo-Finnish War by Robert Sherwood, which was abruptly forgotten after the Reds became our heroic allies), and George M. Cohan in *I'd Rather Be Right,* a political satire with an FDR-like hero, drew nearly $700,000 box office, compared with $980,-000 on Broadway.

The first year of war, however, nearly ruined Broadway, as people stayed away from the theater in droves. No less than fifty-four plays flopped, and only six were considered bona fide hits. One play scheduled to open on December 10 was an early direct casualty of war. Called *The Admiral Had a Wife* and starring Uta Hagen and Alfred Drake, it was a jolly comedy of Navy life set in Hawaii involving the machinations of an ambitious Navy wife against a background of roaringly funny examples of nepotism, inefficiency and other less than flattering perspectives on shore duty. Even though the flagrant unpreparedness at Pearl Harbor lent truth to the playwright's thesis, the producers hurriedly canceled it on December 8; nobody, it seemed, was in a mood to laugh at the peacetime Navy.

The 1942–43 season saw a wave of hastily produced war plays. Most appeared briefly, then beat a hasty retreat, routed by the withering fire of the critics. One element they had in common was a good deal of noise emanating from the sound-effects men in the wings; the intent was evidently to subject the audience to as near an experience of war as Broadway artifice could muster. All of which caused George Jean Nathan to write testily after being assaulted by something called *The Wookey:* "Thinking quickly back over the war plays of all history, I cannot recall one of any authentic quality that was not practically soundless."

The only play that occupied the critics more than passingly was John Steinbeck's *The Moon Is Down*. With the exception of a few firebrands, the critical reaction was on the whole more restrained than to the book version. Richard Lockridge of the New York *Sun* spoke for many when he wrote: "By making his invaders more sinned against than sinning Mr. Steinbeck has dissipated his drama. The drama needs two hostile forces face to face. Here are pleasant, reasonable people on one side and on the other disembodied orders from 'the capital.' Mr. Steinbeck proves himself tolerant to a fault and his play suffers. So, I suspect, does his argument."

The failure of serious dramatists to deal satisfactorily with war themes exemplified by the 1941–42 season in general and Steinbeck in particular (after all, he was one of our best writers) set a standard of mediocrity which held during the remainder of the war years. The only other major effort was Maxwell Anderson's *The Eve of St. Mark,* a drama telling of the growing up and finding of love by a young man who goes off to war and ends up on a small island in the Philippines. Many critics thought the boy an impossible prig (the young hero and a buddy meet a couple of tarnished women in a bar; while the females are temporarily absent, the buddy says wolfishly, "Now what do we do?" to which the hero replies, "We take the bus back to camp and crawl into our own truckle beds") and the poetic Andersonian language hollow and rhetorical. Others noted beautiful moments in the play, especially those flashbacks to the boy's growing up on an Ohio farm, but as for the play's ultimate success, they seemed to divide squarely between those who admired its sentiment and those who opposed its muddled idealism. The former school was represented by John Mason Brown of the New

York *Post,* who wrote, "Whether *The Eve of St. Mark* is a good play or not seems almost beside the point. It is deeply affecting. It speaks to the heart irresistibly even when the head says No." Speaking for the naysayers was George Jean Nathan, who wrote, "The present criticism of drama in ratio to the acceptability of its themes is just a small step removed from the older criticism of drama in proportion to its morality, chiefly sexual, and must lead to the same artistically dubious end. . . . Let us be patriotic all, surely, but let those of us whose job is dramatic criticism not confuse it with the job of flying a bomber over Berlin."

Perhaps fittingly, Broadway's most successful efforts on war themes were a musical and a comedy. The musical—more a review or series of sketches—was Irving Berlin's *This Is the Army,* which opened on July 4, 1942. This updating of Berlin's World War I hit, *Yip Yip Yaphank,* with an all-soldier cast (with the exception of Mr. Berlin who reprised "Oh! How I Hate to Get Up in the Morning") delighted the critics and of course the audiences. Aside from the ingratiating cast and the Berlin songs, the show's tasteful simplicity in showing soldiers as they were and its eschewing of hyperbole made it a model patriotic spectacle. As the *New Yorker*'s Wolcott Gibbs wrote: "It was a service show entirely executed by servicemen, and it told more, through the medium of vaudeville, about the qualities that made it possible for a non-military nation to raise an effective fighting force than any ten plays celebrating desperate and rhetorical gallantries on the battlefield." All told, including the movie sale, *This Is the Army* raised $10,000,000 for the Army Emergency Relief Fund.

The comedy was *The Voice of the Turtle* and dealt with a soldier on weekend pass in transit to the battlefront who snatches a few hours of unwedded bliss with a girl in Manhattan. The author, John Van Druten, brought off this rather daring theme with wit and ingenuity; the play had only three characters and a minimal plot, but the dialogue effervesced throughout. Perhaps the war was too peripheral to the play; yet Mr. Van Druten's depiction of the relationships of his characters and the imperatives of love in wartime had the virtue of honesty and probably reflected the young generation's attitudes toward sex more accurately than did Maxwell Anderson's Epworth League strictures on chastity in *The Eve of St. Mark.*

A less successful serviceman show was Moss Hart's *Winged Victory,* which followed a group of wholesome, naïvely inarticulate all-American boys through flight training. On the plus side were the realistic training

scenes staged by director Hart. But the boys themselves and their inevitable sweethearts and moms were more sentimental stereotypes. As
described by critic Wolcott Gibbs there were "the nerveless student who
failed his flight test, the illiterate who delivered what Mr. Hart must
hopefully have regarded as the profound, intuitive philosophy of the
common man, and even, at the end, that handiest of all stencils, the pilot
who learned about the birth of his son while he himself was confronted
with death." There was even a note of unwitting condescension in Mr.
Hart's characterizations. The airmen were brainless, happy-go-lucky little
boys, or as one of their wives puts it: "They're such kids, Mom—such
babies . . . it's [flying's] all they think about. They talk about it like
kids, as though it were some wonderful party they were going to." The
American boy-man was not a new figure in the imagination of wartime
writers, and perhaps he existed, but it is doubtful he was flying B-17's
over Germany or B-19's over Japan.

With the exception of a few noble failures, such as Lillian Hellman's
The Searching Wind, which attempted to damn isolationists for all time,
and modest successes such as John Hersey's *A Bell for Adano,* Broadway failed to mirror the larger real-life drama convulsing the world.
New York *Times* critic Lewis Nichols summed up: "The final play about
the weariness, the hatred, the savagery, and the pathos of the Second
World War has yet to reach Broadway."

Indeed, it appeared that Broadway, becoming increasingly prosperous as war money flowed into the box office, became more and more
escapist as the war went on. There were big musicals, notably *Oklahoma!,* which debuted in 1943, and *Carousel,* also by the Rodgers-
Hammerstein team, and their derivatives such as *Bloomer Girl* and *Up
in Central Park. Oklahoma!* was, of course, quickly hailed as a landmark
musical with its integration of plot and songs and brilliant employment
of ballet. But it also embodied cheerful, folksy Americana, a sort of
nostalgic harking back to bucolic Arcadian times when the rugged
American peasantry, pioneer species, engaged in a constant round of
festivities involving dance and song. The same could be said for the other
musicals mentioned, all period pieces, all wonderfully entertaining. Only
On the Town, about three sailors loosed upon Manhattan, had any con-
temporaneity to it.

The escapist temper of the theater reached its zenith in the 1944–45
season, which was Broadway's most prosperous yet. There were ninety-
five openings—eighteen more than 1942–43—of which twenty-four were

considered by the New York *Times* to have been successful—*i.e.,* run for at least 100 performances. The biggest hits were *Harvey,* a bit of optimistic whimsy about a dipsomaniac with a six-foot invisible rabbit for a pal; *Anna Lucasta,* about a Negro prostitute; *I Remember Mama,* an adaptation by John Van Druten of the book *Mama's Bank Account,* about a lovable Norwegian matriarch; *The Late George Apley,* from the Marquand novel about a bloodless but ultimately lovable Boston aristocrat; and *The Glass Menagerie,* a delicate, poetic play of illusions which marked the debut of Tennessee Williams. Other than *A Bell for Adano,* the only serious war-theme plays were *The Streets Are Guarded,* by Laurence Stallings, and *The Hasty Heart,* by John Patrick. Stallings' effort, an exercise in muddled metaphysics, was a flop, which was ironic, for Stallings, with Maxwell Anderson, had written one of the best American World War I plays, *What Price Glory? The Hasty Heart* was a boisterous but essentially hollow story about a very unpleasant Scotsman who is dying in an Army hospital in the South Pacific. The only other offerings on the war were *Foxhole in the Parlor,* an overwrought drama about an overwrought, psychoneurotic soldier obsessed with delivering his personal formula for world peace to the United Nations Organization, and some comedies including *Soldier's Wife, Dear Ruth* and *Kiss Them for Me.* (Wartime comedies seemed usually to involve brave wives following their soldier-husbands or a heterogeneous group of people thrown together by the housing shortage.)

As wartime prosperity waxed, so did the Hollywood money flowing into Broadway's coffers. In 1942 a record $300,000 was paid for Steinbeck's *The Moon Is Down;* by 1945, with the sale of *Harvey* to the movies for $750,000, this record had been broken many times over. Broadway itself saw a new audience: the war workers out on the town. The spectacle of front rows filled with men in their shirt sleeves became common. Ticket scalpers did a roaring business; tickets to *Oklahoma!,* for example, were selling for $25 each on the black market. Theaters were at a premium, and when the producer of *The Red Mill* tried to rent the Shuberts' 46th Street Theater, he was charged an unprecedented 5 percent of the gross for the privilege. Still, even though business was up, some plays failed, as they always will; during the 1944–45 season eleven musicals, representing a total investment of $1,735,000, flopped badly. On the road, in the entertainment-starved war towns, the public might pay to see anything, but the Broadway playgoer remained somewhat discriminating about his entertainment—possibly because he was willing (and financially able) to pay a premium to see the latest hit, rather than settle for a so-so production. So free with his money was the wartime theatergoer that a raise in the federal amusement tax from 10 to 20 percent in 1944 did not put the slightest crimp in business.

Broadway became a mecca for servicemen also; they were given free tickets to shows through the USO and many saw their first stage play in this manner. Also popular was the Stage Door Canteen located in the basement of the 44th Street Theater, once the home of the Little Club. There servicemen could get free food and beverages and dance with pretty starlets or converse with stage luminaries doing volunteer chores. There were always lines of men outside waiting to get in.

People's avid interest in the war news provided a shot in the arm for magazine journalism. If there had been no paper shortage, magazine circulation would have increased even more than it did (paper quotas came to 75 percent of prewar usage). Advertisers fought for precious space, wined and dined the magazine's advertising salesmen in a temporary reversal of roles and, in 1944, poured $100,000,000 more advertising dollars into the magazines' coffers than they had in 1942. Actually, profits remained about the same because of rising costs and increased staffs.

This emphasis on journalism marked the wartime course of the American magazine. It meant swollen staff boxes, as the list of "assistant" or "roving" editors—*i.e.*, men out in the field—lengthened. The *Reader's Digest* had 19; *Collier's*, 27; the *Saturday Evening Post*, 13. The *Time-Life-Fortune* complex at one time had thirty editor-reporters on the spot. This expansion was in response to a mixture of shrewd editorial exploitation and the boundless thirst of readers for long, in-depth, vivid reports from the battlefields, copiously illustrated with the new photojournalism pioneered by *Life* in 1936 and brought to maturity in wartime. How much the public was really edified is moot, but there is no doubt that standards of reporting were raised, that stories were more comprehensive and that magazines mobilized increased research staffs to supplement the efforts of the reporter.

On the other hand, there was a rather tasteless exploitation of the news to sell copies. The magazines, for a time, fell into a prophets-of-doom stance—perhaps reflecting the mood of frustration and gloom of the early war years. As Eric Hodgkins of Time, Inc., wrote after the war: "Bad news was often more salable than good news, and usually, in the war's early days, was much more plausible. The magazines from 1939 onward for a while fairly drooled of doom."

By 1944 the attitude had changed, and the editors confessed that they had known all along that America was the mightiest country in the world. Nonetheless, in their editorials, which drew unprecedented readership during the war, they continued to lecture Washington on its massive bunglings, profiteering, excessive taxes and all-round incompetence. Then, too, some of the new journalism sounded precisely like the old. There were many portentous titles, for which the reader could easily fill in the blanks with whatever was the fashionable topic of the moment:

"THE MYTH OF_____" "AFTER_____WHAT?"
"HOW GOOD IS OUR_____?" "WHY_____ FAILED"
"CRISIS IN_____" "_____: MASTERPIECE
OR MENACE?"

True, the increased revenues of magazines afforded a greater editorial independence. As Frederick Lewis Allen of *Harper's* said: "It is much easier to forget about money and edit for glory than it used to be." But the advertiser's dollar was not scorned, and *Collier's* magazine was proud to announce: "We feel that the advertisers who are reporting progress on their part in the war are making an important and valuable contribution to morale on the home front."

Advertisers were indeed anxious to identify their product with the war effort. Some insinuated that use of their product helped the civilian do his home front job—although the connection was often rather far-fetched. Others implied that their product was more or less single-handedly winning the war.

Examples of the first kind included this puff for Dr. West's Toothbrushes: "Take good care of yourself . . . you belong to the U.S.A. America has a job to do. A job that calls for full physical efficiency of everyone. We owe it to our family, to ourselves to be well and keep well." (By preventing gum trouble, of course, Dr. West's helped one keep well.) A similar golden rule of good health was sounded by Kleenex: "Don't be a public enemy! Be patriotic and smother sneezes with Kleenex to help keep colds from spreading to war workers—America needs every man—full time!"

The advertisers whose products were connected with the war often ran pictures of combat, coupled with an inspirational message on how their products were roundly smashing the Axis—be it ball bearings ("the subject of ball bearings is on everybody's lips these days"), cotton cloth ("cotton cloth can help win an air fight"), or wire rope ("back of every attack is wire rope"). Readers were educated about "the gun that comes out of an oil well" (gun barrels were bored with oil as a saturating lubricant) by an oil company or told that the reason a soldier was sleeping soundly in his hammock (*"His* cradle won't drop") was that the advertiser's product, a metal fastener, was "30% stronger than specified." Readers of an advertisement captioned "The Great Gift to the Mothers of Men!" were perhaps a little surprised to learn that though the "great gift" was sulfa drugs, the advertiser was an air-conditioning company. (Air conditioning was used to cool the plant where sulfanilimide was manufactured.)

The purpose of much of this advertising, of course, was to keep the product's name before the consumer's eye, looking ahead to the brimming cornucopia days of peace when these wares would again be available. A rather fulsome example of this was a shoe company's ad, captioned "Angel in Muddy Boots," which showed a pretty nurse ministering to a wounded GI. The GI is having a reverie about the girl, peace and, of all things, shoes:

> I remember you . . . you are the girl with flying feet who led the way to laughter . . . you are all the girls I ever liked who brightened a fellow's life . . .
> You didn't always wear muddy boots. . . .
> Someday peacetime living will come again. Someday there will be girls again who . . . fly over sun-flecked lawns with the lilt of summer in their hearts and rainbows on their feet.

Sex, the advertiser's staple, was toned down. When it found its way into the ads, it was swathed in veils of sentiment. Such ads bore down on the theme of reunion of husband and wife in the happy postwar world. Most popular of this type were the silverware company's ads that showed peaches-and-cream-complected, blond, blue-eyed girls and handsome, clean-cut soldiers embracing in a reunion kiss. The running title was "Back Home for Keeps." The phrase caught on; thousands wrote in for copies of the ads, and Irving Berlin wrote a song with that title.

An exception to the tame boy-girl themes of most ads were the perfume company blurbs, which spoke of sudden encounters, of overwhelming passion, of—though this was distantly implied—men intoxicated by a whiff of perfume dragging the scented maid straight to the boudoir. "This is It," went one advertisement, capitalizing on a popular catch-phrase of the times. "The starry eyes . . . the fireworks in the blood-stream . . . this is what the songs sing about . . . this is what little girls are made for." Another panted: "A moment bright with rapture, and suddenly you know . . . you are whirling through space, *lost* . . . you've found yourself for the first time! This is the beginning of your life. This is love, love, love. . . ." Even more explicit was the company which promised: "He will if you wear it; she will if you give it."

Despite their sheer escapism, no one seemed to mind the romantic ads, but the "brag" ads stimulated a wave of GI complaints or, at least, horse laughs. When a company making some minor part or other advertised "Who's Afraid of the Big Focke-Wulf?" a bomber pilot tore out the ad, wrote "*I* am" across it and got his entire squadron to sign their names before sending it to the advertiser. Another serviceman complained: "As soon as a pea canner runs short of peas he shouts 'Canned peas have gone to war!' and as soon as an umbrella maker starts building parachutes he has us in Berlin."

Some of the advertisers themselves began to satirize the pompousness and self-aggrandizement of their competitors and after 1942 the advertising industry's war-planning group, the War Advertising Council, was able to eliminate a good percentage of the brag ads by moral suasion. The council was in charge of coordinating the wartime public service activities of advertising with the government's publicity demands. By channeling government war propaganda into advertising, it forestalled the government's doing its own advertising, a proposal put forth by several officials in 1942.

Also lurking in the council's mind was the Treasury Department view that advertising should no longer be deducted as a legitimate business expense. In exchange for the council's cooperation the Treasury ruled that advertising in "reasonable" amounts would be considered a deductible business cost. The end result was that businesses took out ads for war bond campaigns, scrap metal and salvage drives, recruitment of nurses, conservation of materials, fuel and rubber conservation, early mailing of Christmas packages, greater use of V-mail letters and so on.

The businessmen paid for the space, and advertising agency personnel contributed their time gratis. According to Ray Rubicam, of Young and Rubicam, more than $1 billion of space and radio time was "donated" by businesses. The media themselves also donated pages to advertising whatever government campaign happened to be current. For example, the anti-inflationary plea "Use it up, wear it out, make it do or do without" was featured in a monthly page by more than 400 magazines.

Advertising reversed itself by urging people *not* to buy some things (the New York Telephone Company reversed its traditional slogan "Don't write—telephone" and urged: "Use the mail wherever time permits this method of communication").

Some products managed a tie-in with their wartime messages, notably the hat company which combated loose talk with the slogan "Keep it under your Stetson." This was followed by stories of betrayed troop movements under snappy captions such as "Idle words make busy subs," and "The less said, the less dead."

Indeed copywriters found in the war ads ample scope for their talents. Some of the products that rolled off their assembly lines:

"Can you pass the mail box with a clear conscience?" (V-mail)
"I have freed a Marine to fight. You can do it too!" (Women
     Marines)
"The food you save can help win the war."
"Joe needs long-distance lines tonight." (decrease telephone calls)
"Careful, son—don't let that money bite you." (anti-spending)
"You've done your bit, now do your best."

Nor were the copywriters above using a hate-the-enemy approach. In one such spread, three young girls were lined up in a Nazi headquarters while a typical Prussian type of officer leered at them. A HIGH HONOR FOR YOUR DAUGHTER was the headline, and the text went on to explain to fathers what would happen to their little girls if the Nazis won:

> You they may cast aside and put to some ignominious task, such as scrubbing the sidewalks or sweeping the streets. But your daughter . . . well, if she's young and healthy and strong, a Gauleiter with an eye for beauty may decide she is a perfect specimen for one of their experimental camps. A high honor for your daughter.

One of the most widely acclaimed ads was calculated to make the reader misty-eyed, rather than stimulate his adrenaline. It was called "The Kid in Upper 4" and was a plea by the railroads for the civilian traveler to put up with some inconvenience so that the Kid in Upper 4, on his way to war, could get some sleep. The copy described what the Kid was thinking about:

> Wide awake . . . listening . . . staring into blackness . . . thinking of . . . the taste of hamburgers and pop . . . the feel of driving a roadster over a six-lane highway . . . a dog named Shucks or Spot, or Barnacle Bill. . . . There's a lump in his throat and maybe a tear fills his eye. It doesn't matter, Kid. Nobody will see . . . it's too dark.

The Kid in Upper 4, widely considered the best example of war-message advertising, caught perfectly the amalgam of subconscious idealized emotions Americans had toward their soldiers. He was usually young, freckle-faced, clean-minded, sweet-tempered; somewhere he had a mother who worried over him (his dad was a vaguer figure). He was, in short, the young son leaving the nest for the first time, still attached to the apron strings of Mom's loving concern. His crying—something Americans ordinarily consider sissyish or womanish—was, strangely, expected and forgiven, for, if he were too "manly," if he gruffly quelled his homesickness as unseemly and through his military training grew into someone tough and ready to kill, where would that leave Mom? She would have lost her little boy.

As for the role of Mom in wartime, Philip Wylie commented: "I cannot think, offhand, of any civilization except ours in which an entire division of living men has been used, during wartime, or at any time, to spell out the word 'mom' on a drill field."

Advertising was an effective tool when part of a properly mounted campaign directed toward an already-popular goal. Such were the War Bond drives, in which just about every promotional stunt the combined brains of Madison Avenue, Hollywood and the Treasury Department's War Finance Division—plus hundreds of thousands of local drive chairmen—could dream up was employed. The energetic and sometimes gross and tasteless ballyhoo emanating from Hollywood's bond cavalcades were undoubtedly effective, yet the backbone of the effort was probably the advertisements on radio, in newspapers and magazines, on billboards, on the movie screen and hundreds of other places which could catch the public eye or ear. In other words, what was needed during a campaign were the daily pleas tirelessly hammering home the importance of buying bonds.

In the Third War Loan drive of September, 1943, for example, Secretary of the Treasury Henry Morgenthau sparked an intensive advertising effort aimed at saturating every possible medium of communication, from radio to milk bottle tops and matchbox covers, with exhortations to "Back the Attack" and buy E bonds (whose low face value made it the "little man's" bond). The intensive campaign produced results markedly superior to the Second War Loan. For example, while 71 percent of the nonfarm population had known about the Second War Loan, 86 percent knew about the Third; an even greater improvement was achieved with people living on farms.

But for all its good work in spreading the word about War Bonds, advertising continued to work at its main job of moving civilian goods off the shelves—those that were available—and providing the stuff for dreams of the postwar world when scarcity would be ended and civilian amenities would be back from war.

Escapism was a thread running through all the mass media, but unquestionably war news was the big, continuing story, the story that sold newspapers. Evidence of this came during a deliverers' strike in 1945 in New York City. Roper pollsters asked a cross section of New Yorkers which parts of the newspaper they missed most. The most often named were: news 31.5 percent; "war news" and "foreign news," 26.5 percent; comics, 15.2 percent; editorials, 14.2 percent; sports, 12 percent; and advertisements, sales, 11.3 percent. And when the New York *Times* set up special counters at Times Square to sell papers during the strike, more than 150,000 copies were bought in a day, with lines forming five blocks long.

Like the magazines the papers met their readers' demand for eyewitness reports from the front by dispatching reporters overseas in large numbers—700 were abroad at a given time, and a battalion of reporters, more than 400 strong, covered the Normandy invasion. The papers too were hampered by the paper shortage and the rising cost of newsprint. They responded by using thinner paper, cutting back on pages, classified ads, holiday editions, out-of-town subscriptions and so on. A shortage of chlorine at the pulp mills gave many a tattletale gray look because of the inadequate bleaching of the newsprint. Reporters were given deferments as essential, and there were all-out attempts to recruit women reporters. During 1944, more than 80 percent of the journalism school graduates were women. The increase in costs caused the nickel paper to become commonplace.

Censorship was voluntary on the part of the newspapers, but it caused them constant concern and was the chief topic of complaint at every meeting of the American Society of Newspaper Editors. Elmer

Davis' OWI, charged with coordinating the information the federal government released, came in for much criticism. It was in the thankless position of being caught between demanding reporters and governmental agencies which often sought to release as little news as possible, especially if it reflected adversely in any remote way on their performance. The military were especially niggardly at times.

In general, whenever requested to withhold news for security reasons, newsmen routinely complied, so that items as important as D Day plans or speculation about the use of uranium in making explosives— *i.e.*, the atom bomb—were kept completely out. But in some cases, when a reporter thought he had a legitimate story of service boondoggling and was ordered not to print it, his paper did so anyway. One of the most famous of these incidents was the appearance in the New York *Times* of Hanson Baldwin's series on inefficiency in the South Pacific in 1942. And the most famous break of censorship during the war, the prerelease of the announcement of the German surrender by Ed Kennedy of the AP, was justified on the grounds that since the war was over, security considerations no longer obtained.

At the same time, the press had to contend with a plethora of self-aggrandizing news releases from the myriad Washington wartime agencies —what we call news management today—all designed to show how the agency was doing a tremendous job and to minimize any appearance of dissension among its heads.

Bruce Catton recalled a memo circulated in the War Production Board in late 1942 stating that: "The deficiencies of WPB are naturally seized upon by press and radio with more glee than its successful achievements. Methods must be found, therefore, to give true value to WPB's really significant results." The memo went on to give a specific suggestion on how this might be done:

> Whenever possible, predictions and quotas should be a-voided, except when understatement is used in full confidence that figures will be exceeded. Predicting 60,000 of something and making 50,000 is a failure. Predicting 45,000 and making 50,000 is a success. *The public has no way of knowing whether the original quota is adequate or not. (In fact, most public officials are also at sea* [my italics].)

But production goals were tossed out as much in a spirit of exhortation as of informativeness. More disturbing was the attitude of an assistant to Donald Nelson who appended this endorsement to the memo:

The whole direction of the public relations activities under
the new set-up will be changed to one of pre-testing the public
reaction and planning the whole public relations program, *not
to satisfy the newspapers and the radio, but to get a more favorable reaction toward the WPB and to eliminate so far as possible
the controversies of one kind and another which emanate from
this agency in the form of news stories.* Rather than be forced
to make explanations for announcements which have reached the
press . . . the policies established will, to a large extent, eliminate
stories of a controversial nature unless an analysis of the public
reaction before the release is made makes it clear that the reception will be what is desired [my italics].

The memorandum was not officially adopted by the WPB, but its
recommendations were followed in practice by the agency.

Since there were numerous newspapers that were unrelenting, even
biased critics of the government, the average reader did not subsist
solely on a diet of spoon-fed government pap. The press *was* free, which
included freedom to be bad and to slant the news in its news columns as
well as on its editorial pages, as had been the Chicago *Tribune*'s—
to name but one—habit for many years.

The war news, if not always coherent in terms of the big pictures,
certainly flowed in a large quantity—200,000,000 words in 1944, enough
for 1,000 editions of the New York *Times*.

In the early months of the war suppression of news was constant—
the Pearl Harbor disaster being the most flagrant. Casualty lists were not
printed for a year. Not until 1943 did the OWI finally receive authorization to release grim photos showing American dead. An extreme attitude
of the military was expressed by the brass hat who said there should be
only two stories: (1) "We have been attacked" and (2) "The enemy
has surrendered." General Eisenhower, normally cooperative with the
press, was guilty of suppressing legitimate, non-military-secret news when
he asked correspondents not to write about the slapping of a soldier
by General George Patton, on the grounds that such publicity would be
harmful to the troops' morale.

Patton, a ruthless, driving general and combat leader but a crude,
often cruel man personally, had become enraged upon seeing an apparently healthy GI sitting on a bed in a hospital in Sicily. When
told the man was suffering from an acute combat neurosis,
Patton shouted: "You dirty no-good son of a bitch! You cowardly
bastard! You're a disgrace to the Army and you're going right back to
the front to fight." He then slapped the man and ordered a doctor

to discharge him. A correspondent present sent an account of the incident to General Eisenhower, pointing out that the GI had had malaria, that his combat record was good, and that he had, previous to the slapping, asked to be sent back to his unit. Eisenhower investigated, then shot off a letter to reprimand Patton and relieve him of his command. Still, not one correspondent wrote up the story which had become common knowledge, and it was not made public until a month later when Drew Pearson revealed it on his radio program. (Most newsmen were critical of Pearson's breach of faith, just as in 1945 they were critical of Ed Kennedy's premature V-E Day story, even though security was not involved.)

But these incidents aside, the newspapers' chief fault lay in their chronic overoptimism, which was, more often than not, the fault of the editors and headline writers in the home office rather than the correspondents. For example, for six consecutive days the New York *Daily News* reader was given the identical impression that the American Army was on the verge of capturing Cherbourg:

First day: STORM CHERBOURG, CITY ABLAZE
Second day: YANKS HIT CHERBOURG IN FLAMING FINALE
Third day: YANKS STORM CHERBOURG FROM THREE SIDES
Fourth day: YANK BAYONETS SLASH PATH INTO CHERBOURG
Fifth day: YANKS STORM CHERBOURG'S LAST HEIGHTS
Sixth day: CHERBOURG IS OURS

Every other week, it seemed, some newspaper or another was headlining REMNANTS OF JAP FLEET SUNK, and in alternate weeks: REMNANTS OF JAP MERCHANT NAVY SUNK. Of course, the services themselves frequently suppressed the really bad news, such as the German breakthrough in the Battle of the Bulge and the destruction wreaked by Japanese kamikaze attacks on the Navy off Okinawa in 1945.

The correspondents themselves were not above embroidering the news, if it meant more sales to wire-service subscribers. One reporter based in New Guinea devised a story that was surefire. Natives had discovered the remains of a Jap bomber, so the resourceful correspondent calculated the date the bomber was probably shot down and compiled from flight logs a list of the American pilots in the air that day. He then wrote a short story on the shooting down of the Japanese plane, concluding: "The enemy could have been shot down by any of the following pilots:" followed by a list of thirty-five names and hometowns. He explained to an Australian colleague: "This story will go on the wire all over the States. Most of the papers will chuck it anyway. But I'll bet you ten bucks there'll be 35 newspapers which will carry an almost identical headline: 'Hometown Boy Downs Jap Bomber.' And the funny thing is that every one of the 35 papers will credit the kill to a different guy."

Exaggerations of GI exploits reached their apogee in the early months of war, when the papers, desperate for good news, seized on every rumor or shred of a story of an American success. When the British and Canadian commandos raided Dieppe in 1942, one headline had it AMERICANS LAND IN FRANCE, accompanied by a story which proclaimed: "The electrifying slogan of World War I, 'the Americans are coming,' is now heard in Belgium and France. The Russians repeat it, the Italians whisper it and Hitler says it in his nightmares." (Actually, about 200 American soldiers were along on the raid.) During the battle for the Philippines, newspapers reported a wholly fictional Battle of Lingayen Gulf, which had resulted in a smashing American victory. In some ways the saddest exploit, though, was the "sinking" of the Japanese battleship *Haruna* by Captain Colin Kelly, who allegedly put his Flying Fortress in a suicide dive after telling his crew to bail out. Actually the plane had only damaged a Japanese transport with its bombs, released by another premature hero, Meyer Levin, the bombardier. Kelly had gone down with his crippled plane, after ordering his crew to parachute.

But if the press catered to its audience's presumed need for heroes— or doomsaying or heartening victories—it also rose to occasions of great reporting. Indeed, some of the dispatches from the fighting front partook of almost classic simplicity and power. This description by the AP's Kenneth L. Dixon of American troops moving into Germany was reminiscent of the war classic *The Red Badge of Courage:*

> As seen from a ditch, the two tall trees made a perfect frame through which the column slowly advanced.
>
> Ten paces apart, company A was moving into the combat line.
>
> The men walked upward along a gradually rising ridge, entering the picture one by one. Each drab, muddy outline held the scene a moment as it topped the crest. It seemed suspended there against the gray smokey sky just before it stumbled on.
>
> All along the rainswept slope, the wet earth seemed to boil with muddy mortar bubbles bursting and splashing around the men.
>
> Through it all the doughboys walked slowly, grim, strained —ten paces apart.

Sometimes when a shell landed too close they hit the dirt, but mostly they just kept moving. Twice men were hit. The column paused briefly. Then it flowed forward again, with sticky reluctance, like heavy motor oil on a cold morning.

The best of the newspaper writers were able to convey with stark directness the GI's world, without resorting to clichés or fustian. The soldiers were not depicted as soldiers, the military; they were civilians in uniform, guys like you and me or our sons and brothers—in short, Us. True the little-guy talk might become a cliché, but in the best reporting there was an easy familiarity that was a natural descriptive outgrowth of a democratic army.

If not the best, certainly the most widely read and loved of the correspondents was Ernie Pyle, who had spent his prewar years as a "tramp" newspaperman in the Southwest, writing features. Pyle entered the war as a correspondent for the Scripps-Howard papers, covering the invasion of North Africa. A small, dapper man, terribly shy, suffering from a plethora of ailments real or imagined, he found himself in war by writing about what the ordinary soldier saw, felt, thought, said.

The turning point had come one day in North Africa when Pyle and another soldier had dived into a ditch under intense strafing from a flight of Stuka dive bombers. When the firing stopped, Pyle turned to his companion and gasped: "Whew! That was close, eh?" The other didn't answer; he was dead. In a daze Pyle went on to his assignment— a press conference for a French general—but was unable to write his story. He cabled his editor that he could not carry out the assignment and instead wrote about the soldier who had died with him in a ditch. He had found his point of view.

Pyle was not a heroic man, and his war was an antiheroic one perfectly in tune with the men who were fighting in it—men like those two archetypical GI's Willie and Joe, whom the cartoonist Bill Mauldin had caught so well with his pen. Pyle concentrated on details—the debris of shoes, cigarettes, writing paper left behind by the dead on Normandy beach, for example. He conveyed a quick, ingenuous sympathy for the GI's, and he made individual deaths as important as the loss of a friend. One of his best columns (he appeared six times a week in 310 papers with more than 12,000,000 readers) told of a company commander named Captain Waskow, who was revered by his men. Captain Waskow had been killed in the hills of Italy; his body was brought down on muleback and laid beside the road. The men in the company passed by slowly, one by one:

One soldier came and looked down, and he said out loud: "God damn it!"

That's all he said, and then he walked away.

Another one came, and he said, "God damn it to hell anyway!"

He looked down for a few last moments and then turned and left.

Another man came. I think he was an officer. It was hard to tell in the dim light, for everybody was grimy and dirty. The man looked down into the dead Captain's face and then spoke directly to him, as though he were alive: "I'm sorry, old man."

Then a soldier came and stood beside the officer and bent over, and he too spoke to his dead Captain, not in a whisper but awfully tenderly, and he said: "I sure am sorry, sir."

Then the first man squatted down, and he reached and took the Captain's hand, and he sat there for a full five minutes holding the dead hand in his own and looking intently into the dead face. And he never uttered a sound all the time he sat there.

Finally he put the hand down. He reached up and gently straightened the points of the Captain's shirt collar, and then he sort of rearranged the tattered edges of his uniform around the wound, and then he got up and walked away down the road in the moonlight.

Pyle himself had long been dogged with the infantryman's fatalistic belief that his luck was running out; in 1945, during the Battle of Iwo Jima, it did. Ernie Pyle died in a foxhole, hit by a Japanese bullet.

If the newspapers sometimes attained near-sublime heights, they also managed to dig their toes into the comfortable mulch of feature material which they printed war or peace. There were the usual articles on celebrities, children, dogs and other transitory subjects. A list of titles taken from a collection of the best feature stories in a war year conveys what the reporters were writing about in a nonwar vein:

"How Grandma Learned to Read"

"Halstead Street Found Most Typical of Chicago and Its People"

"I Answer Letters to the Lovelorn"

"Lou Gehrig: A Great Ballplayer Passes On"

"He [Irving Berlin] Still Hates to Get Up in the Morning;
    Sleeps till 2 P.M."

"International Education Urged"

"Who's Afraid of Those Big (But Not Bad) St. Bernards?
    Everyone, Especially Youngsters"

Because of wartime uncertainties, both global and domestic, astrology and advice to the lovelorn features acquired increased popularity.

The *doyenne* of American manners, Emily Post, worked overtime to revise her code to fit special wartime situations. On the knotty problem of meeting weekend guests who arrive by train when one's gasoline supply is curtailed, she ruled that the hosts need not, unless all incoming guests could be picked up in one trip. Hosts located far from public transportation were permitted to send a letter along these lines: "Our house is a mile from the bus stop, and there is no conveyance. So be prepared to walk and don't bring a heavy bag, because there is no way to get it here except to carry it."

Miss Post also strongly urged guests to bring food of their own or expect to do without. Because of the fuel shortage, a guest need not fear embarrassing his host by bundling up in winter—both indoors and out: "No matter whom you go to stay with this winter . . . be sure to take warm clothing. . . . To wear woolen underwear is supposed to be the answer. . . ." Just how flexible Miss Post could be in order to win the war was revealed when she gulped down her standards and told the OWI that it was all right for female war workers to hitch a ride to the job. Of course, she hastily added, the feminine hitchhiker should confine her talk to the weather, and, don't you know, the traditional thumb was a bit vulgar—better the ride seeker should discreetly display her plant ID card.

A staple in the average newspaper's bill of fare was the comic page. From the newspapers' standpoint the comics were lucrative in drawing and keeping readership. It was estimated that the Hearst papers derived 60 percent of their entire income from syndicating their home-grown comic strips. The daily comic pages had a total readership of 70,000,000. The ten most popular strips during the war in order of size of readership were: (1) "Joe Palooka"; (2) "Blondie"; (3) "Li'l Abner"; (4) "Little Orphan Annie"; (5) "Terry and the Pirates"; (6) "Dick Tracy"; (7) "Moon Mullins"; (8) "Gasoline Alley"; (9) "Bringing Up Father"; (10) "The Gumps".

This list, of course, represented no radical change in comic-reading habits; all were longtime favorites. Although the war did witness the birth of a few new strips—"Kerry Drake," "Penny," "Johnny Hazard," "Bruce Gentry" and preeminently Bill Mauldin's "Up Front," which won a Pulitzer Prize in its first year of syndication in the States and later underwent a transition to peacetime under the evolving titles "Sweating It Out," "Back Home" and "Willie and Joe"—the major changes in the comic strip field wrought by war were in subject matter and presentation. And even here the field remained fairly conservative.

A number of comic heroes—and heroines—joined up, but about as many stayed home, where they were immersed in home front problems and plugged various government drives or else fought spies and saboteurs. Among the enlistees were: Joe Palooka (who remained a democratic Pfc throughout the fray, while his sidekick Jerry made lieutenant as a flyboy); Terry (who twenty-five years later is still barging in on various wars); Slats of "Abbie and Slats" (Army); Snuffy Smith (Army) and Barney Google (Navy); Dick Tracy (a commission in naval intelligence, but the peerless nose continued to fight crime on the home front in the form of the usual bizarre characters, *viz.,* Pruneface, 88 Keys, Flattop, Laffy, the Summer Sisters, Brow, Gravel Gertie and Breathless); Skeezix (Army); Harold Teen (Navy—Shadow and the rest of the gang did war work); Mickey Finn (Coast Guard); Scorchy Smith (Fifth Air Force all the way); Smilin' Jack (Air Force); and Tillie the Toiler (WAC— her sisters, Fritzie Ritz and Winnie Winkel, did war work and married a GI, respectively).

Others that, for often obvious reasons, ignored the war were: "Buck Rogers," "Alley Oop," "The Captain and the Kids" and "The Katzen- jammer Kids," "Mutt and Jeff," "Napoleon" and "Uncle Elby," "Pop- eye" and "Prince Valiant" and, most notably, "Superman." More or less in the thick of home front activities were "Blondie," "Bringing Up Father," "The Neighbors," "Out Our Way," "Li'l Abner" and "Little Orphan Annie."

The comics, like the radio soap operas, represented a unique blend of fantasy and reality in their readers' minds. No one except a few far- gone schizophrenics thought they were real people, yet close followers of a strip would bombard their creators with advice on the story line or corrections of small details. There were things that a certain character just wouldn't do, and if the reader didn't like it, he said so. For example, early in the war Ham Fisher's Joe Palooka was shown shooting a Nazi soldier in the back, while Bateese slugged another Nazi, egged on by Jerry, who is saying: "Bite 'im, Bateese!! Sic 'im!" The sight of clean-cut, 100 percent-American Joe doing such a dastardly thing as shooting some- one in the back—however dastardly the victim—aroused his fans' boyish sportsmanship. To the complaints Fisher, who was by that time hip-deep in war, replied toughly: "No good soldier is going to be polite in a real war. Why should Joe?"

Another absolute taboo was death. When a rumor—untrue—spread in 1945 that Skeezix would be killed in the war, complaints poured into newspaper offices. The switchboards of the New York *Daily News* and the Chicago *Tribune* were clogged with calls for three days before the rumor was downed. And when Dick Tracy eliminated Flattop, obituary notices appeared in papers throughout the country.

The most celebrated "death" was that of Daddy Warbucks in Harold Gray's "Little Orphan Annie." Gray, a curmudgeonish man, had for years used his strip as a vehicle for attacking the New Deal and defending the virtues of old-fashioned monopoly capitalism, as personified by "Daddy." Throughout the war, Gray had groused (through Annie) in his usual fashion about rationing, overweening labor unions, the plight of the businessman and so on. No one bothered him much, even though he was, after all, criticizing the government in wartime—actually a good many people sharply agreed with him that the war was a New Deal plot to assure the eventual triumph of Communism. By 1945 Gray, also a shrewd businessman not undevoid of a public relations sense, decided that Daddy had had it with the New Deal and sent him, in a state of despair over his beloved country, to his doom. Daddy's death set off another one of those waves of reader protests, which may or may not have been just what Gray was looking for. At any rate, soon after Roosevelt's death, Daddy made a reappearance, remarking somewhat tastelessly that "the climate is different around here recently."

Politically, Gray had his counterweight in the liberal Ham Fisher, an avidly pro-Roosevelt man. He had won the Chief's personal gratitude by enlisting Joe in the Army before the war, thus supporting the defense effort and showing that the life of a $21-a-month private was not as bad as Mom thought. Fisher continued to plug the war effort in his strip and even presented the President as a character in it—with the latter's permission. (Gray did his bit for the war effort, too, for that matter; a pet organization of Annie's called the Junior Commandos stimulated a large number of boys and girls to collect scrap.)

Apolitical was Superman, however; he sat out the war in a kind of noncombatant status. Not that he was a conscientious objector; rather his creators, Jerry Siegel and Joe Schuster, simply decided that Superman's invincibility would make him an improbable wartime character. It was all right to leap tall buildings in a single bound in pursuit of the mythical malefactors of Metropolis, but it might pall if Superman were daily engaged in wiping out the Axis, especially when real American GI's weren't finding it so simple.

After the fall of France, the authors had pitted Superman briefly against the Axis. He had been depicted as ripping up by the roots the now German-held Maginot line, causing the real-life Nazi Storm Trooper magazine *Das Schwarze Korps* to brand him a Jewish-American pluto-crat. In peacetime, as an expression of simplistic protest against the German victory, Superman's action was acceptable, but when America was at war, such exploits would become tasteless and perhaps set off cries of derision from real GI's. So the two authors made their decision: Superman—or rather his alter ego, mild-mannered reporter Clark Kent, would be 4-F for the duration. They accomplished this ingeniously. Kent reported for his preinduction physical and was given an eye test, where-upon his Supermanly attribute of X-ray vision betrayed him. Instead of the chart before him, he read the one in the next room through the wall. And so it was that the only man of steel on the Allied side bore the Russian name of Stalin.

Taking up the slack were the comic books, whose fantastically en-dowed heroes were not loath to whip the Axis. Monthly, bimonthly or quarterly, stalwarts such as Batman and Robin, Flashman, Plastic Man, Captain America, Captain Marvel, the Green Lantern, the Spirit *et al.* defeated a variety of biliously yellow-skinned Japs and fat Germans, whose speech was interlarded with such Teutonisms as *"Achtung!"* *"Kamerad!"* and *"Götterdämmerung!"* (used as an oath). Within their color-smudged pages, an absolute freedom of the imagination flourished; there were no inhibitions about fantasy clashing with wartime realities. For in this genre of *lumpen* literature the young reader was king (although it should be added that comic books had a substantial GI readership too). In his private garden of fantasy, the child's war tended to be a simple contest between all-powerful, all-good superheroes and nasty, nightmarish villains. It was thus permissible for a hero of superhuman powers to be unleashed against the enemy, for to the child *they* were unreal, superhuman figures too.

Adults had their own fantasy life, but it fed on reality—front-page news stories. Much of the same escapist fare that always appeared domi-nated the front pages, having nothing, of course, to do with the war. Indeed, the average newspaper made sure to supply its reader with a gaudy carnival of sex, murder and disasters.

Thus, in 1942 one of the leading stories was the Coconut Grove nightclub fire in November. Eight hundred revelers, many of them specta-tors at the Holy Cross-Boston College football game earlier in the day, had crowded into the Boston nightclub which was festooned with artificial tropical flora in keeping with its name. A busboy replacing a light bulb lit a match, and the supposedly fireproof greenery ignited. The flames leaped around the room, from paper palm to paper palm—and then spread to screaming patrons, turning them into blazing torches. In frenzied panic, people rushed for the exit, a revolving door that quickly became jammed as people tried to push on both sides. Bodies piled up like cordwood at the door as people were trampled or overcome by smoke and flame. In all, 484 died. The tragedy set off a belated crusade for stricter fire regulations for nightclubs.

The hectic love life of Errol Flynn became public property in 1943. Flynn, who had divorced Lily Damita the previous year, had been making the most of his restored bachelorhood, specializing in the bobby-sox brigade. First came a charge of statutory rape from a seventeen-year-old aspiring actress named Betty Hansen, who said the Hollywood swashbuckler had had his wicked way with her in the bedroom of a friend's bachelor apartment. What with all the publicity, another seventeen-year-old named Peggy Satterlee was stimulated to recall that, come to think of it, Flynn had statutorily raped *her* too, aboard his yacht *Sirrocco*. Ambitious Los Angeles DA John Dockwiler combined the two cases and announced he intended to prosecute Flynn to the fullest extent of the law, which was five years in San Quentin, hence the term "San Quentin quail."

Though a serious matter for the actor, Flynn's trial became a circus. His shrewd lawyer, Jerry Geisler, was able to attack successfully the characters of the two young ladies. Betty had cooperated most willingly in her "violation" because she hoped Flynn would help her get a movie contract, while Peggy was no stranger to fornication, having been involved in several escapades—the wages of one such sin being an abortion. In somewhat girlish language the girls told Mr. Geisler what had happened in great detail—to the delectation of newspaper readers everywhere. Peggy, attired demurely in pigtails and bobby sox but exhibiting a rather precocious figure, testified that Flynn had on the fateful night given her a potion—rum in hot milk—then later entered her room and forced her to have intercourse with him. Before dawn he lured her into another connection, first showing her the moon. His line on that occasion —"Darling, look out the porthole. You see that glorious moon?"—became a catchphrase of the trial and soon another phrase, "In Like Flynn," meaning just that, entered the language. Geisler's forensic skills won the day, and the jury of nine women and three men returned a verdict of not guilty. Flynn consoled himself during the trial by flirting with a voluptuous cigarette counter girl in the courthouse lobby named Nora Eddington, age eighteen; soon after, he married her. The two did not live happily ever after.

Sex reared its headlines again in 1944, when Charlie Chaplin was tried for violation of the Mann Act. It was alleged that he lured a protégée, a starlet named Joan Barry, from California to New York for purposes of having sexual relations with her. The actress had already slapped a paternity suit on him in 1942, after which, Chaplin, his career at a low ebb, married eighteen-year-old Oona O'Neill, daughter of the playwright Eugene O'Neill. The Mann Act was thrown out, but the next year Miss Barry's paternity suit reached the courts, and their love life was dragged out for all to see. There were spicy stories of lovemaking on a bear rug before the fire, and trial followers snickered when it was revealed that after one amorous encounter, Chaplin, naked, flexed his muscles and delivered the immortal line: "You know, Joan, I look something like Peter Pan, don't you think?"

The case was finally decided in 1946, and although a blood test proved conclusively that Chaplin was not the father of Miss Barry's baby, he was ordered to pay support. Chaplin's wartime fall from grace was due in part to the revelations of his sexual peccadilloes, but he was also heavily criticized for his speeches in favor of a second front to aid the Russians. People thought in 1942 that such a call was premature and that Chaplin was showing an inordinate favoritism for the Russians. Besides, the fact that he was an alien demanding action from the U.S. government did not win him friends among the staid gentry. (Ironically, while Chaplin's career was strangled at the box office, Flynn's popularity rose.)

Another headline case had darker sexual overtones. This involved the murder of his wife, beer heiress Patricia Burton Lonergan, by a strange young man named Wayne Lonergan. Mrs. Lonergan's body was discovered in their luxurious Beekman Place apartment brutally beaten. The murder weapon was a brass candlestick. Expert detective work established the guilt of her husband, and he was convicted and sentenced to life imprisonment. As one New York cabby was alleged to have said, it was "the kind of case that gives degeneracy a bad name."

Another sensational murder case was the killing of Sir Harry Oakes in the Bahamas. His son-in-law, Alfred de Marigny, a suave, shady type was indicted, but the jury finally acquitted him and ordered him deported. The case remained unsolved, although there is evidence that gambling interests and organized crime seeking to gain a foothold on the island may have been behind the slaying.

Café Society antics were always good copy. The stormy married life of Gloria Vanderbilt and her husband Pat DiSicco made a running story during the war. DiSicco had a penchant for nightclub brawls and once took on a Texan who turned out to be an expert in the art and flattened him twice. The DiSiccos were finally divorced, but Miss Vanderbilt was again in the news when she married Leopold Stokowski, the famed conductor.

One of the stellar figures on the front pages in 1945 was a 130-pound bull mastiff named Blaze. What pushed him into notoriety was the fact that he was owned by Colonel Elliott Roosevelt, who was of course the son of the President and who was also the husband of actress Faye Emerson.

In January all public hell broke loose. It seemed that an eighteen-year-old sailor, Seaman First Class Leon LeRoy, had arrived in New York and learned that his father had died while he was at sea. He was immediately granted an emergency leave to visit his mother in Antioch, California, and put aboard an Army Transport Command flight out of Newark, with a C priority. When the plane landed in Dayton, Ohio, for refueling, LeRoy and two other servicemen, also on C priorities, noticed that a crate containing a large dog and addressed to Miss Faye Emerson, Los Angeles, was loaded aboard; the crate took up three seats. The men and dog continued on uneventfully to Memphis, where a load of urgent war material destined for the West Coast was at the airport. The local ATC officer routinely checked the priorities and it came out that the dog had an A, or top, priority, while the cargo of war materials had a B priority. Since the servicemen had only C's and there was not room for them, war materials and dog, they were bumped off the flight.

Seaman LeRoy was forced to hitchhike, losing his leave papers en route and being picked up by the MP's before finally managing to make it to Antioch, where he spilled the whole story to reporters. The other servicemen aboard corroborated LeRoy's tale, and still another serviceman, it later came out, had been bumped off the plane at Dallas and had to borrow $98 from the Red Cross to take a commercial flight.

These revelations set off a storm of criticism. Here was a perfect example of the "Roosevelt arrogance" by which a dog, as long as he fell under the mantle of Roosevelt family privilege, was more important than three ordinary servicemen trying to visit bereaved mothers and sick wives.

To top it all off, shortly after the incident, the President sent to Congress a list of colonels recommended for promotion to brigadier generals; among the names was that of Elliott Roosevelt. The timing was ill advised, to put it mildly, and even a loyal Roosevelt Democrat like

Senator Albert B. "Happy" Chandler could wail, "Why do they have to pick *this* time for it?" Congress was in an uproar, calling for an investigation, and the New York *Herald Tribune* poured out daily editorials.

The same paper noted in one: "We would not go so far as to say that the story of Elliott Roosevelt's dog has blanketed the news of the great Russian offensive, but we venture to guess that as a subject of discussion from coast to coast it is a strong rival." A letter to the editor from an Ohio lady reflected the sentiments of many on the Roosevelt promotion: "Do you mean to say, for God sakes, that any Roosevelt can just make himself a general if he wants to?"

The denouement came when General Harold L. George, commandant of the ATC, issued a 900-word report on the incident absolving Colonel Roosevelt and any other Roosevelts from blame. The man responsible for the dog's high priority was Colonel Ray W. Ireland, assistant chief of staff for priorities and traffic, headquarters Air Transport Command, who said he had awarded it on his own volition as a favor to the President's family. There had been no request from on high that he do so. Mrs. John Boettiger (Anna Roosevelt) had called to ask if Blaze could be shipped to the coast but had asked for no priority treatment. The ATC was reprimanded and ordered henceforth not to transport animals of any kind. But the priority system, which could classify an ordinary soldier below a dog or cargo of freight, continued along its merry way.

One popular section of the wartime newspaper was the sports page. During the war, professional sports proved to be one of the most popular divertisements despite the loss to the armed services of most of the skilled performers and a shortage of young talent.

Perhaps hardest hit, yet still followed as avidly as ever, was professional baseball. Of some 5,700 players in the major and minor leagues, more than 4,000 went into the service. The immediate victims of this decimation of the player rosters were the minor league farm clubs. Out of forty-one such leagues in existence before Pearl Harbor, only nine were able to continue through the war. Adding to the minor leagues' woes was the banning of night baseball in some parts of the country—a ban which continued until 1944. This meant not only were they short of players, they were also short of customers, for most of their games were played at night. As for the majors, they bore the ban in stride and resorted to twilight games instead.

Baseball as a morale builder was recognized by the President as early as January 15, 1942, in a letter to the commissioner of baseball, Judge Kenesaw Mountain Landis:

> Baseball provides a recreation which does not last over two hours or two hours and a half, and which can be got for very little cost. . . . . [If] 300 teams use 5,000 or 6,000 players, these players are a definite recreational asset to at least 20,000,000 of their fellow citizens—and that in my judgement is thoroughly worthwhile.

The Great American Game responded to the President's confidence by performing admirably under trying circumstances. The War Department sponsored broadcasts of the World Series games to GI's all over the world via shortwave radio, while at home, major league baseball enjoyed a popularity greater than at any other time in its venerable history, even though the quality of play declined.

During the ensuing 1942 season, stars not in the service were subjected to a good deal of verbal abuse from the fans on the obvious, if simplistic, grounds that if they were healthy enough to engage in a strenuous sport, they were healthy enough to serve. Even the heretofore sacrosanct Joe DiMaggio of the Yankees was booed. DiMaggio soon went in, as did Bob Feller, Ted Williams, Bill Dickey, Johnny VanderMeer, Phil Rizzuto, Hank Greenberg, Peewee Reese, Schoolboy Rowe, Virgil "Fire" Trucks, Joe Gordon, Johnny Mize, Johnny Beazley, Dom DiMaggio, Pete Reiser, Hugh Casey and many others. Thereafter, the cries of "favoritism" at those who were classified 4-F for such things as flat feet and punctured eardrums dwindled and steadily increasing attendance in 1944 and 1945, reversing the trend of the previous two years, showed that the fans were happy.

The players who remained were for the most part obvious castoffs, rejects or overage fathers. As the level of the talent barrel sank to the bottom, managers felt an increasing pressure to fill out their rosters with a variety of substitutes—like a housewife stretching her meat ration for the week. Some of the players had deferments for doing essential work in defense plants and played in their spare time, as it were, after putting in a hard day at the plant. (This was largely true in the minor leagues.) 4-F's were in high demand, as were foreign players from Cuba and Mexico. Finally, there were the old-timers who were able to add three or four years to their careers.

By 1945 baseball had sunk to what *Time* magazine called "somewhere between AA and A—but still baseball." (In normal times, AA represented the top level of minor league baseball—the American Association, International League and Pacific Coast League. A-1 was the next level down—*e.g.*, the Southern Association—and so on through A, B, C, and D.) "Rosters," the magazine said, were "as full of unknown names as Y.M.C.A. hotel registers."

The owner of one of those unsung names was Pete Gray, who joined the American League champs, the St. Louis Browns. What distinguished Gray was not his batting average, but his way with a bat. Gray batted one-handed, having only one arm (the left). At a time when disabled veterans were returning from the fighting front in increasing numbers, he became a symbol of how to overcome a handicap courageously. He was the most talked-about rookie of the year and a drawing card at the box office. Although obviously a wartime exotic, Gray had made himself a master of the drag bunt by way of compensating for being an otherwise weak hitter. He was an excellent outfielder, trapping the ball in his glove, then in a quick motion throwing the ball in the air, cramming his glove under the stump of his right arm and quickly plucking the ball and throwing it with his now bare hand. Gray lasted one season in the majors. He played in 77 games and batted .218, with 51 hits—all but 8 of which were singles.

In a way, it seemed only fitting that Gray should join Luke Sewell's Browns, who were perhaps the shining light of wartime's ersatz baseball. The year 1944 was destined to go down as the Year the Browns Won the Pennant, the first in their long tenure of lackluster servitude in the American League. Their roster boasted such indelible names as Denny Galehouse, a thirty-two-year-old Ohio farmer who had never seen a World Series before, Mark Christman (thirty-one), Nelson Potter (thirty-three), Jack Kramer (twenty-six), Gene Moore (thirty-five), Milt Byrnes (twenty-eight), Don Gutteridge (thirty-two), Frank Mancuso (twenty-six), George Caster (thirty-seven), Sig Jakucki (thirty-five), Chet Laabs (thirty-two), George McQuinn (thirty-five) and Mike Kreevich (thirty-six). Perhaps the only authentic star on the team was the twenty-four-year-old shortstop Vern "Junior" Stephens, who led the league in runs batted in and was second in home runs.

The series matched the Browns against their fellow townsmen, the Cardinals, who had dominated the wartime season by winning pennants in 1942, 1943 and 1944. Estimable as the one-city series was from the standpoint of curtailing wartime travel, the confines of Sportsman's Park did not bring the Browns good fortune, even though most of the St. Louis fans rooted for them as underdogs. The powerful Cards, who had breezed through their own league to win by 14½ games, captured the Series four games to two. The following year the Browns finished third, in 1946, seventh, and, in the remainder of their history, before the franchise was moved to Baltimore in 1954 (and the name forever dropped, as though baseball were trying to deny that they had ever existed), they never came close to repeating their glorious triumph of 1944.

Although the level of play was of low quality during their war, those who carried on came up with a number of notable performances. Outstanding was Mel Ott, the playing manager of the New York Giants, who, with his raised-leg batting stance that was compared to a dog making an approach to a fire hydrant, continued to pull home runs into the short right-field bleachers of the Polo Grounds. In those last years of his career, Ott broke a staggering number of National League records including RBI's, total bases, walks, runs scored, total hits and extra base hits. In 1945 it looked as though Ott would also lead his Giants to a pennant, for the club won twenty-five out of its first thirty-two games and pulled away to the longest lead in major league history. But the Giants collapsed in midseason, losing twenty-one out of twenty-nine games during one stretch, and faded from contention.

The Dodgers lived up to their sobriquet of "Dem Bums" by similarly blowing a large lead in the 1942 race. They maintained first-division play during the war, led by their veteran batting stars, Dixie Walker, Billy Herman, Augie Galan and Goody Rosen but never threatened the Cardinals' domination.

The latter were noted for their pitching, fielding (their 1943 team fielding average of .982 set a record) and aggressive baserunning. Their infield was built around the lithe, graceful shortstop Marty "Slats" Marion, who drew comparisons to Honus Wagner. But there were also Terry Moore and Enos Slaughter (both in service by 1943), Whitey Kurowski, and catcher Walker Cooper for hitting power, and on the mound, Walker's brother Morton, Harry "the Cat" Brecheen and Ted Wilks, who in 1944, his freshman year, led the league in won-lost percentage.

Manager Joe McCarthy's Yankees dominated the American League in 1942 and 1943, winning the world's championship in the latter year. But the loss of such greats as Phil Rizzuto, Charley "Red" Ruffing, Buddy Hassett, Joe DiMaggio, Bill Dickey and Joe Gordon to the services took its toll; the Yanks finished third in 1944 and fourth in 1945. Standouts for the wartime Yanks were John Lindell, a converted pitcher who hit 18 home runs and batted in 102 runs in 1944, third in the league in both departments, George "Snuffy" Stirnweiss, who won the American League batting championship in 1945 with an average of .309, the lowest in many years. Spurgeon "Spud" Chandler was the club's pitching stalwart, along with Hank Borowy, who was sold to the Cubs in 1945, in time to help them win the National League pennant.

The Detroit Tigers, managed by Steve O'Neill, mounted strong contenders during the war and also led the league in attendance for three consecutive years, reflecting both the large Motor City war worker population and the down-to-the-wire pennant races in which the Tigers were involved. The Tigers' most outstanding asset was their pitching, the bulwarks of their staff being Hal Newhouser, who won twenty-nine games in 1944 and twenty-five in 1945, and Paul "Dizzy" Trout, who led the league in ERA in 1944.

The year 1945 was marked by the return of discharged servicemen to baseball, and two of them made significant contributions to the Tiger cause. Hank Greenberg, out of the Army, played seventy-eight games and hit thirteen home runs, the last of which, a grand-slammer, clinched the pennant for Detroit on the final day of the season. Greenberg's hitting also contributed to the Tigers' four-games-to-three victory over the Cubs in the World Series, and Virgil "Fire" Trucks, released from the Navy only a few days before the end of the season but allowed to play in the Series under a special rule for returning servicemen, contributed a victory to the Tiger cause.

The Tigers' opponent in the 1945 series, Charlie Grimm's Chicago Cubs, were a powerful hitting club with a fair pitching staff, bolstered by the midseason acquisition of Borowy from the Yanks. Borowy went on to win eleven games and lose only two. Other Cub pitching aces were Hank Wyse, Paul Derringer and Claude Passeau, who threw a one-hitter in the Series. Although eclipsed by other hitters in 1945, Bill Nicholson was the Cubs' leading power hitter, leading the league in both home runs and RBI's in 1943 and 1944. Phil Cavarretta was National League batting champ in 1945 with a hefty .355 average. Third baseman Stan Hack and outfielder Andy Pafko were also outstanding; Hack finished fourth in batting with a .323 average, and Pafko was third in RBI's with 110.

Other players who were standouts on noncontenders included pitcher Bucky Walters of the Reds, who won twenty-three games to lead the league in victories in 1943; Truett "Rip" Sewell of the Pirates, who won twenty-one games in 1943 with his famous "balloon ball" (a looping pitch thrown twenty-five feet in the air which crossed the plate at a downward angle that made it difficult to hit); Lou Boudreau, the young shortstop-manager of the Cleveland Indians, who won the 1944 American League batting championship with an average of .327; Tommy Holmes, the Boston Braves veteran who batted .352 and hit a league-leading twenty-eight home runs in 1945; Ed Heusser of Cincinnati who led the league in ERA percentage in 1944; Jim Tobin of the Braves, who pitched two no-hitters in 1944; Joe "Ducky" Medwick of the Giants, who finished second to Dixie Walker in batting in 1944; Luke Appling, the durable White Sox shortstop and champion foul-ball hitter, who led the American League in batting in 1943 with .328, 60 points less than his league-leading average of 1936; Ace Adams, the New York Giant relief specialist, who set a major league record by pitching in seventy games in 1943; and Bobby Doerr, the young Boston Red Sox second baseman who was most valuable player in 1944 and second in hitting. These men, who could play in any league, wartime or peacetime, helped the game retain some of its prewar star quality; but it was the remnants, the retreads, the too young and too old, the temporarily promoted minor-leaguers in the supporting cast who kept the game alive.

It was not only the somewhat deteriorated quality of its players that gave baseball a wartime cast. The conditions under which the game was played were altered in many ways. To accommodate war workers, games in some cities started at odd and exotic times, ranging from 10:30 A.M. (Newark and Milwaukee in the minors had 9:30 games) to 9:30 P.M. The twilight games started around 5:30. Restrictions promulgated by the Office of Defense Transportation curtailed travel and played havoc with scheduling. In 1943 the traditional spring training junkets to the Southern climes were halted. Teams were confined to an area north of the Potomac and Ohio rivers and east of the Mississippi (with the exception of the St. Louis clubs, which trained at home)—a boundary popularly known as the Landis-Eastman Line after commissioner Landis and the head of the ODT.

So the teams fanned out to university field houses and worked out the kinks in aging muscles amid the chilly Northern March wind. In 1945 the All-Star Game was canceled, and seven games between American and National League teams were held, with the receipts going to Army-Navy Relief. The Dodgers-Senators game featured Lieutenant Bert Shepard, a veteran who had lost a leg in combat, pitching four innings (his only major league appearance). The Senators won, 4–3, and Shepard was patriotically credited with the victory.

Baseball contributed in a variety of other ways to war campaigns. Proceeds of individual World Series games were turned over to war relief. During scrap drives, youngsters bearing aluminum pots, old hot-water bottles or whatever they could snitch from attics and basements were admitted free of charge. Special games were held with admission being a war bond. One of the most unusual of the latter was a three-way game in New York between the Giants, Yankees and Dodgers. Each team went to bat six times in the same nine-inning game against rotating opponents; the final score was Dodgers 5, Yankees 1, Giants 0, and the Fifth War Loan was $56,500,000 richer. Receipts from the annual All-Star Games went to the Baseball Equipment Fund, which was used to buy sports equipment for the services. The fan's traditional right to a ball hit into the stands was suspended during the war; he was supposed to throw it back for use by the fund. Those who procrastinated about doing so found themselves the objects of boos and chants of "Throw it back, throw it back"—repeated until the unpatriotic fan had complied.

The other sports answered their manpower problems in a variety of ways. Professional football, for example, had an advantage over baseball in that its games were played only on weekends. As a result, players could hold down essential defense jobs (thus acquiring a deferment) during the week and play on weekends, practicing in their after-work hours. Some servicemen even played while on weekend passes—Sid Luckman, the Chicago Bears' star quarterback, being one example. Certain teams had their troubles, however. The Cleveland Rams suspended play during the 1943 season when their owner and coach went into the service, and in the same year the Pittsburgh Steelers and the Philadelphia Eagles combined teams and were known as either the Phil-Pitt Eagles or the Steagles (the next year Pittsburgh paired up with the Chicago Cardinals). Rosters were filled out with an assortment of 4-F's and other players, including Bronko Nagurski, who emerged from a six-year retirement to help the Bears win the National Football League championship in 1943.

Attendance continued to be good, although below prewar highs, for there were still enough stars in action to divert the fans. Among the standouts were Cecil Isbell and Don Hutson of Green Bay, Sammy Baugh of Washington, Luckman, Bill Paschal of New York and Steve Van Buren of Philadelphia. The Chicago Bears remained the most consistent challengers, winning the championship in 1941, losing it in 1942 to the Redskins, and regaining it the next year. Green Bay edged out the Giants in the 1944 play-off, and the revived Cleveland Rams with rookie quarterback Bob Waterfield beat the Redskins in 1945, after a Sammy Baugh pass from behind his goal line hit a goalpost (an automatic safety in those days). Unlimited substitution was permitted, and teams lent players to other squads that were short in a further effort to beat the manpower squeeze.

The war delivered college football both a blow and a reprieve. The blow, of course, was the decimating of the campus population by the draft: There were no college deferments in those days. Some schools dropped the sport entirely for a season or so, while others played informal schedules. In the 1943 season the Navy allowed V-12 and V-5 cadets on campus to play, but the Army barred its men in various training programs from intercollegiate sports on the grounds they should be devoting full time to their studies. As a result, schools with Navy training units were able to mount strong teams, while those with Army training programs gave up the sport. Among the latter were Alabama, Tennessee, Florida, Mississippi State, Fordham, Syracuse, Stanford, Oregon, and Washington State. Most of these schools managed to return to action in 1944 with teams composed of 4-F's and freshmen, the latter having been made eligible under a special dispensation.

It was not all roses for the Navy-staffed teams, however; as men moved through the training cycle, they were likely to be transferred. Hence, a man might play half a season for one school, half for another—and on some occasions find himself opposing his former teammates or a team he had played earlier. Schools that were world-beaters in October might be doormats by December.

By 1944 most of the stars in the V-12 programs had graduated and gone on to military duties; in their place came a crop of young unknowns. Nonetheless, the game limped through the season, and overall attendance, which had dropped during 1942 and 1943, was up 18 percent. This rise probably reflected the easing of restrictions on pleasure driving as much as it did any spurt of renewed interest.

Into the vacuum formed by the decimation of the collegiate ranks came the service teams, and on the sportswriters' Top Ten list in 1943 appeared such names as Great Lakes Naval Training Center, Iowa Pre-Flight, Del Monte Pre-Flight and March Field, which of course played college schedules, mounted teams made up of former college and professional stars and were guided by top coaches such as Bernie Bierman,

Jim Crowley and Wallace Wade. Because of turnovers in their ranks, these teams had their ups and downs too, and it was the two service academies at Annapolis and West Point—especially the latter—that emerged as the wartime powerhouses. They could attract the cream of the upcoming young players and keep them in school long enough to develop them into a cohesive unit.

Indeed, in 1944–45, Army dominated the national football scene, winning all eighteen of its games during that period by lopsided scores. The Army squad was considered by most sportswriters to be not only the best college eleven, but also superior to any of the other service or professional teams then in action. In 1944 Colonel Earl Blaik's Black Knights scored 504 points to their opponents 35, running up 59–0 and 67–7 scores over, respectively, Notre Dame and Penn, their only serious civilian challengers. Their closest call was Navy, which they beat 23–7. In 1945 it was a similar story, with Michigan coming nearest in a 28–7 loss.

Army featured an explosive T-formation attack—a style of play which became increasingly popular among colleges during the war and one which George Hallas' Chicago Bears had perfected to dominate the pro game in the late thirties and early forties. Army's attack was drilled to military precision by Coach Blaik; the linemen blocked like scythes, but even worse—from the viewpoint of the opposition—were Army's two explosive backs, Felix "Doc" Blanchard, "Mr. Outside," and Glenn "Junior" Davis, "Mr. Inside." Blanchard was a bruising 205-pound fullback with speed and tremendous drive, and Davis was a skittering, breakaway runner capable of sudden accelerations that left would-be tacklers stumbling in his wake. With such players as Doug Kenna, Dale Hall and Max Miner backing them up, there was no one who could come close to Army.

But it was horse racing that cut itself the fattest slice of the wartime prosperity pie. As Dan Parker, sports editor of the New York *Daily Mirror,* wrote: "America was off on the damndest gambling binge in its history. Almost everyone was playing the horses." Attendance, which had averaged 15,000,000 prewar, passed the 17,000,000 mark by 1944; on-track betting totaled $1.2 billion nationwide in that year, compared with $705,000,000 in 1943, and at least twice that through bookies. In New York it was calculated that the average bet was $12 per race, and the average fan spent $91.22 during an entire afternoon at the track. In the 1945 season, even though the tracks were closed between January 3 and May 9 (see Chapter VII), betting and attendance were even higher: bets totaled $1.4 billion, attendance 17,200,000. People with money to spend and little to spend it on poured it into racing's coffers—in hopes of having even more money with nothing to spend it on. Or perhaps affluence bred dreams of even greater affluence, while providing the gambler with basic working capital.

Be that as it may, racing drew considerable criticism that transcended any puritanical hatred of gambling. Although the sport's official spokesman offered a variety of patriotic rationalizations—*e.g.*, that by parting ordinary citizens from their dollars, it was a powerful anti-inflationary measure; that it "improved the breed" and thus helped the U.S. Cavalry (the Army had phased out all its horse cavalry units); that it built morale on the home front; and that it offered a painless form of taxation (this while racing lobbyists in Washington successfully fought against a federal betting tax)—when it came to actually doing something positive, racing responded sluggishly under government's whip. Following the imposition of gas rationing, racetrack parking lots continued to be filled with cars, although this was obvious pleasure driving. When the Office of Defense Transportation ordered the tracks to close down their parking lots, several simply ignored the order. The ODT also asked for the suspension of the 1943 Kentucky Derby—also to no avail. Bond sales at the tracks were anemic, the owners naturally fearing it would cut into the take.

At last, the track owners awoke to the bad image they were generating and took steps to close the parking lots, encourage bond sales and make donations from receipts to war charities. Track public relations men did not allow these patriotic gestures to go unnoticed.

Then, in 1945, retribution set in: James Byrnes ordered all tracks closed and racing banned to save gasoline and encourage frugality by discouraging wagering. The ban unleashed an anguished howl from the owners. Following the ban, some of the smaller owners had to sell or destroy horses because they couldn't afford to feed them. Others, unable to get gasoline, remained stranded near the Southern racecourses in Miami and New Orleans, where they had gone for the winter season. Others shipped their horses to Mexico City, where they competed in the Hippodrome of the Americas' season. All this was hard on their pocketbooks, but it was beneficial for the horses; normally overworked, they now had a chance to rest up, and juveniles that were customarily pushed too fast into competition had time to mature.

Despite its disgrace of being the only sport to be banned during the war for nonessentiality to the war effort (auto racing, with its obvious dependence on scarce tires and rubber, was blacked out completely by the war), the sport of kings put on a top-grade show. A galaxy of great names swept past the cheering stands—Whirlaway, first horse to surpass the $500,000 mark in all-time winnings; Count Fleet, triple crown winner in 1943; Shut Out, Alsab, Pensive, Hoop Jr., Twilight Tear, Busher, and Bounding Home.

The ban on horse racing in 1945 had repercussions in other sports, most notably basketball, for while the tracks were closed, the gambling money gravitated to other action, and college basketball was the leading beneficiary of this dubious interest. As a result, the sport had the first gambling scandal in its history: Five Brooklyn College players were expelled from school for taking bribes from a couple of small-time bookies, Henry Rosen and Harvey Stemmer. Fortunately, that appeared to be the extent of the corruption of the college sport in that year.

With goaltending and freezing ended by rule changes, the college game opened up, although there was still a dominance of tall men. There was also a continued dominance by Western teams in the postseason championship games. Stanford won the NCAA tournament in 1942; then, in 1943, Wyoming, sparked by its hot-shooting Kenny Sailors, a master of the then novel one-hand jump shot, won both the NCAA and a special "national championship" tourney for the benefit of the Red Cross against the National Invitational Tournament winner, St. John's; Utah, a slow starter, picked up late-season steam and performed the same feat against St. John's at the close of the 1943–44 season, which also saw the breakup of the famed University of Illinois "Whiz Kids," who entered the service en masse. In 1945 the Red Cross tournament pitted two giants, Bob Kurland (7 feet) of Oklahoma A & M and George Mikan (6 feet 7 inches) of DePaul. Oklahoma and Kurland won the duel by a score of 72–44.

If basketball continued to please the crowds, boxing fell upon evil days. Its great heavyweight champion, Joe Louis, entered the service in 1942, deeply in debt to the government for back taxes, although he had donated his last two purses to charity. Joe served as a sergeant in special services, giving exhibitions for the troops and operating as a kind of government symbol of Negro solidarity behind the war effort. Undoubtedly he had contributed more to the revival of the sport in the late thirties than any other fighter; his legendary comeback victory over the German Max Schmeling took on political implications far beyond the prize ring.

The deadpan slow-talking Louis, né Joe Louis Barrow, was also honest in a sport that had more than its share of corruption. Born in rural Alabama and transplanted to the black ghettos of Detroit at age twelve, he never got beyond the fifth grade; yet he could say, after fighting twenty fights in four years against all comers, not one of which was even slightly tainted: "I want to fight honest so that the next colored boy can get the same break I got. If I 'cut the fool,' I'll let my people down." His fights drew 50,000,000 listeners, the greatest radio audiences in history, except for two speeches of President Roosevelt. He would be sorely missed by the fight game. Joe was also credited with naming the war; he called it "God's war."

Following Louis' classification of 1-A in 1941, other fighters streamed into the services. What was left were the 4-F's and an increasing number of medical discharges from the services. The latter, it should be said, were not medicaled out for combat wounds but for such things as flat feet, punctured eardrums, "buzzing noises in the head" and other injuries which had been suffered in the ring. The number of these medical rejects (there were more than 300 of them in 1944 alone) who promptly began engaging in fisticuffs caused a good deal of criticism, with the result that the government recalled several, including featherweight champion, Willie Pep, for non-strenuous duties.

Prewar titles were frozen, since all the champs were in the service and service regulations forbade them to fight during off-duty hours. As a result, promoters created something called duration champs in order to lure the crowds in. They came and paid $12 to $15 tops at Madison Square Garden, for example, to see fighters whom promoter Mike Jacobs would "be afraid to use as semi-finals on $5 cards before the war," as Dan Parker wrote. The quality of the fighters was symbolized by the discovery by the California Boxing Commission, during a routine prefight physical exam that a fighter named Luther "Slugger" White had one glass eye. And this was by no means White's maiden fight.

One small plus to boxing's dismal war years was the opening up of opportunity to Negro fighters, who, with their higher rejection rate because of poor education and so on, were available in somewhat larger numbers than whites—in any case, more than 75 percent of the active fighters were Negroes. Whereas before the war, promoters shied away from all-black matches, now out of desperation they matched black fighters and found that crowds accepted it without complaint.

Such were the nation's pastimes and amusements, spectator sports and recreations, entertainments and escapes during the war—the substitutes and ersatz gaiety that nonetheless relieved the tedium of daily life.

IX

WAR NERVES

On June 21, 1943—the wost day of the Detroit race riots—the most ferocious in more than twenty-five years, 25 Negroes and 9 white persons were killed, 800 injured; property damage was more than $2,000,000. War production during "bloody week" fell off 6 percent in the arsenal of democracy. Absenteeism ran to 20 per cent in the war plants, and the WPB estimated that in the first two days of riot 2,000,000 man-hours were lost. The nation was both sickened and disgusted; radio commentators agreed it cast a blight on the pretensions of a nation fighting a world war for democratic ideals. Many were quick to blame the riot on Axis provocateurs; other observers saw it as a case of overstrung "war nerves." The underlying causes, however, were not so simple.

It was no secret to readers of the national press that racial tensions had been festering in Detroit for at least twelve months. *Life* magazine had printed a story a year before called "Detroit Is Dynamite." Anti-Negro hate mongers such as Father Coughlin, the Reverend Gerald L. K. Smith, and J. Frank Norris had found an avid reading public for their tracts in the city, although Coughlin had lost his radio program and Smith's newspaper had been banned. The Ku Klux Klan was active among the thousands of Southern po' whites who had migrated to Detroit for defense jobs. Certainly, there were a number of fundamentalist lay preachers whose teachings emphasized hatred of the Negro, and their ranting could be heard on the radio every Sunday.

Among the Negro population there was widespread discontent over the way Negroes were being excluded from participation in the war effort. One poll of Detroit blacks found that 83 percent felt they weren't "getting as much chance as they should to help win the war." What they meant, for one thing, was that they were still being excluded from the higher paying war jobs. Negroes made up about 10 percent of the Detroit population but held only 8.4 percent of the jobs. At 55 of 185 major war plants less than 1 percent of the employees were Negroes. Their opportunities for promotion were less than those of the white workers. Only recently at the Packard plant, when 3 Negro workers were upgraded, 3,000 whites had walked out in protest, with the encouragement of management. In housing, too, Negroes were at the short end of the stick. Some of the migrants from the South (about 60,000 of them between 1940 and 1943 as against 440,000 whites) were given housing in the government projects, but most of the rest, as well as the native Detroiters, were boxed into the Negro slum known as Paradise Valley. There rents were two or three times higher than other areas; houses were decrepit; people were crammed together in too small living space. White workers, of course, had housing problems of their own, but a white Southern migrant had a better chance of living decently in a white neighborhood than did a Negro in the ghetto, for while 50.2 percent of all Negro dwellings were substandard, according to a 1941 survey of the Detroit Housing Commission, only 14 percent of the white dwellings were so graded. Still, the housing problem for whites was acute, with many of them forced to live in trailers, tents, tar-paper shacks or "fox-hole homes"—excavated basements for houses that would never be built, which the inhabitants covered over with a roof. This increased tensions among white immigrants and led to clashes between whites and Negroes over federal housing. In February, 1942, when a group of Negroes tried to move into the Sojourner Truth Homes—a housing project set aside for them—a mob of whites, demanding the houses for themselves, attacked and repulsed them. Eventually only 14 Negro families moved in, under Guard escort. Negroes also had a grudge against the police, who they felt treated them unfairly. An example of such treatment came out in a report on the Sojourner Truth riots made by the Office of Facts and Figures. The report observed: "Police seem bent on suppressing Negroes . . . to keep the peace and . . . the choice is . . . made from the fact that the Negro group is smaller. . . ." The Detroit police department of about 3,000 men was under strength because of the inroads of the draft; the men left tended to be over worked and poorly educated. Many came from the South and had no love for Negroes. On the other hand, Negroes accounted for 65 percent of the crimes committed in the city. Clashes had also broken out on a small scale between Negroes and sailors stationed at the Navy Arsenal near the Belle Isle bridge. Finally, the local Negro press was calling for justice and equality for Negroes; their cries were emotion-laden, but they were helping form a Negro consciousness and a unified sense of injustice.

An immediate sore point was the segregation of Negro GI's in the Army. Negroes knew that their brothers in service were being given menial and service jobs. Typical was the story of the Negro biochemist who, after training as an armorer, ended up as a laborer. Certainly they read almost weekly in the Negro press about lynchings in the South, of ill-treatment of Negro GI's in Southern towns, of murders that went unpunished, such as the on-duty Negro MP who was shot by a white Southern deputy. (An added humiliation was that Negro MP's were not permitted to carry weapons in some parts of the South.) Southerners dismissed the incident as a "nigger killing"; when government pressure forced the case to trial, the local jury quickly found the sheriff innocent. When they learned that the Red Cross was segregating Negro and white blood, many Negroes tore up their pledge cards in anger. Some of them may have even heard of the Negro scientist, Dr. Charles R. Drew, who perfected a method of preserving blood plasma, for which he was awarded the Spingarn Medal by Harvard. The irony of Dr. Drew's own blood being segregated probably provided a bitter laugh for a sophisticated few. But the large majority of Negroes living in Paradise Valley were not sophisticated. They were merely tasting what was slowly opening up for them—in some war plants there were now good jobs for Negroes—and this made them all the more bitter at the vestiges of prejudice surrounding them which hemmed them into their ghetto and segregated their way of life.

If the Negro's resentment was the flint, the newly arrived white Southerner's attitude was the steel. A social worker concluded: "[The Southern whites] have moved into the best areas and have no basic community ties. They constitute a thoroughly dislocated element in the population." Finding themselves in a big, dynamic Northern city, a wartime city short of everything from housing to space at the bar, recruited by large corporations seeking a docile, nonunion labor supply, rootless, lost, defensive in the manner of backwoods people, they sought something to cling to from back home. One such certainty was that in the South "they knew how to keep niggers in their place." Negroes down there worked as handymen or in the fields; they didn't elbow next to you on the assembly line or compete for the higher paying job. The tensions and frustrations of his life made the red-neck itch for some kind of explosion, but he had no way of letting it out—unless against the Negro.

So the flint and the steel were poised. It took only a sudden jar to strike them together and set off the spark that inflamed the city for nearly two days, and kept it in a state of shock and tension after that.

Sunday night, June 21, a hot summer night. The picnickers—85 percent of them Negroes—who had streamed across the bridge to Belle Isle for a breath of air were heading homeward. Then around 8 P.M. a fight broke out on the bridge. Nobody recalled exactly why, but apparently some Negro teen-agers had jostled a sailor and his girl. It may have been these were members of a gang of Negro boys and girls who had gone to Belle Isle with the express purpose of driving all the whites off and claiming the island for their own race and who had been starting sporadic fights with other whites earlier. At any rate the fight spread along the bridge, over which a line of cars filled with picnickers was flowing. The Navy Arsenal was nearby, and apparently hearing that their buddies were being attacked, about 200 sailors joined the fray; by 10:30 fights were raging. Then a black boy raced downtown to a Negro social club in Paradise Valley where drinking and dancing were in progress. He announced excitedly on the microphone that a Negro woman and her baby had been thrown off the bridge by whites. Parallel rumors that a group of Negroes had raped and killed a white woman on the bridge were also licking out across the city. These pretexts were all that was needed.

The Negroes from the social club, many of them shady types, hoods and fancy men, set to work wrecking stores owned by whites in the vicinity. A mob of 500 formed in Paradise Valley and stoned whites in cars. A mob of Negroes stopped a streetcar carrying 50 white factory workers and beat up the surprised occupants. By 5 A.M. the white rioters were mobilizing and beginning to retaliate. White mobs at Woodward and Charlotte avenues stoned passing Negroes' cars. As the patrons of the all-night Roxy and Colonial theaters emerged at the movie's end, the Negroes among them were pulled out and systematically beaten by groups of whites, while policemen sat in two squad cars and indifferently watched.

By 6:15 A.M. the first death was reported, a Negro; admissions to the hospitals were running at the rate of one a minute. At 9, Mayor Edward J. Jeffries, Jr. called Governor Harry F. Kelly and asked him to declare martial law and request federal troups. The governor refused, reluctant to take such a drastic step; his procrastination was fatal.

Monday—"Bloody Monday"—saw large mobs of whites, perhaps 10,000 of them, ranging up and down Woodward Avenue, one of the city's main thoroughfares, in search of Negroes to beat up or kill. When school let out at 1:30, many students joined the rioters. Four white boys hanging around poolrooms were caught up in the excitement. "Let's go out and kill a nigger," one of them said. They got into a car and drove around searching, and spotted Moses Kisko, fifty-eight, waiting for a streetcar. One of the boys leaned out of the window and shot Kisko dead. The white mob divided up into hunting packs; when they spotted a lone Negro, a cry would go up—"Get him!"—and they ran after the hapless victim.

Observers noted that most of the active rioters were young, but that with them were older men who stood behind them and urged them on. There were also women in the mob, who acted, according to the Detroit *News,* "with a savagery that exceeded that of the men." There was an obscenity, cruder than the scatological kind in their cries, as when one drunken man, spotting a Negro motorman driving a trolley, yelled: "Here's some fresh meat!" Others seemed preternaturally excited, as if drugged. One nineteen-year-old participant recalled the event, the words tumbling out: "Jesus, but it was a show! We dragged niggers from cars, beat the hell out of them, and lit the sons of bitches' autos. I'm glad I was in it! And those black bastards damn well deserved it." Among those arrested, 60 percent were under thirty-one, 48 percent under twenty-one. To many of the teen-age youths it was a thrilling spectacle. They had no more feeling for the dead than for the Japanese John Wayne was mowing down in a war movie. One sixteen-year-old, "too scared" himself to kill, recalled the spree he witnessed in exhilarated terms: "Oh, there were about 200 of us in cars. We killed eight of 'em. . . . I lost my nerve I guess, but my pals didn't. I saw knives being stuck through their throats and heads being shot through, and a lot of stuff like that. It was really some riot. They were turning over cars with niggers in them, you should have seen it. It was really some riot."

Meanwhile, the police forced Negroes back into the Paradise Valley area, where looting spread—mostly "stores of decidedly exploitive character," in the words of a white Detroit civic leader. Whites caught in the area were knifed. At 8:30 P.M. on Monday a mob surged east on Vernon Street, bent on attacking the police who were penning them into their ghetto. Snipers began firing from the Negro Frazer Hotel, but the police repulsed the charge and cleaned out the snipers. Although some whites were knifed and a handful shot, most Negro rage focused on the police, and there was a feeling that Paradise Valley had to be defended against invasion, whether by police or by others. William H. Baldwin of the National Urban League later criticized the police, saying they "behaved with deplorable callousness." There were numerous cases of police shooting to kill on suspicion of looting in Negro districts and an equal number of instances where police stood by passively when Negroes were being attacked or even killed. One Negro expressed the view of many toward the police: "Word got around awful fast. Those police are *murderers*. They were just waiting for a chance to get us. We didn't stand a chance. I hate 'em. Oh, God, how I hate 'em. But the fellows who had guns were ready to go. They were saying, 'If it gets tight, get two whites before you go.'"

Finally, Governor Kelly requested federal troops at 9:45 P.M. Monday; they were long overdue. The 701st MP battalion, which had been ready for hours, quickly moved in on Woodward Avenue. By 11:30 quiet had been restored. At midnight President Roosevelt signed a proclamation ordering in federal troops, and the next day 6,000 soldiers rolled into the city. They put down the riot without firing a shot.

The city government later issued a white paper (aptly named) on the riot, blaming mostly Negroes, the Negro press and the NAACP for starting it. (As an example of the kind of inflammatory thinking these groups were purveying, the report observed: "A theme repeatedly emphasized by these [Negro] papers is that the struggle for Negro equality at home is an integral part of the present world wide struggle for democracy.") Attorney General Francis Biddle in his report to the President found "no evidence of any Axis or Fascist or Ku Klux Klan involvement." Congressman Martin Dies, however, had his own theory: The riots were fomented by Japanese-Americans illegally released from their detention camps. He threatened to hold hearings but later dropped the idea.

Attorney General Biddle also took note (1) that there was no rioting in neighborhoods where Negroes and whites were integrated; (2) that Negro and white students at Wayne State University attended classes as usual throughout "Bloody Week" without incident; and (3) that Negroes and whites continued to work together on the assembly line without any friction. Indeed, labor leaders such as UAW head R. J. Thomas were active in seeking to end the riots or at least deploring them; from top business executives, however, there was only silence. Negro leaders also were active in trying to make peace, as were many white churchmen and other civic leaders. But only federal troops it seemed could have stopped the mayhem. Although there were local hoodlum elements among them—Italian and Syrian gangs especially—no one really doubted that the majority of the white rioters were immigrant Southerners (in contrast with the Negroes, of whom 74 percent of those arrested had lived in Detroit longer than five years).

The Detroit riots were neither the first nor the last of their kind during the war years. There had been riots in Mobile (in which 12 Negro shipyard workers who were promoted were attacked by white co-workers and beaten badly enough to require hospitalization) and Beaumont of less severity, and in August, 1943, Harlem exploded in a riot that left 6 dead, 543 injured and $6,000,000 in damage. (It was touched off by false rumors that a policeman had killed a Negro GI and was squarely a Negroes-against-the-police riot, although, at bottom, it was a reflection of the same kinds of Negro discontent as obtained in Detroit.) For the remainder of the war, however, the racial scene was relatively quiet. More positive voices began to be heard. Wendell Willkie, for one, campaigned for better treatment for Negroes. Numerous commissions on interracial understanding were formed across the nation. People were beginning to face up to the race problem. As Roy Wilkins of the NAACP said: "Hitler jammed our white people into their logically untenable position. Forced to oppose him for the sake of the life of the nation, they were jockeyed into declaring against his racial theories—publicly." The public began to connect the racist doctrines of the Nazis with the parallel theories of racial superiority held by Senator Theodore Bilbo, Congressman John Rankin and other diehard Southerners. On the other hand, Japanese propaganda was making a straightforward pitch to American Negroes on racial lines, calling on them to desert the white man in his fight against the colored races of the world. Only a few hours after Cleo Wright, a Negro, had been burned to death in 1942 by a Mississippi lynch mob, a Japanese propagandist was on the air describing the event. In another 1942 broadcast this theme was presented: "Democracy, as preached by Anglo-Americans, may be an ideal and a noble system of life, but democracy as practiced by Anglo-Americans is stained with the bloody guilt of racial persecution and exploitation." Few Negroes paid any attention to this, but at least one organization was formed having as its goal "an Ethiopian-Pacific movement envisaging a coalition of Africa and Japan in an Axis-dominated world." Its leaders were indicted for subversive activities.

The publication of Gunnar Myrdal's *An American Dilemma* in 1944 was considered a milestone in the history of American race relations. A number of other serious treatises on the Negro came out, while Richard Wright's *Black Boy,* Saunders Redding's *No Day of Triumph* and Lillian Smith's *Strange Fruit* all constituted strong fictional presentations of the problem. Carey McWilliams, who himself made several notable contribuions to the study of minority races in the United States, said hopefully at the war's end that "more progress has been made, in this five-year period, toward a realistic understanding of the issues involved in what we still call 'the race problem' than in the entire period from the Civil War to 1940."

But McWilliams himself realized that along with this increased awareness, as well as the actual betterment of the Negroes' lot that was a dividend of wartime prosperity, there was a growing fear in the South that the Negroes were going too far too fast, that the ancient privileges of the white man were threatened. Even "liberal" Southern editors such as Virginius Dabney and David L. Cohn began to warn about "the delicate race problem" and counsel conservatism. As for the more extreme Southerners, they girded themselves for a massive postwar effort to repress the Negro (except for Senator Bilbo; his final solution to the race problem was send them back to Africa, and the sooner, the better). An expression of the South's anxiety was the wild racial rumors that continued to be circulated. Many were unbelievably vile, but a few received wide acceptance and became almost articles of faith. The most notable of the latter were the Eleanor Clubs, already mentioned.

Most hopeful of all were developments in Washington and in the upper South. Although its powers were limited, the FEPC applied vigorous moral persuasion and was able to open up thousands of defense jobs to Negroes. The Supreme Court in the *Smith v. Allwright* case struck down the white primary device in Texas, which had been used to keep Negroes out of Southern politics by barring them from membership in the Democratic Party. In the South—at least the upper South—Negroes were losing their passivity and fear and organizing to obtain their rights. Membership in the NAACP had increased from 100,000 at the beginning of the war to 500,000 in 1944, with most of the recruits in the South. Some Southern whites were speaking out for Negro rights. The prestigious Atlanta *Journal* called for a four-point program of Negro betterment, including the right to vote in primary and general elections. A few liberal politicians such as Governor Ellis Arnall of Georgia, and

Senators Claude Pepper of Florida and Lister Hill of Alabama countered the voices of Bilbo and Rankin in Congress. Still the Bourbons (with their power of filibuster) were powerful enough to prevent passage of an antilynching law and repeal of the poll tax in federal elections and to cripple the FEPC at the war's end.

The poisoned relations between black and white in America irrupted in violent incidents of social disorder. But prejudice against other racial and religious groups were also quickened by war's emotional intensifications. A virulent strain of anti-Semitism broke out in Boston, especially among Irish Catholics. The local church hierarchy was politically conservative, and Father Coughlin's anti-Semitic tract *Social Justice* was sold in front of Catholic churches after Sunday mass. Irish politicians reflected the anti-British, anti-Russian and anti-New Deal sentiments of their constituents. One reporter estimated—perhaps too ungenerously— that nine-tenths of Boston's Irish were anti-Semitic. However that may be, there were a series of ugly anti-Semitic incidents and rumors. After the tragic Coconut Grove nightclub fire of 1942, rumors spread making the club's owner, Barnett Welansky, a Jew, the scapegoat; some people even believed that the accidental fire was a Jewish plot against the Irish Catholics (most of the revelers, Boston College and Holy Cross fans, were Catholic). A poem called "America's Fighting Jew" was widely circulated. The title was intended sarcastically and echoed a persistent canard that Jews had started the war for their own profit and that they were evading the draft and letting Christians do the fighing. Several hoodlum attacks on Jewish schoolchildren occurred after the Irish Evacuation Day exercises in March, 1943, at which Representative Hamilton Fish and Father Edward Lodge Curran, whose views reflected those of Coughlin and the Christian Front, spoke.

Of course, Jews for the most part supported the war vigorously and contributed many of their sons to the armed forces. Citizens on New York's Lower East Side were among the most active in the entire city in various war drives, while on the campus of CCNY, which had a large Jewish enrollment, students participated in every war program and complained because they weren't asked to do enough. Later, as the full extent of Nazi persecution of the Jews came to be known, Jewish groups began to agitate harder for a resettlement of Jewish refugees in Palestine and more liberal refugee quotas in this country. But the government, especially Congress and the State Department, greeted their pleas with stony indifference, and the American people in general seemed apathetic, ill informed or else actually hostile to the idea. Most American Jews, however, supported the war as Americans and because of a hatred of Fascism dating back to the thirties. The wealthy European Jews who had fled the Nazi pogroms of the thirties and settled on Manhattan's Upper West Side, bringing with them diamonds and any other valuables they could carry, became more vociferous in the cause of refugees. But to most non-Jewish Americans it was as though the nation's immigration laws were engraved on stone. They were willing to support large aid programs for starving Europeans, but they were not willing to open their gates (except a tiny crack) for any of war's victims. They had no comprehension that Nazi persecution had in effect made the few surviving Jews truly homeless. On the other hand, anti-Semitism in American life eased somewhat when, in 1945, movies of the concentration camps were shown in the nation's theaters. For the first time, many people realized what anti-Semitism, carried to its logical extreme, meant.

Unlike World War I, there was no anti-German hysteria (nor was there any anti-Italian feeling). Perhaps symbolic of this attitude was a minor isolated event early in the war. A Lutheran minister in Illinois, with a large German-born congregation, timidly asked the governor if it was all right if he continued his services in German. Permission was granted as a matter of course, and indeed as though none need have been asked. A few thousand German and Italian aliens considered to be subversive by the Justice Department were rounded up after Pearl Harbor, and there were attempts by local authorities to exclude others from coastal areas. In all, 3,100 Japanese, 3,000 Germans and 85 Italian dangerous enemy aliens remained in detention camps. Others living in certain areas were severely curtailed in their movements for a time. Among these were some famous *émigrés* living in California, including Thomas Mann, Erich Maria Remarque, Leon Feuchtwanger and Bertolt Brecht. The restrictions were eventually lifted, and Mann became a propagandist making eloquent broadcasts to the German people. Brecht co-authored the script for an excellent movie about the underground, *Hangmen Also Die.* At the time of their restrictions, Feuchtwanger's colored maid was quoted as saying, "Well, I guess it's tougher over here for refugees even than for colored folk."

A number of German-American Bund leaders were among a large group indicted for sedition, but there was no movement to blame all Americans of German descent, probably because they were a large proportion of the population and most of them citizens who had been here for generations. It was the newly arrived, the pariah groups, that bore the brunt of prejudice wherever it showed its face.*

Mexican-Americans had long suffered discrimination in California, where they were segregated, lumped together with Negroes in the use of public swimming pools, insulted daily by the police and kept on menial jobs, mainly picking in the fields. This long-standing prejudice coalesced during the war into a hatred for the Mexican teen-agers, the *pachucos,* who wore those outlandish zoot suits and thus were highly visible. Actually, zoot-suitism was a nationwide phenomenon, which began among slum teen-agers, both Negro and white. In Detroit, zoot-suiters took on aspects of organized juvenile gangs and were frequently involved in fights, while in other cities they were not particularly violent.

Central to the zoot-suit cult was dress, argot and jitterbug dancing. Their clothes were immortalized in the song "I Wanna Zoot Suit":

> I wanna zoot suit with a reat pleat.
> With a drape shape and a stuff cuff
> To look sharp enough to see my Sunday gal
> I want a reave sleeve with a ripe stripe
> And a dressed seat with a glad plaid,
> In the latest fad to see my Sunday Sal.
> I want to look keen so my dream will say,
> "You don't look like the same beau."
> So keen that she'll scream,
> "Here comes my walkin' rainbow–"
> So make a zoot suit with a reat pleat,
> With a drape shape and stuff cuff
> To look sharp enough to see my Sunday gal.

The suits consisted of long, loosely cut coats (called fingertips) which had wide, padded shoulders and reached to mid-thigh. Pants ("drapes") ballooned out below the waist and around the legs, but were cut tight around the ankles—*i.e.,* pegged. Thick shoes, a wide-brimmed hat, a long watch chain, a T-shirt or sport shirt with long collar points, buttoned without a tie and a ducktail haircut completed the ensemble. It was

---

* Some light on whom Americans hated/loved was provided by a 1942 Gallup Poll which queried respondents on whom they considered "good as we are in all important respects" or "not as good as we are" or "definitely inferior." Only five nationalities— Canadians, English, Dutch, Scandinavians and Irish—were considered by a majority "good as we are." Germans ranked seventh (after the French); South Americans ninth; "Jewish refugees" tenth, followed by Poles, Russians, Chinese, Spaniards, Italians, Mexicans, and Japanese, in that order. Africans and other colored races were not included in the list.

a bizarre and colorful outfit—worn both for vanity and as a kind of uniform to set the zoot-suiter apart from the rest of society—a sort of defiantly pariah elite. It had the added virtue of being radically different from conventional clothes and so was a method for shocking outsiders. Zooters' outfits could cost as high as $100 and provided a way of impressing the girls with one's style and affluence, even for a slum boy.

The zooters' argot provided them with elements of a secret society. In Los Angeles among the *pachucos* it was a mixture of jive musician's slang, English, Spanish, and *pachucana,* the special language of the underworld. The heart of the zoot-suiter's way of life was jitterbugging; it provided a kind of orgiastic release for his pent-up energies. Zoot-suiters played hard, drank a lot, fought over girls, crashed parties and broke them up by starting fights, and sometimes engaged in criminal activity. But on the whole they were simply poor kids seeking escape from drab lives and exploding in the moral vacuum of wartime life.

It was the Mexican zoot-suiters of Los Angeles who were finally singled out for physical attack. For months bad blood had been building up between them and sailors because of fights and the stabbing and robbing of lone sailors Although these incidents were few—social workers had said that the *pachucos* had a low rate of crime—the sailors decided it was time to retaliate. There were ample warnings of trouble, but naval authorities did not restrict their men, and the sailors went on a rampage, beating up anyone who was wearing the hated clothing. The action of the police was characteristic of their treatment of the *pachucos.* They arrested the zoot-suit wearers and let the sailors go free, even though the latter had started the riot. Governor Earl Warren appealed for restraint on both sides, and the Navy took steps to rein in its men. But the city fathers of Los Angeles revealed their understanding of the riot's cause when, in their infinite wisdom, they passed an ordinance forbidding the wearing of zoot suits within the city limits of Los Angeles.

The city fathers' wisdom to the contrary, the *pachucos* were essentially a surface phenomenon—that is, whatever their life-style, they were still underprivileged kids, caught between the old Mexican way of life and life in an America where they were at the bottom of the social ladder. More fundamental was the problem of the Mexican farm laborers, especially the contract laborers, or *braceros,* who came over the border to work on crops. For years they had been exploited by Western farmers who paid them bare-subsistence wages and let them live in intolerable squalor. Frequently, they were left stranded and penniless between crop seasons. In wartime, their labor was needed to harvest the crops. This need, plus the active interest the Mexican government was taking in the treatment of its citizens in the United States, enabled the government to step in and regulate working conditions more strictly. Workers were imported by and under the protection of the U.S. government, minimum wages were paid under a contract, and housing and hygenic conditions were strictly regulated. In Montana, for instance, a group of *braceros* working on local crops found that they were unwelcome in the nearby town, and signs had been put up to tell them this in blunt terms. A Mexican representative assigned to looking out for the workers investigated and complained of the conditions to the U.S. government. The War Food Administration, which was responsible for them, intervened and the discrimination was quickly ended. The Jim Crow treatment of *braceros* in Texas was so deep-rooted, however, that the Mexican government refused to allow any workers to go there. The FEPC was also able to open up industrial jobs for Mexicans. In Los Angeles, for example, in 1944, 17,000 were working in the shipyards whereas before the war there had been none.

By far the most serious blot on the record of treatment of the races was the relocation of the West Coast Japanese and their incarceration in detention centers. Here was a case where racial prejudice, plus economic envy and greed, was, through wartime callousness, raised into a national policy that was approved all the way up to the President of the United States. One of the unfortunate by-products of the hysteria rife along the West Coast during the early months of the war was to give license to the wholesale denial of the rights of a group of American citizens. Military necessity was the official justification for the removal of 110,000 Issei and Nisei, two-thirds of them American citizens, from their homes; but long-standing prejudice in the Pacific coast states, especially California, where more than 80 percent of them lived, was the hammer which bludgeoned public opinion into acquiescence in this drastic denial of rights which established dubious constitutional precedents.

During the first weeks of war, no one worried about the West Coast Japanese. Then reports of sabotage incidents, all of them later proved untrue, began to appear in the papers. There were several "arrow" rumors; one Japanese farmer's field of flowers was found to be pointing arrowlike at a nearby airport; a truck farmer in the Ivanhoe district was alleged to have planted tomatoes so they formed a crude arrow pointing to an air training field. (The arrows were in the imaginations of the beholders and in any case of dubious value to Japanese bombers. Arrow rumors occurred in the East Coast, too; one, false, in 1942, was traced to a Mitchel Field public information officer.) The Hearst San Francisco *Chronicle* began agitating for removal and printed a lurid report of an FBI raid on "a deadly nest of saboteurs" near the Mare Island Naval Base, breathlessly describing the cache uncovered in the raid: a set of Navy signal flags, five illegal radios, at least two guns and two illegal cameras.

Other voices began to take up the cry about the potential danger of a group of aliens living along a coastline which might be (as it was then believed) subject to invasion at any time. What the security problem came down to was that there was no way of telling who was and who was not a loyal American, in the event of an invasion.

Despite all the rumors, no clear-cut espionage and sabotage by Japanese-Americans had been (or ever was) reported; nonetheless, in February California's Attorney General Earl Warren found this a bad sign. It was "significant," he said, that there were no reports of sabotage and fifth column activities. "I take the view that is the most ominous sign of the whole situation. It convinces me more than perhaps any other factor that the sabotage that we are to get, the fifth column activities that we are to get, are timed just like Pearl Harbor was timed and just like the invasion of France, and of Denmark, and of Norway, and all of those other countries."

Under these circumstances there was little the Japanese-Americans could do to prove they would not commit sabotage—no use mentioning that the FBI had already rounded up the Americans of Japanese descent it considered potentially dangerous or disloyal. For this was a matter of a *race*. "A Jap is a Jap," said General DeWitt, the Army man who had been vigorously, if erroneously, warning of enemy bombing planes in California skies throughout December, in his report recommending that the Japanese be interned. This sentiment was echoed in Washington, in perhaps more extreme form, by Congressman Rankin who said: "Once a Jap, always a Jap . . . you cannot regenerate a Jap, convert him and make him the same as a white man any more than you can reverse the laws of nature." It was stated more politely by Los Angeles Mayor Fletcher Bowron, who wondered, "When the final test comes who can say but that 'blood will tell?' " And looking at it solely from the standpoint of security, Attorney General Warren concluded: "When we are dealing with the Caucasian race [*i.e.*, German and Italian aliens] we have methods that will test the loyalty of them." Also in currency was the erroneous idea that Japanese-Americans had dual citizenship (actually the Japanese government had renounced this claim back in 1925).

Other voices were less moderate—and more self-interested. The Western Growers Protective Association, an organization of Southern California vegetable raisers, was eying the rich Japanese-owned truck farms, well aware that they produced nearly 40 percent of the total California crop, which in turn was 22 percent of the nation's total. The chance of picking up this land at eviction-sale prices or renting it cheaply was tempting, so their collective voice began to speak with great fervor and demagoguery. They proposed that all Japanese caught with guns be executed; they advocated not the relocation elsewhere in the United States of the Japanese, but their transportation 500 miles *west* of California, out in the Pacific Ocean. American Legion groups joined the hue and cry; one Legion official seconded the growers' proposal and recommended "old broken chicken crates" as "the most suitable craft" for transporting them. The main idea, of course, was not to relocate the Japanese but to deport them permanently from California. Later, in testimony before the Tolan Committee on the question of evacuation, the growers and their allies, the Grower-Shipper Vegetable Association, confined themselves to testifying that no vegetable shortage would result if the Japanese land were expropriated.

Another patriotic group, with a history of anti-Japanese agitation that went back to the turn of the century, was the Native Sons of the Golden West, who really wanted deportation but realized this might be impractical for the duration. Worried that during their incarceration the Japanese would "multiply," they recommended that the sexes be segregated throughout the detention. Others expressed similar fears that the concentration camps would become "breeding farms" because, as everybody knows, "Japs multiply like rabbits." One California Congressman suggested the detainees be offered "the alternatives of sterilization or deportation."

The great debate was carried to Washington by the California Congressional delegation, all of whom save Senator Sheridan Downey and Representative Jerry Voorhis favored incarceration. Some began chafing under the delay, and Representative Ward Johnson said, "Let's move these Japanese out and talk about it later." The others preferred to act under at least flimsy legal cloak. Representative Leland Ford sought to address himself to the argument that probably most of the Japanese were loyal citizens. Since we, the responsible officials, cannot determine who is a loyal Japanese and who isn't, Ford reasoned, then *they* must determine this for us by *voluntarily* going en masse into confinement. In Ford's own words: "by permitting himself to be placed in a concentration camp, he would be making his sacrifice and he would be willing to do it if he is patriotic and working for us."

As their next step, the California delegation, with the support of their colleagues from Washington and Oregon, began putting strong pressure on the Attorney General and the Secretary of War. Both of these agencies had not been enthusiastic about the mass detention of Japanese-Americans in the past. Attorney General Biddle had made several statements against the wholesale locking up of all enemy aliens, while the War Department did not want to be saddled with the responsibility for carrying out the operation. But pressure built, and the Attorney General received hundreds of letters, many from hysterical women, running four to one in favor of relocation. Meanwhile the Pacific coast states Congressional delegations adopted a resolution favoring evacuation (according to Morton Grodzins, in his book *Americans Betrayed,* the measure had been co-authored by the president of the Los Angeles Chamber of Commerce and its Washington lobbyists). Under this pressure, the executive branch, including the Attorney General's Office, began to back and fill. On February 18, the House debated the bill, and voices were raised in criticism of it, but on February 19, FDR made the debate academic by signing Executive Order 9066 authorizing the Secretary of War and appropriate military commanders "to prescribe military areas . . . from which any or all persons may be excluded." Persons of Japanese descent were soon thereafter duly ordered excluded from the Pacific coast war zone and were evacuated to inland areas, the movement to be carried out by the Army, while a new agency, the War Relocation Administration, was created to look after the detainees' welfare.

Signs began to appear on mailboxes in front of neat little farms around Los Angeles reading EVACUATION SALE—FURNITURE MUST ALL BE SOLD. The evacuees could take along only what they could carry; they would have to provide furniture in their new homes out of their own pockets. A host of bargain hunters descended on the farms to pick up furniture, stoves, refrigerators and so on at cut rate prices. In Los Angeles' little Tokyo, stores with Japanese names closed up, pathetic signs in the windows:

> Many thanks for your patronage. Hope to serve you in near future. God be with you till we meet again.
>
> Mr. and Mrs. K. Iseri

But many of the evacuees already felt in their hearts they would not be returning to a place where so much hatred surrounded them—hatred that could suspend the Constitution itself. Little Tokyo emptied to become an all-Negro neighborhood called Bronzeville.

The evacuation was orderly; the people cooperated stolidly, perhaps a little fearfully. Such was their cooperation that *Life* was moved to praise their patriotism and good sense in realizing the necessity for the measure. Some perhaps were glad to leave because they feared for their safety. Indeed, one of the many reasons advanced for the necessity of the evacuation was the danger of violence, and thirty-six cases of assaults on Japanese, including seven murders, had been reported between Pearl Harbor and April, 1942. Eighteen of the assailants were Filipinos, who had a particular rage against the Japanese; it was rumored that hot-blooded Filipinos in one area were drawing names of Japanese out of a hat, marking them for murder.

The evacuees were herded into temporary reception centers at race-tracks and fairgrounds, while officials decided what to do with them. The facilities were inadequate, and people driving by the temporary center at the Santa Anita Racetrack liked to joke that they hoped the re-locatees would remain there permanently as hostages against Japanese bombing. But the order expelling the Japanese did not envisage where they would be resettled. Originally the idea was that they be allowed to go where they liked so long as they remained away from the restricted coastal zones, but citizens and governors, especially in the Western states, raised such a howl against Japanese being allowed into their area that this seemed unfeasible. Most states feared that the evacuees would settle down permanently, and they did not want these people who multiplied like rabbits and worked for less than white man's wages. Besides, it was an expression of patriotism to say, "No Japs wanted here."

Finally, the WRA decided to set up detention centers in isolated areas in the West. The one at Heart Mountain in Wyoming was slapped together by a group of workmen, some carpenters in name only, for a cost-plus fee of $5,000,000. The centers resembled Army camps with tar-paper hutments or barracks partitioned into family-sized apartments each 20 by 100 feet. The Heart Mountain camp was designed to accommodate (and in fact did) 11,000 people in 456 barracks. There were community toilets and showers and a mess hall. Not forgotten was the barbed-wire fence that surrounded the camp, with watchtowers manned by rifle-wielding guards at each corner. There was to be no mistaking that this was a prison and the detainees were in it.

The prisoners were loaded into trains and shipped to the various centers. One, at Tule Lake, California, was reserved for those considered "disloyal" or who wished to return to Japan after the war was over. Its population would reach 18,000, of whom one-fourth were children. Many of the rest were people with close relatives in Japan or first-generation Issei.

The earliest inhabitants of Heart Mountain began to arrive in October, 1942. Having stored or sold their furniture, they found themselves faced with living in bare apartments furnished only with an army cot, a mattress and an army blanket. From the lush California valleys they were dropped down in a barren, forbidding part of Wyoming, where the temperatures went down to 30 below in the winter and where there were sandstorms, blizzards and high winds. One of the internees wrote a poem in the camp newspaper, the Heart Mountain *Sentinel,* that summed up his feelings:

> Snow upon the rooftop
> Snow upon the coal;
> Winter in Wyoming—
> Winter in my soul.

Eventually, the inhabitants bucked up their courage and set to work making their places livable. They succeeded remarkably in establishing a functioning society in the camp. They elected their own officials, held town meetings and set up a variety of group recreational and educational courses. All internees, except the schoolchildren, worked at jobs, for which they were paid $12 to $19 a month. They ate in mess halls, and food was sometimes scanty, as witness this poem that appeared in the *Sentinel:*

> When servings are a little bit lean
> Off we plod to the nearest canteen.
> Trekking to the store for extra nutrition
> Has grown into an expensive tradition.

The WRA set up stores for the inhabitants, selling canned goods, newspapers, dry goods and so on; the profits were returned to the residents or used for community projects. Discarded CCC clothes were distributed and coal stoves finally installed in each apartment. Gradually the inhabitants began to acquire some amenities. They planted trees to beautify the camp and keep down the Wyoming dust. They grew their own vegetables and in all reclaimed by irrigation 2,700 acres of arid land near the base. Most of the men were soon let out on pass to work on farms in the surrounding areas at going wage rates for field hands (although nearby townspeople in Powell and Cody demanded that they be confined to the camp). Their labor was badly needed, and internees were credited with saving the 1942 beet crop in Utah and Colorado.

By late 1942 the government was quietly instituting a policy that would relocate the internees elsewhere in the country. The original outcry against them was forgotten or irrevelant in many states, and by the end of 1944 more than 34,000—mostly Nisei—had resettled, largely in the Midwest and East. Among those remaining, however, many were reluctant to leave out of apathy or fear of the reception they would get. The barbed wire surrounding their camps had become symbolic not of a force penning them in but of protection against a hostile outside world. Several newspapers continued to harass the internees throughout the war, accusing them of being "coddled" and served better food than were American civilians. ("Coddling" charges were a favorite theme of some newspaper editors. There were stories of German and Italian POW's, such as one which had the German prisoners sitting in the dining car of a crowded train, feasting luxuriously on chicken and white bread, while hungry civilians peered pathetically through the glass at them. The purpose was always the same: to confirm American griping at food shortages by "exposing" how the "bureaucrats in Washington" were mucking up.) Newly elected Wyoming Senator E. V. Robertson, a Republican, delivered speeches in the Senate about the "pampering" at Heart Mountain, tying it in with the general food shortage and alleging that the Japanese in the camp were better housed and fed than "75% of the people of Wyoming." The Denver *Post,* with circulation in mind, played the story for all it was worth, saying in one column that "The Japs who are being petted and pampered and coddled there are the same kind of Japs that American boys are fighting in the Pacific. They are the same breed of rats as those over in Japan who have murdered American prisoners." (Anti-Japanese feeling ran particularly high in April, 1943, after the government revealed that captured members of the Doolittle raid on Tokyo had been tortured.) In 1944, Senator Robertson began hinting that all American-born Japanese in the centers should be deported to Japan after the war, thereby catering to the view of many of his constituents who feared that the Japanese in their area would settle permanently. He admitted that "handling them" would be a "ticklish problem" because so many were American citizens. The fact that Robertson himself was not born in the United States did not deter him.

When, in December, 1944, the government announced that the West Coast was no longer a war zone and the Japanese could return to their homes if they wished, the fangs were really bared and the true motives behind the Japanese relocation were revealed. Hearst and other papers began to agitate for permanent deportation of Japanese aliens or else "sharing" California's "Jap problem" (110,000 people in a population of 7,000,000) by dividing them up among the other forty-seven states. They even called for rescinding the citizenship of all native-born Japanese. And so it was obvious: The reason for the relocation in the first place was to expel all Japanese permanently. It was, in a manner of speaking, Hearst's final solution to the Yellow Peril.

Many of the internees reciprocated the feeling and vowed to relocate somewhere else or pathetically clung to the security of the center. Others threw off their depression and apathy and decided they would return to California after all. Eventually, 90,000 of them did, and in 1945, public opinion in California slowly began to change. Church groups worked to dispose their congregations toward the returnees, and Governor Earl Warren made speeches urging that the returnees be welcomed and sent telegrams to every mayor, sheriff and Legion post in the state urging fair treatment.

Even so, fifty-nine acts of violence against returning Japanese were reported during 1945, and signs reading NO JAPS ALLOWED greeted repatriates in many small towns. Most infamous was the action of the Hood River, Oregon, American Legion Post in removing from its Honor Roll the names of all local Japanese-Americans who had fought in the war. (In all, some 17,660 Japanese Americans, many volunteers, served in the U.S. Army; a few thousand remained loyal to Japan.)

Just a day after the War Department announced that the detainees could return to the West Coast, the Supreme Court handed down its decisions in two cases questioning the constitutionality of the entire relocation program. In the Korematsu case, the Court held the evacuation was a valid exercise of the executive branch's war power, but in *Ex parte Endo* it said that no one could be detained without reasonable grounds for questioning his loyalty. The War Department's action in releasing all detainees made the decision academic; still, the precedent of detention—even if it was detention for "disloyalty"—remained and still remains.

X

THE WAR IS OVER!

*He was the commander-in-chief, not only of our
armed forces, but of our generation.*

—YANK

Obviously, many of the problems which were most crucial to the
Roosevelt government of the thirties and which the New Deal was designed to alleviate were solved stunningly by war, notably unemployment, business stagnation and chronically anemic farm prices. In fact,
the changes brought on by war were signaling faster than a jammed
switchboard that a new America was in the making.

Many of the New Deal programs had, of course, achieved perma-
nency and the war did not disturb them. Social Security, unemployment
compensation, old age benefits, TVA, the SEC, the Wagner Act and many
others had found a permanent niche in the government structure. Prosperity may have softened the workingman's dependence on the New Deal,
but his quest for economic security, colored by memories of the Depression, was at bottom as strong as ever. The most fiercely held goal
of the labor unions was not to give up any of the gains achieved before
the war.

The conservative and reactionary forces in Congress wanted no
serious rocking of the boat either and they were ever wary that some
wartime measures that would expand the New Deal were being slipped

over on them. The trained hounds of Congress sniffed each and every wartime innovation carefully for the forbidden New Deal scent (however they might define it at the moment), and when their keen noses flashed a warning, they raised a baying in committees and on the floor and in the press.

The New York *Times* reported early in February, 1943, that there was in Washington "a disposition to inquire into how broadly the war is being used to conceal programs of industrial and social reform of which many elements of Congress and other segments of the Washington population have long been suspicious." And the *Times*' Mark Sullivan wrote:

> The war came to America at a time when the Roosevelt Administration was in the midst of what is called social advances. At once President Roosevelt announced that the war would not be permitted to interfere—that the social gains must be not only kept but enlarged. The result is, as it has often been put, the Administration is trying to do two things at the same time— carry on a social revolution and conduct a war. There are few thoughtful people who believe that both can be successfully carried on together.

This was patent nonsense, of course. Almost nothing that could be described as reform took place during the war. Knowing he was blockaded by Congress, Roosevelt had shelved such ideas as he had along those lines for the duration and, in any case, had little time for them. Certain members of his administration, notably Vice President Henry Wallace and Secretary of the Treasury Henry Morgenthau, may have indeed sought to channel expedient war policies into liberal ends, but Wallace was merely ineffectual and the others were put on the sidelines in favor of the wartime team of Wall Streeters and big businessmen.

The Justice Department's vigorous enforcement of the antitrust statutes, including investigation of American firms that had cartel agreements with large German firms—notably Standard Oil's with I. G. Farben— ground to a halt after Congress gave the business-minded War Production Board a say in such cases. There may have also been some kind of tacit agreement between the administration and business whereby antitrust enforcement was deliberately laid aside on the condition that big business cooperate wholeheartedly with the war production effort. Be that as it may, the loose alliance of Southern Bourbons and Midwest farm bloc and other Republicans had acted effectively to hamstring Attorney

General Thurman Arnold, who finally resigned in disgust and became a federal judge.

Another victory of the conservative coalition was the torpedoing of the OWI's Domestic Branch, which was loudly accused of being a personal propaganda organ for FDR and the New Deal. Although the OWI quickly halted its program of issuing pamphlets discussing domestic issues and many of its "liberal" members resigned, Congressmen still found fault with some of its overseas propaganda, mainly a brochure for soldiers which portrayed Roosevelt as wartime leader. The Republicans were worried about the soldier vote in 1944, and abetted by their Southern allies who feared the votes by normally disenfranchised Negro GI's from their states, the GOP did all it could to water it down.

Another manifestation of Congressional anti-New Dealism centered on the Farm Security Agency which had been set up to help the small farmer, especially in the South, thus earning the enmity of the Bourbons, who wanted a steady supply of cheap tenant labor. The agency was put in dire jeopardy several times, but was always saved at the eleventh hour, even though its appropriations were frequently reduced. Otherwise the New Deal survived, and in their 1944 platform the Republicans were careful to incorporate most of its programs, promising merely that they would administer them better but not expand them.

Even so, when the progressive forces tried to expand New Deal programs on the books, they were stopped cold by the coalition. Various measures aimed at broadening the coverage of Social Security, increased public health facilities, medical care and health insurance were stillborn. Civil rights measures such as the antipoll tax and antilynching bills and the FEPC were squelched or eviscerated. In one speech the notorious Representative Rankin called New York State's FEPC Law "the greatest betrayal of the white Americans of New York that state has ever known" and then went on:

> As I said on this floor some time ago, the white Gentiles of this country still have some rights left, and should be protected from the persecutions they are now compelled to endure. If this drive continues they will be driven entirely from the business world and from the professions, as well as from public life. Remember that something like 98 per cent of the men who are dying on the high seas and the battle fronts of the world to protect American institutions in this war are white Gentiles. Yet when one speaks up on their behalf on this floor, in the press, on the radio, or elsewhere, we hear the whine of "anti-Semitism," or the cry of "race prejudice."

Where the legislative and executive branches were destined most frequently to clash was over the wartime agencies, spawned in profusion by Roosevelt's fertile employment of the executive order, and in the field of foreign affairs, where he bypassed the Senate's advice and consent with executive agreements. The conservatives' natural distrust of Roosevelt caused them to see him at times as the great prestidigitator, switching the policy peas with dazzling rapidity under one agency shell, then another. In addition, he was labeled a "poor administrator," a man who might appoint four men to do the job of one or one man to do the job of four. And this suspicion, usually expressed in speeches heavy with partisan rancor, also made the activities of Roosevelt's agents constantly vulnerable to attack. Whenever Congress felt its traditional independence was in jeopardy, it revolted. Thus, even such a New Deal loyalist as Senator Alben Barkley of Kentucky, the majority leader, was moved to rebel in 1944, after FDR had vetoed a tax bill, saying it gave relief "not for the needy but for the greedy." The harsh language of the veto message, the unprecedentedness of a President vetoing a revenue measure were too much for him. He resigned (although he reconsidered after FDR sent him a "Dear Alben" letter full of charm and apology), and the Senate defiantly overturned the veto by a large majority.

Opposed by the coalition, labor resorted to political pressure from the grass roots up. Sidney Hillman, who regarded himself as labor's chief spokesman in Washington, saw that Roosevelt needed labor's votes and set out to deliver them in the 1944 election.

Although the Republican candidate Dewey began with an effective low-key campaign against the "tired and quarrelsome old men" of the incumbent administration, Roosevelt was never in serious danger. Almost contemptuously he wiped out Dewey with his maiden campaign speech before the Teamsters Union in which he employed finely-honed *reductio ad absurdum* to Republican attacks on "my little dog Fala." (The Republicans had charged—falsely—that a destroyer had been diverted to pick up Fala, left behind in the Aleutians on a Presidential trip.)

Yet the Chief needed a strong electoral mandate, one that would sweep into office a more firmly Democratic Congress, thus recouping the losses suffered in the 1942 off-year election, when the Republicans picked up 40 seats in the House and 5 in the Senate, reducing the Democratic majorities to 222 to 209 and 58 to 38, respectively. There were many explanations for the Democratic debacle in 1942—general disgruntlement with the way the war was going, apparent confusion in

Washington, continuance of the farmers' return to the Republican Party begun in 1940 after their wholesale diaspora during the Depression, traditional off-year reaction and the absence of the President from the head of the ticket. But a major factor was the loss of two of Roosevelt's largest constituencies—labor and the twenty-one to thirty age-group, both of which were heavily affected by war's dislocations. The young were among the first to migrate to defense work and of course first to be called into service, where in 1942 they had no vote. Workingmen, young or old, who were part of the gigantic migration of 1941–42 to the defense centers, fell afoul of residency requirements in their new precincts or simply did not bother to register.

Obviously, in 1944, the labor vote must be got out. This Hillman tried to accomplish through the Political Action Committee, an offshoot of the CIO. Thousands of PAC members canvassed door to door, getting voters registered. Its brochure *Political Primer for All Americans* urged: "Let's quit blaming the politicians and face the responsibility of full citizenship. Let's become politicians ourselves." Fully confident that a big vote meant a big Democratic vote, the PAC aimed at stimulating participation among the previously apathetic. But its propaganda also stressed FDR in his above-politics role as Commander in Chief and symbol of the United States. One poster showed a kindly Roosevelt profile amid waving hands, black and white, and hats identifiable as those of workingmen and farmers; a child was in the background and the caption read, simply: "OUR FRIEND."

The PAC's efforts and the labor and ethnic vote in the big cities were given credit for Roosevelt's 3,500,000 plurality (the electoral votes ran 432 to 99); only one major city, Cincinnati, went for Dewey. The Democrats also recorded gains in the House, increasing their margin to 243 to 190. Still, 60 of those Democrats were anti-New Deal members of the coalition. On the other hand, the strength of Dewey's showing—he received more votes than any other losing candidate in history except Willkie, although the nation's population had increased 3,000,000 since 1940—revealed a strong current of opposition to the President. Most of it came from the farm states of the Midwest, ten of which Dewey carried. Farmers continued to be riled by labor shortages, what they saw as Washington's favoritism to big labor, the OPA, subsidies and price fixing; others were just plain anti-Roosevelt for a variety of reasons and could not stomach a fourth term for the President—"Are we going to be voting for Roosevelt *forever?*" wailed one Midwestern lady. Rumors that Roosevelt was in ill health, fueled by an unflattering picture of him in the newspapers making a speech at the Bremerton Navy Yard, fed this anti-Roosevelt feeling.* So threatening did these rumors become that the President's physician, Vice Admiral Ross T. McIntire, was called upon to issue a statement on the matter. After saying he wished the Chief would get more exercise in the White House pool and gain back eight or nine pounds, McIntire summed up: "Nothing organically wrong with him at all. He's perfectly O.K." This did not put the rumors to rest, and during the campaign Roosevelt repeatedly and deliberately exposed himself to rainy weather, riding hatless in an open car or speaking, unsheltered, at the podium in an obviously deliberate effort to show he was hale.

The campaign had roused the President's combative instincts and perhaps brought about a remission of a deterioration in health that was increasingly noted by those around him, including William Hassett, Roosevelt's private secretary, who had begun worrying as far back as April, 1944, about the Boss' loss of zest, the lackluster way he talked— no longer the sparkling stories, the banter—and the deterioration of the President's usually bold signature into a spidery scrawl. In a narrow sense then, those who raised the health issue, whether they knew it or not, had cause, and perhaps they felt vindicated by his death. No one will ever know whether or not Roosevelt even considered retirement— beyond the face value of his statement in a letter to Democratic Chairman Bob Hannegan: "For myself I do not want to run. . . . All that is within me cries out to go back to my home on the Hudson River. Reluctantly, but as a good soldier, I repeat that I will accept and serve in this office, if I am so ordered by the Commander in Chief of us all—the sovereign people of the United States." Certainly after Dewey's attacks nettled him, he dropped his previously announced intention not to campaign; certainly he despised Dewey, whom he dubbed the "All-American boy"—and he probably got a laugh from his tart-tongued cousin Alice Longworth Roosevelt's description of Dewey's running mate, John Bricker as "an honest Harding."

So labor helped Roosevelt forge a victory on his terms, and the labor-urban coalition alone would have reelected him. He had been, under rather devious circumstances, making overtures to Wendell Willkie

---

* An examination in August, 1944, by Lt. Comm. Howard G. Bruenn at Bethesda Naval Hospital confirmed that the President had suffered a minor heart attack at Bremerton. Hypertensive heart disease was diagnosed and the President was put on a strict medical regimen. His physician, Admiral McIntire, was informed of the diagnosis, but the President himself was apparently not told.

to form a new "truly liberal" Democratic party, joined by the liberal wing of the Republicans. Willkie was interested, but apparently Roosevelt leaked the news and Willkie pulled out, not wishing to appear a traitor to his party. Nonetheless, Roosevelt's victory was such that he did not need the South's 127 electoral votes; had he lived, he might have moved further to shed the Southern millstone, as Harry S. Truman was to do in 1948, albeit not entirely by choice.

Roosevelt's supporters represented a cluster of attitudes: admiration and faith in him as national leader, unwillingness to "change horses in the middle of the stream," a coolness toward Dewey's personality and his youth and "inexperience" (as FDR characterized him), worries about postwar economic security and a consequent greater faith in the Democrats' ability to guarantee jobs. (Roosevelt had revived memories of the "Hoover Depression" and, more positively, promised 60,000,000 jobs in the postwar era—a figure he seems to have more or less pulled from his hat.) Other factors included satisfaction with the way the war was going on the battlefronts (a few weeks before the election Eisenhower's troops had penetrated German soil, while MacArthur had fulfilled his "I shall return" pledge by wading ashore on Leyte Island in the Philippines; these achievements had a symbolism on the home front far weightier than their military value), general satisfaction with wartime prosperity (Roosevelt emphasizing a national income in 1944 of $150 billion, an all-time high, and of course a corresponding all-time low of fewer than 1,000,000 unemployed) and a wave of anti-isolationism. The last is worthy of note; in concrete terms it meant the defeat of several Senators, including Gerald P. Nye, and Representatives, including Ham Fish, who were considered "isolationist." The Republicans cried "purge" and saw sinister motives in penalizing men for their prewar voting; nonetheless, the people, belatedly pro-Woodrow Wilson, responded to Roosevelt's allusions to the undermining of the League of Nations after the last war by a handful of Republican Senators.

Partly as a result of this overwhelming mandate and partly because Roosevelt assiduously wooed Congressional support, internationalist measures passed the legislative branch by overwhelming majorities: the 1944 Fulbright (House) and Connally (Senate) Resolutions favoring U.S. participation in an international organization and paving the way for the Dumbarton Oaks Conference which drew up a preliminary UN Charter; the ratification of the UN Charter itself by the Senate, and authorization of reciprocal tariff reduction agreements and the approval of the Bretton Woods agreements (which provided for an international bank). Significant Republican opposition formed only against the reciprocal trade measures.

Roosevelt himself, though he frequently stooped to petty partisanship, became, in his Commander in Chief role, a truly heroic national figure. Never before was there an American war with so little disunity among the military men who ran it. Their publicly smooth cooperation—with perhaps the exception of MacArthur, who was jealous of the priority given to defeating the Nazis and the neglect of the Pacific theater—and their succession of victories after the initial dark days of 1942 won them the staunch, uncritical support of the American people. Even the irascible George Patton, after his public reprimand by Eisenhower, retained a large reservoir of popularity and was accorded a cordial welcome upon his return to the country in 1945. For this harmony the Commander in Chief must take considerable credit. Similarly, relations with the Allies functioned with unprecedented smoothness, and such machinery for international cooperation as Lend-Lease made possible a vast pooling of matériel, men and services with a minimum of national rivalries. As wartime leader, Roosevelt reached the zenith of his powers.

Although in Washington there was a surface spectacle of bureaucracy run amok, Roosevelt instinctively downgraded the importance of the nation's capital to the war and sought rather to secure the participation of the people outside Washington—of big business primarily (and small business, to a lesser degree), of the farmers and labor and the ordinary people. As for his performance behind what Cousin Teddy called the "bully pulpit" of the Presidency, Roosevelt was sometimes faulted for not adequately enunciating our war aims. Vague declarations about the Four Freedoms (from fear and want and of speech and religion), about an international town meeting of the world with some kind of muscle backing it up, about an economic bill of rights for all men were Roosevelt's attempts at articulations, but there was—even discounting the hindsight of twenty-five years—a disturbing cloudiness to these words, a high-sounding nebulosity. If Roosevelt did have a kind of instinctive grand design for the postwar world, the details were by no means filled in (it was like the little sketches he used to draw on pieces of paper). But his real achievement went back to the prewar years, to his recognition of the menace of aggressive Fascism. The menace loomed steadily larger, and the people clearly recognized and understood it by 1942. It was a real threat, a threat to our coasts and even our homes. Then, when the tide turned and the menace receded, it became a question of getting it over with, by any means possible—though the original goal—destruction of Fascism—remained. People were more concerned about immediate discomforts and the threat to their jobs posed by a postwar depression than they were by any "war aims" or vision for the postwar world.

There was, of course, no question of a return to isolationism, as after the last war, and support for America's belonging to a new League of Nations rose from 39 percent in 1939 to an overwhelming 81 percent in 1944. Roosevelt had played a part in this change in attitude, if for no other reason than for the accuracy of his cautious prophecies and for his continued reminders of the pernicious errors of the isolationists' doctrine. Both parties were united behind his view, and the tradition of politics stopping at the water's edge—of the so-called bipartisan foreign policy—was forged in this wartime unity. Roosevelt administered this trust superbly, and the crises in confidence were few and minor. Yet all in all, when the war ended, Americans had little idea of what to expect from the postwar world or what the nation should be doing about it. The most prominent spokesman on the nature of the postwar order, Vice President Wallace, was little heeded. Even Wendell Willkie with his book *One World* went no farther than Roosevelt did in terms of concrete programs. Ideologically, then, the war was fought on a high-octane gaseous mixture of slogans, hopes and yearnings.

Whatever were Roosevelt's plans for the postwar world, his death in April, 1945, put them to rest. On April 12 at 3:55 P.M. Eastern War Time, while sitting for a portrait, the President was struck down by a cerebral hemorrhage. By 5:48 P.M. the press service teletypes, which had clattered steadily throughout four years of war, giving the good news and the bad, tapped out the White House's bare announcement that Roosevelt had died. The first relay to the nation came when CBS's John C. Daly broke into *Wilderness Road,* a children's program, to make the announcement. Seconds later NBC interrupted *Front Page Farrell,* ABC, *Captain Midnight,* and Mutual, *Tom Mix*—all children's programs. The children would be, it seemed, the first to know.

The word spread rapidly—"Did you hear the news? President Roosevelt died." People were uncomprehending, struck by a tremendous blow. Statesmen and politicians compulsively composed tributes, grief-stricken. "God, God, how he could take it for us all," said Representative Lyndon Johnson of Texas, who had been an FDR protégé. "He was the one person I ever knew—anywhere—who was never afraid." An old Jewish lady on New York's Lower East Side was asked if she'd heard the radio. "For what do I need a radio?" she replied. "It's on everybody's face." And the country fiddler Bun Wright, who had planned to play for the President at a barbecue in Warm Springs that same day, said simply: "What a good man to leave us. What a good man." Not all were grieving. A man in the elevator of a Park Avenue hotel sneered: "So he's finally dead. Isn't it about time?" The elegant, genteel wife of a prominent Wall Street lawyer surprised herself by promptly turning around and slapping the man.

That night the body was borne in a massive 800-pound bronze casket to the Presidential train and placed in the car named Ferdinand Magellan, draped in a flag and flanked by a military guard. As the cortege left Warm Springs, Petty Officer Graham Jackson, with tears in his eyes, played "Going Home" on his accordion. People watched the train pass through the warm Southern night, scarcely able to believe that this vital, optimistic, cheerful, plainspoken man, who had become a fixture of a generation, was no longer alive. In Charlotte, North Carolina, there were 10,000 people waiting patiently for a look; when the train arrived, they all sang "Onward, Christian Soldiers," and the Negroes —standing separately from the whites—sang spirituals. A few whites joined in. The Negroes waited all along the line, and, as a reporter observed, though most had never had a chance to vote for him, they all came to pray for him. A Georgia Negro named Nelson Waters summed it up, perhaps: "He made a way for folks when there wasn't no way."

The next morning at 9:50 the train arrived in Washington, and with little delay the funeral procession began moving up Delaware Avenue and turned west on Constitution. A silent, tearful crowd lined the streets behind ranks of young soldiers, while twenty-four Liberator bombers droned in the sky above. The casket on a black-draped caisson drawn by six white horses turned onto Pennsylvania Avenue and approached the White House entrance. At the gate a Negro woman stood moaning: "Oh, he's gone. He's gone forever, I loved him so. He's never coming back." And another woman echoed: "Oh Lord he's gone forever and forever and forever . . ." The caisson moved up the drive.

Everywhere, the nation was observing the day of mourning; at 4 P.M., when the funeral would begin, everything would stop. That morning rumors of other deaths spread through New York. First, it had been Jack Dempsey—this rumor was traced to the wording of a "closed" sign on the ex-pugilist's restaurant. But there were no explanations for the other "deaths" people talked about—of Harry Hopkins, Governor Herbert Lehman, Charlie Chaplin, Frank Sinatra, Al Jolson, Errol Flynn,

Babe Ruth, Jack Benny and Jimmy Walker. The New York *Times'*
switchboard received 10,500 calls in the space of an hour from people
asking about the rumors. So momentous was this death, it seemed, that
people, by some contagion of shock, immediately began to envision the
demise of other national idols. One other striking thing happened: Just
before four o'clock, a thunderstorm moved into the city; the streets fell
dark as night, and hard rain pelted down; then, as suddenly as it had
come, the black cloud moved away. Promptly at four the radios fell
silent; all telephone service stopped; the teletypes clicked out the word
"SILENCE" over and over. Subway trains groaned to a halt, and the
passengers bowed their heads; on a trolley in Times Square the passengers
stood, while pedestrians knelt where they were in front of the out-of-town
newspaper stand.

The following day the body was borne to Hyde Park for burial.
The country squire who had become the quintessential democratic leader
—of whom Anne O'Hare McCormack wrote, "He did not stoop and
he did not climb; he was one of those completely poised persons who
felt no need to play up or play down to anybody"—was laid to rest
on his ancestral estate, amid the wafting fragrances of April's first blos-
soms. The identity of the date—April 14—and that of Lincoln's assassination did not go unremarked; the coincidence of two wartime leaders
being struck down, one by an assassin, the other by mortal weariness
of the flesh was compelling. Many recalled Walt Whitman's threnody
"When Lilacs Last in the Dooryard Bloom'd," with its haunting juxta-
position of spring flowers and death. And Millard Lampell's folk cantata
for radio about Lincoln's funeral train, *The Lonesome Train,* became
the most widely played radio program in America. Transcriptions of
it were broadcast everywhere in America, and the Decca phonograph
record was played in school assemblies and before other groups. The
deaths of the two leaders became merged; Lincoln's funeral train became
Roosevelt's:

> A lonesome train on a lonesome track
> Seven coaches painted black.
> They carried Mr. Lincoln down,
> The train started, the wheels went round,
> You could hear the whistle for miles around,
> Crying, Free – dom!
>   Free – dom!

But the President's death was but one cataclysm in what was perhaps
the most eventful year in human history. As the war rushed at breakneck

speed to its end, Roosevelt's memory receded quickly into the distance, like one high mountain among many passing by a train window. People listened and read in mounting excitement as the Allied armies broke across the Rhine into Germany. They watched newsreels with their pictures of corpses piled high in Belsen concentration camp and saw the blasting to rubble of the great swastika at the stadium in Nuremberg, scene of so many of those pagan Nazi rallies full of ferocious songs, massed flags and raised, heiling arms, all centered on the short man with a vague smile on his face, the author, if one man could be, of all this misery, who now was missing, presumed dead, in the ruins of Berlin.

The war continued in a crescendo of ferocity. Berlin fell; then Germany surrendered in May. In the United States people heard the news one day early because of a leak by an AP correspondent; still, like reasonably well-disciplined soldiers, they waited until the official announcement the next day, May 7, before breaking loose in full celebration. In Manhattan paper poured out the windows by the ton, and all over the country whistles sounded, guns boomed, church bells rang, and people went inside the churches for prayers.

Now attention focused on the Pacific theater, where Japanese resistance was becoming more fierce, more fanatical and more costly in American lives. Iwo Jima fell, and Joe Rosenthal's photograph of the flag raising was splashed over all the papers. Okinawa was finally mopped up after nearly three months of fighting, at a cost of 39,000 American casualties, including 13,000 dead. American B-29's in blocks of 500 dropped tons of incendiary bombs on Japanese cities with impunity, wiping out 46 percent of Tokyo alone, killing 90,000 civilians. The raids were so commonplace that few gave them second thought; forgotten was the great elation of 1942, when General Doolittle's puny force of B-24's had dropped a few bombs on Tokyo and Yokohama and scurried to the Chinese mainland for hazardous crash landings.

In Washington the Senate ratified the United Nations resolution and the Bretton Woods agreement, and in April delegates from around the world met in San Francisco to wrangle about the Charter of the United Nations Organization. Americans overwhelmingly approved emergency aid to devastated Europe through the United Nations Relief and Rehabilitation Administration. They also began to have a line on the relative unknown who had become their President upon FDR's death, and they wholeheartedly approved of Harry S. Truman. Brisk, efficient, with an image of impeccable honesty from his Truman Committee days, when he kept an unrelenting eye on chicanery and waste in the war industries, he enjoyed a Gallup Poll rating of 84 percent approval before he left for the final Big Three conference at Potsdam—the high water-mark of Allied cooperation. There was little comparing of Truman with Roosevelt; people simply willed him Roosevelt's mantle of wartime lead-ership. And with the war marching inexorably to a successful conclusion, with a harmonious relationship with Congress, Truman seemed to have Roosevelt's magic, yet without the residue of ill feeling that had accumu-lated during the latter's twelve years in office. There was a heady opti-mism in the air, a sense of great events marching toward consummation. The final showdown with Japan, only partially sobered by predictions that the battle for the Japanese mainland would cost perhaps 175,000 American lives, was imminent.

Then came the Presidential announcement of the dropping of an atomic bomb on Hiroshima: "Sixteen hours ago an American airplane dropped one bomb on Hiroshima, an important Japanese army base. That bomb had more power than 20,000 tons of TNT. It is an atomic bomb. It is a harnessing of the basic power of the universe."

Few people understood nuclear fission or even could imagine an atom, except as a sort of ultimate, infinitesimally small particle of matter, rather as the ancient Greeks had conceived of it. Editorial writers busily trotted out their most portentous clichés: "dawn of a new era" . . . "vast possibilities for good or evil" . . . "boon to mankind or the doom of civilization as we know it" . . . "revolutionizes warfare" . . . "makes current weapons of war obsolete" . . . "a Frankenstein's monster." At first, people only saw it as a new, terrible but logical end product in the evolution of increasingly violent weapons of war; they trusted science almost as a god. A second bomb was dropped at Nagasaki, and five days later the war was over, and people gave themselves up to an orgy of celebrations from coast to coast. Servicemen rushed up to pretty girls in the street and kissed them. Two million massed in Times Square, as though it were New Year's Eve, cheering the *Times'* electric sign. The celebration continued from 7 P.M. on August 14, when the President announced the news, until late at night on the following day. People snake-danced, played leapfrog, formed la conga chains in the streets; 5,000 tons of paper, confetti and miscellaneous other litter poured from office windows in New York. It was a wild carnival, a Mardi Gras, a spontaneous explosion of relief and a mass blowing off of steam. Yet a Chicago reporter wrote: ". . . everybody talked of the 'end of the war,' not 'victory.' " After the cheers had died, the hangovers passed, the ringing in the eardrums faded, people began to look ahead to what for four years they had dreamed of—the Postwar World. It seemed not a very secure world after all, either in America or abroad. Here was an America unscathed by war, its arms victorious in far-flung corners of the earth, with allies who were staunch comrades at arms; yet when the hush descended, when the din of war stopped it seemed that this same world, so long totally engaged in war, was now full of an ominous, uneasy, weary silence. The slogans and ideals and exhortations that had sustained the daily grind of a war effort in which every man was but one small cog in the great machine of Victory now faded into the past, to be replaced by the ambiguities of peace.

America had surely fulfilled its "rendezvous with destiny" by helping destroy the Axis threat, but what now? No one knew, and people buried themselves in their daily lives again, in the shortages, in the dreams of buying a new car to replace the worn-out wartime jalopy, of plentiful steaks and nylons and whiskey; of stores filled with polite, smiling clerks anxious to solicit one's business; of new houses filled with the glittering gadgetry that wartime science was already promising—yes, even of factories powered by atomic energy. People saw many problems in the world, for now they thought about the world and had come to believe that America had a peace-keeping role to play in it and must be militarily prepared so that Pearl Harbor would never happen again. Yet their hopes and fears would come down to an immediate desire for normality. "Bring the boys home" and end controls—those were the two most urgent demands. As they looked back (when they did) on the war period, it became an increasingly unreal dislocation of the normal, almost like a dream—a rapid, often grand shuffle of events, of black arrows on maps spearheading a cross-hatched tide of military advances. Now they stood as if on a mountain of power compared to the prewar times. They had plenty of money in their pockets—more than $140 billion in Savings and War Bonds held by individuals and a pent-up demand for consumer items. (Yet there were millions of workers with no savings —it was estimated that the lowest half, by income, of all United States families held only 3 percent of total liquid assets [and had incomes of less than $2,000 a year], while the top 10 percent families held 60 percent—indicating that if a postwar momentum of demand were to be maintained, jobs would have to be found.) The big corporations had strengthened their power; there was $26 billion worth of new factories in existence, $6 billion of it unusable in peacetime, in addition to a prewar plant valued at $40 billion. Corporate cash reserves for postwar expansion were upwards of $20 billion. There was an aircraft industry (prewar plant capacity, worth $114,000,000; postwar worth, nearly $4 billion) and a massive shipping industry that eyed the future with uncertainty. There was a work force of more than 51,000,000 men and women, but some of the 6,600,000 in jobs geared only for wartime production were already being laid off. Unions looked to keeping the wartime pay gains based on overtime, and all eyed the 12,000,000 returning servicemen with apprehension, as threats to their livelihood. The needs of civilian life had been allowed to go to seed in the interests of war production; now people saw that 5,000,000 new houses were needed at once—and they could not be built. At the same time, a stockpile of more than $90 billion surplus war goods was at hand, much of it with little civilian usefulness. Scientists were heady with triumph for they had played a key role—yet some of them had learned a "sense of sin" for their work on the atomic bomb. . . .

At Willow Run the people started moving out of the "temporary" government housing in spring as the plant cut back on its work force. By June the exodus was general. People would simply walk into the office, toss their keys on the desk and drive off, back to where they came from. Children left school in droves even before the term was up. A steady procession of trailers moved along Holmes Street. By Christmas, 1945, where once 13,000 war workers had lived, there were now only 600 families. The cold wind blew between the rows of empty gray prefabricated houses, and over at the bomber plant the machinery was silent and the wind swirled up fine clouds of snow on the empty runways. In 1946 the Edsel Ford Post of the American Legion in Willow Run made a formal request to the War Department for a B-24 bomber to serve as a sort or reminder of the war and what had gone on at the plant. Washington agreed, and bomber number 139, a combat veteran, was flown from Washington. The Legionnaires after much effort towed the bomber into an empty bit of land across from their post and parked it under an apple tree. Time passed, and the Willow Run plant was taken over by Henry J. Kaiser and his partner, Joseph Frazer, who thought they could make cars. Number 139 suffered the depredations of souvenir hunters and small boys playing "war" crawling over its hospitable fuselage. Finally, it became little better than a pile of junk, an eyesore; in 1950 a scrap metal company hauled it away.

Notes

I. PRELUDE: SATURDAY

13 "Twenty-five bucks a week": "Twenty-five Bucks a Week" by Henry Myers, Edward Ellison, Jay Gorney. © 1941 Mills Music Corporation.

15 "a national appeal": *Wall Street Journal*, December 6, 1941.

16 " 'Blue Star' Girls": New York *Times*, December 6, 1941.

19 "Students seem to be": *New York Times Magazine*, December 7, 1941.

21 "The American people may feel": quoted in New York *Times*, December 6, 1941.

21 "Curious hodgepodge of Communist": New York *Herald Tribune*, December 5, 1941.

21 "I don't want to set": "I Don't Want to Set the World on Fire" by Eddie Seiler, Sol Marcus, Bennie Benjamin and Eddie Durham. © 1941 Cherio Music Publishers, Inc.

22 "CLOSED Until Further Notice": quoted in New York *Times*, December 6, 1941.

22 "In saying farewell": quoted *ibid*.

22 "There is not enough": quoted *ibid*.

22 "There is not a single": quoted *ibid*.

23 "A tulip garden by an old Dutch mill": "My Sister and I" by Hy Zaret, Joan Whitney, Alex Kramer © 1941 Broadcast Music Corporation.

23 "There'll be bluebirds over": "There'll Be Bluebirds over the White Cliffs of Dover" by Nat Burton and Walter Kent. © 1941 Shapiro, Bernstein & Company, Inc.

24 "If we should take": by Benjamin Baker, New York *Times*, December 6, 1941.

II. IN THE EVENT OF AN AIR RAID, WALK DO NOT RUN

25 "There's a crazy man": quoted in Rosebery, 5.

25 "If there are Jap": Manck (typescript).

25 "I don't think there's": quoted in New York *Times*, December 10, 1941.

26 "There are more damned": quoted in Rosebery, 5.

26 "We've got to show": *ibid.*, 6.

27 "another evidence of the": New York *Times*, December 8, 1941.

27 "to make sure Texas": quoted *ibid*.

27 "I have a boy": quoted *ibid*.

28 "My country has done": quoted *ibid*.

28 "Less than 1,000 Japanese": quoted *ibid*.

30 "definitely no enemy": quoted *ibid.*, December 11, 1941.

31 "Am I embarrassed": quoted *ibid*.

31 "This is the time": quoted *ibid*.

32 "This is war . . .": quoted *ibid.*

34 "There is no need": quoted in McElroy (typescript).

34 "An auxiliary fire department": quoted in Manck (typescript).

35 "It hasn't been definitely": quoted *ibid.*

35 "new technique, to seek": quoted in New York *Times*, January 2, 1942.

35 "The war will come": *ibid.*

35 "Rejoice, be happy": *ibid.*

37 "glamour is not needed": quoted in McElroy (typescript).

37 "If that is the prime": quoted in New York *Times*, February 6, 1942.

37 "Enemy raids": quoted *ibid.*

37 "instruction in physical fitness" quoted *ibid.*

38 "He is a Jew": quoted *ibid.*

39 "There are a number": quoted in Manck (typescript).

40 "I want to tell": quoted in *Harper's Magazine*, August, 1942.

41 "Abercrombie and Fitch recommends": *New Yorker*, January 10, 1942.

42 "sounds like rolling thunder": Conner.

42 "We're close enough": quoted in Morehouse, 34.

43 "never give the war": *ibid.*, 207.

43 "It may come to pass": *Collier's*, March 14, 1942.

44 "for were they not": quoted in Watters, 70.

44 "California can handle those": quoted in Morehouse, 64.

44 "They are prepared to": *Life*, April 6, 1942.

46 "The opening night of": New York *Herald Tribune*, June 13, 1942.

46 "People come [to Times Square]": quoted in Meyer Berger, *New York Times Magazine*, March 10, 1942.

47 "Guess they've gone out": quoted in Johnson, 137.

48 "blackout of civilization": quoted in Watters, 62.

48 "the awesome night": quoted *ibid.*, 83.

48 "does something to you": quoted *ibid.*, 82.

49 "Bed rooms need not": *House & Garden*, February, 1942.

49 "Dimout Suedes": New York *Times*, March 11, 1942.

49 "Time spent by employees": quoted in *Business Week*, January 10, 1942.

50 "there was no blackout": quoted in *New Republic*, March 30, 1942.

51 "I solemnly swear": quoted in Manck (typescript).

53 "personal thrill it gave": Hartzell, 126.

53 "all through 1942 the accent" quoted in Manck (typescript).

53 "If incendiary bombs fall": "What to Do in an Air Raid."

55 "A word-of-mouth campaign": quoted in Larson, 77.

56 "In building shelters consider": *House and Garden*, March, 1942.

56 "Remember what I was": quoted in Morehouse, 33–34.

57 "Have we got to": quoted in Larson, 67.

57 "beyond the realm of": quoted *ibid.*, 66.

57 "I would be better": letter from Stella Ross in New York *Times*, January 6, 1942.

57 "Why are we sure": letter from Katherine I. Gannon in New York *Times*, February 18, 1942.

58 "Immediately before entering": quoted in Rosebery, 10.

60 "The questionnaires were delivered": *Harper's Magazine*, August, 1942.

60 "Don't think they're scared": quoted in *Saturday Evening Post*, June 6, 1942.

61 "That's just housework!": quoted in *Harper's Magazine*, August, 1942.

61 "The Nursery School will": *New Yorker*, January 10, 1942.

61 "There are sections": quoted in Manck (typescript).

61 "A big job is": quoted in *Harper's Magazine*, August, 1942.

61 "who knows little about": quoted *ibid*.

61 "the third likeliest target": quoted *ibid*.

III. THE CHANGING LANDSCAPE: WAR BRIDES, WAR TOWNS AND WASHINGTON

63 "We ain't war-scared": quoted in Morehouse, 12.

64 "Why, people were sleeping": *ibid*., 154.

64 "I had two stores": *ibid*., 155.

65 "most severe contraction": *Business Week*, February 19, 1942.

65 "aside from truck production": quoted in Catton, 95.

66 "Gentlemen, I think the country": quoted in Janeway, 228.

66 "we built many new": quoted *ibid*., 308.

70 "The bus rumbles down": Dos Passos, 89.

70 "Once I was westbound": quoted in Menefee, 87.

71 "Maybe you don't know": quoted in Dos Passos, 66.

71 "Go to war": quoted in Menefee, 78.

73 "You're as pleasant as": "Scatter Brain" by Johnny Burke, Frankie Masters, Kahn Keene and Carl Bean. © 1939 Bregman, Vocco and Conn, Inc.

73 "The stars at night": "Deep in the Heart of Texas" by June Hershey and Don Swander. © 1941 Melody Lane Publications, Inc.

73 "From Natchez to Mobile": "Blues in the Night" by Johnny Mercer and Harold Arlen. © 1941 Remick Music Corporation.

73 "snowy plains where great": Dos Passos, 34.

74 "It took me twenty-nine": quoted in Wilson, 48.

75 "a milling crowd; soldiers": Dos Passos, 91–92.

75 "more like a Western mining camp": Menefee, 51.

76 "a hole that": quoted in *National Geographic*, January, 1942.

76 "We used to go": quoted *ibid*.

76 "The flies we get": quoted in Meyer, 175.

77 "These are the lowest": quoted in Menefee, 53.

78 "What's good enough for": quoted in Meyer, 197.

78 "Those folks in houses": *ibid*., 198.

78 "Haven't you heard there"; "They work all week"; "The reason you see"; "The hillbillies will": quoted in *Harper's Magazine*, July, 1944.

79 "There's a Star Spangled": "There's a Star Spangled Banner Waving Somewhere" by Paul Roberts and Shelby Darne. © 1942 Bob Miller Inc.

80 "Never have I met": quoted in Meyer, 51, 52.

81 "Fur. Apt., no streetwalkers": quoted in Menefee, 83.

81 "Families are sleeping": quoted *ibid*.

81 "I can't help realizing": Menefee, 72.

82 "Temporary houses which have": Straus, 211.

83 "lack of wholesome recreational": quoted in Menefee, 111.

83 "Professional gamblers": *ibid*., 112

84 "The real estate business": quoted in Straus, 212.

85 "This brings me to": Meyer, 156.

85 "In the San Fernando Valley": *ibid*., 152–53.

85 "You mean you": quoted *ibid*., 146.

85 "I'm just waiting for": *ibid*., 153.

86 "I'll tell you a": quoted, National Conference of Social Work, 121.

86 "Miss Bessie, why don't": quoted in Meyer, 205.

86 "It's Saturday night": Muncie *Evening Press*, February 7, 1944.

89 "What substitute do we": quoted in Robinson, 195.

89 "The young soldier": quoted *ibid.*, 195.

90 "I never realized it": quoted in *Smith College Studies in Social Work*.

91 "aircraft did it for": quoted in Morehouse, 54.

92 "a reasonable length of": New York *Times*, April 21, 1942.

94 "We must learn to wait": *PM*, September 25, 1942.

95 "Paradoxically her thoughts": *New York Times Magazine*, April 21, 1942.

95 "There's always some woman": quoted in *Life*, September 9, 1944.

96 "Saturday night": "Saturday Night Is the Loneliest Night of the Week" by Sammy Cahn and Jule Styne. © 1942 Barton Music Corporation.

96 "U.S. women have changed": *Time Capsule/1945*, 51.

96 "I work half a day": *ibid.*, 51–52.

97 "You will find that": *ibid.*, 52.

97 ". . . many mothers of school": Castendyck, "Juvenile Delinquency in War-time," *Federal Probation*, July–September, 1942.

99 "Men, on the other hand": quoted in Rosebery, 111.

99 "Won't someone help": quoted *ibid*, 111.

100 "Times Square on New Year's": Menefee, 38.

100 "Washington is the loneliest town": quoted in Dos Passos, 164.

100 "If I were you": *ibid.*, 180–81.

101 "affects even the secretaries": quoted *ibid.*, 148–49.

102 "Well, we have the two": quoted *ibid.*, 149.

102 "Yes there's no money": quoted *ibid.*, 151.

103 "Christ it's the tar": quoted *ibid.*, 141.

103 "You work in a": quoted *ibid.*, 141.

104 "a tirade filled with": quoted in "The Man at the Microphone," 38.

105 "Suppose you and I": quoted in Catton, 203.

IV. COST-PLUS

107 "We are going to": quoted in Catton, 112.

109 "the most workable and": quoted in William H. Jordy, *Nation*, May 8, 1943.

110 "I don't like it": quoted in Meyer, 5.

111 "[Roosevelt] was counting on": Janeway.

111 "business-minded men": *Kiplinger's Newsletter*, January 24, 1942.

112 "A priority is something": quoted in Rosebery, 125–26.

112 "Washington's a funny town": *ibid.*, 109.

112 ". . . the man who got": quoted in Novick *et al.*, 376.

113 "it was also due": Sherwood, 554.

119 "This movement spread all": Nelson.

119 "We could figure a way": quoted in *Business Week*, February 7, 1942.

120 "The price of vegetables": quoted in Dos Passos, 115.

121 "Just what the lack": quoted in Rosebery, 98.

121 "The corset and brassiere": *ibid.*, 99.

122 "In Ed Massey's barbershop": *Time Capsule/1944*, 32.

122 "Her resultant vivacious spirit": quoted in Rosebery, 87.

123 "She wears it proudly": quoted *ibid.*, 88.

124 "There is, for instance": *New Yorker*, February 7, 1942.

124 "Instead of pussyfooting around": *Life*.

125 "Some day after this": Simmons and Meyer, III, 242.

130 "Success in anything depends": quoted by L. E. Davies, *New York Times Magazine,* January 25, 1943.

130 "The principle is the": Vinde, 58.

132 "We looked at each other": quoted by Henry J. Taylor, *Saturday Evening Post,* December 22, 1942.

133 "A British observer, D. W. Brogan": in Goodman, 21–22.

134 "Please for God's sake": quoted in *Time Capsule/1945,* 53.

V. GIVE US THE TOOLS

138 "I may be dumb": quoted in Dos Passos, 48.

138 "Any employee who": quoted in Lever and Young, 196.

139 "Our policy is not": quoted in Meyer, 265, 266.

140 "We have good wages": *ibid.,* 264.

142 "A good union would": *ibid.,* 284.

142 "Attention, Associates . . .": quoted in Dos Passos, 38.

143 "I believe that": quoted in Meyer, 24.

145 "You know there's": quoted in Dos Passos, 40–41.

146 "Detroit . . . where Irvin Caesar's": *Daily Variety,* October 29, 1943.

147 "He wears a thin": Dos Passos, 90.

147 "We may not be": quoted in Menefee, 54.

150 "If only we could': Wilder, 185–86.

152 "had pondered seriously": Rosebery, 80.

153 "This is a lot": quoted *ibid.,* 75.

153 "I know your home": quoted *ibid.,* 71.

153 "As long as we're": quoted *ibid.,* 71.

153 "After a date": quoted *ibid.,* 72.

153 "I flunked in charm": quoted *ibid.,* 74.

153 "That new foreman is": quoted *ibid.,* 77.

154 "The traditional maidenly modesty": Lerner, 21, 20.

154 "I won't have": quoted in Rosebery, 82–83.

154 "My observations are": quoted *ibid.,* 81.

166 "continued sharp discrimination": quoted in *Labor Fact Book 8,* 86.

167 "in the long run": Dos Passos, 126.

VI. WILL THIS PICTURE HELP WIN THE WAR?

168 "we felt it wise": letter, in Mellet correspondence, BMP files.

168 "Because of the war": New York *Times,* January 4, 1942.

170 "Aged 37, Henry Fonda": *Daily Variety,* August 26, 1952.

170 "Jimmy Stewart": *Fortune,* April, 1942.

170 "Bob Cummings": *Photoplay,* November, 1942.

170 "Clark Gable shouldn't": Kyle Crichton in *Collier's,* January 9, 1943.

170 "The American motion picture": letter, Mellett correspondence, December 18, 1941, BMP files.

171 "freedom of the screen": quoted in *Fortune,* April, 1942.

171 "Whether it was foresight": transcript of meeting of January 15, 1942, BMP files.

172 "At least 20 pictures": *Vital Speeches,* September 15, 1941.

172 "[Joseph Kennedy] apparently threw": Mellett correspondence, November 19, 1940.

173 "The applause in": letter, Mercey to Mellett, May 11, 1941.

173 "The Committee is exercising": *ibid.*

174 "Guess what the Hollywood": *Photoplay,* December, 1942.

174 "If you were privileged": *Daily Variety,* October 29, 1944.

174 "No longer are actresses": *ibid.,* October 29, 1944.

175 "A training school plane": *Life,* April 13, 1942.

175 "No more he-man build up": *Daily Variety,* October 29, 1944.

178 "thrilling newsreels of": New York *Herald Tribune,* November 25, 1942.

179 "In the movies you": *Photoplay,* December, 1942.

179 "The war-year of 1943": *Daily Variety,* October 29, 1943.

179 "Old process of long": *ibid.*

180 "This is my friend": undated clipping, Sonny Tufts file, Library of the Performing Arts, New York City.

180 "That may be, but": *Daily Variety,* October 19, 1942.

180 "Don 'Red' Barry has": New York *Times,* December 3, 1942.

181 "HOW TO TELL YOUR": *Time,* December 22, 1941.

181 "OK, you Yankee Doodle": *God Is My Co-Pilot* (film).

183 "It was not long": memo from Fred Polangin, August 13, 1942.

183 "At every opportunity, naturally": *General Information Manual for the Motion Picture Industry,* BMP files.

184 "In crowds unostentatiously show": *ibid.*

184 "Show colored soldiers in": *ibid.*

184 "Does the picture tell": *ibid.*

184 "This will enable us": letter, Fred Polangin to George Bagnal, United Artists, December 2, 1942, BMP files.

185 "Our producers and their": *Hollywood Reporter,* December 9, 1942.

185 "This is the only": telegram, Nelson Poynter to Mellett, January 1, 1943, BMP files.

185 "the Hays Office has": Agee, 74.

186 "presentation of wartime England": Review of *White Cliffs of Dover,* BMP files.

186 "Don't make blanket condemnation": (paraphrased), reviews in BMP files.

187 "window dressing" and "At the conclusion": reviews, BMP files.

190 "For one thing tell": *Life,* March 2, 1942.

190 "fails to suggest that": Agee, 27.

190 "many in the audience": letter, Mellett correspondence, BMP files.

190 "I was rather shocked": *ibid.*

192 "phoniest war film ever": *Documentary Newsletter,* August, 1942.

192 "But, Jerry, there *are*": Bessie, 80

200 "You have managed to": letter in BMP files.

201 "a garrulous youngster": New York *Times,* May 4, 1943.

201 "formidable and ruthless": review in BMP files.

202 "Many millions of reflective": quoted in Goodman, 10–11.

203 "The central character . . .": *New Republic,* October 18, 1943.

209 "This time we will": "This Time" by Irving Berlin. © 1942 by Irving Berlin. © renewed 1969 by Irving Berlin.

211 "Oh, we didn't want": "We'll Knock the Japs Right into the Laps of the Nazis" by Ned Washington and Lew Pollock. © 1942 Mills Music, Inc.

211 "You're a sap": "You're a Sap, Mr. Jap" by James Cavanaugh, John Redmond and Nat Simon. © 1941 Mills Music, Inc.

212 "If I said it, nobody": letter to Editor, *Life,* November 2, 1942.

212 "You stay in the": quoted in *Daily Variety,* October 29, 1943.

215 "Imagine what the enemy": "Wait Till the Girls Get in the Army, Boys" by Al Goodhart and Kay Twomey. © 1942, Advanced Music Corporation.

215 "After you wash": "GI Jive" by Johnny Mercer. © 1943, Capitol Songs. Copyright assigned 1960 to Commander Publications, Hollywood, California.

216 "They're either too young": "They're Either Too Young or Too Old" by Frank Loesser and Arthur Schwartz. © 1943, M. Witmark & Sons, New York.

218 "I'm getting tired": "I'm Getting Tired So I Can Sleep" by Irving Berlin. © 1942 by Irving Berlin. © renewed 1969 by Irving Berlin.

218 "Thanks for the dream": "Thanks for the Dream" by Al Stillman, Xavier Cugat, Raymond Gonzales, Jr. © 1943 Sam Fox Publishing Company.

218 "When I Go to Sleep": "Linda" by Jack Lawrence. © 1946 Warock Music, Inc.

218 "Dream when you're": "Dream" by Johnny Mercer. © 1944 Capitol Songs.

219 "You'll never know how": "It's Been a Long Long Time" by Sammy Cahn and Jule Styne. © 1945 Edwin H. Morris & Company, Inc.

219 "He's just a fellow": "Fellow on a Furlough" by Bobby Worth. © 1943 House of Melody.

224 "The platform on which": quoted in Goodman, p. 386.

225 "Ordinarily, we Americans are": Corwin, *More by Corwin*, 257.

225 "They're going to die": quoted in Goodman, 389.

226 "dollar-a-year men": Norman Corwin in Goodman, 393–94.

226 "Our soldiers don't care": Domestic Radio Bureau files.

226 "GUY: [The Negro] gets": *ibid.*

227 "PEASANT: This dam has": *ibid.*

227 "We're marching on": *ibid.*

228 "ANNOUNCER (FORCEFUL)": *ibid.*

228 "Stating the simple honest": letter to New York *Times*, April 16, 1942.

228 ". . . but you, America": Domestic Radio Bureau files.

229 "The house I live in": "The House I Live in" by Lewis Allen and Earl Robinson © 1942 by Lewis Alland and Earl Robinson. Used by permission of Chapell & Company, Inc.

229 "NARRATOR: You're a chief": Barnouw, 254.

231 "Almost every chapter": *New York Times Magazine*, December 21, 1943.

231 "You never know when": quoted in Goodman, 385.

232 "an alarming trend": quoted *ibid.*, 382.

232 "After twenty-five years": quoted *ibid.*, 382.

232 "Lord God of fresh": Corwin, *Untitled and Other Radio Dramas*, 483.

VII. SHORTAGES AND MR. BLACK

234 "Roses are red": quoted in Rosebery, 179.

235 "For one thing": Morehouse, 71.

237 "We suspect that there": quoted in Catton, 163.

237 "Personally I'm not worried": quoted *ibid.*, 162.

240 "I came back to": Simmons and Meyer, II, 172.

241 "It's only fair to": quoted in Rosebery, 211.

245 "I only hope": quoted *ibid.*, 179.

245 "Aw shucks, nothin' but": quoted *ibid.*, 179.

246 "Now we're all sharing": quoted *ibid.*, 180.

246 "We respectfully suggest": quoted *ibid.*, 180.

247 "It's wonderful what": quoted *ibid.*, 181.

247 "What was right for": Dameron, 30.

249 "room, radio, good salary": quoted in Rosebery, 168.

249 "Just a moment": quoted *ibid.*, 168.
251 "to keep the flower": *House & Garden,* February, 1942.
258 "PLEASE BE NICE": quoted *ibid.*, 182.
260 "You'll never get": quoted in Menefee, 79.
260 "I'm goin' back to": quoted in Janeway, 328.
260 "The most conservative miners": Meyer, 230.
261 "A man couldn't do": Dos Passos, 234.
263 "389,419,000 patriotic": *Time Capsule/1944,* 66.
264 " 'Yep,' said the man": *ibid.*, 32.
264 "on the point of": quoted in Catton, 215.
265 "the damndest crime"; quoted *ibid.*, 211.
265 "the repudiation of democracy," quoted in Drury, 403.
265 "not only for war production": *ibid.*, 404.
267 "really any transaction where": quoted in *Book of the Year,* 1945.
267 "We have relied": quoted in Clinard, 680.
268 "Rifles with silencers": Lever and Young, 140–41.

VIII. PLEASURES, PASTIMES, FADS AND FOLLIES

273 "In a world where": quoted in Goodman, 448.
277 ". . . the publishers": *ibid.*, 463–64.
281 "It's no gag that": quoted in Green and Laurie, 529–30.
281 "the Kohinoor": Maurice Zolotow in *Saturday Evening Post,* February 13, 1942.
282 "You gotta keep in": quoted in *ibid.*
282 "flashy, elaborate floor": Green and Laurie, 509.
283 "It's getting so I": quoted in Zolotow, *ibid.*
283 "a mechanism for social": *ibid.*
283 "Every time those Nazis": quoted *ibid.*
283 "It's a certainty": quoted in Green and Laurie, 510.
283 "So turn off the heat": quoted in *Time Capsule/1945,* 52.
283 "Any crum-bum what": quoted in Green and Laurie, 510.
283 "New York is still": quoted *ibid.*, 511.
284 "Anyway 1 A.M. was OK": *ibid.*, 511.
285 "I'd get tired of": quoted in *Song Hits,* July, 1942.
287 "Thinking quickly back over": quoted in Goodman, 466.
287 "By making his invaders": *ibid.*, 468.
287 "Now what do we": quoted in Goodman, 455.
288 "Whether *The Eve of St. Mark":* quoted in Goodman, 476.
288 "The present criticism": quoted *ibid.*, 476.
288 "It was a service": *ibid.*, 469.
289 "the nerveless student": *ibid.*, 476.
289 "They're such kids": quoted in Goodman, 471.
289 "The final play": quoted in Goodman, 482.
292 "Bad news was often": Goodman, 408.
292 "It is much easier": quoted *ibid.*, 418.
292 "Take good care": *Life,* December 20, 1943.
292 "Don't be a public": *ibid.*
293 "I remember you . . .": quoted in Goodman, 433–34.
294 "The starry eyes . . .": *ibid.*, 440.
294 "A moment bright with": quoted *ibid.*, 400.
294 "As soon as a pea canner": quoted *ibid.*, 431.

295 "Use the mail whenever": quoted in Rosebery, 171.
295 "You they may cast": *Life*, December 20, 1943.
296 "Wide awake . . . listening": quoted in Goodman, 438.
296 "I cannot think, offhand": quoted in *Time Capsule/1943*, 211.
298 "The deficiencies": quoted in Catton, 75.
299 "The whole direction": quoted *ibid.*, 75.
299 "You dirty no-good": quoted in *Time Capsule/1943*, 161.
300 "First day: STORM CHERBOURG": quoted in *Time Capsule/1944*, 241.
300 "This story will go": quoted in Johnson.
301 "The electrifying slogan": quoted *ibid.*
301 "As seen from a ditch": quoted in Goodman, 342.
303 "One soldier came": Pyle, 107.
304 "Our house is": quoted in Rosebery, 155.
304 "No matter whom you": *ibid.*, 155.
305 "No good soldier is": quoted in *Time*, November 30, 1942.
306 "the climate is different": quoted in Goodman, 492.
311 "Why do they have": quoted *ibid.*, 429.
311 "We would not go": *ibid.*, 328.
311 "Do you mean to say": *ibid.*, 330.
312 "Baseball provides a recreation": quoted in *Book of the Year 1943*, 98.
312 "somewhere between AA and A": *Time Capsule/1945*, 196.
319 "America was off on": Goodman, 295.
322 "I want to fight": quoted in *Time Capsule/1941*, 174.
322 "be afraid to use": Goodman, 301.

IX. WAR NERVES

324 "Police seem bent on": quoted in McClun and Lee, 75.
325 "[The Southern whites] have moved into": quoted *ibid.*, 92.
327 "Let's go out and": quoted *ibid.*, 38.
327 "Jesus, but it was": quoted *ibid.*, 80.
327 "Oh, there were about": quoted *ibid.*, 8.
328 "behaved with deplorable callousness": *ibid.*, 41.
328 "Word got around awful": *ibid.*, 78.
328 "A theme repeatedly emphasized": *ibid.*, 69.
328 "no evidence of any": quoted *ibid.*, 60.
329 "Hitler jammed our white": quoted in Goodman, 94.
329 "Democracy, as preached by": quoted *ibid.*, 91.
329 "an Ethiopian-Pacific movement": quoted *ibid.*, 91.
330 "more progress has been made": *ibid.*, 98.
333 "I wanna zoot suit": "I Wanna Zoot Suit" by Ray Gilbert and Bob O'Brien. © 1942 by Greene-Revel, Inc.
336 "I take the view": quoted in Grodzins.
336 "Once a Jap, always": *ibid.*
336 "When the final test": *ibid.*
336 "When we are dealing": *ibid.*
337 "Let's move these Japanese": *ibid.*
337 "by permitting himself": *ibid.*
338 "Many thanks for your": from photo in Stegner, 67.
340 "Snow upon the rooftop": quoted in Larson, 301.
340 "When servings are": quoted, *ibid.*, 301.
341 "75% of the people": *ibid.*, 308.

341 "The Japs who are": *ibid.*, 310.
341 "handling them" "ticklish problem": *ibid.*

X. THE WAR IS OVER!

343 "He was the commander": quoted in Asbell, 120.
344 "a disposition to inquire": quoted New York *Times*, February 13, 1942.
344 "The war came to": quoted in Hinshaw, 173.
345 "the greatest betrayal": quoted in Barnouw, 151.
347 "Let's quit blaming": quoted in *Time Capsule/1944*, 61.
348 "Nothing organically wrong": *ibid.*, 18–19.
348 "For myself I do": *ibid.*
351 "God, God, how he": quoted in Asbell, 90.
351 "He was the one": quoted *ibid.*, 92.
352 "For what do I": quoted *ibid.*, 75.
352 "So he's finally dead": *ibid.*, 75.
352 "What a good man": *ibid.*, 92.
352 "He made a way": *ibid.*, 120.
352 "Oh, he's gone": *ibid.*, 172.
353 "He did not stoop": *ibid.*, viii.
353 "A lonesome train": "The Lonesome Train" by Millard Lampell and Earl Robinson. © 1944 Sun Music Company, Inc.
355 "everybody talked of": quoted in Goldman, 4.

Selected Bibliography

PERIODICALS

(Issues of September, 1941–September, 1945
consulted by individual numbers or serially)

American Sociological Review
Atlantic Monthly
Business Week
Collier's
Daily Variety
Documentary Newsletter
Fortune
400 Songs to Remember
Harper's Magazine
Hollywood Quarterly
The Home Front Digest
Home Front Letters
House & Garden
Life
Motion Picture Herald
Nation's Business
National Geographic
New Republic

Newsweek
Parent's Magazine
Photoplay
Popular Mechanics
Saturday Evening Post
Smith College Studies in Social Work
Song Hits
Theater Arts
Time
Top Hits
Variety
Victory WPB
Vital Speeches
War Manpower
Woman's Home Companion
Yank
Your Hit Parade

NEWSPAPERS

Milwaukee *Journal*
New York *Herald Tribune*
New York *Times*
PM
St. Louis *Post-Dispatch*

PAMPHLETS

Chamber of Commerce of the U.S., War Service Division, *War Survey*, April 27, 1944–June 28, 1945.

Consumer Education Study, *My Part in the War*, 1943.

Office of Civilian Defense, Handbooks, G.P.O., 1942: *Handbook for Air Raid Wardens, Handbooks for Auxiliary Firemen, Handbook for Demolition and Clearance Crews, Handbook for Firewatchers, Handbook of First Aid, Handbook for Messengers, Handbook for Rescue Squads, Handbook for Road Repair Crews, Notes on City Gas, Handbook for Drivers' Corps Members, Handbook for Auxiliary Police, Handbook for Emergency Feed-*

ing and Housing Corps, Fire Protection in Civilian Defense, Protection against Gas, Institution of Auxiliary Fire Equipment, Community Air Raid Shelters, Luminescent Materials, First Aid in the Prevention and Treatment of Chemical Casualties, Treatment of Burns and Prevention of Wound Infection, A Technical Manual on the Preservation and Transfusion of Whole Human Blood Plasma, Development of Car-Sharing Campaigns, Guide for Planning and the Local Victory Garden, Volunteers in Consumer Training Programs, Volunteers in Nutrition, Volunteers in Family Security, Volunteers in Recreation, Volunteers in Library Services, Volunteers in Health, Medical Care and Nursing, Volunteers in Child Care, Volunteers in Schools, Casualty Record Book, Morgue Record Book.

U.S. Tariff Commission, *War Changes in Industry Series,* Washington, D.C., U.S. Government Printing Office. (undated)

Office of Civilian Defense "What to Do in an Air Raid." Illustrated by Milton Caniff, Washington, D.C., U.S. Government Printing Office, December, 1941.

UNPUBLISHED MANUSCRIPTS

Manck, Elwyn A., *Civilian Defense in the United States* (Typescript), 1946.

McElroy, Robert, *Narrative Account of the Office of Civilian Defense* (Typescript), 1945.

FILES

Bureau of Motion Pictures; Domestic Radio Bureau (Office of War Information), National Archives, Washington, D.C.

BOOKS

ABRAMS, RAY H., *Preachers Present Arms.* Scottsdale, Pa., Herald Press, 1933, 1969.

ADAMS, HENRY H., *1942 The Year That Doomed the Axis.* New York, David McKay Company, 1967.

ADAMS, JAMES TRUSLOW, *The March of Democracy,* Vol. VI. New York, Charles Scribner's Sons, 1943, 1944, 1945.

AGEE, JAMES, *Agee on Film.* Boston, Beacon Press, 1958.

ANGELL, NORMAN, *Let the People Know.* New York, The Viking Press, 1942, 1943.

ASBELL, BERNARD, *When F.D.R. Died.* New York, Holt, Rinehart & Winston, 1961.

BALL, LAMAR Q., *Georgia in World War II.* State of Georgia, 1946.

BARNOUW, ERIK, *Radio Drama in Action.* New York, Rinehart & Company, 1945.

BAXTER, JAMES PHINNEY, *Scientists Against Time.* Boston, Little, Brown & Company, 1947.

BESSIE, ALVAH, *Inquisition in Eden.* New York, Macmillan Company, 1965.

BLUM, JOHN MORTON, *Years of War 1941–1945 From the Morgenthau Diaries.* Boston, Houghton Mifflin Company, 1967.

BROOKS, THOMAS, R., *Toil and Trouble.* New York, Dell Publishing Company, 1964.

BROWN, WILLIAM B., *et al., America in a World at War.* New York, Silver Burdett Company, 1942, 1943.

BROWNE, LEWIS, *See What I Mean?* New York, Random House, 1943.

BUCHANAN, A. RUSSELL, *The United States and World War II,* Vol. I and Vol. II. New York, Harper & Row, 1964.

BUREAU OF THE BUDGET, *The United States at War*. Washington, U.S. Government Printing Office, 1946.

BURTON, JACK, *The Blue Book of Hollywood Musicals*. New York, Century House, 1953.

BURNS, JAMES MACGREGOR, *Roosevelt: The Lion and the Fox*. New York, Harcourt, Brace & World, 1956.

CARLSON, JOHN ROY, *Under Cover*. Philadelphia, The Blakiston Company, 1943.

CARNES, MAX PARVIN, *The Hoosier Community at War* (Vol. IX, Indiana War History Series, Indiana in World War II). Bloomington, Ind., Indiana University Press, 1961.

CARPOZI, GEORGE, *Clark Gable*. New York, Pyramid Books, 1961.

CASTLES, MRS. JOHN V., *History of the Civilian Defense Volunteer Office of the City of New York, 1941–1945*. New York, 1946.

CATTON, BRUCE, *The War Lords of Washington*. New York, Harcourt, Brace & Company, 1948.

CHILDS, MARQUIS, *I Write from Washington*. New York, Harper & Brothers, 1942.

COFFIN, TRISTRAM, *The Armed Society*. Baltimore, Penguin Books, 1964.

CONNER, WILLIAM H., and DE VALINGER, LEON, JR., *Delaware's Role in World War II*. Dover, Delaware, State Archives Commission, 1955.

CORSON, JOHN J., *Manpower for Victory*. New York, Farrar & Rinehart, 1943.

CORWIN, NORMAN, *More by Corwin*. New York, Henry Holt and Company, 1944.

——, *Untitled and Other Radio Dramas*. New York, Henry Holt and Company, 1945, 1947.

DAMERON, KENNETH, ed., *Consumer Problems in Wartime*. New York, McGraw-Hill Book Company, 1944.

DAVIS, C. K. *In Abundance and on Time*. Bridgeport, Remington Arms Company, 1944.

DAVIES, JOHN LANGDON, *American Close-up*. London, John Murray, 1943.

DE SEVERSKY, ALEXANDER P., *Victory Through Air Power*. New York, Simon and Schuster, 1942.

DIRECTOR OF SELECTIVE SERVICE, *Selective Service in Wartime*. Washington, Government Printing Office, 1943.

DOS PASSOS, JOHN, *State of the Nation*. Boston, Houghton Mifflin Company, 1943, 1944.

——, *The Great Days*. New York, Popular Library, 1958.

DRURY, ALLEN, *A Senate Journal 1943–1945*. New York, McGraw-Hill, 1963.

DUPUY, R. ERNEST, and CARTER, HODDING, *Civilian Defense of the United States*. New York, Farrar & Rinehart, 1942.

EDITORS OF *Look*, *Movie Lot to Beachhead*. Garden City, New York, Doubleday, Doran and Company, 1945.

EDMISTON, JAMES, *Home Again*. New York, Doubleday & Company, 1955.

ENCYCLOPAEDIA BRITANNICA, *Britannica Book of the Year*. Chicago, Encyclopaedia Britannica Inc., 1942, 1943, 1944, 1945.

FARRINGTON, S. KIP, JR., *Railroads at War*. New York, Coward-McCann, 1944.

Film Daily Yearbook, 1942, 1943, 1944, 1945.

FURNAS, J. C., and the staff of the *Ladies Home Journal*, *How America Lives*. New York, Henry Holt and Company, 1941.

GARCEAU, JEAN, with COCKE, INEZ, *Dear Mr. G—*. Boston, Little, Brown & Company, 1961.

GIBBS, PHILIP, *America Speaks*. New York, Doubleday, Doran and Company, 1942.

GIRDNER, AUDRIE, and LOFTIS, ANNE, *The Great Betrayal*. New York, Macmillan Company, 1969.

GOLD, BELA, *Wartime Economic Planning in Agriculture*. New York, Columbia University Press, 1949.

GOLDMAN, ERIC, *The Crucial Decade and After*. New York, Vintage, 1956.

GOODMAN, JACK, ed. *While You Were Gone*. New York, Simon and Schuster, 1946.

GREEN, ABEL, and LAURIE, JOE, JR., *Show Biz from Vaude to Video*. New York, Henry Holt and Company, 1951.

GRODZINS, MORTON, *Americans Betrayed*. Chicago, University of Chicago Press, 1949.

HARTZELL, KARL DREW, *The Empire State at War—World War II*. State of New York, 1949.

HASSETT, WILLIAM D., *Off the Record with F.D.R. 1942–1945*. New Brunswick, New Jersey, Rutgers University Press, 1958.

HERGE, HENRY C. et al., *Wartime College Training Programs of the Armed Services*. Washington, D.C., American Council on Education, 1948.

Highlights from Yank. New York, Royal Books, 1953.

HINSHAW, DAVID, *The Home Front*. New York, G. P. Putnam's Sons, 1943.

HISTORY COMMISSION, WORLD WAR II, OF NEWPORT NEWS, VIRGINIA, *History of the City of Newport News 1941–1945*. Richmond, The Baughman Company, 1948.

HOLLINGSHEAD, A. B., *Elmtown's Youth*. New York, John Wiley & Sons, 1949.

HOSOKAWA, BILL, *Nisei*. New York, William Morrow and Company, 1969.

HURDE, CHARLES, *Washington Cavalcade*. New York, E. P. Dutton & Company, 1948.

ICKES, HAROLD L., *The Autobiography of a Curmudgeon*. Quadrangle Books, 1943.

JANEWAY, ELIOT, *The Struggle for Survival*. New Haven, Yale University Press, 1951.

JOHNSON, GEORGE H., *Skyscrapers in the Mist*. Sydney, Australia, Angus and Robertson, 1946.

JONES, JESSE, *50 Billion Dollars*. New York, Macmillan Company, 1951.

KAPLAN, A. D. H., *The Liquidation of War Production*. New York, McGraw-Hill Book Company, 1944.

KITANO, HARRY H. L., *Japanese Americans*. Englewood Cliffs, New Jersey, Prentice-Hall, 1969.

LABOR RESEARCH ASSOCIATION, *Labor Fact Book 6, 7, 8*. New York, International Publishers, 1943, 1945, 1947.

LARSON, T. A., *Wyoming's War Years 1941–1945*. Laramie, University of Wyoming Press, 1954.

LAWSON, TED, *Thirty Seconds over Tokyo*. New York, Random House, 1943.

LAWRENCE, JEROME, ed., *Off Mike*. New York, Essential Books, 1944.

LEE, ALFRED McCLUNG, and HUMPHREY, NORMAN D., *Race Riot*. New York, The Dryden Press, 1943.

LERNER, MAX, *Public Journal*. New York, The Viking Press, 1945.

LEVER, HARRY, and YOUNG, JOSEPH, *Wartime Racketeers*. New York, G. P. Putnam's Sons, 1945.

LIBBY, FREDERICK J., *To End War*. Nyack, Fellowship Publications, 1969.

LYDGATE, WILLIAM A., *What America Thinks*. New York, Thomas Y. Crowell, 1944.

MALKIN, RICHARD, *Marriage Morals and War*. New York, Arden Book Company, 1943.

"MAN AT THE MICROPHONE, THE" (pseud.), *Washington Broadcast*. Garden City, New York, Doubleday, Doran and Company, 1944.

MAULDIN, BILL, *Back Home*. New York, William Sloane Associates, 1947.

McINTIRE, ROSS T., *White House Physician*. New York, G. P. Putnam's Sons, 1946.

McLUHAN, MARSHALL, *The Mechanical Bride*. New York, Vanguard, 1951.

McVITTIE, J. A., A Report by the City Manager, *An Avalanche Hits Richmond*. Richmond, California, July, 1944.

McWILLIAMS, CAREY, *Prejudice*. Boston, Little, Brown & Company, 1945.

MENEFEE, SELDEN, *Assignment: U.S.A.* Reynal and Hitchcock, New York, 1943.

MEYER, AGNES E., *Journey Through Chaos*. New York, Harcourt, Brace & Company, 1943, 1944.

MILLIS, WALTER, *Arms and Men*. New York, Capricorn Books, 1956.

MOREHOUSE, WARD, *American Reveille*. New York, G. P. Putnam's Sons, 1942.

NATIONAL CONFERENCE OF SOCIAL WORK, *Proceedings*. New York, Columbia University Press, 1943.

NELSON, DONALD M., *Arsenal of Democracy*. New York, Harcourt, Brace & Company, 1946.

NOVICK, DAVID; ANSHEN, MELVIN; and TRUPPNER W. C., *Wartime Production Controls*. New York, Columbia University Press, 1949.

OFFICE OF WAR INFORMATION, *American Handbook*. Washington, D.C., Public Affairs Press, 1945.

OGBURN, WILLIAM FIELDING, ed., *American Society in Wartime*. Chicago, University of Chicago Press, 1943.

OSOFSKY, GILBERT, *The Burden of Race*. New York, Harper & Row, 1967

PERKINS, DEXTER, *The New Age of Franklin Roosevelt*. Chicago, University of Chicago Press, 1957.

PERKINS, FRANCES, *The Roosevelt I Knew*. New York, Harper & Row, 1946.

POLENBERG, RICHARD, ed., *America at War*. Englewood Cliffs, Prentice-Hall, 1968.

RAYBACK, JOSEPH G., *A History of American Labor*. New York, The Free Press, 1966.

ROBINSON, VICTOR, ed., *Morals in Wartime*. New York, Publishers Foundation, 1943.

ROSEBERY, MERCEDES, *This Day's Madness*. New York, Macmillan Company, 1944.

SANDBURG, CARL, *Home Front Memo*. New York, Harcourt, Brace & Company, 1940, 1941, 1942, 1943.

SAYERS, MICHAEL, and KAHN, ALBERT E., *Sabotage!* New York, Harper & Brothers, 1942.

SHERWOOD, ROBERT E., *Roosevelt and Hopkins*. New York, Grosset and Dunlap, 1948, 1950.

SIMMONS, GORDON, AND MEYER, RALPH LOUIS, eds., *This Is Your America*. New York, Literary Classics, Inc., 1943.

SORENSON, CHARLES, *My Forty Years with Ford*. New York, W. W. Norton & Company, 1956.

SPAETH, SIGMUND, *A History of Popular Music in America*. New York, Random House, 1948.

STRAUS, NATHAN, *The Seven Myths of Housing*. New York, Alfred A. Knopf, 1944.

STEGNER, WALLACE, *One Nation*. Boston, Houghton Mifflin Company, 1945.

STOUFFER, SAMUEL A., *et al.*, *The American Soldier.* New York, John Wiley & Sons, 1949.

STOUT, WESLEY W., *Mobilized,* Detroit, Chrysler Corporation, 1949.

STRUTHER, JAN, *Mrs. Miniver.* New York, Harcourt, Brace & Co., 1940.

SWARD, KEITH, *The Legend of Henry Ford.* New York, Atheneum, 1968.

TAYLOR, MARJORIE A., *The Language of World War II.* New York, H. W. Wilson, 1948.

This Is Your America,

Time Capsule, 1941, 1943, 1944, 1945. New York, Time-Life Books, 1967, 1968.

TOLAND, JOHN, *But Not in Shame.* New York, Signet, 1961.

TOULMIN, HARRY AUBREY, JR., *Diary of Democracy.* New York, Richard R. Smith, 1947.

TREGASKIS, RICHARD, *Guadalcanal Diary.* New York, Popular Library Edition, 1943, 1955, 1959.

TURNER, E. S., *The Phoney War.* New York, St. Martin's Press, 1961.

U.S. DEPARTMENT OF COMMERCE, *Small Town Manual.* Washington, D.C., U.S. Government Printing Office, 1942.

————, Bureau of the Census, *Historical Statistics of the United States 1789–1945.* Washington, D.C., U.S. Government Printing Office, 1949.

UNITED STATES DEPARTMENT OF LABOR, BUREAU OF LABOR STATISTICS, *Handbook of Labor Statistics.* 1947, 1950 ed.

VINDE, VICTOR, *America at War,* trans. by E. Classen. London, Hutchinson and Company, 1944.

WAKEMAN, FREDERIC, *Shore Leave.* New York, Farrar & Rinehart, 1944.

WAR RECORDS DIVISION, MARYLAND HISTORICAL SOCIETY, *Maryland in World War II* (Vol. III Home Front Volunteer Services). Baltimore, 1958.

WARNER, W. LLOYD, *et al.*, *Democracy in Jonesville.* New York, Harper & Row, 1949.

WARNER, JACK L., *My First Hundred Years in Hollywood.* New York, Random House, 1964, 1965.

WATTERS, MARY, *Illinois in the Second World War,* Vol. I, *Operation Homefront.* Springfield, Illinois, Illinois State History Library, 1951.

WILDER, MARGARET BUELL, *Since You Went Away.* New York, McGraw-Hill Book Company, 1943.

WILCOX, WALTER B., *The Farmer in the Second World War.* Ames, Iowa, Iowa State College Press, 1947.

WILSON, MARION F., *The Story of Willow Run.* Ann Arbor, University of Michigan Press, 1956.

WISH, HARVEY, *Contemporary America.* New York, Harper & Brothers, 1945.

WOOD, LELAND FOSTER, and MULLEN, JOHN W., eds., *What the American Family Faces.* Chicago, The Eugene Hugh Publishers, 1943.

WOODFORD, FRANK B., and WOODFORD, ARTHUR M., *All Our Yesterdays.* Detroit, Wayne State University Press, 1969.

YOUNG, ROLAND, *This Is Congress.* New York, Alfred A. Knopf, 1943.

INDEX